PEARSON EDUCATION AP* TEST PREP: STATISTICS

FOR

STATS: MODELING THE WORLD,

THIRD EDITION

BOCK—VELLEMAN—DE VEAUX

WRITTEN BY
CARROLL
CARVER
PETERS
RICKS

Addison-Wesley

Boston San Francisco New York
London Toronto Sydney Tokyo Singapore Madrid
Mexico City Munich Paris Cape Town Hong Kong Montreal

ISBN-13: 978-0-13-135964-2
ISBN-10: 0-13-135964-9

8 9 10 11 EBM 15 14 13 12

Addison-Wesley
is an imprint of

www.PearsonSchool.com/Advanced

Acknowledgments

We wish to thank the authors of *Stats: Modeling the World* for letting us share material, and we thank Dave Bock in particular for his trust and confidence in having us write this review book. We also acknowledge Deirdre Lynch, Christopher Cummings, Chere Bemelmans, Sheila Spinney, and the entire Pearson Addison-Wesley publishing team, without whose help this book could not have been produced. Sincere appreciation is extended to the College Board and the Advanced Placement Program for providing content outlines and examination information.

We would also like to thank our statistics colleagues from both the secondary and post-secondary levels for their camaraderie and exchange of ideas and information over the years at the AP Statistics Exam Readings. Our work as readers would not have been as pleasant or as informative without Chief Readers Dick Shaeffer, Roxy Peck, Brad Hartlaub, and Chris Franklin. Our continuing gratitude is extended to Jeff Haberstroh from Educational Testing Services, who has helped us all improve our knowledge and understanding of the examination process over many years.

For the Third Edition, we must also acknowledge the helpful suggestions that came to us from Susan Blackwell, First Flight High School, North Carolina, who reviewed our problem sets, and from the project editor for this edition, Kristin Jobe. We also thank the following statistics educators, whose reviews of the Second Edition helped guide us: Barbara Dobbs, Magruder High School, Maryland; David Cilley, Spring Valley High School, South Carolina; Brendan Murphy, John Bapst Memorial High School, Maine; Paul Myers, Woodward Academy, Georgia; and John Kirk, Rocklin High School, California.

And last, but certainly not least, we all thank our families who supported us throughout the creative, production, and revision processes. Without them we could not have taken on this task nor, indeed, could we ever be teachers, for as we all know, teaching extends long beyond the hours of the workday, week, and year.

About Your AP Test Prep Workbook*

Pearson Education is the leading publisher of textbooks worldwide. With operations on every continent, we make it our business to understand the changing needs of students at every level, from kindergarten to college.

This gives us a unique insight into what kinds of study materials work for students. We talk to customers every day, soliciting feedback on our books. We think that this makes us especially qualified to offer this series of AP* Test Prep Workbooks, tied to some of our best-selling textbooks.

We know that as you study for your AP* course, you're preparing along the way for the AP* exam. By tying the material in the book directly to AP* course goals and exam topics, we help you to focus your time most efficiently. And that's a good thing!

The AP* exam is an important milestone in your education. A high score will position you optimally for college acceptance—and possibly will give you college credits that put you a step ahead. Our goal at Pearson Education is to provide you with the tools you need to excel on the exam—the rest is up to you.

Good luck!

Contents

About the Authors

Anne M. Carroll teaches AP* Statistics at Kennett High School in Kennett Square, Pennsylvania, where she has served on many committees including the Mathematics Leadership Council and Professional Development Committee. She was a reader for the Advanced Placement Statistics examination from 1998 to 2003 and has been a table leader since 2005. Anne was a consultant with the Middle States Region of the College Board before the first exam was given for AP* Statistics. She has also served as a reviewer for AP* Central. She was named the DeVry University Suburban Math Teacher of the Year in 2005 and was a finalist in the Citadel Heart of Learning Award Program in 2006.

Ruth E. Carver is mathematics chairperson and teaches AP* Statistics at Germantown Academy in Fort Washington, Pennsylvania. She has been a reader for the Advanced Placement Statistics examination since 2001 and co-authored the College Board's official *AP* Statistics Web Guide* with Susan Peters. Ruth has received numerous awards, including the 2007 Siemens Foundation AP* Teacher Award; the Presidential Award for Excellence in Mathematics and Science Teaching; the National Education and Technology Alliance STAR Award and "Best of the Best" Award; the Teachers Teaching with Technology, Demana/Waits Vision Award, and the Tandy Technology Prize for Teaching Excellence in Mathematics, Science, and Computer Science. She is a co-founder of the Philadelphia Area Statistics Teacher's Association (PASTA) and a consultant for the Middle States Region of the College Board.

Susan A. Peters taught AP* Statistics at Twin Valley High School in Elverson, Pennsylvania, and was an Advanced Placement Statistics examination reader from 1997 to 2002 and a table leader in 2003 and 2004. She served as a consultant for the Middle States Region of the College Board and co-authored the College Board's official *AP* Statistics Web Guide* with Ruth Carver. She is a co-founder of the Philadelphia Area Statistics Teachers Association (PASTA). She served as assistant editor designate and assistant editor for the *Journal for Research in Mathematics Education* from 2007 to 2009. Susan earned a Master of Applied Statistics degree in 2007 from The Pennsylvania State University and will earn a Ph.D. in Curriculum and Instruction with an emphasis in Mathematics Education in 2009. Her dissertation focuses on the area of statistics education.

Janice D. Ricks is mathematics department leader and teaches AP* Statistics at Marple Newtown High School in Newtown Square, Pennsylvania. She was an Advanced Placement Statistics examination reader from 1997 to 2002 and served as a table leader from 2003 to 2008. Janice has also been a consultant for the Middle States Region of the College Board. She is a co-founder of the Philadelphia Area Statistics Teachers Association (PASTA).

Part I

Introduction to the AP Statistics Examination*

This review guide has been prepared as a supplement to *Stats: Modeling the World,* Third Edition by Bock, Velleman, and De Veaux. The authors hope that users will find this work faithful to the themes, content, and spirit of the Bock text. We also hope that users of other primary texts will recognize the broad-based approach and specific insights of this guide as useful preparation for students.

This Book

So you decided to take AP* Statistics! It was a good choice that will be made even better when you successfully complete the AP* examination. The purpose of this book is to help you do just that. As a supplement to your textbook, this guide will help you to distill important ideas, clarify statistical procedures, and improve your communication so that you can be successful.

This book will present Key Concepts, Skills, and Examples for the AP* curriculum in a compact and student-friendly form. The sequence of material will follow the Pearson Addison-Wesley text by Bock, Velleman, and De Veaux, *Stats: Modeling the World*, Third Edition, but will be keyed to the AP* Content Outline. This guide will offer Clues for Clarity that will enhance your ability to communicate statistical knowledge. It will offer sample examinations with complete solutions and explanations.

This book is not intended to substitute for a full course or a comprehensive treatment of the topics. It is meant, rather, to act as a useful review for students who have previously studied the curriculum topics and now want to solidify their learning through recall and practice.

The Advanced Placement Statistics Curriculum*

As you probably know by now, the AP* Statistics curriculum was designed to provide an introductory course in statistics that is equal in content to the best collegiate courses. It was developed by a team of educators from both the college and high school communities and continues to adapt itself so that a broad base of college programs will offer credit for success in the examination. To find out whether your prospective institution will give credit for your AP* Statistics examination performance, you should e-mail or call the admissions office. You can log on to AP Central at *www.apcentral.collegeboard.com* for up-to-date information about the Advanced Placement Program*.

A course in statistics is especially useful to those pursuing studies in mathematics, the behavioral or social sciences, biology and other applied sciences, economics, and business. In a world of fast and furious data acquisition and interpretation, an understanding of statistics is essential to any informed consumer, voter, or general reader. Your success in the AP* Statistics course, as validated by your success in the examination, marks you as a savvy learner and an informed citizen.

Understanding the Advanced Placement Examination in Statistics

Statistics is one of the most recent offerings in the Advanced Placement Program*. The first examination was administered in 1997, and the program has been growing rapidly. This examination now ranks among the top ten in participation. The examination is given in May during the same two-week window as the other examinations. Your teacher or the AP* coordinator in your school district can give you the exact date for this year's examination. You can also check for this and other information on the AP Central Web site. These dates are determined long in advance, and the dates and times are not flexible. In the event of an emergency, you may qualify to take an alternate examination, but you should not expect to do this, because the qualifying conditions are extremely rigid. Plan your calendar around the examination date, and register with your teacher or coordinator to reserve an examination. Standard fees as determined by the College Board apply.

The topics for AP* Statistics are divided into four major themes, and these themes are reflected in the examination as follows:

Exploratory analysis	20% – 30%
Planning and conducting a study	10% – 15%
Probability	20% – 30%
Statistical inference	30% – 40%

I. Exploring Data: Describing Patterns and Departures from Patterns

Exploratory analysis of data makes use of graphical and numerical techniques to study patterns and departures from patterns. In examining distributions of data, students should be able to detect important characteristics such as shape, location, variability, and unusual values. From careful observations of patterns in data, students can generate conjectures about relationships among variables. The notion of how one variable may be associated with another permeates almost all of statistics, from simple comparisons of proportions through linear regression. The difference between association and causation must accompany this conceptual development throughout.

II. Sampling and Experimentation: Planning and Conducting a Study

Data must be collected according to a well-developed plan if valid information is to be obtained. If data are to be collected to provide an answer to a question of interest, a careful plan must be developed. Both the type of analysis that is appropriate and the nature of conclusions that can be drawn from that analysis depend in a critical way on how the data were collected. Collecting data in a reasonable way, through either sampling or experimentation, is an essential step in the data analysis process.

III. Anticipating Patterns: Exploring Random Phenomena Using Probability and Simulation

Probability is the tool used for anticipating what the distribution of data should look like under a given model. Random phenomena are not haphazard: they display an order that emerges only in the long run and is described by a distribution. The mathematical description of variation is central to statistics. The probability required for statistical inference is not primarily axiomatic or combinatorial, but is oriented toward using probability distributions to describe data.

IV. Statistical Inference: Estimating Population Parameters and Testing Hypotheses

Statistical inference guides the selection of appropriate models. Models and data interact in statistical work: models are used to draw conclusions from data, while the data are allowed to criticize and even falsify the model through inferential and diagnostic methods. Inference from data can be thought of as the process of selecting a reasonable model, including a statement in probability language, of how confident one can be about the selection.

These themes (as provided by the College Board) should guide your review. Always keep in mind that statistics is about seeing the big picture from a series of snapshots. A clear understanding of the way these themes build will help you to build your knowledge efficiently.

You may bring to the examination two calculators with statistics capabilities. You may *not* bring any device with a QWERTY keyboard or any other electronic devices. We highly recommend that you use a graphing calculator with statistical capability throughout the course and that you use this same calculator during the examination. Many students bring a second calculator as a backup. Fresh batteries are a must! You may enhance the capabilities of your calculator only with programs that improve the computational or graphical capabilities; you may *not* have programs that create a template for responses, nor may you incorporate text. Such illegal enhancements constitute cheating. While calculator output is a necessary part of the course and the examination, we strongly discourage *calcu-speak*—a calculator command is not a substitute for clearly communicating procedures and results. We will explain more about this throughout the review in our Clues for Clarity.

The examination will also assume that you are familiar with a variety of computer printouts. Ideally you will have been using some computer software during your classroom instruction and perhaps even in home assignments. Either way, it is important that you review printouts from standard software programs like ActivStats®, Minitab®, DataDesk®, Fathom™, JMP®, and others.

The actual examination is currently formatted and has timing and grade weights as follows:

Multiple Choice—40 questions with 5 answer choices	90 minutes	50%
Free Response	90 minutes	50%
▮ Part A (Equally Weighted)—5 questions	approx. 65 minutes	75% of the 50%
▮ Part B (Investigative Task)—1 question	approx. 25 minutes	25% of the 50%

The Multiple Choice and Free Response sections of the examination are equally timed and weighted. They stand alone with a recommended break in between. You should expect to work the full 90 minutes on both sections. You should, if at all possible, allow time to go back and check your work. The Multiple Choice section is done first; that part of the examination will be sealed and collected at the end of the 90-minute time period.

Although the Free Response section comes with separate directions and suggested times, the entire section is viewed as one. Students may move freely during the 90 minutes from Part A to Part B and back again. We recommend that you spend a few minutes thoroughly reading each question in all of its parts and devising a strategy for answering. You should spend about 8–10 minutes carrying out your solution plan for each of the first five questions. It is extremely important that you devote full time to the Investigative Task since it is more heavily weighted than any of the first five questions. There are more tips along these lines in the Test-Taking Strategies section that follows.

Understanding the Grading Procedure for the Advanced Placement Examination in Statistics

The scoring of the AP* Statistics examination is done in part by machine (Section I—Multiple Choice) and in part by statistics educators (human beings!) who read the answers as you have communicated them (Section II—Free Response). The entire test is valued at 100 points with the Multiple Choice and Free Response sections each contributing 50 points.

In the Multiple Choice section, you are *awarded* 1 point for each correct answer and *penalized* 1/4 point for each incorrect answer. To convert to the possible 50-point total (reflecting 50% of the grade), the number of points earned is multiplied by 1.25. For example, suppose you answered 28 questions correctly but answered 10 questions incorrectly and left 2 questions blank. Here is the way your Multiple Choice section would be graded:

Number correct	28	×	1	=	28
Number incorrect	10	×	−.25	=	−2.5
Number left blank	2	×	0	=	0
POINTS EARNED				=	25.5
MULTIPLE CHOICE SCORE	= 25.5 × 1.25			=	31.875

In the Free Response section, the *reader* assigns a score from 0 to 4 as indicated by the rubric or grading rule developed by the Chief Reader and a select team of statistics leaders. Scoring is done holistically, and the rubric for each question is developed to assist holistic grading. What this means is that the scores reflect a level of knowledge. When an answer scored by the rubric is borderline, the reader may "step back" to look at the overall quality of the answer. This is why *communication* is key. Here is the category template provided by the College Board.

A Guide to Scoring Free Response Statistics Questions
The Category Descriptors

Score Descriptors	Statistical Knowledge	Communication
	■ identification of the important components of the problem ■ demonstration of the statistical concepts and techniques that result in a correct solution of the problem	■ explanation of what was done and why, along with a statement of conclusions drawn
4 Complete	■ shows complete understanding of the problem's statistical components ■ synthesizes a correct relationship among these components, perhaps with novelty and creativity ■ uses appropriate and correctly executed statistical techniques ■ may have minor arithmetic errors, but answers are still reasonable	■ provides a clear, organized, and complete explanation, using correct terminology, of what was done and why ■ states appropriate assumptions and caveats ■ uses diagrams or plots when appropriate to aid in describing the solution ■ states an appropriate and complete conclusion
3 Substantial	■ shows substantial understanding of the problem's statistical components ■ synthesizes a relationship among these components, perhaps with minor gaps ■ uses appropriate statistical techniques ■ may have arithmetic errors, but answers are still reasonable	■ provides a clear but not perfectly organized explanation, using correct terminology, of what was done and why, but explanation may be slightly incomplete ■ may miss necessary assumptions or caveats ■ uses diagrams or plots when appropriate to aid in describing the solution ■ states a conclusion that follows from the analysis but may be somewhat incomplete
2 Developing	■ shows some understanding of the problem's statistical components ■ shows little in the way of a relationship among these components ■ uses some appropriate statistical techniques, but misses or misuses others ■ may have arithmetic errors that result in unreasonable answers	■ provides some explanation of what was done, but explanation may be vague and difficult to interpret and terminology may be somewhat inappropriate ■ uses diagrams in an incomplete or ineffective way, or diagrams may be missing ■ states a conclusion that is incomplete
1 Minimal	■ shows limited understanding of the problem's statistical components by failing to identify important components ■ shows little ability to organize a solution and may use irrelevant information ■ misuses or fails to use appropriate statistical techniques ■ has arithmetic errors that result in unreasonable answers	■ provides minimal or unclear explanation of what was done or why it was done, and explanation may not match the presented solution ■ fails to use diagrams or plots, or uses them incorrectly ■ states an incorrect conclusion, or fails to state a conclusion
0	■ shows little or no understanding of statistical components	■ provides no explanation of a legitimate strategy

There is also a score of a dash (—) that is used to indicate a blank answer or one that is wholly off task. A dash and a zero are both tabulated with values of zero. Recall that the Free Response section is weighted as 50% of the examination score and that the first five questions represent 75% of that 50% weight. Since the exam is scored on a 100-point scale, these five questions represent

37.5 points of the total exam score, while the Investigative Task, representing 25% of the 50%, accounts for the last 12.5 points. The conversion factors for the first five questions and the Investigative Task are 1.875 and 3.125, respectively. Suppose that your answers to the Free Response questions are scored in the following manner:

Question 1	3 points		
Question 2	4 points		
Question 3	4 points		
Question 4	2 points		
Question 5	3 points	Question 6	3 points
	$16 \times 1.875 = 30$		$3 \times 3.125 = 9.375$

Your total score is the sum of the five short-answer scores and the Investigative Task score:

$$30 + 9.375 = 39.375$$

Your weighted score from Section I is added to your weighted score from Section II:

$$31.875 + 39.375 = 71.25$$

This composite score is then subject to the Chief Reader's interpretation of the cut points for that particular examination year's results. These cut points are set shortly after examinations are scored and are based on several factors, including statistical comparability with other years' examinations, the distributions of performance on the various parts of the current year's examination, and the previous three years' grade distributions.

Your results will be available from the College Board by phone, usually by mid-July, and they are mailed out to you and your high school shortly after that. By August your scores are also sent to any college or university that you may indicate in the general information section of your answer packet. If you do not wish to communicate your scores immediately to your institution or if you are unsure of what institution you will be attending, you need not indicate any schools, and the results will go only to your high school and you. You can have them transmitted later to your chosen schools in accordance with College Board policies. There may be a fee for this service.

Test-Taking Strategies for the Advanced Placement Examination in Statistics

You should approach the AP* Statistics examination the same way you would approach any major test in your academic career. Just remember that *it is a one-shot deal*—you must be at your peak performance level on the day of the test. For that reason you should do everything that your coach tells you to do. In most cases your coach is your classroom teacher. It is very likely that your teacher has some experience based on workshop information or previous students' performances that s/he will share with you.

You should also analyze your own test-taking abilities. At this stage in your education, you probably know your strengths and weaknesses in test-taking situations. You may be very good at multiple choice tests but weaker in essays. Or perhaps it is the other way around. Whatever your particular abilities are, evaluate them and respond accordingly. Spend more time on your weaker points. In other words, rather than spending time in your "comfort zone" where you need less work, try to improve your "soft spots." In all cases, concentrate on *clear communication* of your strategies, techniques, and conclusions.

The following table presents some ideas in a quick and easy form. It is divided into two sections: general strategies for approaching the examination day and specific strategies for addressing particular types of questions on the examination.

General Strategies for AP* Examination Preparation

Time	DOs ☺	DON'Ts ☹
Through the Year	■ register with your teacher/coordinator ■ pay your fee (if applicable) on time ■ take good notes ■ work with others in study groups ■ review on a regular basis ■ familiarize yourself with the formula sheets and tables provided by the College Board for the examination ■ use summary templates for statistical procedures ■ evaluate your test-taking strengths and weaknesses—keep track of how successful you are when guessing	■ procrastinate ■ avoid homework and labs ■ wait until the last moment to pull it together for quizzes and tests ■ rely on others for your own progress ■ scatter your work products (notes, labs, reviews, tests) ■ ignore your weak areas—remediate as you go along
The Week Before	■ combine independent and group review ■ get tips from your teacher ■ do lots of mixed review problems ■ check your exam date, time, and location	■ procrastinate ■ think you are the only one who is stressed ■ forget your priorities—this test is a one-shot deal
The Night Before	■ put new batteries into your calculator; check for illegal programs ■ lay out your clothes and supplies so that you are ready to go out the door ■ do a short review ■ go to bed at a reasonable hour	■ study all night ■ get caught without fresh batteries
Exam Day	■ get up a little earlier than usual ■ eat a good breakfast/lunch ■ get to your exam location 15 minutes early ■ bring both pens and pencils to the test site	■ sleep in ■ panic with last-minute cramming ■ take electronic devices (cell phone, iPods, etc.) into the test site ■ take highlighters into the test site
Exam Night	■ relax—you earned it	■ worry—it's over

SPECIFIC STRATEGIES TO USE DURING THE AP* EXAMINATION

Question Type	DOs ☺	DON'Ts ☹
Multiple Choice	■ underline key words and phrases; circle important information you will use ■ look at the answer format so that you do not do unnecessary steps ■ anticipate the likely errors for the type of question being asked—watch out for obvious choices ■ when formulas and calculations are needed, write down what you are doing so that you can check your procedure ■ eliminate as many answers as possible ■ guess only when you are comfortable with the number of possible answers ■ check the units of your answers	■ rush—reading the question correctly is the key to answering the question correctly ■ do unnecessary calculations (sometimes confidence intervals are left in $+/-$ form) ■ fall into the traps your teacher warned you about—a question that looks too easy may have one of these traps built in ■ scribble your work—if you need to review your procedure, you wind up having to repeat it ■ guess haphazardly ■ spend more than 2–3 minutes on any one question; if you don't know, move on ■ close the book until time is up
Free Response (All Questions)	■ look over all the questions before you start and do the ones that seem easiest first ■ read the ***entire*** question in ***all of its parts*** ■ underline what is being asked ■ plan a strategy for answering the question that includes ***statistical evidence, not your opinion*** ■ carry out your strategy by clearly indicating your steps ■ when answering questions about equations and graphs, recall that standard algebraic and geometric terminology and reasoning can be applied along with your statistical knowledge ■ move on to the next part of the question if you cannot answer one part ■ make up a reasonable answer for one part if the next part requires the previous answer ("Suppose my answer to Part A had been a ***p***-value of 0.0235. This would be a significant result for $\alpha = .05$ and would mean that …") ■ state procedures for inference; list necessary conditions (assumptions you have CHECKED); show mechanics ■ write neatly, compactly, and clearly and use all statistical vocabulary ***correctly*** ■ when useful, include graphs/sketches that illustrate your answer; be sure to label axes ■ when the focus of a question is a graph, be sure to scale and label axes (include units as needed) ■ mark up sketches provided to illustrate your thinking ■ use 2 decimal places for ***z***-scores and 4 decimal places for ***p***-values ■ COMMUNICATE CLEARLY—answer the question asked (including YES or NO when indicated), justify your answer, and place your answer in the CONTEXT of the question ■ review your response to make sure that it shows good ***statistical thinking*** and that it answers the question posed (including YES or NO when indicated)	■ feel as though you ***have*** to start with #1 and finish with #6; start with the one you like best ■ forget to answer the ***question asked*** in your haste to write an answer ■ begin without a plan ■ use ***calcu-speak*** ■ move on until you have read what you have written for each part to make sure you have not left out important words, punctuation, or numbers ■ get stuck on a question—if you have no idea how to proceed after thinking about it, move on ■ scribble—a human being must be able to decipher your response ■ waste time erasing unless space is an issue—anything crossed out will not be read as part of your answer ■ just ✓ a list of assumptions—actually show verifications that conditions hold ■ use the words NORMAL, SIGNIFICANT, MEAN, or other key statistical terms unless you are using them as correctly defined ■ round during computation until you reach a final answer ■ run on—you are likely to say something INCORRECTLY that will diminish your previously correct response ■ assume that the size of the space provided is proportional to the answer desired ■ give two different answers—the weaker answer will be selected for scoring

SPECIFIC STRATEGIES TO USE DURING THE AP* EXAMINATION continued

Question Type	DOs ☺	DON'Ts ☹
Free Response: Investigative Task (Additional Strategies)	■ pace yourself—allow a full 25 minutes for this question ■ do easier parts first if possible but remember that if the question is divided into parts, there may be a natural flow from one part to another ■ remember that this problem may ask you to be creative—it may be something you have never seen in class ■ use mathematical understanding from other courses, not just statistics ■ make up reasonable answers for parts you don't know in order to work on other parts	■ panic—take the time to THINK about the question and PLAN your strategy ■ miss labels on graphs and tables; remember to include these labels in your answers ■ leave the question blank; try SOMETHING

Remember that these are general guidelines for success. We will point out specific danger areas and give you those (Clues for Clarity) in our example problems and in the sample solutions.

Topics from the Advanced Placement Curriculum for Statistics

The AP* examination is based on the Topic Outline shown below. For your convenience we have keyed it to the chapters in *Stats: Modeling the World*, Third Edition. Use this outline to keep track of your review. Be sure to cover every topic. Check it off when you have reviewed the topic from your text and then review the topic in this book.

AP* Topic Outline (Excerpted from the College Board's Course Description–Statistics)	Stats Modeling the World Third Edition
I. Exploring data: Describing patterns and departures from patterns	Chapters 4–5
A. Constructing and interpreting graphical displays of distributions of univariate data (dotplot, stemplot, histogram, cumulative frequency plot)	
1. Center and spread	4–5
2. Clusters and gaps	4
3. Outliers and other unusual features	4–5
4. Shape	4
B. Summarizing distributions of univariate data	Chapters 5–6
1. Measuring center: median, mean	5
2. Measuring spread: range, interquartile range, standard deviation	5–6
3. Measuring position: quartiles, percentiles, standardized scores (*z*-scores)	5–6
4. Using boxplots	5
5. The effect of changing units on summary measures	6
C. Comparing distributions of univariate data (dotplots, back-to-back stemplots, parallel boxplots)	Chapters 4–5
1. Comparing center and spread: within group, between group variation	4–5
2. Comparing clusters and gaps	4
3. Comparing outliers and other unusual features	4–5
4. Comparing shapes	4

Topic	Chapters
D. Exploring bivariate data	Chapters 7–10
1. Analyzing patterns in scatterplots	7
2. Correlation and linearity	7
3. Least squares regression line	8
4. Residual plots, outliers, and influential points	9
5. Transformations to achieve linearity: logarithmic and power transformations	10
E. Exploring categorical data	Chapter 3
1. Frequency tables and bar charts	3
2. Marginal and joint frequencies for two-way tables	3
3. Conditional relative frequencies and association	3
4. Comparing distributions using bar charts	3
II. Sampling and experimentation: Planning and conducting a study	Chapters 12–13
A. Overview of methods of data collection	
1. Census	12
2. Sample survey	12
3. Experiment	13
4. Observational study	13
B. Planning and conducting surveys	Chapter 12
1. Characteristics of a well-designed and well-conducted survey	12
2. Populations, samples, and random selection	12
3. Sources of bias in sampling and surveys	12
4. Sampling methods, including simple random sampling, stratified random sampling, and cluster sampling	12
C. Planning and conducting experiments	Chapter 13
1. Characteristics of a well-designed and well-conducted experiment	13
2. Treatments, control groups, experimental units, random assignments, and replication	13
3. Sources of bias and confounding, including placebo effect and blinding	13
4. Completely randomized design	13
5. Randomized block design, including matched-pairs design	13
D. Generalizability of results and types of conclusions that can be drawn from observational studies, experiments, and surveys	Chapters 12–13
III. Anticipating patterns: Exploring random phenomena using probability and simulation	Chapters 11, 14–17
A. Probability	
1. Interpreting probability, including long-run relative frequency interpretation	14
2. "Law of large numbers" concept	14
3. Addition rule, multiplication rule, conditional probability, and independence	14–15
4. Discrete random variables and their probability distributions, including binomial and geometric	16–17
5. Simulation of random behavior and probability distributions	11
6. Mean (expected value) and standard deviation of a random variable, and linear transformation of a random variable	16
B. Combining independent random variables	Chapter 16
1. Notion of independence versus dependence	16
2. Mean and standard deviation for sums and differences of independent random variables	16
C. The normal distribution	Chapter 6
1. Properties of the normal distribution	6
2. Using tables of the normal distribution	6
3. The normal distribution as a model for measurements	6

D. Sampling distributions	Chapters
1. Sampling distribution of a sample proportion	18
2. Sampling distribution of a sample mean	18
3. Central Limit Theorem	18
4. Sampling distribution of a difference between two independent sample proportions	22
5. Sampling distribution of a difference between two independent sample means	24
6. Simulation of sampling distributions	11
7. *t*-distribution	23
8. Chi-square distribution	26

IV. Statistical inference: Estimating population parameters and testing hypotheses	Chapters
A. Estimation (point estimators and confidence intervals)	
1. Estimating population parameters and margins of error	19
2. Properties of point estimators, including unbiasedness and variability	19
3. Logic of confidence intervals, meaning of confidence level and confidence intervals, and properties of confidence intervals	19
4. Large sample confidence interval for a proportion	19
5. Large sample confidence interval for a difference between two proportions	22
6. Confidence interval for a mean	23
7. Confidence interval for a difference between two means (unpaired and paired)	24–25
8. Confidence interval for the slope of a least squares regression line	27

B. Tests of significance	Chapters 20–27
1. Logic of significance testing, null and alternative hypotheses; *p*-values; one- and two-sided tests; concepts of Type I and Type II errors; concept of power	20–21
2. Large sample test for a proportion	20
3. Large sample test for a difference between two proportions	22
4. Test for a mean	23
5. Test for a difference between two means (unpaired and paired)	24–25
6. Chi-square test for goodness of fit, homogeneity of proportions, and independence (one- and two-way tables)	26
7. Test for the slope of a least squares regression line	27

Part II

Review

You are now ready to begin a topic-by-topic review of your statistics course. This review will help you to prepare for the examination.

The sections of the review follow the same sequence as the text *Stats: Modeling the World*, Third Edition (Bock, Velleman, and De Veaux) but can be used by any student and the topics may be taken in any order. The examples are presented in a way that should help you to build an understanding of the format your answers might follow in the Free Response part of the examination. Pay special attention to the (Clues for Clarity) symbols. They will focus your attention on tips directly related to the examination. The clues are intended to help you to communicate your understanding of key statistical concepts.

This review is a capsule view of the course. If you find you need more intensive work in a topic area, we encourage you to refer to your textbook (no matter what text you have been using) and to consult your test coach—your teacher!

Topic 1

Exploring and Understanding Data

The first and most important aspect of "doing statistics" is data: their collection, display, and analysis. In the first part of our review, we will recall the types of visual displays and their appropriateness to the nature of the data. We will also review the numerical values that help us to describe data.

1-1 Graphical Displays

The first step in understanding a data set is to answer the W's:

WHO—Who are the individuals (people, objects, etc.) that we are trying to gain information about? In order to make decisions, we need to know what our *population of interest* is and whether our data are indeed representative of that population.

WHAT—What variables (information) were recorded about each of the individuals? Are the variables **categorical** or **quantitative**?

- **Categorical (qualitative) data**—values that fall into separate, nonoverlapping categories such as marital status or hair color.
  - Numerical values are considered categorical when it does not make sense to find an average for them—for example, nominal data like zip codes and jersey numbers.
  - Data that can be counted and put in a specific order (ordinal data) but not measured are also categorical data. Examples of ordinal data are rankings in events such as horse-race finishes and team standings. A designation of first, second, or third does not tell us how close the competition was.
- **Quantitative (numerical) data**—values that have measurement units such as dollars, degrees, inches, etc.

WHEN, WHERE, HOW, and WHY—

- **When** and **Where**—Knowing when and where the data were collected gives us a context to better understand our data.
- **How**—Whether the data were obtained from a randomized comparative experiment or from a convenience sample will make a difference in our analysis of the data.

- **Why**—Knowing the why can also help us interpret the data. For example, we would be skeptical of any conclusions concerning the harmfulness of second-hand tobacco smoke that were based on data collected by a cigarette manufacturer.

Frequency Distributions—Organizing Data in Tabular Form

Both qualitative (categorical) and quantitative data can be organized into statistical tables that summarize the data and can help identify some of its distinctive features. Categories/classes should be formed in such a way that each item/score can only fall into one category/class. The **frequency** is the **number** of items/scores that fall into that category/class. A variation of the basic frequency distribution is the *relative frequency distribution.* The **relative frequency** is the fraction or ratio that compares the actual frequency of each category/class to the total of all frequencies.

$$\text{relative frequency} = \frac{\text{class frequency}}{\text{sum of all frequencies}}$$

Another variation of the basic frequency distribution is the *cumulative frequency distribution.* The **cumulative frequency** for a category/class is the sum of all frequencies up to and including that class.

Example: Final grades for 42 students in a Basic Algebra class were as follows:

73, 81, 70, 71, 74, 74, 72, 72, 87, 90, 87,
84, 70, 73, 68, 74, 84, 80, 73, 58, 89,

71, 79, 67, 81, 78, 82, 78, 88, 80, 75, 85,
72, 83, 72, 90, 83, 72, 91, 82, 53, 84

The range is 91 − 53 or 38. The table is based on 8 classes. The class width is $\frac{38}{8}$ or 4.75, which rounds to 5.

Final Grades for 42 Basic Algebra Students

Class	Scores	Frequency	Relative Frequency	Cumulative Frequency	Relative Cum. Freq.
1	52–56	1	$\frac{1}{42} = 0.024$	1	0.024
2	57–61	1	0.024	2	0.048
3	62–66	0	0.000	2	0.048
4	67–71	6	0.143	8	0.190
5	72–76	12	0.286	20	0.476
6	77–81	7	0.167	27	0.643
7	82–86	8	0.190	35	0.833
8	87–91	7	0.167	42	1.000
TOTAL		**42**			**1.000**

Notice that Class 3 is an empty class (frequency = 0); therefore, the cumulative frequency and relative cumulative frequency for this class do not change from the class above.

Clues for Clarity

- *All classes are included, even if the frequency of some classes is zero.*
- *All classes have the same width—that is, the class intervals are equal.*

The Three Rules of Data Analysis: Make a picture. ***Make a picture.*** MAKE A PICTURE!

How do you decide which type of visual display is appropriate?

Identify the variable. Is it categorical (counts) or quantitative (measurement)?

Categorical Data

THINK *One-Variable, Categorical Data ⇒ Bar Chart or Pie Chart*

SHOW Bar Chart

Gender of Students
Germantown Academy Senior Class

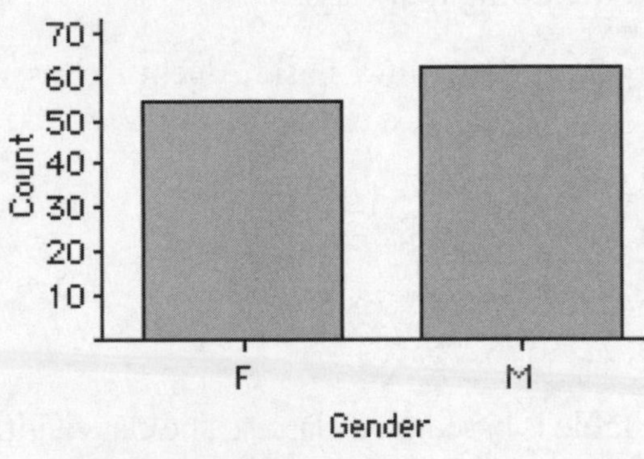

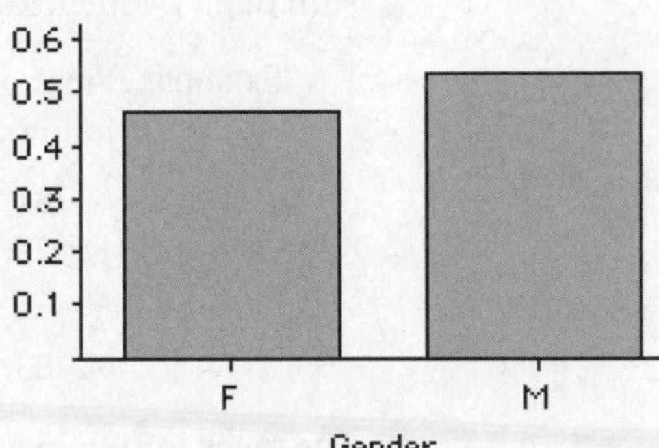

Clues for Clarity

- *Bar charts have spaces between each category of the variable.*
- *The order of the categories is not important.*
- *Either counts or proportions may be shown on the y-axis.*
- *Make sure that your data display has a descriptive title and that both of your axes are appropriately labeled.*

SHOW Pie Chart

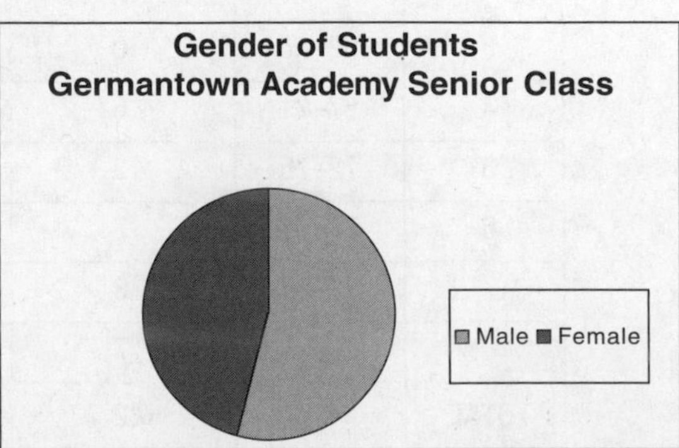

Pie charts show the whole group of cases as a circle. They slice the circle into pieces whose size is proportional to the fraction of the whole in each category.

Describe the Bar Chart/Pie Chart. The senior class at Germantown Academy has an approximately equal distribution of males and females. Males comprise 53% of the class, and females comprise 47% of the class.

Clues for Clarity

- *Describe the distribution in the **CONTEXT** of the data (you will not get any credit on the AP* Statistics exam for generic descriptions that are not in context).*
- *It is not appropriate to describe the shape of the distribution of a categorical variable. Descriptions such as "symmetric" or "skewed" would **not** make sense in describing a bar chart, since the ordering of the bars is arbitrary.*

Two-Variable, Categorical Data (2-way Table or Contingency Table) ⇒ Segmented Bar Graph

Abraham Lincoln H.S. — Summary Table

		Response: no	Response: yes	Row Summary
Grade	10th	16	9	25
	11th	17	8	25
	12th	17	8	25
	9th	20	5	25
Column Summary		70	30	100

S1 = count( )

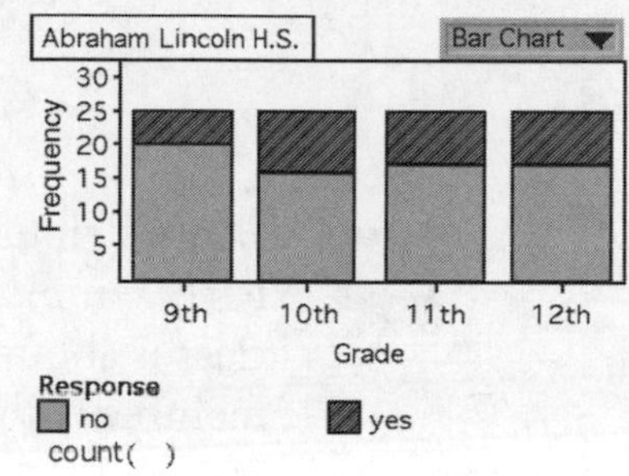

The segmented bar graph represents the responses of students in grades 9 through 12 at Abraham Lincoln High School to the question, "Do you favor changing the current eight-period-per-day schedule to a block schedule with four extended periods?" There does not appear to be much of a difference in opinion about changing to block scheduling between the different grade levels. Most students at Abraham Lincoln High School do not favor the change. About 80% of the ninth-grade students voted no as compared to about 64% of tenth-graders and about 68% of eleventh- and twelfth-graders.

Quantitative Data

One-Variable ⇒ Histogram, Ogive, Stem-and-Leaf Display, Dotplot

Histogram: Histograms group the data into bins of equal width. (Remember to scale each axis as you would a number line.) The number of data values in each bin is the height of the bar.

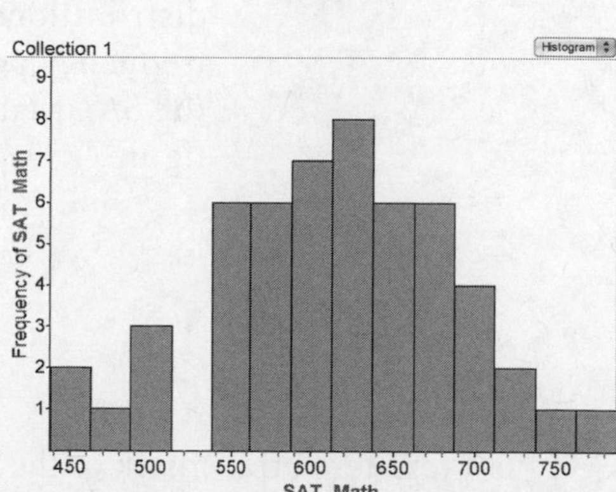

Histograms and other displays of univariate quantitative data are described by their **shape, center, and spread.** Words commonly used to describe shape are unimodal and symmetric (bell-shaped), skewed to the right, skewed to the left, bimodal, and uniform. (Remember that skew is in the direction of the long tail.) From a graphical display we can "eyeball" an approximate center or typical value and we can state the spread as an interval from the minimum to maximum values. Unusual features of the graph should also be noted (gaps, clusters, and outliers).

TI-83/84 **2nd ⇒ StatPlot ⇒ (Choose Plot Location) Enter ⇒ (Choose Histogram)**

TI-*nspire* **Home** ⇒ New Document ⇒ Add Lists & Spreadsheets (enter data into list), move up using NavPad to top of list and name list. (**Important**: You must name each column of data in Lists & Spreadsheet in order to plot the data in Data & Statistics.) Move up using NavPad until list is selected. **Menu** ⇒ Data ⇒ Quick Graph (the default is a dotplot) ⇒ **Menu** ⇒ Plot Type ⇒ Histogram (click key or enter)

TELL

The distribution of SAT*I Math scores has a single peak (is unimodal) and is fairly symmetric with a gap at 525. The typical SAT*I Math score for this class is about 626. There is a good deal of variation in scores among the members of this class, with a low score of about 450, a high score of about 780, and no apparent outliers.

Clues for Clarity

- *The only reason a gap or space would appear between bars in a histogram is that there are no data values in that particular interval.*
- *A **relative frequency histogram** looks just like a frequency histogram except that the vertical axis displays the percentage of cases in each bin instead of the count.*
- *Remember to describe the shape, center, and spread of the distribution in the CONTEXT of the data. You will **not** get any credit on the AP* Statistics exam for generic descriptions that are not in context.*

Ogive: Graphs of cumulative frequency or cumulative relative frequency distributions can be displayed as cumulative histograms or as cumulative frequency polygons called ogives (pronounced "oh-jives"). An ogive using the SAT Math data from the previous example is shown in the following figure.

SAT* is a registered trademark of the College Board.

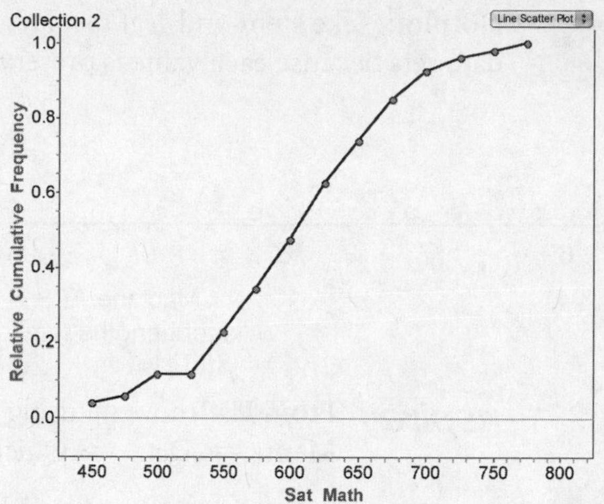

TELL

The slope of each segment of the polygon is related to the rate of increase in the number of data points from interval to interval. Since the slope of the segment from 500 to 525 is zero, there were no students who earned scores in this interval. The sharp decrease in slope after 700 shows that few students scored higher than 700.

SHOW

Stem-and-Leaf Display: Stem-and-leaf displays contain all the information of histograms with the advantage that individual data values are preserved. They are most often used for small- or medium-sized data sets. For larger data sets, histograms do a better job. The leading digit(s) are the "stems," and the trailing digits (rounded or truncated to one digit) are the "leaves."

Example: 5.26, 5.78, 5.82, 6.03, 6.22, 6.47, 6.49, 6.77, 7.10, 7.35, 7.37, 7.46, 8.20, 8.89, 10.66, 12.42

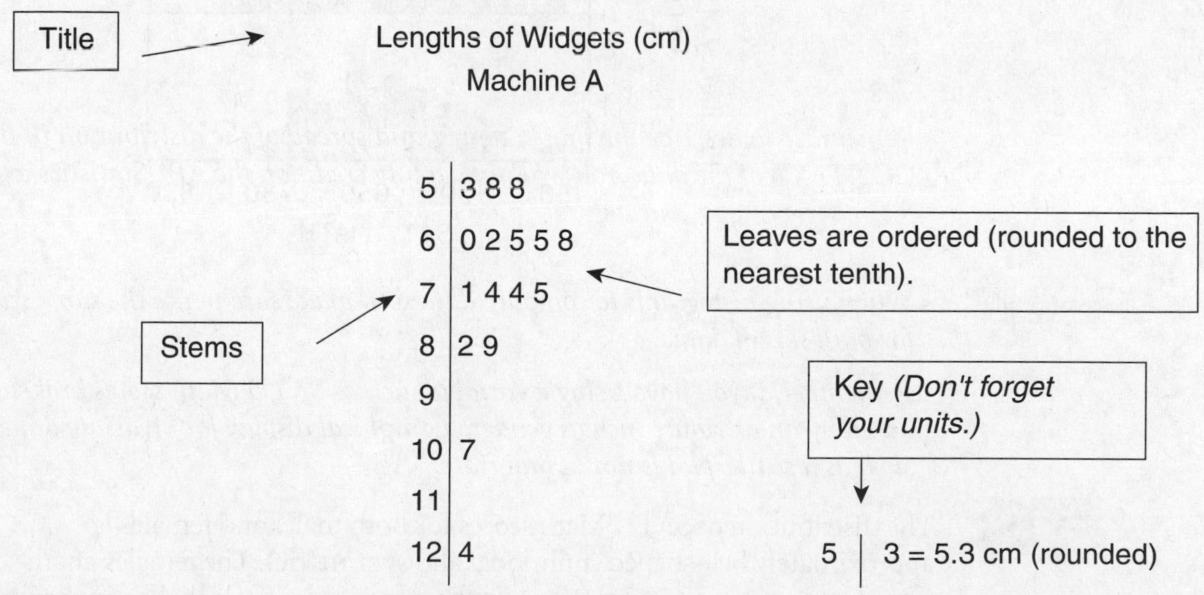

Dotplot: Like stem-and-leaf displays, dotplots are good for displaying small data sets because each value is preserved.

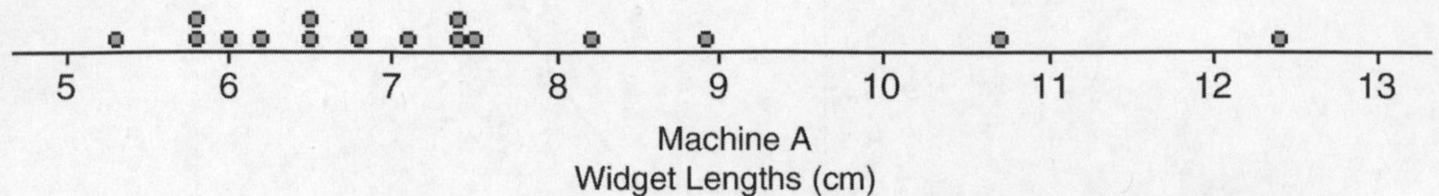

TI-*nspire* From List, move up using NavPad to top until list is selected.
Menu ⇒ Data ⇒ Quick Graph (click key or enter)

The distribution of widget lengths manufactured by Machine A is skewed to the right with possible outliers of 10.7 cm and 12.4 cm. The center, or typical length of a widget produced on that day, is about 7 cm. The process does not seem very stable; there is a good deal of variability in the lengths of widgets produced by this machine (range of 7.1 cm) with gaps at 9 cm and 11 cm. All of these characteristics can be seen in either the stem-and-leaf display or the dotplot.

Using Histograms and Stem-and-Leaf Displays to Compare Data Sets

SHOW

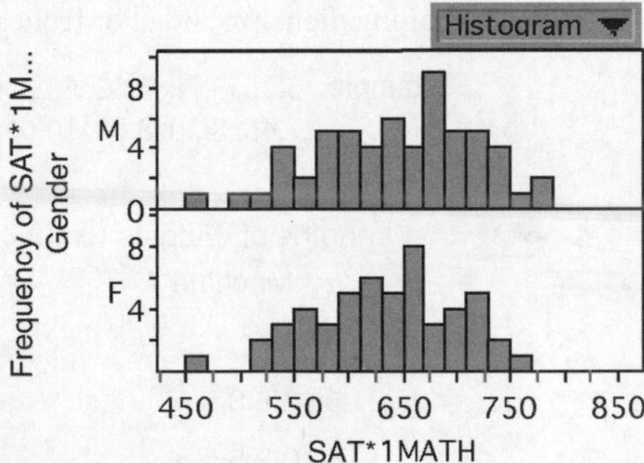

Clues for Clarity

- *When using histograms to compare data sets, make sure to use the same scale for both sets of data.*
- *Remember, if you have a single variable such as SAT*I Math scores broken down by an attribute such as gender, a graphical display for bivariate data such as a scatterplot is **not** appropriate.*

The distribution of SAT*I Math scores for both males and females is approximately bell-shaped (unimodal and symmetric). The females' math score is centered at about 630 points, while the males' score has a slightly higher center at about 640 points. The males' scores have a little more variability (range of 330 points) versus the females' range of 300 points. They both have a low score of around 450, which might be an outlier for the females (note the gap in the data), though probably not for the males since there are data values close to it.

Clues for Clarity

- *When asked to describe two data sets—for example, SAT*I Math scores broken down by gender—make sure that you* ***COMPARE*** *the two data sets (reference similarities/differences in shape, center, and spread) and don't just describe each data set individually.*

Back-to-Back Stem-and-Leaf Display

Lengths of Widgets (CM)

Machine B		Machine A
6 3 2	5	3 8 8
9 9 8 4 3 3	6	0 2 5 5 8
2 1	7	1 4 4 5
1	8	2 9
	9	
	10	7
	11	
	12	4

5| 3 = 5.3 cm (rounded)

The distribution of widget lengths manufactured by Machine A is skewed to the right with possible outliers of 10.7 cm and 12.4 cm; Machine B has a fairly unimodal and symmetric shape. The typical length of a widget produced by Machine A is about 7 cm, while Machine B's distribution is centered a bit lower at about 6.5 cm. Although their centers are relatively close, their variability is quite different. Machine B, with most widget lengths clustered around the center value of 6.5 cm, is much more consistent than Machine A. Machine B did not produce any values that could be considered outliers, unlike Machine A, which had extreme lengths of 10.7 cm and 12.4 cm.

1-2 Describing Distributions Numerically

The Five-Number Summary: Comparing Groups with Boxplots

Another graphical display for univariate quantitative data is a boxplot. A boxplot is based on a five-number summary. The **five-number summary** for a data set consists of the **minimum** value, Quartile 1 (Q1) (25th percentile), the **median**,

Quartile 3 (Q3) (75th percentile), and the **maximum** value. The **interquartile range (IQR)** is the difference between the quartiles, IQR = Q3 − Q1, and is used as a measure of the spread of the distribution.

Finding the Five-Number Summary

We'll start with a small data set.

Example: 5, 47, 3, 16, 8, 7, 1, 22, 20

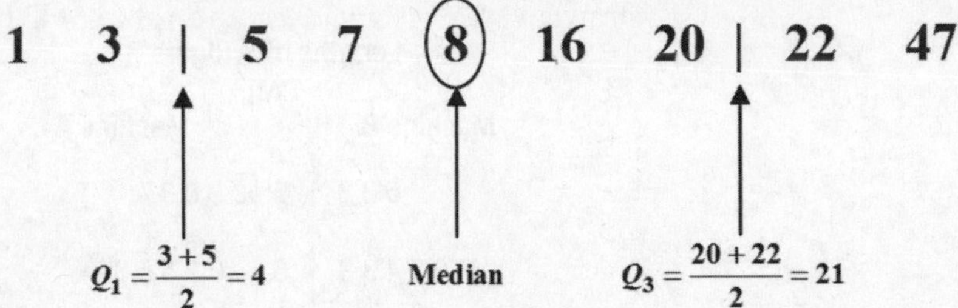

Checking for Outliers

Numerically, values that are at a distance of more than 1.5 times the interquartile range (Q3 − Q1) below Q1 or above Q3 are considered outliers. For this data set

IQR = 21 − 4 = 17

1.5 IQR = 1.5 (17) = 25.5

Q1 − 1.5 IQR = 4 − 25.5 = −21.5
(There are no low outliers since the minimum value is 1.)

Q3 + 1.5 IQR = 21 + 25.5 = 46.5
(Since 47 > 46.5, it is a high outlier.)

The five-number summary can be produced on your calculator from a list.

TI-83/84 **STAT ⇒ CALC ⇒ 1-VAR Stats (Enter List the Data is in) ⇒ ENTER**

Summary statistics for your data appear. Arrow down to see the five-number summary.

TI-nspire From List, move up using NavPad to top until list is selected. **Menu** ⇒ Statistics ⇒ StatCalculations ⇒ One-Variable Statistics, Num of Lists (use arrows to choose number of lists) ⇒ **tab** ⇒ OK (**tab** through selections to choose ×1 List, Frequency List, etc. ⇒ OK ⇒ **ctrl Menu** ⇒ Resize Column Width if necessary), (click key or enter)

Creating a Boxplot Using the Five-Number Summary

For our example data set:

Minimum Value	Q1	Median	Q3	Maximum Value
1	4	8	21	47

- Label and scale a number line appropriate for the given values.
- Draw a vertical line above the value of Q1; this forms the left hinge of the box.
- Draw a vertical line above the value of Q3; this forms the right hinge of the box.
- Draw a vertical line above the value of the median. Complete the box. The box represents the middle 50% of the data.
- Extend the "left whisker" to the minimum value if there are no outliers or to the last data value less than or equal to 1.5 IQRs below Q1 if there are outliers.
- Extend the "right whisker" to the maximum value if there are no outliers or to the last data value less than or equal to 1.5 IQRs above Q3 if there are outliers. Since any value greater than 46.5 is considered an outlier in this data set, the whisker is extended to 22, the largest data value that is not an outlier. The outlier is then represented by a dot or an asterisk. Make sure to give a descriptive title to any visual display you create.

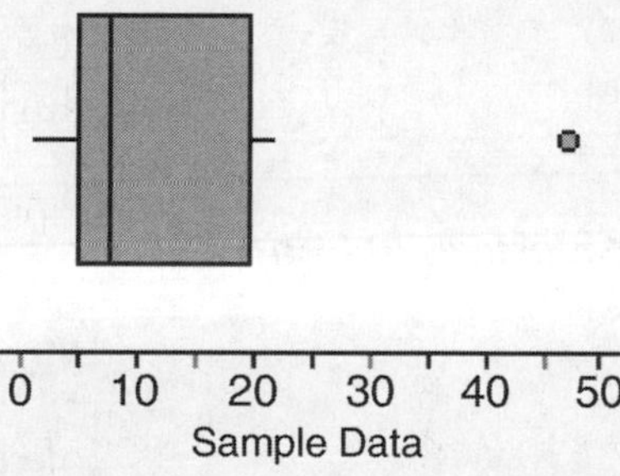

TI-83/84 **2nd ⇒ StatPlot ⇒ (Choose Plot Location) Enter ⇒ (Choose Modified Boxplot)**

TI-*nspire* To do a boxplot: Select the list. **Menu** ⇒ Data ⇒ Quick Graph ⇒ **Menu** ⇒ Plot Type ⇒ Box plot

Using Boxplots to Compare Distributions

Boxplots work well for comparing more than one group because they highlight key aspects of the data. Using a single number line scale and stacking the boxplots (either vertically or horizontally) of the different groups we wish to compare allows us to see which distribution has the higher median (numerical measure of center), which has the greater IQR (measure of spread of the middle 50% of the data), and which has the greater overall range.

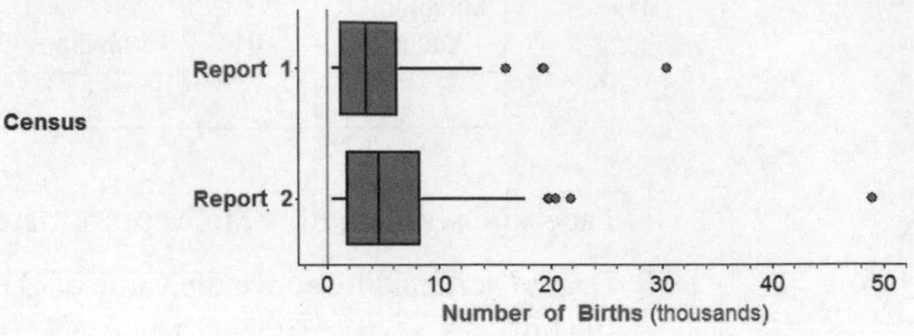

TELL

Both distributions for single teens in the United States giving birth (broken down by state) are skewed to the right. Both have states with values that would be considered outliers, with Report 2's extreme value higher than the extreme for Report 1. The median number of single teens giving birth rose slightly from the first report to the second report. There is less spread in the middle 50% of the data in Report 1 than there is in Report 2. It seems that teen pregnancy is still a problem in the United States and that it has increased during the time period between the two reports.

Measures of Center

Mean: $\bar{x} = \dfrac{\text{sum of values}}{\text{number of values}} = \dfrac{\Sigma x}{n}$ or $\bar{y} = \dfrac{\Sigma y}{n}$. The mean is a good measure of center when the shape of your distribution is approximately unimodal and symmetric.

Median: The middle of a data set when the data have been ordered.

> Note: While the median and the mean are approximately equal for unimodal and symmetric distributions, there is more that we can do and say with the mean than with the median. The mean is important in inferential statistics.

When calculating measures of central tendency, there are some cases in which the values to be averaged differ in relative importance or *weight*. If this is the case, we calculate a **weighted arithmetic mean**. A general formula for computing the **weighted mean** is

$$\text{weighted mean} = \frac{\sum w_i x_i}{\sum w_i}, \text{ where } w_i \text{ is the weight for the value } x_i.$$

Many schools use a weighted mean in computing the final grade for a course.

Example: Suppose your school reports grades quarterly and you take midterm and final exams. If your grades for each quarter count 20% and the midterm and final exams each count 10%, use the following data to compute your final grade for the year:

1st Q	2nd Q	Mid	3rd Q	4th Q	Final E
85	80	82	78	74	71

The weighted mean $= \dfrac{85(20) + 80(20) + 82(10) + 78(20) + 74(20) + 71(10)}{100}$

$= 78.7 \approx 79$ and your final grade for the course is 79.

Measures of Spread (Variation)

Standard Deviation: $s = \sqrt{\dfrac{\Sigma(x - \bar{x})^2}{n - 1}}$ or $s = \sqrt{\dfrac{\Sigma(y - \bar{y})^2}{n - 1}}$. Because its formula contains the mean, the standard deviation is ***not*** resistant to outliers. When using the mean as your measure of center, use the standard deviation as your measure of spread.

Note: You are often given the value for variance. You need to know that this value is just the square of the standard deviation. It would be a pity to get a problem wrong because you didn't know the vocabulary.

Interquartile Range (IQR): IQR = Q3 − Q1 = (upper quartile − lower quartile) = (75%-ile − 25%-ile).

The IQR gives the spread of the middle 50% of the data. Because it does not use extreme values, it ***is*** resistant to outliers. Use the IQR as your measure of spread when outliers are present or if your data are skewed. When using the median as your measure of center, use the IQR as your measure of spread.

Range: Maximum Value − Minimum Value. The range is a single number and is extremely sensitive to outlying values.

Note: The range is a supplementary piece of information; it should ***not*** stand alone as a measure of spread.

Measure of Center	Corresponding Measure of Spread	Resistant to Extreme Values?	When Is It Appropriate?
Mean	Standard Deviation	**NO**	Data are approximately **unimodal** and symmetric (bell-shaped).
Median	IQR	**YES**	Data are strongly skewed or contain outliers.

Clues for Clarity *The standard deviation will equal zero only if all data values are equal. Of course, the variance, range, and IQR will also equal zero in this case.*

The Standard Deviation as a Ruler: Z-scores

To compare data from distributions with different means and standard deviations, we need to find a common scale. We accomplish this by using standard deviation units (*z*-scores) as our scale.

$$\text{Z-scores: } z = \frac{\textbf{data value} - \textbf{mean}}{\textbf{standard deviation}} = \frac{x - \mu}{\sigma}$$

Standardizing data **shifts** the data by subtracting the mean and **rescales** the values by dividing by their standard deviation. **Adding (or subtracting) a constant** to each value of a data set just adds (or subtracts) the same constant to the mean. Measures of spread such as the standard deviation, range, and IQR remain unchanged. Think of it as sliding the graph horizontally.

Multiplying (or dividing) all the data values by a constant value changes both the measures of location (mean and median) and the measures of spread (range, IQR, standard deviation). These measures are multiplied (or divided) by that same value.

Standardizing does *not* change the shape of the distribution of a variable. It changes the center by shifting it to zero and the spread by making the standard deviation one.

Normal Models

Normal models are appropriate for distributions whose shapes are unimodal and roughly symmetric (bell-shaped). A **normal** distribution can be fully described by two parameters, its mean and standard deviation. We use

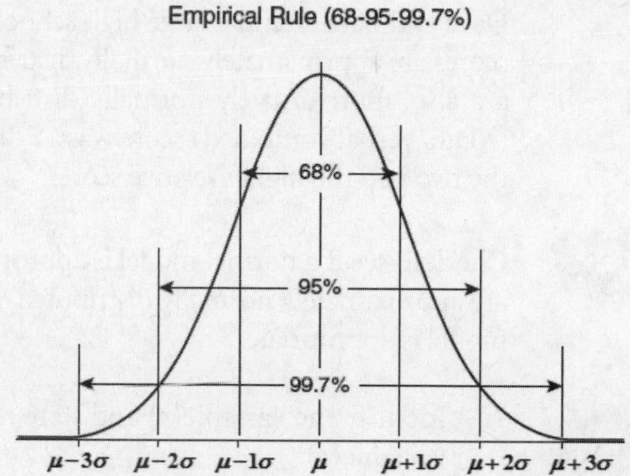

the notation $N(\mu, \sigma)$. The **68-95-99.7% (Empirical) Rule** tells us that in a normal distribution, approximately 68% of the data values fall within one standard deviation (1σ) of the mean, 95% of the values fall within 2σ of the mean, and approximately 99.7%—almost all—of the values fall within 3σ of the mean. The normal distribution with mean zero and standard deviation of one is referred to as the **standard normal distribution $N(0, 1)$**.

Example: Suppose that we know that SAT*I Math scores follow an approximately Normal distribution with mean 500 and standard deviation 100. We use the notation SAT*I Math $\sim N(500, 100)$. This information can be used to sketch the distribution for SAT*I Math scores.

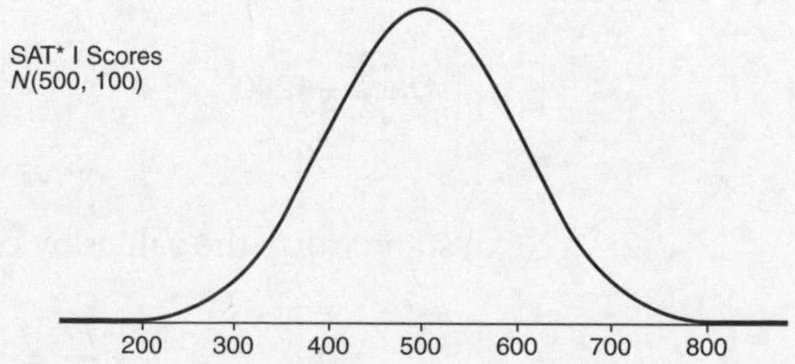

Because the scores are normally distributed, we can say that approximately 68% of students scored between 400 and 600, 95% scored between 300 and 700, and virtually all students scored between 200 and 800.

Finding Normal Percentiles

Dave and Paul attend a large high school, where SAT*I (Math/Verbal combined) scores are approximately normally distributed, $\sim N(1000, 100)$, and ACT scores are also approximately normally distributed, $\sim N(20.6, 5.2)$. If Dave's SAT*I (Math/Verbal combined) score was 1240 and Paul's ACT score was 28.3, which of the two had the higher relative score?

THINK

Check to see if a normal model is appropriate. We are told that both distributions are approximately normally distributed, so using the normal distribution as a model is appropriate.

1. Identify the variable(s) and state the problem in terms of the observed variable(s).
   - Let x = Dave's SAT*I score. Let y = Paul's ACT score. We are told that SAT*I $\sim N(1000, 100)$ and ACT $\sim N(20.6, 5.2)$.
   - Make a picture and identify the value you are interested in on the picture.

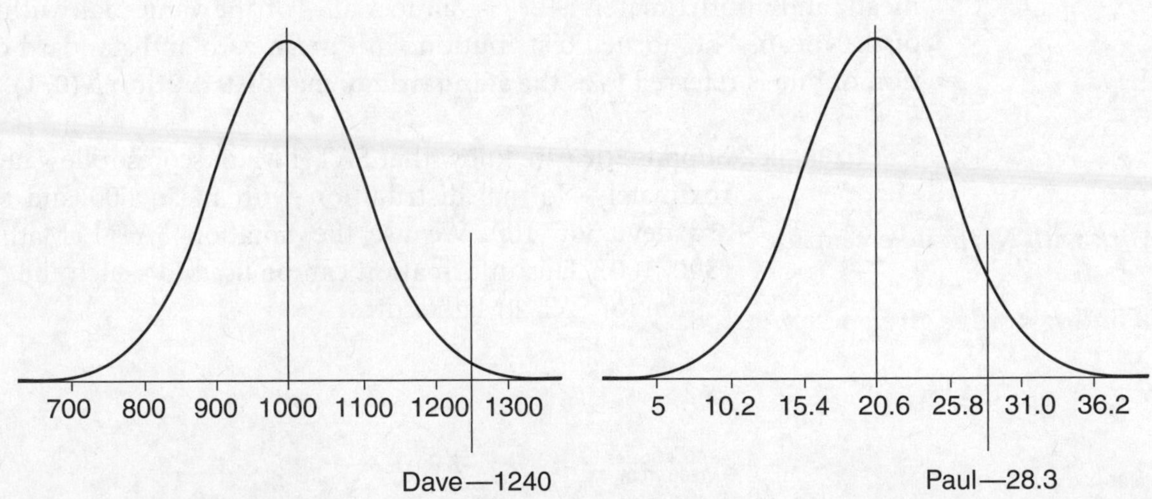

2. Next, standardize the values by converting to z-scores.

$$z_{\text{Dave}} = \frac{x - \mu}{\sigma} = \frac{1240 - 1000}{100} = 2.40$$

$$z_{\text{Paul}} = \frac{y - \mu}{\sigma} = \frac{28.3 - 20.6}{5.2} = 1.48$$

TELL

Dave's score falls 2.4 standard deviations above the SAT*I mean, while Paul's score is only 1.48 standard deviations above the ACT mean. Thus, Dave has scored better than Paul.

Alternatively, you can find the percentage of students who scored below Dave and Paul on their respective tests. Use the normal table to convert your z-scores into percentiles.

TI-83/84 **2nd Distr ⇒ normalcdf (lower bound, upper bound)**

Dave: $P(x < 1240) = P(z < 2.40) = 0.9918 \rightarrow$ normalcdf $(-99, 2.4) = 0.991$

Paul: $P(y < 28.3) = P(z < 1.48) = 0.9306 \rightarrow$ normalcdf $(-99, 1.48) = 0.9306$

TI-*nspire* **Home** ⇒ Calculator ⇒ **catalog** ⇒ normCdf(lower bound, upper bound), (click key or enter)

To find the percentiles on your calculator without first converting to z-scores:

TI-83/84 **2nd Distr ⇒ normalcdf (lower bound, upper bound, mean, standard deviation)**

Dave: normalcdf $(-99, 1240, 1000, 100) = 0.9918$

TI-*nspire* **catalog** ⇒ normCdf(lower bound, upper bound, mean, standard deviation), (click key or enter)

Dave scored higher than approximately 99.18% of the students at his school who took the SAT*I, while Paul scored higher than approximately 93.06% of the students at his school who took the ACT. Dave had the higher relative score.

More Work with Normal Percentiles

Finding a value given a proportion.

Example: Suppose that the high school Dave attends offers a scholarship to students who score in the 99th percentile (top 1%) of the school's students who took the SAT*I. We need to know what SAT*I (Math/Verbal combined) score will be the cutoff for consideration for this scholarship. Recall from the previous example that the SAT*I (Math/Verbal combined) scores for students at this high school are $\sim N(1000, 100)$.

SHOW

- **Make a picture.**
- We need to find the z-score for the shaded area. Since the table gives area to the left of a particular z-score, we want to look up $1 - 0.01$, or an

area of 0.99. The closest area in the table to 0.99 turns out to be 0.9901.

- We find that an area of 0.9901 corresponds to $z = 2.33$.

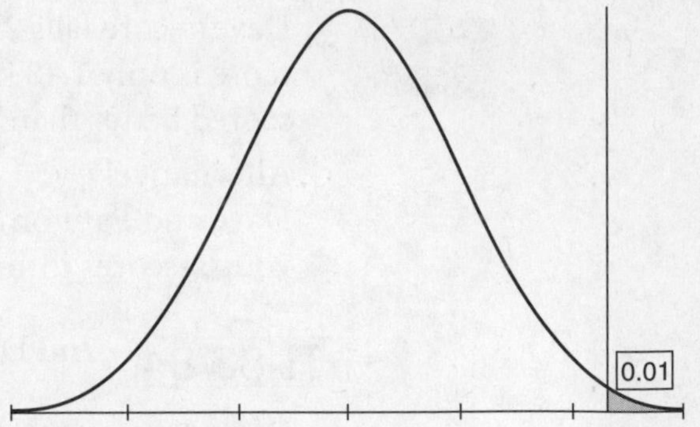

TI-83/84 **2nd Distr ⇒ invNorm (0.99,0,1) = 2.33**

TI-*nspire* **catalog** ⇒ invNorm(0.99,0,1) = 2.32635

We have the *z*-score (2.33) that has an area of 0.01 to the right of it. We need to work backward to find *x*, the SAT*I score at the 99th percentile. Recall, SAT*I (Math/Verbal combined) for students at this school ~ $N(1000, 100)$.

$$z = \frac{x - \mu}{\sigma}$$

$$2.33 = \frac{x - 1000}{100}$$

$$x = 1233$$

Note: It is possible to obtain the cutoff score directly in one step on the TI-83/84; however, you ***must*** round the value up to 1233 since SAT scores are whole numbers.

TI-83/84 **2nd Distr ⇒ invNorm (0.99, 1000, 100) = 1232.63 ≈ 1233**

TI-*nspire* **catalog** ⇒ invNorm(0.99,1000,100) = 1232.63

TELL

In order for a student at this school to qualify for the scholarship, s/he must score at least 1233 on the SAT*I (Math/Verbal combined).

Assessing Normality

How can you tell if the distribution you are dealing with is approximately normally distributed?

Make a picture. ***Make a picture.*** **MAKE A PICTURE!**
To check for normality, you could look at one of the visual displays for univariate data that we have studied (dotplot, stem-and-leaf display, histogram, boxplot). There is a more specialized display that can help you decide whether the normal model is appropriate: the **normal probability plot (NPP)**.

If the distribution of the data is roughly normal, the NPP approximates a diagonal straight line.

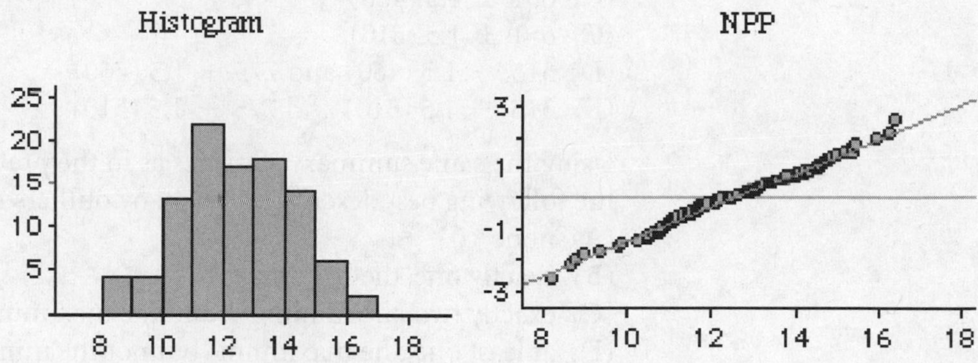

Deviations from a straight line in the NPP indicate that the distribution of the data is not normal.

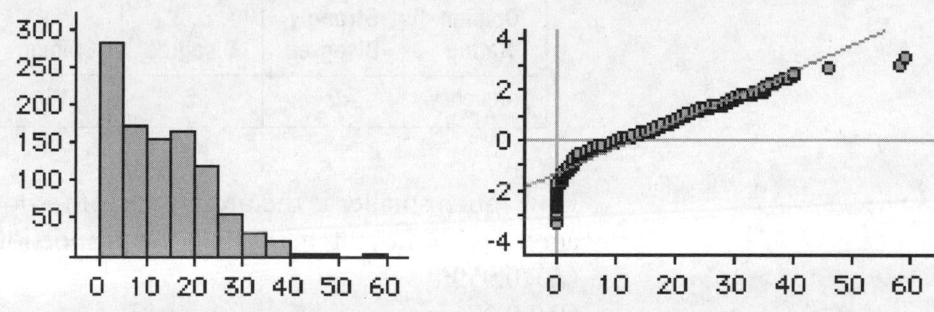

TI-83/84 **StatPlot ⇒ (Choose Plot Location) Enter ⇒ (Choose NPP—the last icon)**

TI-*nspire* From List, move up using NavPad to top until list is selected. **Menu** ⇒ Data ⇒ Quick Graph (the default is a dotplot) ⇒ **Menu** ⇒ Plot Type ⇒ Normal Probability Plot (click key or enter)

Review Questions for Topic 1—Exploring and Understanding Data

Multiple Choice

1. The summary statistics for selling prices (in thousands of dollars) of 35 luxury condominiums are as follows:

$\bar{x}$	S_x	Min.	Q1	Med.	Q3	Max.
651	510	238	315	545	775	2500

Which of the following correctly determines the boundaries for outliers in this distribution?
(A) 545 ± 1.5 (460)
(B) 651 ± 1.5 (460)
(C) 651 ± 1.5 (510)
(D) 315 − 1.5 (460) and 775 + 1.5 (460)
(E) 315 − 1.5 (510) and 775 + 1.5 (510)

2. Using the same summary statistics as in the previous problem, which of the following best describes how many outliers the original data set has?
(A) none
(B) exactly one, the maximum
(C) exactly two, the minimum and the maximum
(D) at least one, the maximum (but not the minimum)
(E) at least one, the minimum (but not the maximum)

3. The table below shows the results of a survey of 34 moviegoers given the statement, "There is too much violence in movies."

Opinion Rating	Strongly Disagree	Disagree	No Opinion	Agree	Strongly Agree
Frequency	2	7	13	5	7

How much smaller is the proportion of respondents who strongly agreed with the statement than the proportion of *all* who disagreed?
(A) 0.059
(B) 0.176
(C) 0.206
(D) 0.265
(E) 0.382

4. Using the cumulative frequency distribution given below, determine which statement is correct:

Less than 60	8
Less than 110	25
Less than 160	35
Less than 210	43
Less than 260	45
Less than 310	46
Less than 360	46
Less than 410	50

(A) 0% of the values are less than 360
(B) 25% of the values are less than 110

(C) 25% of the values are less than 135
(D) 50% of the values are less than 110
(E) 50% of the values are less than 235

5. Match the relative cumulative frequency polygon (ogive) below with the boxplot of the same data.

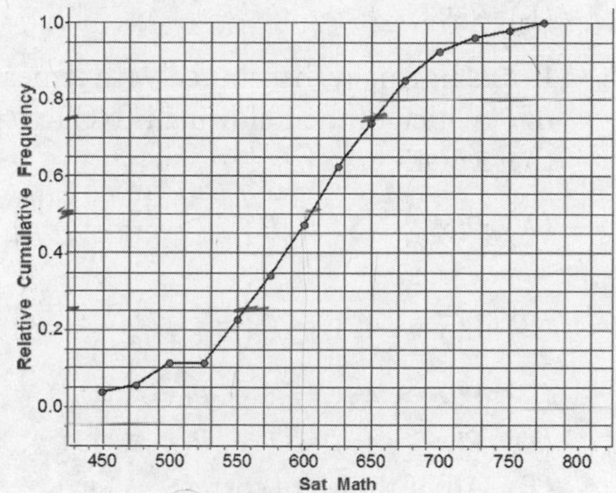

(A)

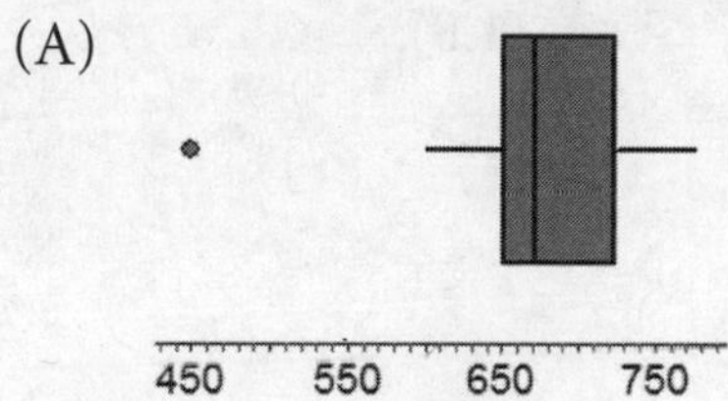

(B)

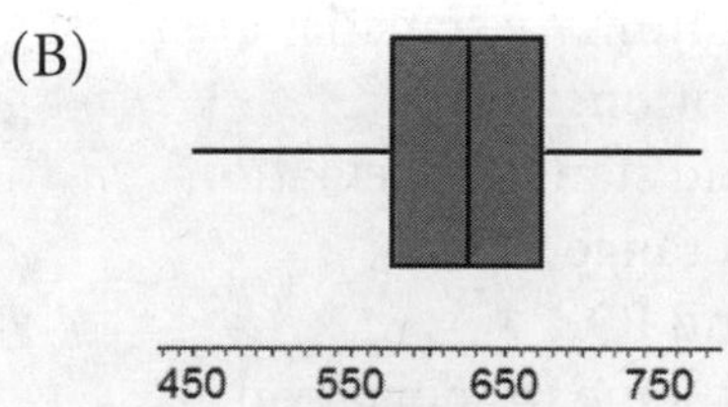

(C)

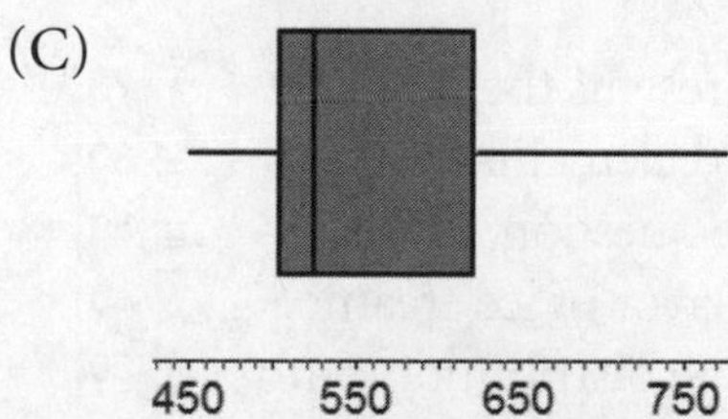

(D)

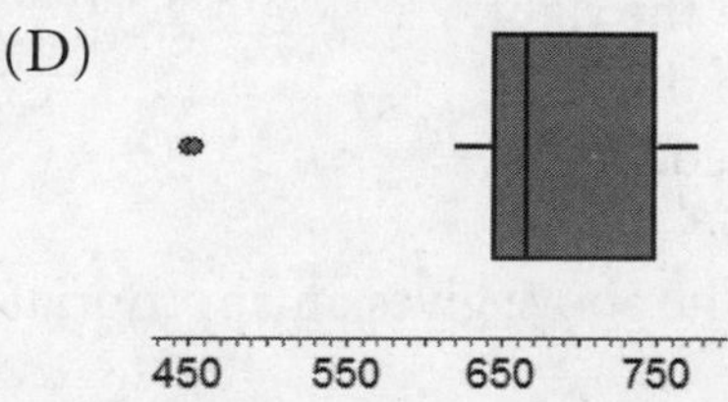

(E) Cannot be determined with the given information.

6. A distribution is ~ $N(25, 5)$. According to the Empirical Rule, approximately what percent of the data would you expect to lie between 20 and 25?
(A) 30%
(B) 34%
(C) 60%
(D) 68%
(E) 95%

7. If X is normally distributed with a mean of 50 and a standard deviation of 8, which of the following is NOT a correct way to find the probability that $x > 45$?
(A) $P(x > 45) = P\left(z > \frac{45 - 50}{8}\right) = P(z > -0.63)$
(B) $P(x > 45) = P\left(z > \frac{50 - 45}{8}\right) = P(z > -0.63)$
(C) $P(x > 45) = 1 - P(x < 45)$
(D) $P(x > 45) = 1 - P(x \leq 45)$
(E) All of these are correct.

8. Find $P(-2.31 \leq z < 1.8)$.
(A) 0.010
(B) 0.046
(C) 0.945
(D) 0.954
(E) 0.975

9. Which of the summary statistics are most appropriate for describing a skewed distribution?
(A) median and standard deviation
(B) mean and range
(C) median and IQR
(D) mean and standard deviation
(E) mode and IQR

10. The graph represents the responses of one hundred elementary school students to the question, "What is your favorite flavor of ice cream?" The shape of the distribution can best be described as

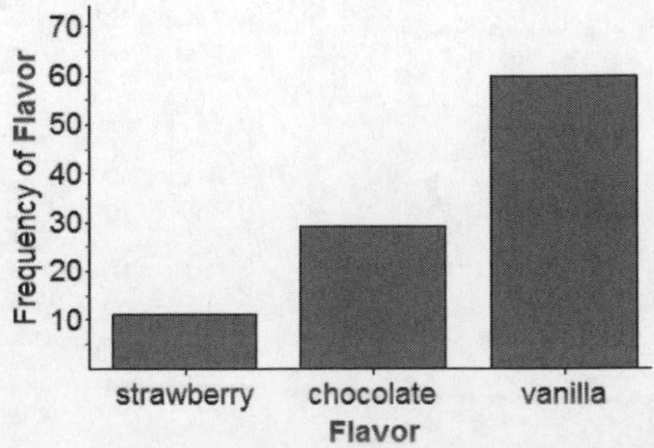

(A) skewed to the right.
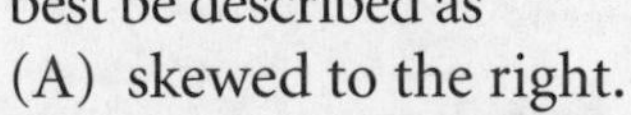
(B) skewed to the left.
(C) bell-shaped.
(D) symmetric.
(E) None of the above gives an appropriate response.

Free Response

The number of highway fatalities per 100,000 vehicle miles for the southwest and northeast regions of the United States over a 35-year period is given in the tables below.

Southwest

145	141	126	127	57	129	126
130	111	117	103	94	96	97
89	93	80	69	82	68	69
83	72	73	74	80	76	67
66	67	57	58	53	61	56

Northeast

113	98	88	81	75	76	75
74	70	63	64	64	60	56
54	53	52	53	55	57	55
57	55	54	53	49	47	45
43	36	34	33	34	34	35

(a) Construct histograms for each of the data sets. Use the same scale.

(b) Use your histograms to compare the two distributions.

(c) Construct side-by-side boxplots of the two data sets.

(d) What do the boxplots show that the histograms do not?

Answers For Topic 1—Exploring and Understanding Data—begin on page 261.

Topic 2

Exploring Relationships Between Variables

2-1 Scatterplots

A scatterplot is used to explore the relationship between two quantitative variables measured on the same cases. We put the **explanatory** or **predictor variable** on the *x*-axis and the **response variable** (the variable you hope to predict or explain) on the *y*-axis.

TI-83/84 **2nd ⇒ StatPlot ⇒ (Choose Plot Location) ⇒ (Choose Scatterplot)**

TI-*nspire* **Home** ⇒ New Document ⇒ Add Lists & Spreadsheets (enter *x*-data into list A, *y*-data into list B), move up using NavPad to list name and name each list, move up using NavPad to top until x-list is selected, press **caps** & right arrow at the same time (this will highlight both x- and y-lists). **Menu** ⇒ Data ⇒ Quick Graph (click key or enter)

Plotting the Data Using Graphs and Geometry

Home ⇒ Graphs and Geometry (to add an application page to the document) ⇒ **Menu** ⇒ Graph Type ⇒ Scatterplot. Press **enter** to open the *x*-values list, scroll down to x-list, and press **enter**, press right arrow on NavPad to open y-values list, and repeat to select y-list. **Menu** ⇒ Window ⇒ Zoom-Data

When analyzing a scatterplot, you will want to discuss:

Direction

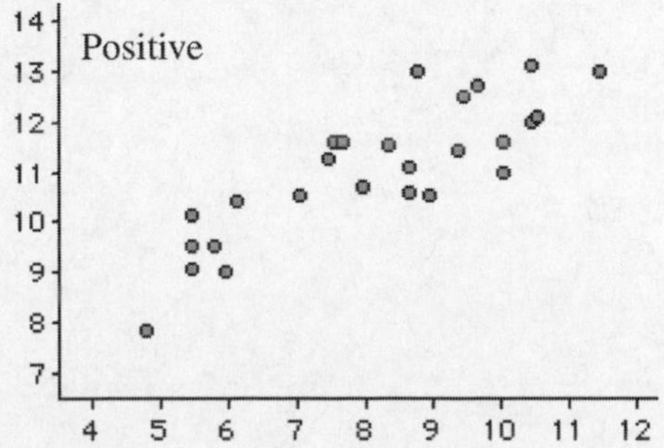

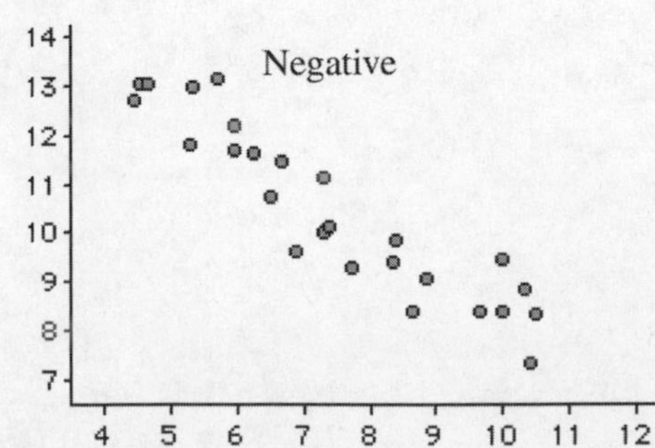

Form

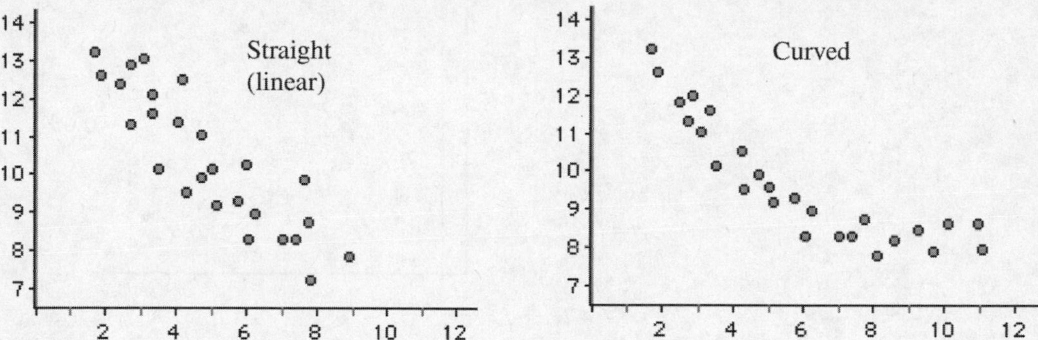

Strength

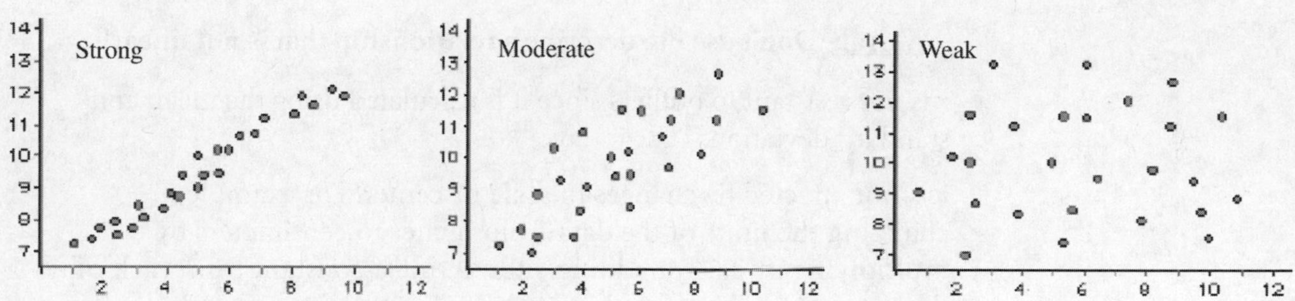

Note: Association does **not** imply causation. The only way to assess causation is through a randomized, controlled experiment.

2-2 Correlation

Correlation describes a linear relationship between two quantitative variables.

Finding the Correlation Coefficient (r): $r = \frac{1}{n-1}\sum\left(\frac{x-\bar{x}}{s_x}\right)\left(\frac{y-\bar{y}}{s_y}\right)$

Facts About the Correlation Coefficient (r):

- The formula uses standardized observations, so it has no units.
- Correlation makes no distinction between explanatory and response variables—correlation (x, y) = correlation (y, x). Correlation *does* require that both variables be quantitative.
- The **sign** of r indicates the **direction** of the association.
- $-1 \leq r \leq 1$: The **magnitude** of r reflects the **strength** of the linear association as viewed in a scatterplot. (An r-value of -1 represents perfect negative correlation; $r = 1$ represents perfect positive correlation; and $r = 0$ represents no correlation.)
- ***r*** measures *only* the strength of a **linear** relationship. It does *not* describe a curved relationship.

Example:

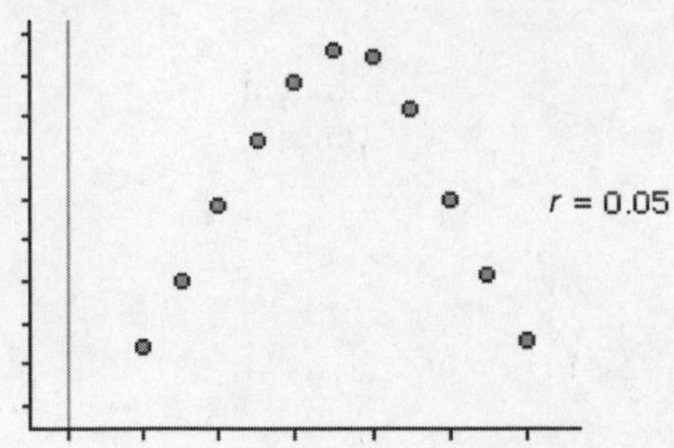

There is obviously a very strong relationship between the two variables in the graph, yet the value of the correlation coefficient, r, is only 0.05.

<u>Moral:</u> **Don't use r to describe a relationship that is not linear!**

- r is ***not*** resistant to outliers since it is calculated using the mean and standard deviation.
- r is not affected by changes in scale or center. For example, changing the units of the data from inches to centimeters by multiplying by 2.54 or adding/subtracting a constant from each of the data values does not change the value of the correlation coefficient.
- Because it is so important, we will repeat it: **A scatterplot or correlation alone *cannot* demonstrate causation.**

2-3 Least Squares Regression Line (LSRL)

The least squares regression line is the line that minimizes the sum of the squared residuals. It is a linear model of the form

$$\hat{y} = b_0 + b_1x \text{ or } \hat{y} = a + bx,$$

where b_0 (or a) is the y-intercept (the predicted value of y when $x = 0$) and $b_1(b)$ is the slope in "y-units per x-unit."

On the calculator, enter your data into lists: explanatory variable *L1* and response *L2* (or lists of your choice).

TI-83/84 STAT ⇒ CALC ⇒ 8:LinReg ($a + bx$) ⇒ L1, L2, VARS ⇒ Y-VARS ⇒ FUNCTION ⇒ Y1

<u>*Note:*</u> Your display on the screen shows LinReg ($a + bx$) *L1*, *L2*, *Y1*. We are creating the LSRL and storing it to *Y1* as a function. The LSRL will now overlay your scatterplot (**GRAPH**).

TI-*nspire* From the scatterplot, **Menu** ⇒ Actions ⇒ Regression ⇒ Show Linear $(a + bx)$. The regression can also be done in the Calculator application.

Clues for Clarity *Be consistent in your choice of form for this equation. Be able to recognize the slope and y-intercept of an LSRL no matter which variables are used to represent them. The AP* formula sheet uses $\hat{y} = b_0 + b_1x$, but you may use either form as long as you identify your variables.*

Facts About the Least Squares Regression Line

- The slope is $b_1 = r\frac{s_y}{s_x}$.
- Every LSRL goes through the point $(\bar{x}, \bar{y})$. Substituting into the equation of the LSRL, we obtain $\bar{y} = b_0 + b_1\bar{x}$ Rearranging and solving for b_0, the y-intercept, we obtain $b_0 = \bar{y} - b_1\bar{x}$.
- R^2, the **coefficient of determination,** indicates how well the model fits the data. R^2 gives the fraction of the variability of y that is explained or accounted for by the least squares linear regression on x. R^2 is an overall measure of how successful the regression line is in relating y to x. *Causation **cannot** be demonstrated by the coefficient of determination.*
- **Residuals** are what are left over after fitting the model. They are the differences between observed data values and the corresponding values predicted by the regression model.

$$\text{Residual} = \text{observed value} - \text{predicted value} = (y - \hat{y})$$

The sum of the residuals is always equal to zero.

Finding Residuals and Creating a Residual Plot

Suppose the LSRL is $\hat{y} = 2 + 3.1x$.

Explanatory Variable x	Observed Data Value y	Predicted Value $\hat{y}$	Residual $y - \hat{y}$
0	1	2	−1
1	6	5.1	0.9
2	8	8.2	− 0.2
3	13	11.3	1.7
4	13	14.4	− 1.4

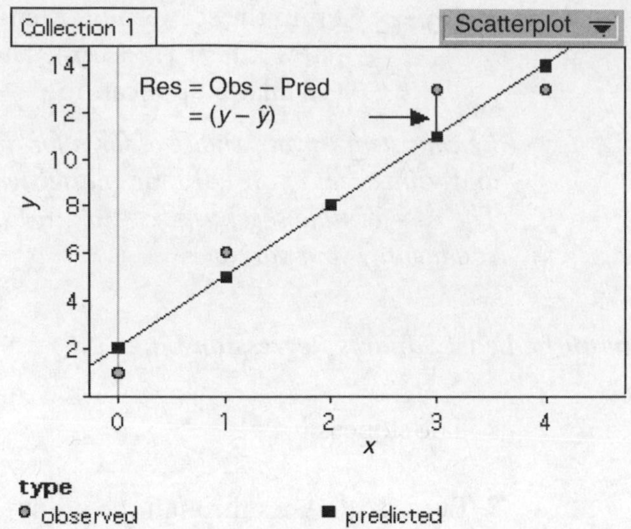

Recall that the residual is the directed distance between the observed and predicted values. A **residual plot** graphs these directed distances against ***either*** the **explanatory** or the **predicted** variable.

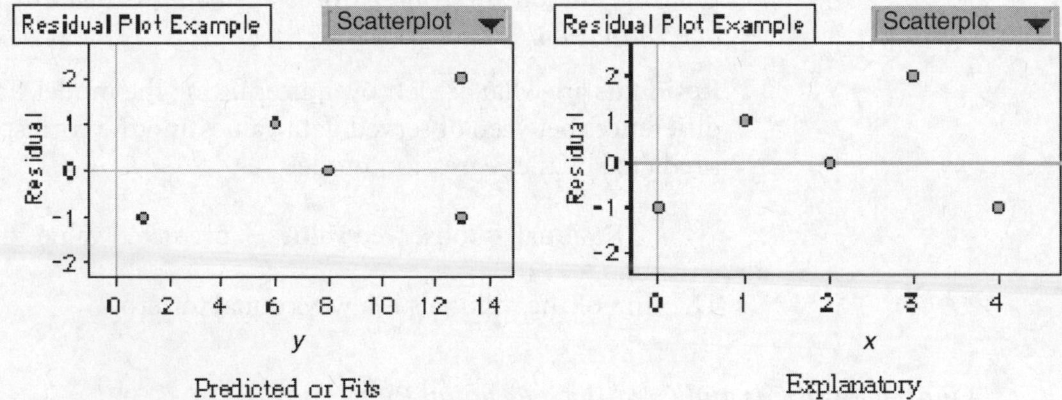

Each time you calculate an LSRL on your TI-83/84, the calculator automatically calculates and stores a list named RESIDS (the residuals for <u>that</u> particular LSRL). To create a residual plot on your calculator, make sure that you calculate the LSRL first.

TI-83/84 **2nd ⇒ StatPlot ⇒ (Choose Plot Location) Enter ⇒ (Choose Scatterplot) ⇒ Xlist: L1 ⇒ Ylist: 2nd ⇒ LIST ⇒ RESID**

TI-*nspire* From the scatterplot, press **enter** to open the *y*-values list and choose {…} stat.resid (click key or enter)

<u>Note:</u> *Remember* that as soon as you calculate a *new* LSRL, the list RESIDS <u>changes</u>.

2-4 Regression Wisdom

No regression analysis is complete without a display of the residuals to check that the model is reasonable. A reasonable model is one whose residual plot shows **no discernible pattern.**

Importance of Checking Your Residual Plot

Because the residuals are what is "left over" after the model describes the relationship, they often reveal subtleties that were not clear from a plot of the original data.

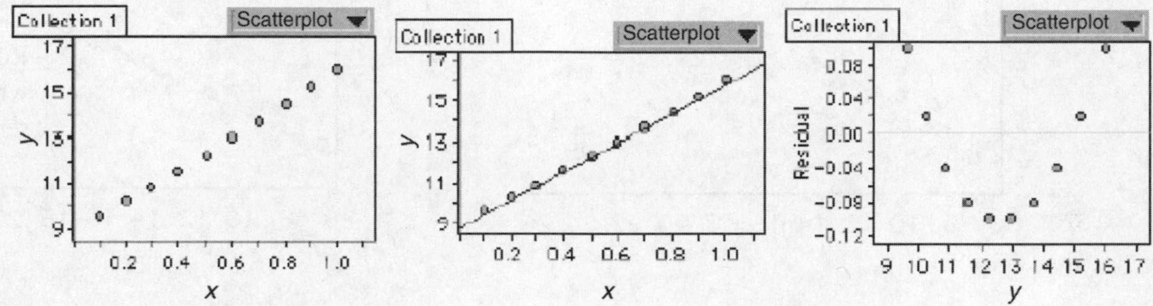

The scatterplot of our data seems to indicate that a linear model will be a good fit. The LSRL $\hat{y} = 8.8 + 7x$ yields an r^2 of 0.9984. The residual plot, however, displays a distinctly curved pattern, indicating that a nonlinear model will be a better fit for the data. The pattern you see in your residual hints at a model that you may need to fit your data.

> **Moral: ALWAYS LOOK AT A RESIDUAL PLOT OF YOUR DATA! Any function is linear if plotted over a small enough interval. A residual plot will help you to see patterns in the data that may not be apparent in the original graph.**

Data Clusters

A residual plot that has no discernible pattern, and otherwise supports your choice of a linear model as the best fit for your data, on close inspection may reveal a group of points that stand away from the central pattern. These observations may lead us to ask the question, "Do your data include distinct subsets?" If you see clusters of data, you may want to create two separate regression models and use these for predictions.

Extrapolation

Making predictions for *x*-values that lie far from the data we used to build the regression model is *very dangerous.* There are no guarantees that the pattern we see in the model will continue.

Outliers and Influential Points

Outlying points can strongly influence regression. A point can be an **outlier** because its x-value is extraordinary, because its y-value is extraordinary, or because it deviates from the overall pattern of the data. We say that a point has *leverage* and we call it an **influential point** if its removal causes the slope of the regression line to change dramatically.

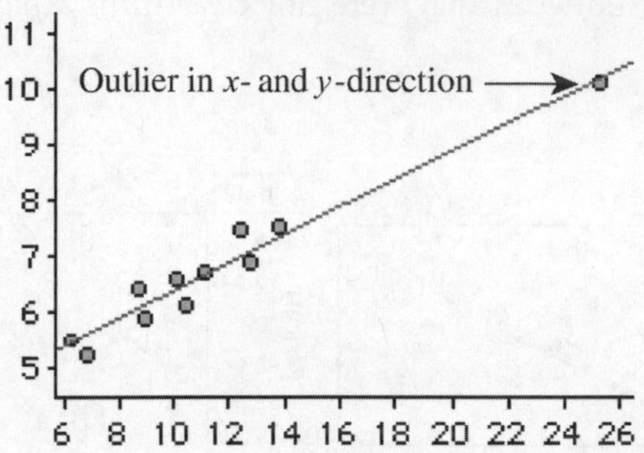

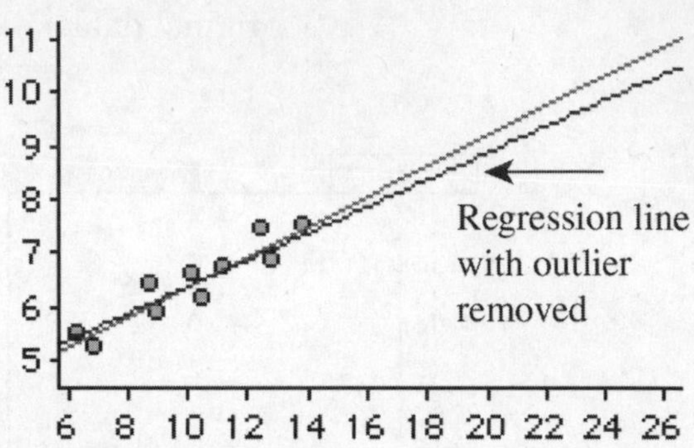

Although the indicated point lies outside the overall pattern of the data set, its removal has little effect on the regression line. It would *not* be considered an influential point.

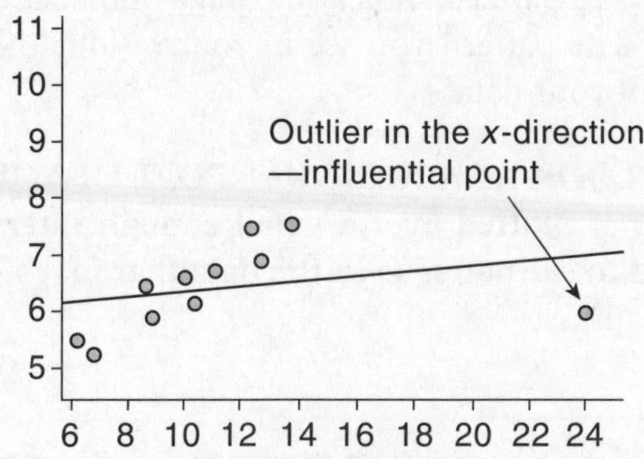

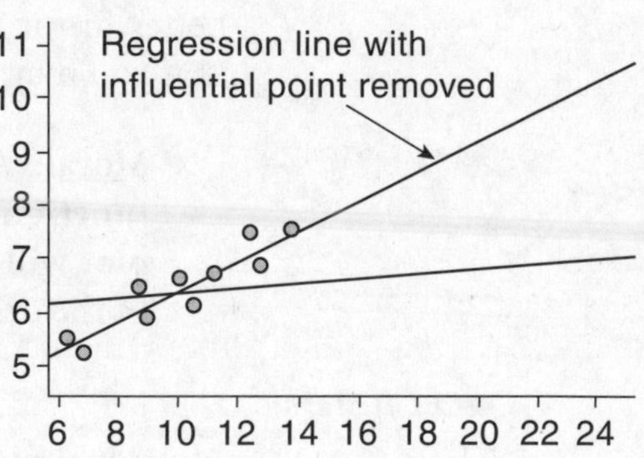

The point in the lower right-hand corner of the graph is an outlier in the x-direction. Its removal causes the slope of the regression line to change dramatically. This point has leverage and *is* an influential point.

Creating and Using a Least Squares Regression Line (LSRL)

Example: A student wanted to see how good she was at predicting distances measured in meters. She randomly selected seven distances to estimate. After recording her estimated distances, she used a range finder to find the actual distances. Below is a scatterplot of the Actual Distances versus Estimated Distances and the corresponding residual plot.

Make a picture.

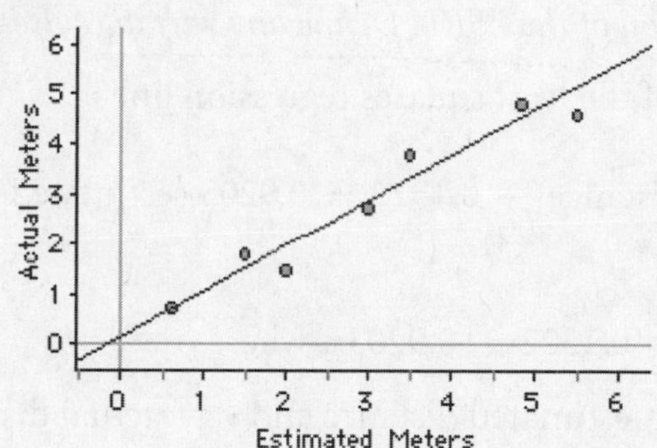

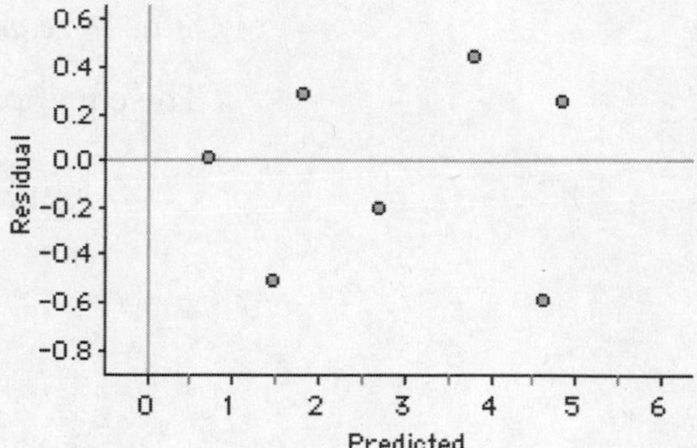

Check conditions for regression:

- The data follow a straight-line pattern.
- There are no outliers in the data.
- A residual plot shows no obvious patterns.

The scatterplot follows a linear pattern with no apparent outliers. The residual plot shows no discernible pattern, so a linear model is appropriate.

Computer outputs are often provided in place of actual data sets. *It is necessary to be able to read computer outputs (like the one shown below) to be successful on the AP* Statistics exam.*

There will be things on the printout that you might not be familiar with. Do not worry about those values. Focus on finding the information you need to write the equation of the LSRL and to describe the strength of the relationship. Recall that you can write the equation of any line if you know the slope and the y-intercept.

Dependent variable is: Actual Distance
No Selector

R squared = 91.2% R squared (adjusted) = 89.5%
s = 0.5549 with 7 - 2 = 5 degrees of freedom

Source	Sum of Squares	df	Mean Square	F-ratio
Regression	16.0489	1	16.0489	52.1
Residual	1.53967	5	0.307934	

	Variable	Coefficient	s.e. of Coeff	t-ratio	prob
y-int. →	Constant	0.132238	0.4266	0.310	0.7691
slope →	Estimated...	0.920311	0.1275	7.22	0.0008

The following are some typical questions that might be asked regarding the LSRL:

1. *State the equation of the LSRL. Define any variables used.*

   The equation of the least squares regression line is

   $$\widehat{\text{Actual distance}} = 0.1322 + 0.9203\ (\text{estimated distance})$$

   or

   $$\hat{y} = 0.1322 + 0.9203x, \text{ where}$$
   $$x = \text{estimated distance and } \hat{y} = \text{actual distance.}$$

2. *Interpret the slope and the y-intercept of the LSRL.*

   $$\textit{Slope} = \frac{\Delta y}{\Delta x} = \frac{\Delta \text{ actual distance}}{\Delta \text{ estimated distance}}$$

   For every additional meter of estimated distance, the predicted actual distance increases by approximately 0.92 meter. (*Remember, all interpretations must be given in context.*)

   The y-intercept is the predicted value of y when x is equal to zero.

   $$\widehat{\text{Actual distance}} = 0.1322 + 0.9203\ (0) = 0.1322$$

   A y-intercept of 0.1322 represents the predicted distance in meters when the distance between the person and the object being measured is zero—the person is holding the object. This value does not make sense in the context of this problem since a person holding an object would not make a prediction other than zero.

3. *State and interpret the correlation coefficient.*

   The correlation coefficient is r, and since we are given that $R^2 = 91.2\%$, or 0.912, then $r = \sqrt{0.912} \approx 0.955$ (r is positive because the slope is positive). The correlation coefficient indicates that there is a strong, positive, linear relationship between the estimated distance and the predicted actual measured distance. (*Remember that r can be either positive or negative. Look at the direction of your line!*)

4. *State and interpret the coefficient of determination.*

   The coefficient of determination, $R^2 = 0.912$, tells us that approximately 91% of the variability in the actual distance can be explained by a linear relationship between the actual distance and the estimated distance. (*Be careful that you do not choose R squared-adjusted because the adjustment has eliminated some of the data values.*)

5. *Predict the actual distance from an object when the estimated distance is 4 meters.*

$$\widehat{\text{Actual distance}} = 0.1322 + 0.9203\,(4) \approx 3.8 \text{ meters}$$

The LSRL predicts that an estimated distance of 4 meters will correspond to a predicted actual distance of about 3.8 meters.

6. *For an estimated distance of 4 meters, the actual distance from the object was 4.2 meters. What is the residual for this data value?*

Residual = observed value − predicted value = 4.2 − 3.8 = 0.4 meter

2-5 Re-expressing Data: Strengthening Relationships

Why Re-express Data?

When we graph bivariate data (in a scatterplot), we sometimes find that a linear model does not fit the pattern of our data. Since we are dealing with two variables, we may find that re-expressing one or both of these variables (transforming our data) will create a graph that is more linear. A few scenarios follow.

To decide which transformation to use, we refer back to our knowledge of functions and their graphs. Inverse functions "undo" the effect of a function. If we see a scatterplot that "feels" exponential, we think of the inverse function, the logarithmic function. Applying the inverse to the data will straighten out curvature.

The process is often one of trial and error. We get a "feel" for a model, try it, then check the residual plot and the coefficient of determination for appropriateness of the model.

- *To make the form of a scatterplot more nearly linear:*

  Take the logarithm of either the x- or y-variables, or both variables, to yield a scatterplot that is more nearly linear.

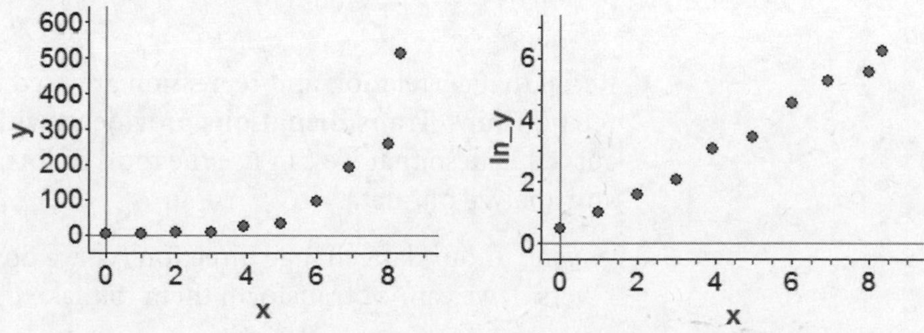

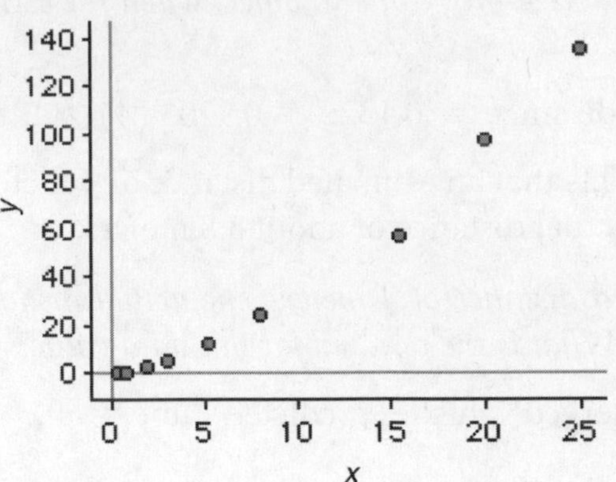

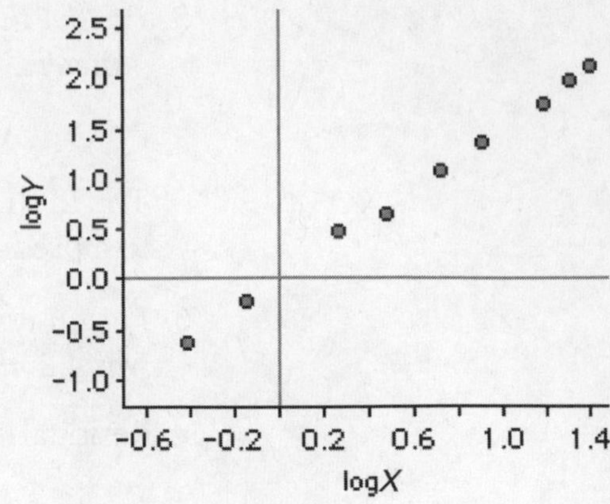

- *To make a scatterplot have a more constant spread throughout rather than follow a fan shape:*

  Take the logarithm of both the x- and y-variables to yield a scatterplot with a linear form and a more constant spread.

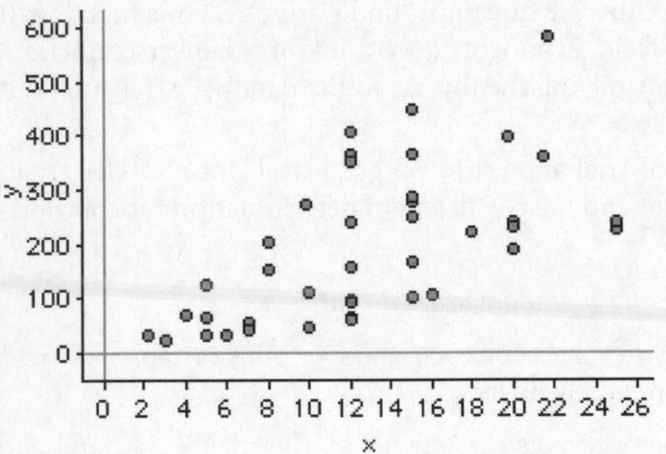

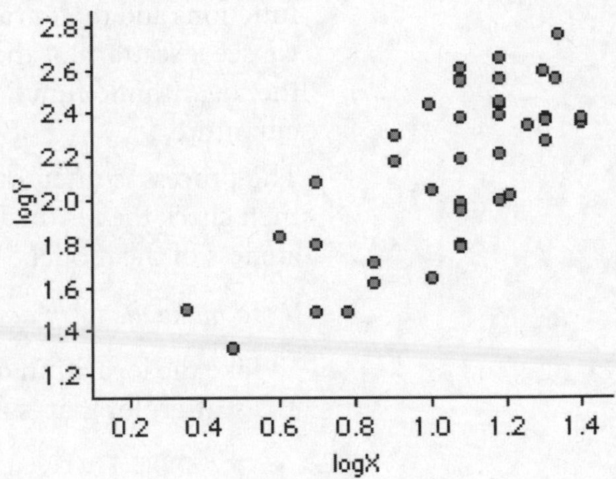

- Recall that correlation and regression are used only to describe *linear* relationships. **Transformations** provide us with a method for straightening curved data so that we can use the tools of linear regression to summarize and analyze our data.

  Note: If our data change direction (curve downward then upward or vice versa), we cannot transform them to make the curve linear.

Using Logarithms to Transform Data

Logarithms can be useful in straightening a scatterplot whose data values are greater than zero. (Remember, you cannot take the logarithm of a nonpositive number!) The table that follows suggests some transformations you might try when you see a familiar pattern in the scatterplot.

Type of Model	Transformation	Re-expression Equation
Exponential	$(x, y) \rightarrow (x, \log(y))$	$\log \hat{y} = a + bx$
Logarithmic	$(x, y) \rightarrow (\log(x), y)$	$\hat{y} = a + b\log(x)$
Power	$(x, y) \rightarrow (\log(x), \log(y))$	$\log \hat{y} = a + b\log(x)$

Remember, after you have made a transformation, you *must* reexamine a residual plot. Your original transformation may not have had the desired effect. Try again!

When you use transformed data to create a linear model, your regression equation is not in terms of (x, y) but in terms of the transformed variable(s).

Why Not Just Use a Curve?

The association between two variables may be curved and not a straight line. Calculators or computers offer nonlinear models to fit curved data (quadratic regression, exponential regression, etc.). This approach has several drawbacks. Lines are easy to understand. We know how to interpret the slope and the y-intercept, and linear models are useful in advanced statistical methods. We give all of that up when we create a model that is not linear. In general, we advise you to stay with a linear model and transform the data when necessary.

Example: A researcher observes the growth of a particular bacteria and records the following results:

Time (hr)	1	2	3	4	5	6	7	8	9	10
Population (in thousands)	2.61	4.19	4.65	5.27	8.46	9.35	13.74	15.06	21.98	29.72

The researcher's goal is to be able to predict the population at any time.

Make a Picture.

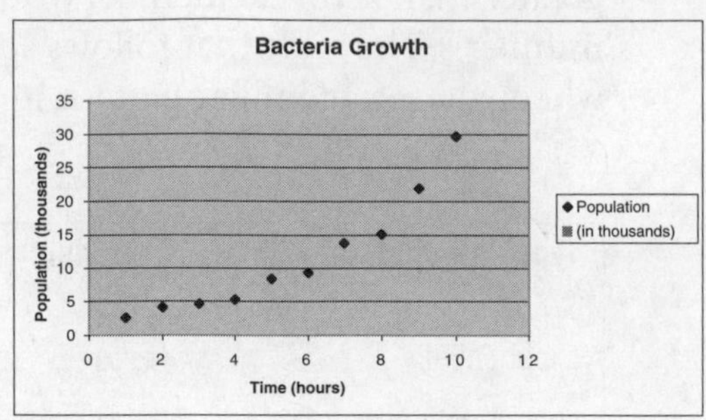

The scatterplot ***does not*** follow a linear pattern, so we will attempt to transform the data to achieve linearity. The data appear to follow an exponential model. A transformation of $y \rightarrow \log y$ is appropriate.

Time (hr)	1	2	3	4	5	6	7	8	9	10
Population (in thousands)	2.61	4.19	4.65	5.27	8.46	9.35	13.74	15.06	21.98	29.72
Log Pop	0.4166	0.6222	0.6674	0.7218	0.9274	0.9708	1.138	1.1778	1.342	1.473

Make a New Picture.

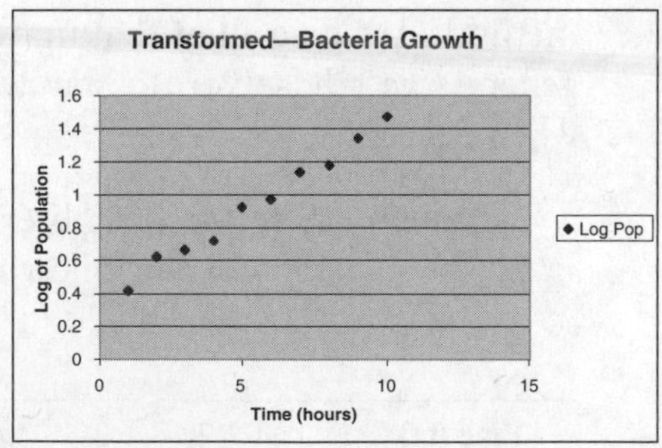

Check Conditions for Regression:

- Data now follow a linear pattern.
- There are no apparent outliers.

Find the LSRL for the Transformed Data:

You can use your calculator to find the equation of the least squares regression line. A computer analysis might look like the following.

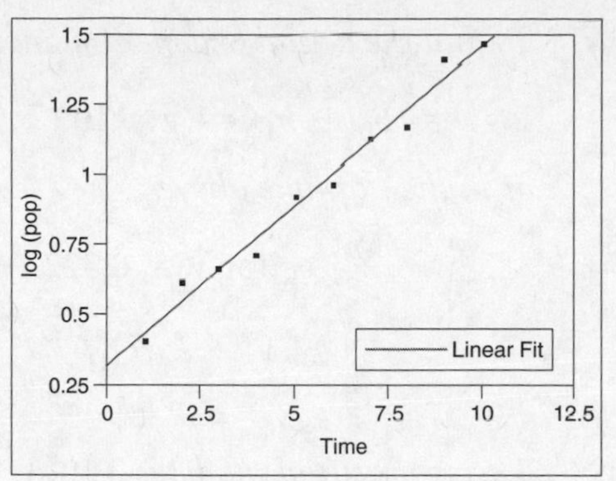

Linear Fit
log(pop) = 0.3223247 + 0.1147608 Time

Summary of Fit

RSquare	0.982117
RSquare Adj	0.979882
Root Mean Square Error	0.049729
Mean of Response	0.953509
Observations (or Sum Wgts)	10

Parameter Estimates

Term	Estimate	Std Error	*t* Ratio	Prob > |*t*|
Intercept	0.3223247	0.033972	9.49	<.0001
Time	0.1147608	0.005475	20.96	<.0001

A residual plot confirms that the LSRL of the transformed data is a better fit.

State the equation of the least squares regression line for the transformed data. Define any variables used.

The equation of the least squares regression line is
predicted log of pop = 0.3223 + 0.1148 *time*

or

$\log \hat{y} = 0.3223 + 0.1148x$, *where* x = *time in hours and*
y = *population in thousands.*

Suppose we want to predict the population at 15 hours.

$$\log \hat{y} = 0.3223 + 0.1148x = 0.3223 + 0.1148(15) = 2.0443$$

$$\text{But } \log \hat{y} = 2.0443 \Rightarrow 10^{2.0443} = \hat{y} \approx 110.74.$$

Our prediction for the population of this bacteria at 15 hours is 110.74 thousands of bacteria, or approximately 110,740 bacteria.

Clues for Clarity *To find the actual exponential model from the transformed LSRL:*

$\log \hat{y} = b_0 + b_1 x \Rightarrow \hat{y} = 10^{b_0 + b_1 x} = 10^{b_0}(10^{b_1})^x$ where $10^{b_0} = a$ and $10^{b_1} = b$

or in the example above

$$\log \hat{y} = 0.3223 + 0.1148x \Rightarrow 10^{0.3223+0.1148x}$$

$$= 10^{0.3223}\, 10^{0.1148x} \approx 2.10(1.3025)^x \approx \hat{y}.$$

The exponential model is $2.10(1.3025)^x \approx \hat{y}$.

Review Questions for Topic 2—Exploring Relationships Between Variables

Multiple Choice

1. The scatterplot shows the batting average and the number of home runs by each player on a summer baseball team.

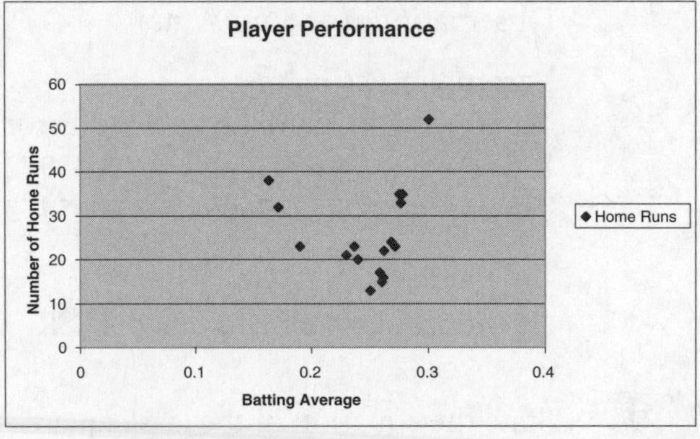

Which of the following best describes the plot?
(A) possibly linear, very scattered
(B) positive, linear, somewhat scattered
(C) negative, linear, somewhat scattered
(D) nonlinear, quadratic, somewhat scattered
(E) nonlinear, exponential, very scattered

2. A scatterplot shows a linear association, and a residual plot for the linear regression shows no pattern. The regression yielded the following.

Regression Statistics	
Multiple R	0.967039
R Square	0.93516443
Adjusted R Square	0.92976146
Standard Error	27.87746
Observations	14

Coefficients	
Intercept	− 1.2338362
Explanatory Var.	2.70155319

Which of the following is *false*?

(A) The LSRL is a good linear model for this data.
(B) The high R value means that it is reasonable to assume a cause-and-effect relationship between the two variables.
(C) Because a new LSRL after removal of one of the points is $\hat{y} = 16.72 + 2.15x$, the point that was removed can be considered an influential point.
(D) For every unit increase in x, the y-value will increase by approximately 2.701 units.
(E) The association is strong and positive.

3. Twenty types of beef hot dogs were tested for calories and sodium (mg). The hot dogs averaged 156.85 calories with a standard deviation of 22.64, and the sodium level averaged 401.15 mg with a standard deviation of 102.43 mg. The correlation was given as $r = 0.887$. The equation of the LSRL predicting sodium level from number of calories is
(A) $\hat{y} = -228.30 + 4.01x$
(B) $\hat{y} = 22.64 - 156.85x$
(C) $\hat{y} = 102.43 - 401.15x$
(D) $\hat{y} = 4.01 - 228.33x$
(E) $\hat{y} = 78.19 + 0.196x$

4. Data that follows an exponential model in (x, y) can be re-expressed as a linear model if you plot
(A) $(\log x, y)$
(B) $(x, \log y)$
(C) $(\log x, \log y)$
(D) (x, y^2)
(E) $(x, \sqrt{y})$

Use this scatterplot and computer printout for questions 5–9.

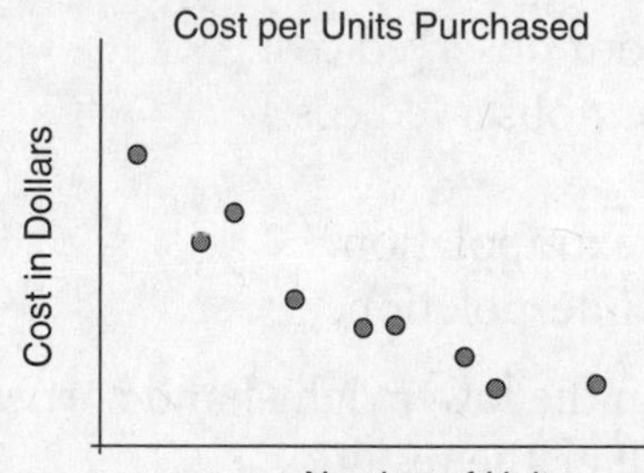

SUMMARY OUTPUT	
Regression Statistics	
Multiple R	0.941101163
R Square	0.885671399
Adjusted R Square	0.866616632
Standard Error	0.80341784

	Coefficients	*Standard Error*	*t Stat*
Intercept	8.661	0.6899	12.55
Units	−0.5042	0.0739	−6.81

5. The correlation and coefficient of determination are
(A) −0.94 and 0.97
(B) −0.94 and 0.89

(C) -0.93 and 0.94
(D) 0.89 and 0.94
(E) 0.94 and -0.89

6. Write the equation of the least squares regression line.
   (A) $\hat{y} = -0.50 + 0.07x$
   (B) $\hat{y} = -0.50 - 0.866x$
   (C) $\hat{y} = 8.66 - 0.50x$
   (D) $\hat{y} = 8.66 + 0.69x$
   (E) $\hat{y} = 12.55 - 6.81x$

7. Because of inflation, the cost per unit increases by 25 cents. The correlation for the revised data will be
   (A) $0.25 \times$ original correlation.
   (B) $0.25 +$ original correlation.
   (C) $25 \times$ original correlation.
   (D) $25 +$ original correlation.
   (E) original correlation.

8. Which of the following is a correct interpretation of the coefficient of determination?
   (A) Approximately 89% of the data is explained by the least squares regression line.
   (B) Approximately 89% of the least squares regression line is explained by the data.
   (C) Approximately 89% of the variation in the cost can be explained by its linear relationship with number of units purchased.
   (D) Approximately 89% of the variation in the number of units purchased can be explained by its linear relationship with the cost.
   (E) None of these is a correct interpretation.

9. The residual for 8 units purchased is -0.8074. This tells us that our predicted cost is
   (A) higher than our observed cost.
   (B) lower than our observed cost.
   (C) wrong.
   (D) the result of extrapolation.
   (E) the result of interpolation.

10. If the data point in the lower right-hand corner of the graph is removed, which of these will be the result?

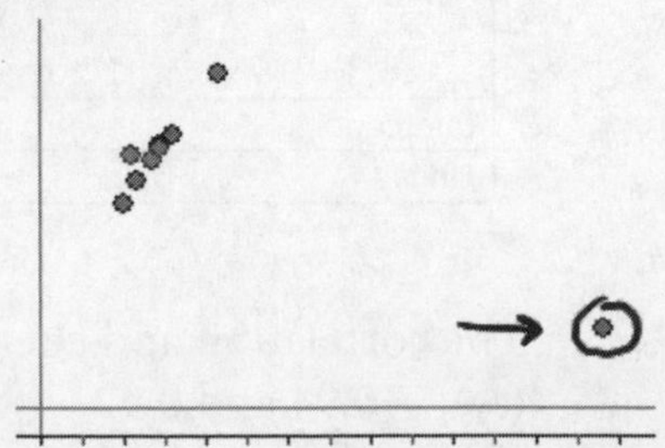

(A) The slope of the least squares regression line will decrease and the correlation will increase.
(B) The slope of the least squares regression line will increase and the correlation will increase.
(C) The slope of the least squares regression line will decrease and the correlation will decrease.
(D) The slope of the least squares regression line will increase and the correlation will decrease.
(E) The slope of the least squares regression line and the correlation will remain the same.

Free Response

The table of data shows the average highway mileage (mpg) based on car engine size (liters).

Engine Size (liters)	1	1.3	1.5	1.6	1.8	1.9	2.0	2.2	2.3	2.4	2.5	2.8
Hwy Mileage (mpg)	47	43	39	38	33	36	32	30	29	31	28	28
Engine Size (liters)	3.0	3.2	3.4	3.7	4.0	4.3	4.4	4.6	5.0	5.5	5.7	6.0
Hwy Mileage (mpg)	26	25	28	24	24	23	23	24	22	20	23	19

(a) Make a scatterplot of the data.

(b) Find the equation of the least squares regression line (LSRL) for the data.

(c) Does a linear model seem appropriate for this data? Why or why not?

(d) Re-express the data using logs of one or both variables and create a new model. Explain your choice. Is this model better? Why or why not?

(e) Estimate the highway mileage for a car with an 8.0 liter engine. Is your model a good predictor for the highway mileage for such a car?

(f) Calculate the residual for a 2.0 liter engine.

Answers for Topic 2—Exploring Relationships Between Variables—begin on page 263.

Topic 3

Gathering Data

We have reviewed how to look at data. But data analysis is meaningful only if the data truly reflect what we are trying to study. In other words, good methods of collecting data are essential to reaching meaningful conclusions. We will now review the key ideas about data collection.

3-1 Understanding Randomness

Random Outcomes

A random event is one whose outcome we cannot predict. This fact may suggest that random events are totally chaotic and therefore not very useful in modeling real-world situations. Although the outcomes of individual trials of a random event are unknown, over the long run a pattern emerges. For example, we cannot predict with any certainty the outcome of a single toss of a fair coin; however, if tossed many times, we know that, in the long run, the coin will show heads about half of the time. It is this long-run predictability that makes randomness a useful tool in reaching conclusions and making intelligent decisions about real-world situations.

Simulation

Simulation is a powerful tool for gaining insight into events whose outcomes are random.

Example: Your school decided to hold a raffle to defray the cost of tickets to the senior prom. The breakdown of ticket sales was as follows:

Students: 650 tickets

Faculty: 325 tickets

At an assembly, the principal reached into a jar and drew three winning tickets. To everyone's dismay, all three ticket winners were members of the faculty. The students cried foul. Their argument was that, given the breakdown of sales between the two groups, it would be nearly impossible for all three winners to be faculty members. They argued that the ticket stubs had not been properly mixed before the drawing. We can use a simulation to determine if the outcome of the drawing could reasonably be expected to have occurred if the tickets were properly mixed.

Performing a Simulation

Identify the trial to be repeated.

In this case the trial to be repeated is the selection of a ticket from the jar.

Outcomes

State how you will model the random occurrence of an outcome.

Since 975 tickets were sold (650 to students and 325 to faculty), we need to look at three-digit random numbers.

- Let 000–649 represent a ticket purchased by a student.
- Let 650–974 represent a ticket purchased by a member of the faculty.
- Skip 975–999. If we get a number in this range, we will discard it and take the next three-digit random number.

If a number appears more than once in a trial, it must be ignored since once a ticket is drawn, it is no longer in the running for the remaining prizes.

Trial

Explain how you will simulate the trial.

Each trial consists of identifying three-digit numbers as either a student ticket (*S*) or a faculty ticket (*F*) until three tickets have been chosen, ignoring numbers that are out of range (*X*) or repeated numbers (*R*).

Define the response variable. What are we interested in knowing? We'd like to know how often all three tickets chosen belong to members of the faculty.

The response variable is whether or not all three tickets drawn belong to members of the faculty. *FFF* = YES; all other combinations = NO.

Mechanics

Run several trials. For the sake of illustration, we ran only ten trials. Calculators and computers allow us to run many trials and to tabulate the results quickly and easily.

Trial Number	Outcomes	All Faculty?
1	*FFF*	YES
2	*SFS*	NO
3	*SSS*	NO
4	*FXSF*	NO
5	*SSS*	NO
6	*FSF*	NO
7	*SSF*	NO
8	*SSF*	NO
9	*SFF*	NO
10	*SSS*	NO

Estimate

Summarize the results across all trials.

FFF (all faculty winners) occurred only once out of ten trials, or 10% of the time.

Interpretation

Describe what your simulation shows and draw your conclusions about the real world.

In our simulation of fair ticket draws, all three prizewinners were faculty members only 10% of the time. While this result could happen, it is not particularly likely. We might be suspicious, but we would need many more trials and a smaller chance of all faculty (*FFF*) winners before we would make an accusation of unfairness.

Clues for Clarity

If you are given a random-number table, follow the steps outlined above and also carefully mark the table so that your method can be duplicated (followed by the reader). You are usually told how many trials to conduct. Indicate the response variable (in this example, yes or no) for each trial.

```
           Yes                            No                        No
  F         F         F   |  S        F         S   |   S        S        S
9 2 1 | 9 5 6 | 6 8 0 | 3 3 1 | 8 2 5 | 6 4 6 | 5 1 0 | 5 8 2 | 0 9 3 |

                     No                           No
  F         X         S          F   |  S         S         S   |   F        S
9 2 3 | 9 8 9 | 2 4 8 | 8 7 9 | 3 3 2 | 0 3 6 | 2 5 0 | 9 4 4 | 3 1 1 |

  No                  No                          No
  F   |     S         S          F   |  S         S         F   |   S        F
7 6 8 | 1 6 1 | 4 0 3 | 9 7 0 | 1 9 8 | 3 7 6 | 7 9 3 | 2 0 6 | 8 3 2 |

  No                  No
  F   |     S         S          S   |
8 2 3 | 3 6 4 | 6 4 8 | 0 4 2 | 9 7 8 2 5 0 9 8 1 9 4 5 5 8 1
```

Wait-time Simulations

In a wait-time simulation, we continue looking at random numbers until the prescribed condition occurs.

Example: Your favorite breakfast cereal, Super Sugar Choco-Balls, is running a promotion. Each box of the cereal will contain one of four different prizes. The only prize that you are interested in obtaining is the computer game Super Snood. The manufacturer advertises that there is an equal chance of getting each of the four prizes. You would like to know, on average, how many boxes of Super Sugar Choco-Balls you will need to purchase before you obtain one that has the prize you desire.

Identify the component to be repeated

In this case, the component is the selection of a box of cereal.

Outcomes

State how you will model the random occurrence of an outcome.

For each box of cereal you choose, the probability of getting a box with the game you desire is 1/4, or 25%. You need to look at two-digit random numbers.

- Let 00–24 represent a box of cereal that contains the game Super Snood.
- Let 25–99 represent a box of cereal that contains any one of the three undesired prizes.

For this simulation, repeated numbers are valid since you may get duplicate undesired prizes before you get the prize you want.

Trial

Explain how you will simulate the trial.

Each trial consists of identifying two-digit numbers as either the desired prize (D) or the undesired prize (U). You continue until you obtain your first two-digit number representing the desired prize.

Define the response variable.

The response variable is the number of boxes of cereal opened until you obtain the desired prize.

Mechanics

Run several trials.

For the sake of illustration, we ran only ten trials. Calculators and computers allow us to run many trials and to tabulate the results quickly and easily.

Trial Number	Outcomes	Number of Boxes of Cereal
1	*UD*	2
2	*UD*	2
3	*UUUUUD*	6
4	*UUUUUUUUD*	9
5	*D*	1
6	*UUUD*	4
7	*D*	1
8	*D*	1
9	*UUD*	3
10	*UUUUUD*	6

Estimate

Analyze the response variable. You want to know how many boxes, on average, you might expect to buy in order to obtain a Super Snood game.

In your first ten trials, you needed 2, 2, 6, 9, 1, 4, 1, 1, 3, and 6 for an average of 3.5.

Interpretation

State your conclusion (in the context of the problem, as always).

Based on this simulation, you estimate that you will need to buy, on average, 3.5 (approximately 4) boxes of cereal to obtain the Super Snood game.

Clues for Clarity *If you are given a random-number table, follow the steps outlined above and also carefully mark the table so that your method can be duplicated. You are usually told how many trials to conduct. Indicate the value of the response variable for each trial.*

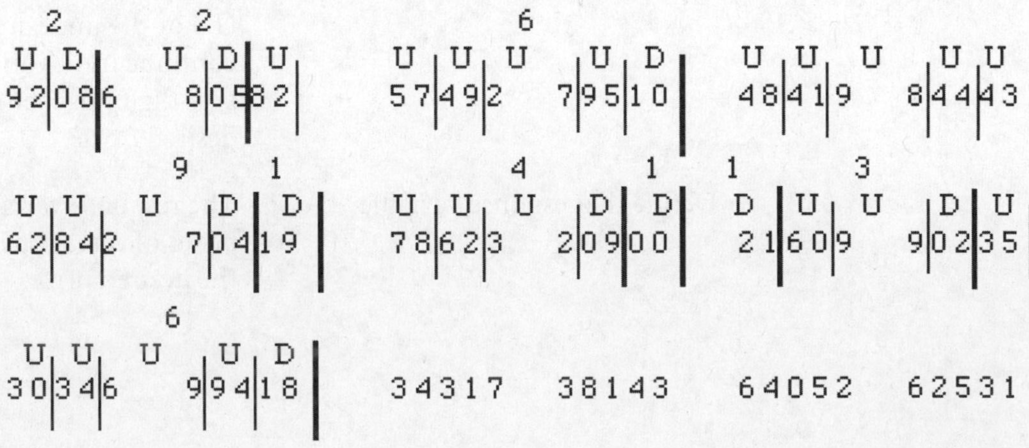

3-2 Sample Surveys

Producing Data

If we are to draw meaningful conclusions from measured or observed data, it is essential that we understand proper data-collection methods. Bad sample designs yield worthless data. There is *no* way to correct for a bad sample.

Basic Concepts and Terminology of Sampling

Population—A population is the entire group of individuals whom we hope to learn about. The population is determined by what we want to know.

Sample—A sample is a smaller group of individuals selected from the population. The sample size is determined by what is practical and representative of the population we are interested in learning about.

- **Sampling Frame**—A sampling frame is a list of individuals from the population of interest from which the sample is drawn. If the sampling frame is not equal to the population of interest and is different from the population in some way that may affect the response variable, the sample will be biased in that same way. For example, if we are interested in obtaining information about high school students in Pennsylvania but obtain our sample of students from a list of private schools, then our sampling frame is not reflective of the population of interest nor is our sample.
- **Census**—A census is a sample that consists of the entire population.
- **Sampling Variability**—Sampling variability is the natural tendency of randomly drawn samples to differ, one from another. Sampling variability is not an error, just the natural result of random sampling. Statistics attempts to minimize, control, and understand variability so that informed decisions can be drawn from data despite variation. Although samples vary, when we use chance to select them, they do not vary haphazardly but rather according to the laws of probability.

Parameters and Statistics

- **Parameter**—A parameter is a number that characterizes some aspect of the population such as the mean or standard deviation of some variable of the population. We rarely know the true value of a population parameter; we estimate it from sampled data. We denote population parameters with Greek letters.
- **Statistic (Sample Statistic)**—Statistics are values calculated for sample data. We use statistics to estimate values in the population (parameters). We denote statistics with standard letters.

Name	Statistic	Parameter
Mean	$\bar{x}$	μ
Standard Deviation	s	σ
Correlation	r	ρ
Regression Coefficient (slope)	b_1	β
Proportion	$\hat{p}$	$p(\theta \text{ or } \pi)$

Sample Size

The sample size is the number of individuals selected from our sampling frame. The size of the population does not dictate the size of the sample. A sample of size 100 may work equally well for a population of 1000 or 10,000 as long as it is a random sample of the population of interest. A ladle of soup gives us the same information regarding the seasoning of the soup regardless of the size of the pot it is taken from as long as the pot is well stirred (random samples). The general rule is that the sample size should be no more than 10% of the population size ($10n < N$).

Sampling Designs

All statistical sampling designs incorporate the idea that chance, rather than choice, is used to select the sample. The sampling design is the method used to choose the sample.

- **Probability Sample**—A probability sample is chosen using a random mechanism in such a way that each individual or group of individuals has the same chance of being selected.
- **Random Sample**—A random sample is chosen using a random mechanism in such a way that the probability of each sample being selected can be computed; random samples may be drawn *with or without* replacement.
- **Simple Random Sample (SRS)**—A simple random sample is a random sample chosen *without* replacement so that, in an SRS of size *n*, an individual could be selected only once for that sample. An SRS of size *n* is one in which each possible *set* of *n* individuals has an equal chance of selection.
- **Stratified Random Sample**—This type of sample divides the population into *homogeneous* groups called **strata**. Strata are made up of individuals similar in a way that may affect the response variable. Simple random sampling is applied within each stratum *before* the results are combined.

Example: A television station is interested in obtaining information from its viewers about the events they are most likely to watch during the Olympics. Because the station's statisticians suspect that men and women differ in their choices of events, a sample that stratifies by gender can help reduce variation in the results.

- **Cluster Sample**—When the population exists in readily defined *heterogeneous* groups or clusters, a cluster sample is an SRS of the clusters. This method of sampling uses the data from all of the individuals from the selected clusters. It is often used to reduce the cost of obtaining a sample.

  Example: A large school wants to sample ninth-grade students to determine their opinions about summer reading requirements. Students are assigned to homerooms alphabetically. Each homeroom can be considered a cluster because it is a heterogeneous grouping of ninth-grade students. To accomplish the school's goal, a random sample of ninth-grade homerooms is selected. All of the students in each selected homeroom (cluster) are asked their opinions about the summer reading assignment.

- **Systematic Sample**—A systematic sample is selected according to a predetermined scheme. For example, we may obtain a list of our population of interest and from that list choose every i^{th} student to be part of the sample. A systematic sample can be *random* if the starting point for the scheme is randomly selected; however, this method can never produce a *simple* random sample because each possible sample of size *n* does not have an equal chance of being chosen. Systematic sampling, where only one random selection is necessary, is used to simplify the sampling process. When there is reason to believe that the order of the list is not associated with the responses sought, this method gives a representative sample.

  Example: The Student Council wishes to survey a sample of 30 students from the senior class about their opinions on the graduation ceremony. The senior class has 350 members. Systematic sampling is used. The seniors are listed alphabetically and numbered in sequence. The sampling scheme is to choose every tenth student. A starting number is randomly selected. The corresponding student and every tenth student thereafter (until 30 students have been selected) is included in the sample. (Note that this method results in only one possible sample of size 30 after the selection of the starting point. The first 30 students in the alphabetical listing, for example, are not a possible sample; thus, the sample is not an SRS.)

- **Multistage Sampling**—This method produces a final sample in stages, taking each sample from the one before it. It may combine several methods of sampling. It can be random but will not produce an SRS.

- **Convenience Sample**—This type of sample is obtained exactly as its name suggests, by sampling individuals who are conveniently available. Convenience samples are very unlikely to represent the population of interest because it is unlikely that every member of this population is conveniently available. Convenience samples are not probability samples nor are they random. As a method, convenience sampling may lead to bias.

Sources of Bias

Bias is any systematic failure of a sample to represent its population of interest. It is very important to reduce bias. The best defense against bias is randomization. There is no way to recover from a biased sample or a survey that asks biased questions. *Remember, you can* reduce *bias, but you can never completely eliminate it.*

These are some sources of bias:

- **Undercoverage Bias**—A sampling scheme that differs from its population of interest by excluding or underrepresenting some part of the population results in undercoverage bias.
- **Response Bias**—Anything that influences responses falls in the category of response bias. Examples are respondents lying because of the survey method or because the wording of questions produces strong feelings or confusion.
- **Nonresponse Bias**—Nonresponse bias occurs when individuals selected for the sample fail to respond, cannot be contacted, or decline to participate.
- **Voluntary Response Bias**—When choice rather than randomization is used to obtain a sample, the sample may suffer from voluntary response bias. People with strong opinions tend to be overrepresented.

3-3 Design of Experiments

Observational Study Versus Randomized Comparative Experiment

Observational Study

In an observational study, researchers observe individuals and record variables of interest but do *not* impose a treatment. It is not possible to prove a cause-and-effect relationship with an observational study.

Experiment

An experiment differs from an observational study in that the researcher deliberately *imposes a treatment.* An experimenter must identify at least one *explanatory variable* to manipulate and at least one *response variable* to measure. In an experiment, it is possible to determine a cause-and-effect relationship between the explanatory and response variables.

Example: Researchers believe that diuretics may be as effective in reducing a person's blood pressure as a conventional drug (Drug A), which is much more expensive and has more unwanted side effects.

Explanatory Variable — Type of Medication

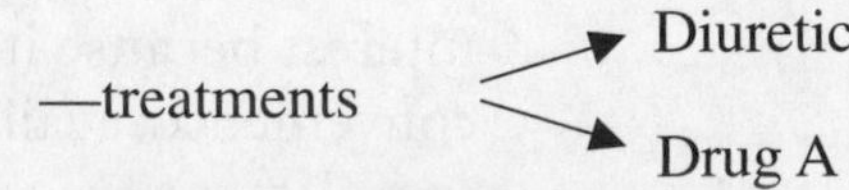

Response Variable — Change in Blood Pressure

Completely Randomized Experiment

Subjects are randomly assigned to a treatment group. The researcher then compares the subject groups' responses to each treatment. In this case we would compare the change in blood pressure for each of the treatments, a diuretic and Drug A.

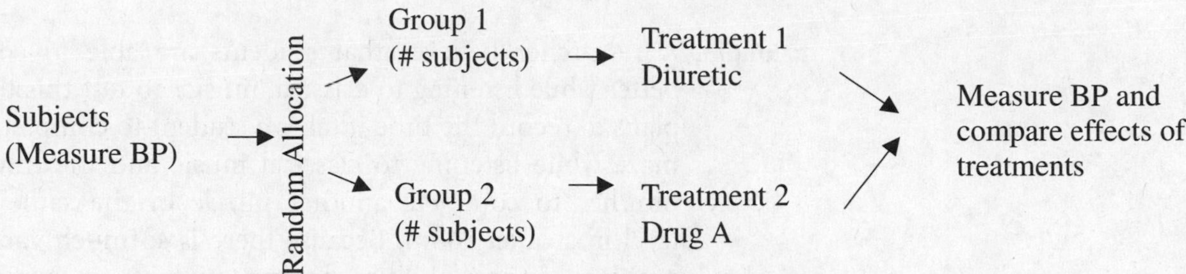

It is not necessary to start with a random selection of subjects. The randomization occurs in the random assignment to treatment groups.

- **Block Design**—If our experimental units (subjects) differ in some characteristic that may affect the results of our experiment, we should separate the groups into **blocks** based on that characteristic and then randomly assign the subjects *within* each block. In effect, we are conducting parallel experiments. We use blocks to *reduce variability* so that we can see the effect of the treatments. The blocks themselves are ***not*** treatments.

  Suppose the researchers in our diuretics versus Drug A example have reason to believe that men and women respond differently to blood pressure medication. In this example, gender would be the blocking variable.

  Note: Our goal is to be able to assess a cause-and-effect relationship between the treatment imposed and the response variable (what we are interested in measuring). **Blocking reduces variability** so that the differences we see can be attributed to the treatment that we imposed.

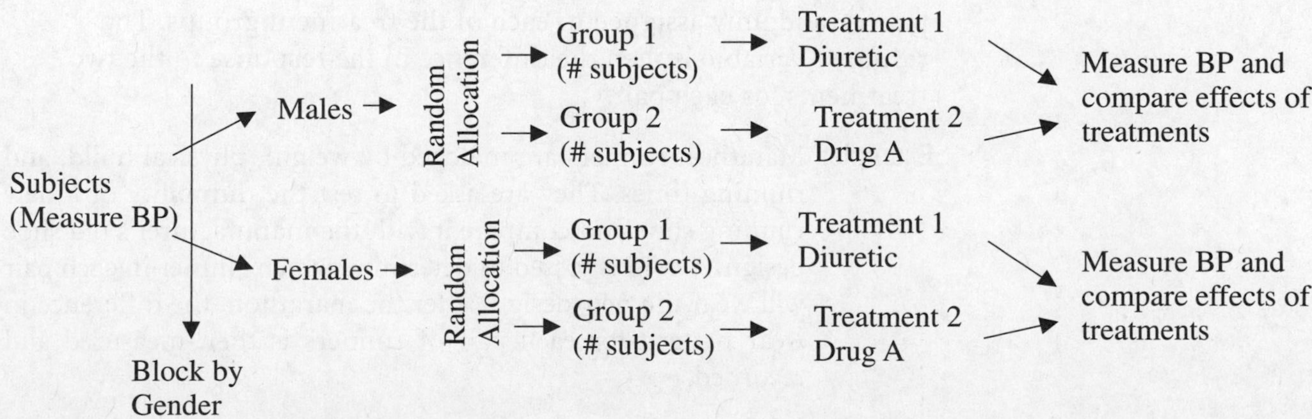

Clues for Clarity *Blocking is to experimental design as stratifying is to sampling design.*

- **Matched-Pairs Design**—A matched-pairs design is a form of block design. We will consider two types.

  - **One Subject:** A common form of matched-pairs design uses just one subject, who receives both treatments. The order in which the subject receives the treatments is randomized.

Example: A researcher believes that students are able to concentrate better while listening to classical music. To test this theory, she plans to record the time it takes a student to complete a puzzle maze while listening to classical music and the time it takes him/her to complete another puzzle of the same difficulty level in a quiet room. Because there is so much variability in problem-solving abilities among students, a matched-pairs design will be used to reduce this variability so that any difference recorded can be attributed to the conditions under which the student completed the puzzle.

Each student will complete a puzzle under each of the conditions. A coin will be flipped to determine whether the task will first be done in a quiet room or while listening to classical music. The difference in the time it takes to complete each puzzle (Quiet—Music) is recorded for each student.

Clues for Clarity *When matching individuals to themselves, it is important to randomize the order of the treatment. In our example, it is possible that an individual may become better at solving puzzles with experience. If each subject were to solve a puzzle without music first, then solve one with music, we might incorrectly attribute increased skill to music when experience instead may have caused the difference.*

  - **Two Subjects:** Another type of matched-pairs design involves two subjects. The two subjects are paired based on common characteristics that might affect the response variable. One subject from each pair is randomly assigned to each of the treatment groups. The response variable is then the difference in the response to the two treatments for each pair.

Example: Marathon runners are matched by weight, physical build, and running times. They are asked to test the durability of a new running shoe and compare it with the manufacturer's old shoe design. A coin is tossed to determine which runner in each pair will wear the new design. After the marathon, the difference in wear pattern for each pair of runners is then measured and recorded.

The Four Principles of Experimental Design

1. **Control**—Good experimental design reduces variablility by controlling the sources of variation. **Comparison** is an important form of control. Every experiment must have *at least two* groups so that the effect of a new treatment can be compared with either the effect of a traditional treatment or the effect of no treatment at all. The control group is the group given the traditional treatment. It may also be given no treatment or a **placebo** (a treatment known to have no effect).

2. **Randomize**—One source of variation is **lurking variables**, variables that we did not think to measure but that can affect the response variable. Randomization to treatment groups reduces bias by equalizing the effects of lurking variables. It does not eliminate unknown or uncontrollable sources of variation but spreads them out across the treatment levels and makes it easier to detect differences caused by the treatment.

3. **Replicate**—One or two subjects do not constitute an experiment. We should include many subjects in a comparative experiment. Our experiment should also be designed in such a way that other researchers can replicate our results.

4. **Block**—Although blocking is not *required* in an experimental design, it may *improve* our design. If our experimental units (subjects) are different in some way that may affect the results of our experiment, we should separate the groups into blocks based on that characteristic.

Other Considerations in the Design of Experiments

- **Blinding**
  - **Single-Blind:** An experiment is said to be single-blind when the subjects of the experiment do not know which treatment group they have been assigned to *or* when those who evaluate the results of the experiment do not know how subjects have been allocated to treatment groups.
  - **Double-Blind:** An experiment is said to be double blind when *neither* the subject *nor* the evaluators know how the subjects have been allocated to treatment groups.
- **Confounding**—An experiment is said to be confounded if we cannot separate the effect of a treatment (explanatory variable) from the effects of other influences (**confounding variables**) on the response variable.

  Example: Suppose we want to test the effectiveness of a meditation program in relieving workers' stress. We create a control group (a group who does not get any treatment but whose stress levels are also monitored). If there are outside influences that reduce stress, they will also affect this group. By including a control group in our experiment, a confounding variable (like better weather, news of a bonus, a change in management) will act equally on both groups, and any change in stress levels can be attributed to the explanatory variable, meditation.

- **Statistical Significance**—When an observed difference is too large for us to believe that it is likely to have occurred by chance, we consider the difference to be statistically significant.
- **The Placebo Effect**—The placebo effect is the tendency in humans to show a response whenever they think a treatment is in effect. Well-designed experiments use a control group so that the placebo effect operates equally on both the treatment group and the control group, thus allowing us to attribute changes in the response variable to the explanatory variable.

Review Questions for Topic 3—Gathering Data

Multiple Choice

1. The Women's Health Study randomly assigned nearly 40,000 women over the age of 45 to receive either aspirin or a placebo for over 10 years to examine the effect of aspirin on cancer risk to healthy women. This long-term trial was best conducted as
   (A) a census.
   (B) an observational study.
   (C) a randomized comparative experiment.
   (D) a single-blind randomized comparative experiment.
   (E) a double-blind randomized comparative experiment.

2. In the previous problem, suppose that the researchers suspected that women over the age of 55 may respond differently to the treatment. Given that a random sample of 40,000 women over the age of 45 has already been chosen, the study would have been improved by
   (A) a stratified sample, with strata determined by age.
   (B) a stratified sample, with strata determined by gender.
   (C) a block design, with blocks determined by age.
   (D) a block design, with blocks determined by gender.
   (E) a double-blind completely randomized design.

3. Researchers were interested to know whether internal vehicle temperatures vary by outside temperatures. To evaluate this, temperature rise was measured continuously over a 60-minute period in a dark sedan on 16 different clear, sunny days with outside temperatures ranging from 72°F to 96°F. The researchers' method of analysis is best described as
   (A) a census.
   (B) a survey.
   (C) an observational study.
   (D) a randomized comparative experiment.
   (E) a single-blind randomized comparative experiment.

4. Respondents to a randomly distributed questionnaire answered the question, "Do you agree that nuclear weapons should never be used because they are immoral?" The study that uses the results of this questionnaire will *most* likely suffer from which type(s) of bias?
   (A) undercoverage
   (B) voluntary response
   (C) response
   (D) nonresponse
   (E) all of the above

5. A statistics teacher decides to compare this year's students to all those she has taught over the history of the course. She will use the students' examination performances as the method of comparison. Which of the following is true in this context?
   (A) The mean performance of this year's students is a parameter.
   (B) The mean performance of this year's students is a statistic.
   (C) The mean of all except this year's students is a parameter.
   (D) The mean of all students is a statistic.
   (E) None of these is true.

Use the information below for questions 6–8.

Left-handedness is the preference for the left hand over the right for everyday activities such as writing. Studies indicate that about 93% of the population may be characterized as right-handed. Researchers would like to conduct a study to determine if left-handed teens differ significantly in their ability to memorize facts than right-handed teens.

6. The explanatory variable in this study is
   (A) ability to memorize facts.
   (B) age.
   (C) handedness.
   (D) researchers.
   (E) none of the above.

7. A random-number table is used to simulate the number of teens selected before a left-handed teen is found. A proper assignment of digits is
   (A) let the digits 0–6 represent a left-handed teen and 7–99 represent a right-handed teen; ignore repeats of numbers 7–99 until you get a number from 0–6.
   (B) let the digits 0–6 represent a left-handed teen and 7–99 represent a right-handed teen; count repeats of numbers 7–99 and continue until you get a number from 0–6.
   (C) let the digits 00–06 represent a left-handed teen and 07–99 represent a right-handed teen; ignore repeats of numbers 07–99 until you get a number from 00–06.
   (D) let the digits 00–06 represent a left-handed teen and 07–99 represent a right-handed teen; count repeats of numbers 07–99 and continue until you get a number from 00–06.

(E) let the digits 01–07 represent a left-handed teen and 08–100 represent a right-handed teen; count repeats of numbers 08–100 and continue until you get a number from 01–07.

8. Suppose the researchers concluded that the average number of words memorized by left-handed teens was statistically significantly higher than the average number memorized by right-handed teens. In this context, statistically significant means that
(A) the number of words memorized by left-handed students exceeded the number memorized by right-handed students.
(B) the average number of words memorized by left-handed students exceeded the average number memorized by right-handed students.
(C) right-handed students tend to not do as well as left-handed students in memorizing words.
(D) it would be unlikely to observe an average difference as large as was observed by chance variation.
(E) a randomized, controlled experiment was conducted.

9. Pollsters are interested in conducting a survey to determine if students who belonged to an online social network during college continued with it after graduation. They plan to randomly select 50 people from a list of registered voters. A problem with the proposed plan is that the
(A) sampling frame may be different from the population of interest.
(B) sample size is too small.
(C) sample is a systematic random sample.
(D) sample was not stratified by political party.
(E) sampling design should incorporate multistage sampling.

10. The purpose of randomization in an experiment is to
(A) make the experiment seem fair.
(B) make the treatment groups as similar as possible.
(C) make the treatment groups as different as possible.
(D) create the blocks in an experiment.
(E) reduce variability within treatment groups.

Free Response

1. A political party's position on a ballot is often determined by random selection. For the last 10 years, the Innovators have never had the coveted first position on the ballot; this position has always gone to either the Old-timers or Preservationists. The Innovators have cried foul. Use the random-number table below to test the likelihood of the disputed result. Clearly communicate your scheme, conduct 10 trials, and report your results.

32813	90372	59627	94240	12957
11832	26220	79684	53312	26114

2. Researchers at a company that manufactures health and beauty products are working on a new foot lotion formula for women with extremely dry feet. They plan to test the new formula against their current product. Fifty women with extremely dry feet have been identified and have volunteered to participate in a clinical trial over a period of 6 months.

   An experimental design considered by the researchers is to divide the volunteers into two equal groups, one of which will use the new formula for the first 3 months and then use the current product. The other group will use the current product first and then use the new formula. The experiment is to be double-blind. At the end of each 3-month period, the researchers will measure foot dryness and will compare the results of the two treatments at the end of the trial.

   Propose an alternative design and explain why your design is better.

Answers for Topic 3—Gathering Data—begin on page 265.

Topic 4

Randomness and Probability

We generally collect data so that we can use it to draw conclusions or make decisions. Those conclusions and decisions are not based on certainty but on likelihood. An understanding of probability is key to our ability to use data analysis.

4-1 From Randomness to Probability

Dealing with Random Phenomena

Random phenomena differ from chaotic events in that they settle down and exhibit predictable behavior in the long run. It is precisely this long-run predictability of randomness that allows us to make decisions based on statistics.

Probability

The probability of an event is its **long-run** relative frequency.

Vocabulary

- **Trial**—A trial is a single attempt or realization of a random phenomenon (for example, rolling a pair of dice).
- **Outcome**—The outcome of a trial is the value measured, observed, or reported for each trial (for example, the sum of the faces shown on the dice).
- **Sample Space**—The sample space (*S*) of a random phenomenon is the set of all possible outcomes. There are 36 possible ordered arrangements when two dice are rolled. These 36 outcomes constitute the sample space.

Die 1

Die 2	1	2	3	4	5	6
1	(1,1)	(1,2)	(1,3)	(1,4)	(1,5)	(1,6)
2	(2,1)	(2,2)	(2,3)	(2,4)	(2,5)	(2,6)
3	(3,1)	(3,2)	(3,3)	(3,4)	(3,5)	(3,6)
4	(4,1)	(4,2)	(4,3)	(4,4)	(4,5)	(4,6)
5	(5,1)	(5,2)	(5,3)	(5,4)	(5,5)	(5,6)
6	(6,1)	(6,2)	(6,3)	(6,4)	(6,5)	(6,6)

- **Event:** An event is a collection of outcomes. We identify results in order to attach probabilities to them. An event might be the probability of rolling a sum of 7. Events are usually designated by capital letters. Let A = the probability of rolling a sum of 7 when two dice are rolled. Then

$$P(A) = \frac{6}{36} = \frac{1}{6}.$$

Example: In the casino game Craps, two dice are rolled and bets are made about the sum of the two dice. A bet that the next roll of the dice will show a sum of 7 pays 4:1 odds. Although the outcome on an individual roll of the dice is random, there is predictability in the long-run behavior. The graph shows the cumulative proportion of obtaining a 7 when two dice are rolled 500 times. Notice that the graph settles down and approaches the theoretical value of $\frac{1}{6}$.

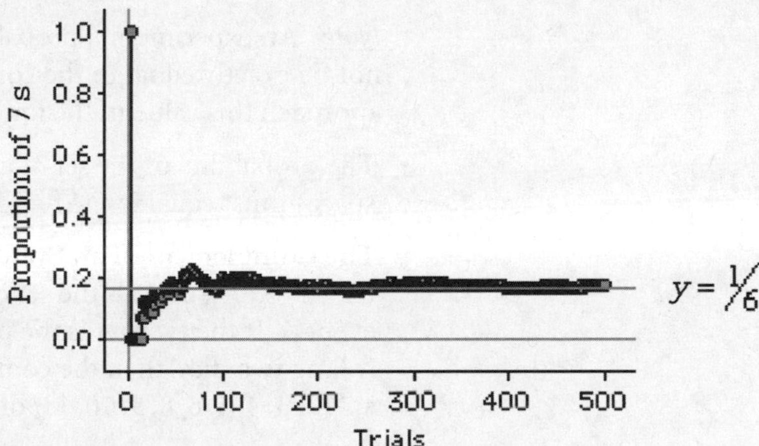

- **The Law of Large Numbers:** The Law of Large Numbers states that the long-run relative frequency of repeated independent events gets closer and closer to the true relative frequency as the number of trials increases. We saw this law at work in the example above. In the long run, if you roll two dice many times, a sum of 7 will occur about $\frac{1}{6}$ of the time.
- **Independence:** Two events are independent if the occurrence of one event does not alter the probability that the other event occurs. If you roll two dice and obtain a sum of 7, the result of that roll has no effect on the next roll, so the two rolls are independent. But if you draw an ace from a deck of cards $P(\text{ace}) = \frac{4}{52}$ and without replacing it draw a second card, the probability that the second card is also an ace is $P(\text{ace}) = \frac{3}{51}$. These events are *not* independent. (We will give a more formal definition of independence later.)

Formal Probability

Probability Rules

- The probability of an event is a number from 0 to 1 that reports the likelihood of the event's occurrence. For any event A,

$$0 \leq P(A) \leq 1.$$

- **Theoretical Probability of an Event A** (when all possible outcomes are equally likely):

$$P(A) = \frac{\text{number of elements in } A}{\text{number of elements in the sample space } (S)}$$

- The theoretical probability of rolling a sum of 7 when two dice are rolled is $P(\text{sum} = 7) = \frac{6}{36} = \frac{1}{6}$.
- **Empirical (Experimental) Probability of an Event A:**

$$P(A) = \frac{\text{number of successes}}{\text{total number of observations}}$$

  Note: An experimental probability arrived at by simulation will probably not be exactly equal to the corresponding theoretical value, but it should approach this value in the long run.

- The probability of the set of all possible outcomes of a trial (sample space) must equal 1: $P(S) = 1$.
- **The Complement of an Event A:** The complement of an event A (A^C, $\sim A$, A', or $\overline{A}$) is the set of all possible outcomes that are *not* in the event A. If the event A is the probability of obtaining a sum of 7 when rolling two dice, then the complement of A would be any sum that is not a 7 (2, 3, 4, 5, 6, 8, 9, 10, 11, or 12).
- The probability of the complement of an event is 1 minus the probability that the event occurs, $P(A^C) = 1 - P(A)$.
- **Addition Rule for Disjoint (Mutually Exclusive) Events:** Two events, A and B, are **disjoint** if they cannot occur together. The probability that one *or* the other *or* both occur is the sum of the probabilities of the two events.

$$P(A \text{ or } B) = P(A \cup B) = P(A) + P(B)$$

Disjoint Sets A and B

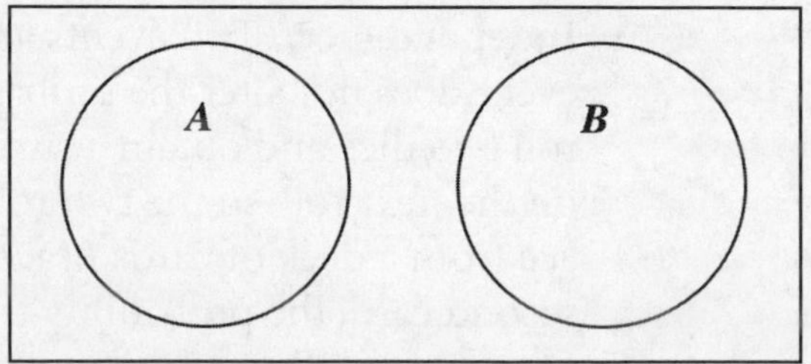

- **General Addition Rule:**

$$P(A \text{ or } B) = P(A \cup B) = P(A) + P(B) - P(A \cap B),$$

where $A \cap B$ is the intersection of sets A and B (values that both sets have in common). Elements in the intersection region are counted when A is counted and again when B is counted. We need to subtract $P(A \cap B)$ so that it is not counted twice. If A and B are disjoint, then the number of elements contained in both sets is equal to zero, $P(A \cap B) = 0$.

- **Multiplication Rule for Independent Events:** For two *independent* events A and B, the probability that both A *and* B occur is the product of the two probabilities.

$$P(A \text{ and } B) = P(A \cap B) = P(A) \times P(B),$$

provided that A and B are *independent.*

This rule can be extended to more than two independent events.

Example: An event consists of flipping a coin and rolling a die. What is the probability that the coin shows tails and the die shows a 6? Both of these events are independent, so the product rule applies. Let A = obtaining a tail and B = rolling a 6. Then $P(A \text{ and } B) = P(A) \times P(B)$. We will use a tree diagram to illustrate the sample space.

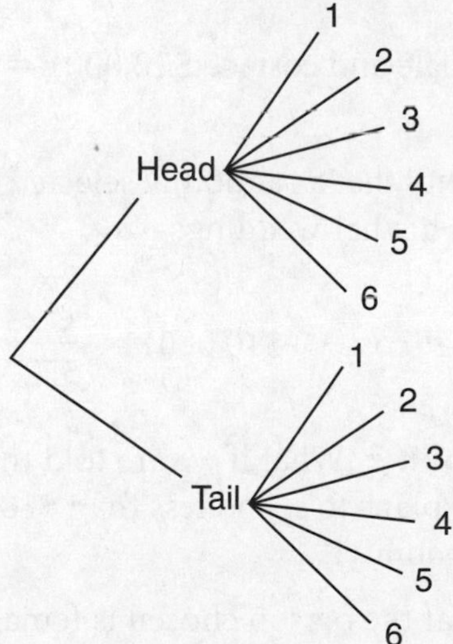

The probability of obtaining a tail and a 6 is

$$P(A \text{ and } B) = \frac{1}{2} \times \frac{1}{6} = \frac{1}{12}.$$

There are 12 possible outcomes when flipping a coin and rolling a die; only one of them corresponds to getting a tail ***and*** a 6.

- **Conditional Probability and the General Multiplication Rule:** What if the events are *not* independent?

Example: A bridal magazine wants information regarding college students' attitudes about wedding costs. Students from a large college campus are randomly selected to take part in a survey. Students who respond yes to the question, "Do you plan to marry some day?" are then asked how much they plan to spend on their wedding. The results of the survey are summarized in the table below.

	Cost ≤ $10,000	Cost > $10,000 and ≤ $20,000	Cost > $20,000	Total
Male	147	23	5	175
Female	5	120	72	197
	152	143	77	372

We will consider the 372 responses as our sample space.

- What is the probability that a randomly selected person from our survey group is female?

$$P(\text{female}) = \frac{197}{372}$$

- What is the probability of selecting a female who plans to spend less than $10,000 on her wedding?

$$P(\text{female and cost} < \$10{,}000) = \frac{5}{372}$$

- What is the probability that a randomly selected student plans to spend less than $10,000 on his/her wedding?

$$P(\text{cost} < \$10{,}000) = \frac{152}{372}$$

- **Conditional Probability:** What if we are told that the randomly selected person who plans to spend less than $10,000 is female? Does that change the probability?

  Because we know that the person chosen is female, we restrict our sample space to the 197 *females*. The probability that a selected student plans to spend less than $10,000 on a wedding given *that we know the student selected is female* is $\frac{5}{197}$.

  This is called a **conditional probability** because the second event is conditioned upon the first event having occurred. We use the notation

$P(\text{cost} < \$10{,}000|\text{female})$ to represent the probability that the planned cost of the wedding is less than \$10,000 given that the person selected is female.

Notice that

$$P(\text{cost} < \$10{,}000|\text{female}) = \frac{P(\text{cost} < \$10{,}000 \text{ and female})}{P(\text{female})}$$
$$= \frac{5/372}{197/372} = \frac{5}{372} \times \frac{372}{197} = \frac{5}{197}.$$

In other words, for any two events A and B,

$$P(B|A) = \frac{P(A \cap B)}{P(A)}.$$

- **General Multiplication Rule:** We can transform the formula for conditional probability to give us a general rule for the probability of two events occurring, whether those events are independent or not. This is the general rule:

  $$P(A \text{ and } B) = P(A \cap B) = P(A) \times P(B|A).$$

  The probability that events A and B both occur is the probability that A occurs times the probability that B occurs *given that A has already occurred.*

- **Formal Definition of Independence:** Informally, we defined two events as independent if the outcome of one does not influence the probability of the other. Formally, the events A and B are independent whenever

  $$P(B|A) = P(B).$$

  The probability of B occurring given that A has already occurred is just the probability of B (knowing the outcome of A didn't give us any additional information).

- If two events are independent, $P(B|A) = P(B)$, then the general rule $P(A \text{ and } B) = P(A \cap B) = P(A) \times P(B|A)$ becomes $P(A \cap B) = P(A) \times P(B)$.

  Note: Disjoint events **cannot** be independent. If A = {student is a sophomore} and B = {student is a junior}, then A and B are disjoint. Are they independent? If you find out that A is true, does that change the probability of B? If A is true, then B cannot be true. So they can't be independent. Looking at this from a mathematical point of view, if A and B are disjoint,

  then $P(A \cap B) = 0$ and $P(B|A) = \dfrac{P(A \cap B)}{P(A)} = \dfrac{0}{P(A)} = 0$. But if A and B are independent, $P(B|A) = P(B)$. Since $P(B) \neq 0$, A and B cannot be both disjoint and independent.

Conditional Probability Practice

Example: Suppose there is an outbreak of a rare disease in the United States. It is estimated that 1 in every 1000 people will contract the disease. A diagnostic test is available that is 97% accurate (i.e., returns a positive result) for people who have the disease and 95% accurate (i.e., returns a negative result) for people who do not have the disease. Given that a person has tested positive for the disease, what is the probability that the person actually has the disease?

THINK

Define the events we are interested in and their probabilities.

Let D = has disease
and N = no disease.
$+$ = tests positive for disease
$-$ = tests negative for disease

Figure out what you want to know in terms of the events.

We want to know the probability that a person has the disease given that s/he tests positive for it $P(D|+)$.

SHOW

Use the definition of conditional probability to **write the event** whose probability you want to find.

$$P(D|+) = \frac{P(D \cap +)}{P(+)}$$

Draw a tree diagram.
Multiply along the branches to find the four possible outcomes. Check to see that they total 1.

$0.001(0.97) = 0.00097$
$0.001(0.03) = 0.00003$
$0.999(0.05) = 0.04995$
$0.999(0.95) = 0.94905$
$0.00097 + 0.00003 + 0.04995 + 0.94905 = 1$

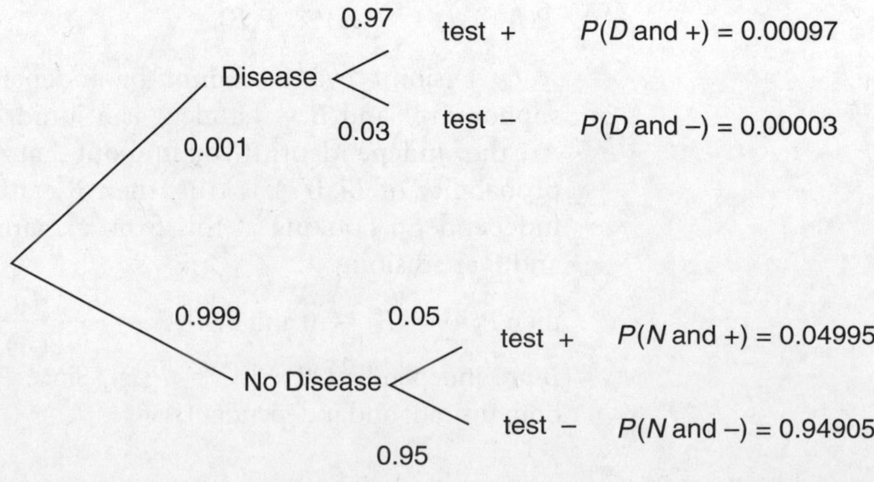

Add the probabilities corresponding to the condition of interest—in this case, testing positive. We can add the probabilities from the tree twigs that correspond to testing positive because the tree shows disjoint events.	$P(+) = P(D \cap +) + P(N \cap +)$ $= 0.00097 + 0.04995$ $= 0.05092$
Fill in all the values in the formula and solve.	$P(D \mid +) = \dfrac{P(D \cap +)}{P(+)}$ $= \dfrac{0.00097}{0.05092} = 0.01905$

State your conclusion.

The chance of having this disease given that you tested positive is less than 2%.

Another Method for Solving a Conditional Probability Problem

Pick a value to represent the number of people in your population. (It is a good idea to choose a large enough value so that you end up with whole number values—this is not necessary to get the correct answer, it just makes more sense when the number of people in a category is a whole number.)

Let the population = 100,000 people.

Make a two-way (contingency) table.

	Disease	No Disease	Total
Tests Positive			
Tests Negative			
Total			100,000

Calculate the probabilities for each cell in the table.

Disease total = 0.001(100,000) = 100

No-disease total = 100,000 − 100 = 99,900

Disease and tests + = 100(0.97) = 97

Disease and tests − = 100 − 97 = 3

No disease and tests + = 99,900(0.05) = 4995

No disease and tests − = 99,900 − 4995 = 94,905

Fill in the chart.

	Disease	No Disease	Total
Tests Positive	97	4995	5092
Tests Negative	3	94,905	94,908
Total	100	99,900	100,000

Find the desired probability from the table.

$$P(D|+) = \frac{97}{5092} = 0.01905$$

State your conclusion.

The chance of having this disease given that you tested positive is less than 2%.

4-2 Random Variables

A random variable assumes any of several different values as a result of some random event. Random variables are denoted by a capital letter such as X, and the values that the random variable can take on are denoted by the same lowercase variable $(x_1, x_2, \ldots)$. All possible values that the random variable can assume, with their associated probabilities, form the probability distribution for the random variable.

Types of Random Variables

Continuous Random Variable

A continuous random variable is one that can take on any numeric value within a range of values. The range may be infinite or bounded at either or both ends. The probability distribution of a continuous random variable is described by a density curve. The probability of any given event is given by the area under the curve over the values of x that make up the event. A density curve lies above the x-axis and has an area beneath it of 1.

Discrete Random Variable

A discrete random variable is a random variable that can take on a finite number of distinct outcomes.

- **Expected Value of a Random Variable**—Although we cannot predict the outcome of any single event of a random variable, the expected value of a random variable is its theoretical long-run average. It is the center of its distribution and is denoted by μ or $E(X)$. It is a weighted average.

$$\mu = E(X) = \sum x\,P(x)$$

- **Standard Deviation of a Random Variable**

$$\text{Var}(X) = \sigma^2 = \sum (x - \mu)^2\,P(x)$$

$$\text{SD}(X) = \sigma = \sqrt{\text{Var}(X)}$$

Example: At a carnival, a game of chance involves spinning a wheel that is divided into 60 equal sectors. The sectors are marked as follows:

$20 – 1 sector

$10 – 2 sectors

$5 – 3 sectors

No Prize – 54 sectors

The carnival owner wants to know the average expected payout for this game and the amount of variablility (as measured by the standard deviation) associated with it.

THINK

Define the random variable.

Let X = the amount of payout.

SHOW

Make a table.
List the possible values (x) of the random variable X and their associated probabilities.

X	\$0	\$5	\$10	\$20
$P(x)$	$\frac{54}{60}$	$\frac{3}{60}$	$\frac{2}{60}$	$\frac{1}{60}$

Find the expected value.

$$\mu = E(X) = \$0\left(\frac{54}{60}\right) + \$5\left(\frac{3}{60}\right) + \$10\left(\frac{2}{60}\right) + \$20\left(\frac{1}{60}\right) \approx \$0.92$$

Find the standard deviation.

$$\sigma \approx \sqrt{(0-0.92)^2\left(\tfrac{54}{60}\right) + (5-0.92)^2\left(\tfrac{3}{60}\right) + (10-0.92)^2\left(\tfrac{2}{60}\right) + (20-0.92)^2\left(\tfrac{1}{60}\right)} \approx \$3.23$$

State your conclusion.

In the long run, the carnival owner can expect a mean payout of about \$0.92 on each game played, with a standard deviation of about \$3.23.

<u>*Note:*</u> You can find the mean and standard deviation of a random variable on the TI-83/84. Put the values of the random variable in *L1* (or any list) and their corresponding probabilities in *L2*.

TI-83/84 **STAT ⇒ CALC ⇒ 1-Var Stats L1, L2**

TI-nspire From List, use NavPad to move to top until x-list is selected, press **caps** & right arrow at the same time (this will highlight both x- and freq-lists). **Menu** ⇒ Statistics ⇒ Stat Calculations ⇒ One-Variable Statistics, Num of Lists (1) ⇒ **tab** ⇒ OK (**tab** through selections to choose x1 List, Frequency List, etc.) ⇒ OK ⇒ **ctrl Menu** ⇒ Resize Column Width (if necessary), (click key or enter)

Example: Refer to the carnival game in the previous example. Suppose the cost to play the game is \$1. What are a player's expected winnings?

THINK

Define the random variable.

Let X = the amount won by the player. Since it costs \$1 to play, we need to subtract that amount from the amount paid to him if he wins the game.

SHOW

Make a table.
List the possible values (x) of the random variable X and their associated probabilities.

X	−\$1	\$4	\$9	\$19
$P(X)$	$\frac{54}{60}$	$\frac{3}{60}$	$\frac{2}{60}$	$\frac{1}{60}$

Find the expected value.

$$\mu = E(X) = -\$1\left(\frac{54}{60}\right) + \$4\left(\frac{3}{60}\right) + \$9\left(\frac{2}{60}\right) + \$19\left(\frac{1}{60}\right)$$
$$\approx -\$0.08$$

State your conclusion.

In the long run, the player can expect to lose about 8 cents for every game he plays. (Since we previously calculated the carnival owner's expected payout, \$0.92, we could have calculated the expected winnings for the player by subtracting this value from the cost to play the game: \$1 − 0.92 = \$0.08.)

Clues for Clarity *When you are asked to calculate the expected winnings for a game of chance, don't forget to take into account the cost to play the game.*

Operations on Random Variables

Let X be a random variable with mean μ_x and variance σ_x^2 and let Y be a new random variable such that $Y = a \pm bx$. The mean (expected value) and variance of this new random variable are given by the following.

$$\mu_Y = \mu_{(a \pm bX)} = a \pm b\mu_X$$
$$\sigma_Y^2 = \sigma_{(a \pm bX)}^2 = b^2\sigma_X^2$$
$$\text{and } \sigma_Y = \sigma_{(a \pm bX)} = \sqrt{b^2\sigma_X^2} = b\sigma_X$$

More About Means and Variances

- The mean of the sum of two random variables is the sum of the means of the random variables.
- The mean of the difference of two random variables is the difference of the means of the two random variables.

$$\mu_{X \pm Y} = E(X \pm Y) = E(X) \pm E(Y)$$

- If the random variables are **independent**, the variance of their sum or difference is always the ***sum*** of the variances.

$$\sigma_{X \pm Y}^2 = \text{Var}(X \pm Y) = \text{Var}(X) + \text{Var}(Y)$$

Recall: Variances of **independent** variables add; **STANDARD DEVIATIONS DO *NOT* ADD!**

Example: Two golfers plan to enter a tournament where the score will be determined as a team score. Golfer X has a mean score of 85.4 with standard deviation 3.2. Golfer Y has a mean score of 89.6 with a standard deviation of 4.1. What is their expected team score and the variation associated with it?

We can apply the rules for combining two random variables to answer this question.

$$\mu_{X+Y} = E(X + Y) = E(X) + E(Y) = 85.4 + 89.6 = 175$$

We have no reason to assume that their scores are not independent, so

$$\sigma_{X+Y}^2 = \text{Var}(X + Y) = \text{Var}(X) + \text{Var}(Y) = (3.2)^2 + (4.1)^2 = 27.05$$
$$\sigma_{X+Y} = \sqrt{\text{Var}(X + Y)} = \sqrt{27.05} \approx 5.2.$$

The golfers can expect a team score of 175 with standard deviation 5.2.

Combining Normal Random Variables

When two random variables have Normal models, their sum or difference also has a Normal model. This fact allows us to apply our knowledge of

Normal probabilities to questions about the sum or difference of independent random variables.

Example: The local supermarket has pints of strawberries on special. The strawberries are packaged as either medium or large. Since you love strawberries, you decide to pay the extra money for a container of the large ones, while your frugal friend decides to purchase the medium-sized package. On the way home from the market, you both decide to eat some of the fruit you bought and each take a strawberry from your respective containers. Surprised to find that your friend's strawberry is larger than yours, you decide to gather some data. Your supermarket buys its produce from a large distribution center, where large strawberries have a mean height of 6.1 cm with a standard deviation of 1.2 cm, and medium strawberries have a mean height of 4.8 cm with a standard deviation of 1.6 cm. Further, the heights of strawberries are approximately normally distributed. Given this information, if a person were to select from strawberries sold at the distribution center a random strawberry classified as large and a random one classified as medium, what is the probability that the medium strawberry will have a greater height than the large one?

THINK

Define the random variables.

Let L = a large strawberry and M = a medium strawberry. Then

$\mu_L = 6.1$ cm and $\sigma_L = 1.2$ cm

$\mu_M = 4.8$ cm and $\sigma_M = 1.6$ cm.

What are you trying to find?

You want to find the probability that a randomly selected medium strawberry has a greater height than a randomly selected large strawberry.

$P(\mu_M > \mu_L)$ or $P(\mu_M - \mu_L) > 0$

SHOW

Define a new random variable to represent the difference of the two variables.

Let $\mu_D = \mu_{(M-L)}$; then μ_D follows a normal distribution centered at

$$\mu_{(M-L)} = \mu_M - \mu_L = 4.8 - 6.1 = -1.3$$

with standard deviation of

$$\sigma_{(M-L)} = \sqrt{\sigma_M^2 + \sigma_L^2} = \sqrt{(1.2)^2 + (1.6)^2} = \sqrt{4} = 2.$$

Make a picture.

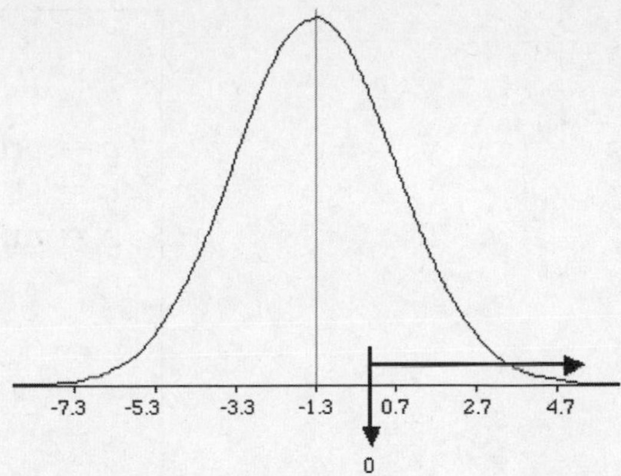

This display represents the distribution of the differences (Medium − Large) in strawberries. We are interested in the case where a medium strawberry is bigger than a large one (difference is greater than zero).

Calculate the desired probability.

$$P(\mu_D > 0) = P\left(z > \frac{0 - (-1.3)}{2}\right)$$
$$= P(z > 0.65) \approx 0.2578$$

State your conclusion.

About 25.78% of the time, a randomly selected medium strawberry will have a greater height than a randomly selected large strawberry.

4-3 Probability Models

Previously we looked at situations involving two possible outcomes (success and failure) and used simulations to help us understand their probabilities. Situations like this often occur in real life. We will look at the theoretical probabilities associated with two particular models, the geometric and the binomial.

The Geometric Model

- Each observation falls into one of two settings: *success* or *failure.*
- The probability of success, p, is the same for each observation.
- The observations are all independent.
- The variable of interest is *the number of trials required to obtain the first success.*

Geometric Probability Model

$p =$ probability of success
$q = (1-p) =$ probability of failure
$X =$ number of trials until the first success occurs

$$P(X = x) = q^{x-1}p$$

$$\text{Expected value: } \mu = \frac{1}{p}$$

$$\text{Standard deviation: } \sigma = \sqrt{\frac{q}{p^2}}$$

Example: Your favorite breakfast cereal, Super Sugar Choco-Balls, is running a promotion. Each box of cereal will contain one of four different prizes. The only prize that you are interested in is the computer game Super Snood. The manufacturer advertises that there is an equal chance of getting each of the four prizes. You would like to know, on average, how many boxes of Super Sugar Choco-Balls you need to purchase before you obtain one that has the prize you desire. Additionally, suppose you are only willing to purchase seven boxes of the cereal. What is the probability that it takes exactly seven boxes to get a Super Snood game? What is the probability that you obtain the game you desire by opening seven or fewer boxes?

<u>Note:</u> Recall that, to solve this problem previously, we did a simulation. Now we can answer this question with a theoretical probability using a geometric model.

Define the random variable and specify the model.

Let $X =$ the number of boxes of Super Sugar Choco-Balls opened until you obtain the first Super Snood game.

You can model X with a geometric model with $p = \frac{1}{4} = 0.25$.

Check to see that the conditions for the model are met.

Conditions for using the Geometric Model:

- *There are two outcomes.*
  Success = Super Snood game
  Failure = any other prize
- *The probability of success, p, is the same for each observation.*
  The probability of obtaining the desired game on each trial is $\frac{1}{4}$.

- *The observations are all independent.* We are assuming that each store has a representative sample of the prizes.
- *The variable of interest is the number of trials required to obtain the first success.* You are interested in how many boxes of cereal you must open until you find a Super Snood game.

Find the expected value.

$$E(X) = \mu_X = \frac{1}{p} = \frac{1}{0.25} = 4$$

Calculate the probability that your first success occurs on the seventh trial.

If success occurs on the seventh trial, then the first six trials must have resulted in failure.

$$P(x = 7) = (1 - 0.25)^6(0.25) \approx 0.0445$$

TI-83/84 **2nd ⇒ DISTR ⇒ geompdf (p, x) geompdf (0.25, 7)**

TI-*nspire* **Home** ⇒ Calculator ⇒ **catalog** ⇒ geomPdf(p, x)

Calculate the probability of success in less than or equal to seven trials.

You are interested in the probability that success occurs on the first, second, . . . , or seventh trial.

$$\begin{aligned} &P(X \leq 7) \\ &= P(x = 1) + P(x = 2) + P(x = 3) + P(x = 4) \\ &\quad + P(x = 5) + P(x = 6) + P(x = 7) \\ &= 0.25 + (1 - 0.25)(0.25) + (1 - 0.25)^2(0.25) \\ &\quad + (1 - 0.25)^3(0.25) + (1 - 0.25)^4(0.25) \\ &\quad + (1 - 0.25)^5(0.25) + (1 - 0.25)^6(0.25) \\ &\approx 0.8665 \end{aligned}$$

TI-83/84 **2nd ⇒ DISTR ⇒ geomcdf (p, x) geomcdf (0.25, 7)**

TI-*nspire* **Home** ⇒ Calculator ⇒ **catalog** ⇒ geomCdf(p, x)

State your conclusion.

You would expect to open about four boxes of the cereal on average before obtaining one with the desired prize. The probability that it takes seven boxes of cereal before you get the game you desire is about 4.5%, and the probability that you get the Super Snood game by opening seven or fewer boxes is about 87%.

The Binomial Model

- Each observation falls into one of two settings: *success* or *failure*.
- There is a fixed number n of observations.
- The n observations are all independent.
- The probability of success, p, is the same for each observation.

Binomial Probability Model

n = number of trials
p = probability of success
$q = 1 - p$ = probability of failure
X = number of successes in n trials

$$P(X = x) = \binom{n}{x}p^x(1 - p)^{n-x}, \text{ where } \binom{n}{x} = \frac{n!}{x!(n - x)!}$$

Mean: $\mu = np$

Standard deviation:

$$\sigma = \sqrt{np(1 - p)}$$

Example: A basketball player at Wissahickon High School makes 70% of her free throw shots. Assume each shot is independent of the others. She shoots five free throws.

- What are the mean and the standard deviation of the distribution?
- What is the probability that she makes exactly four of them?
- What is the probability that she makes fewer than three of her shots?

Define the random variable and specify the model.

Let X = the number of free throw shots made of the five taken.

We can model X with a binomial model, $n = 5$ and $p = 0.70$.

SHOW

Check to see that the conditions for the model are met.

Conditions for using the Binomial Model:

- *There are two outcomes.*
  Success = make shot
  Failure = miss shot
- *There is a fixed number of observations.*
  $n = 5$
- *The observations are all independent.*
  We are told to assume that each shot is independent.
- *The probability of success, p, is the same for each observation.*
  The probability of making a free throw is 0.70.

Find the expected value and standard deviation.

$E(X) = \mu_X = np = 5(0.70) = 3.5$

$SD(x) = \sqrt{np(1-p)}$

$= \sqrt{5(0.70)(0.30)} \approx 1.025$

Calculate the probability that there are exactly four successes.

$P(X = 4) = \binom{5}{4}(0.70)^4(1 - 0.70)$

$= 0.36015$

TI-83/84 **2nd ⇒ DISTR ⇒ binompdf (n, p, x) binompdf (5, 0.70, 4)**

TI-*nspire* **Home** ⇒ Calculator ⇒ **catalog** ⇒ binomPdf(n,p, x)

Calculate the probability of fewer than three successes.

Fewer than 3 successes would mean that she made 0, 1, or 2 of her shots.

$P(X < 3) = \binom{5}{0}(1 - 0.70)^5$
$+ \binom{5}{1}(0.70)(1 - 0.70)^4$
$+ \binom{5}{2}(0.70)^2(1 - 0.70)^3$
$= 0.16308$

TI-83/84 **2nd ⇒ DISTR ⇒ binomcdf (n, p, x) binomcdf (5, 0.70, 2)**

TI-*nspire* **Home** ⇒ Calculator ⇒ **catalog** ⇒ binomCdf(n,p, x)

State your conclusion.

The average number of free throws she can expect to make out of five attempted is $3.5 \approx 3$ with a standard deviation of ≈ 1.025. If she takes five free throw shots, the probability that she makes exactly four of them is about 36%, and the probability that she makes fewer than three of them is about 16%.

Clues for Clarity *The difference in conditions between the binomial and geometric models is in the number of trials. The binomial requires a fixed number of trials to be set in advance. The geometric has no fixed number of trials and is often used to model wait-time. In other words, we continue conducting trials until we get our first success.*

Normal Model as an Approximation to the Binomial

The Normal distribution can be used as an approximation for the binomial distribution provided that the number of successes and failures is at least ten ($np \geq 10$ and $nq \geq 10$). It is convenient to use this method of approximation when the number of trials is large and beyond the ability of the calculator to compute probabilities.

Example: A shipment of ice cream cones has the manufacturer's claim that no more than 15% of the shipment will be defective (broken cones). What is the probability that, in a shipment of 1 million cones, Dairy Heaven Corporate Distribution Center will find more than 151,000 broken cones?

Define the random variable and specify the model.

Let X = the number of defective cones in the shipment (successes).

We can model X with a binomial model, $n = 1{,}000{,}000$ and $p = 0.15$. *(Most calculators will not handle a problem of this magnitude.)* We can use the Normal model with $\mu = np$ and $\sigma = \sqrt{npq}$ as an approximation.

Check to see that the conditions for the model are met.

Conditions for using the Normal Model to approximate binomial probability:

$np \geq 10$ and $nq \geq 10$

$1{,}000{,}000(0.15) > 10$ and

$1{,}000{,}000(0.85) > 10$

Find the mean and standard deviation of the distribution.

We need to find the mean and standard deviation of the distribution.

$$\mu = np \text{ and } \sigma = \sqrt{npq}$$

$$\mu = 1{,}000{,}000(0.15) = 150{,}000$$

$$\sigma = \sqrt{1{,}000{,}000(0.15)(0.85)}$$

$$= \sqrt{127{,}500} \approx 357.07$$

Calculate the probability of 151,000 or more successes.

$$P(X > 151{,}000) = P\left(z > \frac{151{,}000 - 150{,}000}{357.07}\right)$$

$$\approx P(z > 2.80) \approx 0.0026$$

State your conclusion.

In a shipment of 1 million cones, the probability of getting more than 151,000 defective cones is approximately 0.26%.

Review Questions for Topic 4—Randomness and Probability

Multiple Choice

1. The Safe Drinking Water Hotline routinely tracks requests for information about water quality. The table below shows the sources of some of its calls.

Source	*Telephone*	*E-mail*
Laboratories	44	3
Citizens	1875	118
Consultants	234	19
Environmental Groups	62	1
Governmental Groups	83	7
Schools	64	2
Other	369	14

What is the probability that a request comes from a school given that it is an e-mail request?

(A) $\frac{1}{62}$

(B) $\frac{1}{63}$

(C) $\frac{1}{82}$

(D) $\frac{1}{117}$

(E) $\frac{64}{90,123}$

2. At Kennett High School, 5% of athletes play both football and some other contact sport, 30% play football, and 40% play other contact sports. If there are 200 athletes, how many play neither football nor any other contact sport?
(A) 20
(B) 70
(C) 80
(D) 100
(E) 130

3. The Correcto Publishing Company claims that its publications will have errors only twice in every 100 pages. What is the approximate probability that Anne will read 235 pages of a 790-page book published by Correcto before finding an error?
(A) 0.02%
(B) 2%
(C) 5%
(D) 16%
(E) 30%

4. The theoretical probability of rolling a 2 or a 6 on one roll of a die is $\frac{1}{3}$. A student who tries to reproduce this probability by counting successes in repeated trials is most likely to come closest to $\frac{1}{3}$ with
(A) one roll of the die.
(B) two rolls of the die.
(C) three rolls of the die.
(D) ten rolls of the die.
(E) one hundred rolls of the die.

5. For the sake of efficiency, a shoe company decides to produce the left shoe of each pair at one site and the right shoe at a different site. If the two sites produce shoes with a number of defects reflected by $\mu_1 = 0.002, \sigma_1 = 0.15$ and $\mu_2 = 0.005, \sigma_2 = 0.18$, what is the mean and standard deviation for the number of defects for pairs of shoes produced by this company?
(A) $\mu = 0.00035, \sigma = 0.165$
(B) $\mu = 0.00035, \sigma = 0.0549$
(C) $\mu = 0.007, \sigma = 0.0549$
(D) $\mu = 0.007, \sigma = 0.2343$
(E) $\mu = 0.007, \sigma = 0.33$

6. The probability of a certain genetic trait in the general population is 27%. What is the expected number of people you would need to observe before finding one person with this trait?
(A) About 4
(B) About 10
(C) About 27
(D) About 73
(E) Not enough information is given to answer the question.

7. A recent survey of students at John Tukey High School revealed that 18% of the students are in favor of changing the dress code. If you randomly select 15 students from this school, what is the probability that at least three of these students are in favor of the proposal to change the dress code?
(A) 0.18^3
(B) $(0.18)^3\,(0.82)^{12}$
(C) $\binom{15}{3}(0.18)^3\,(0.82)^{12}$
(D) $1 - \left[\binom{15}{0}0.82^{15} + \binom{15}{1}(0.18)(0.82)^{14} + \binom{15}{2}(0.18)^2\,(0.82)^{13}\right]$
(E) $1 - \left[\binom{15}{0}0.82^{15} + \binom{15}{1}(0.18)(0.82)^{14} + \binom{15}{2}(0.18)^2\,(0.82)^{13} + \binom{15}{3}(0.18)^3(0.82)^{12}\right]$

8. On a recent test in an introductory economics course, the mean grade was 42 with variance of 9. Suppose that the distribution of students' scores on this test is given by the random variable X. The professor decides to curve the test by multiplying each score by 1.5 and then adding 7 more points to the result. The new mean and standard deviation for the scores are
(A) 63, 4.5
(B) 63, 7.5
(C) 70, 4.5
(D) 70, 7.5
(E) 70, 20.25

9. Given two events A and B, if the probability that A occurs is 0.3, the probability that B occurs is 0.4 and the probability that A or B occurs is 0.55, then the $P(A|B)$ is
(A) 0.120
(B) 0.220
(C) 0.375
(D) 0.500
(E) 0.700

10. A game of chance involves rolling a fair die. If the die shows a 1, you win \$4; if it shows a 2, you win \$0.50; and if it shows any other number, you win nothing. If the cost to play the game is \$1, what are a player's expected winnings?
    (A) Lose \$0.08
    (B) Lose \$0.25
    (C) Win \$0.08
    (D) Win \$0.25
    (E) Win \$0.75

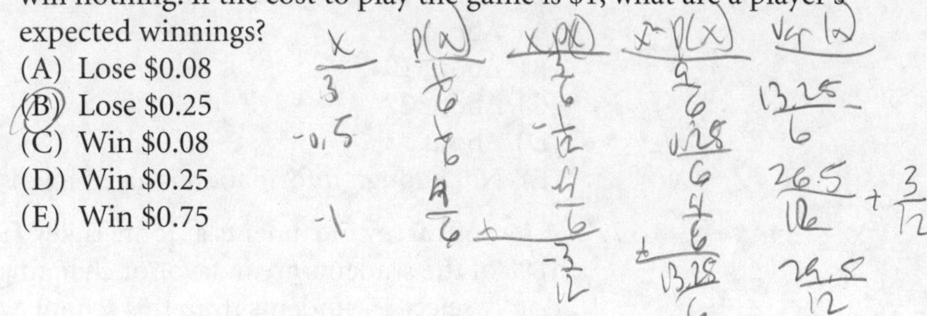

Free Response

Over time, a student analyzes her ability to guess correctly after narrowing down multiple choice answers in a 5-selection question. She discovers that if she narrows her answer set to 2 or 3 choices, her probability of getting the right answer is 0.8, but if she still has 4 or 5 choices left, her probability of choosing correctly decreases drastically to 0.1. Assuming that in general she can narrow her choices to 2 or 3 choices 70% of the time, what is the probability that she will answer a question correctly any time she must guess? Justify your answer.

Answers for Topic 4—Randomness and Probability—begin on page 267.

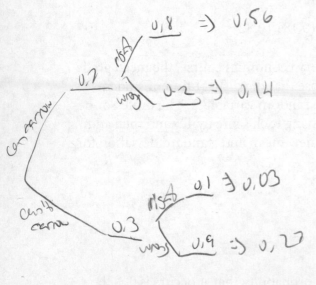

Topic 5

From the Data at Hand to the World at Large

The fourth major theme of statistics is **inferential statistics**. Inferential statistics helps investigators draw conclusions about a population based on a sample drawn from that population. Since not every sample, no matter how carefully selected, may be truly representative of the population, there are risks involved in inference techniques. Probability can be used to quantify those risks. First, we have to understand something about how sample statistics behave. We need to know what conditions must be met in order for our estimates about the population to be meaningful. We also need to imagine what would result if we were to take *all* possible samples of a given size from the same population. Why are these models important? Remember, our goal is to be able to move "from the data at hand to the world at large."

5-1 Sampling Distribution Models

The world as we know it is quite different from the world of our grandparents. We are inundated with information and try to make decisions based on our ability to analyze and understand this information. Statistics help us to make better decisions by allowing us to assess risks (*How serious are the dangers of Hormone Replacement Therapy?*), to make predictions (*How long will the polar ice caps remain intact?*), and to determine how certain things are related (*Are short people more prone to heart attacks?*).

In order to answer questions such as these, statisticians collect data from samples. For each sample collected, the results could be different. So, how does a statistician arrive at a "good conclusion" if the results are affected by the sample selected?

Sampling Distributions

To draw a conclusion about some aspect of a population (the mean income of the adult residents or the proportion of teen smokers in a particular town), we often rely on a random sample drawn from the population of interest. Since there are a large number of possible samples *of which we will draw only one*, it is important to understand how *our* sample is related to all of the samples that could be drawn; that is, we must understand the sampling distribution of a sample statistic.

A **sampling distribution** is the distribution of a statistic, such as $\bar{x}$ or $\hat{p}$, from *all possible* samples of a given size (n) from a population of size N. A certain proportion (p) of the population may display a particular characteristic. In each randomly selected sample of size n, that same characteristic will be seen in a proportion ($\hat{p}$) of the sample. We use $\hat{p}$ (our sample proportion) as an **estimate** of p (the population proportion). The same is true for the sample mean ($\bar{x}$) as an **estimate** of the population mean (μ).

At right is a histogram of the income for *all* of the residents of a certain town. The mean income is $16,439 with standard deviation $21,580. The shape of the distribution is skewed right.

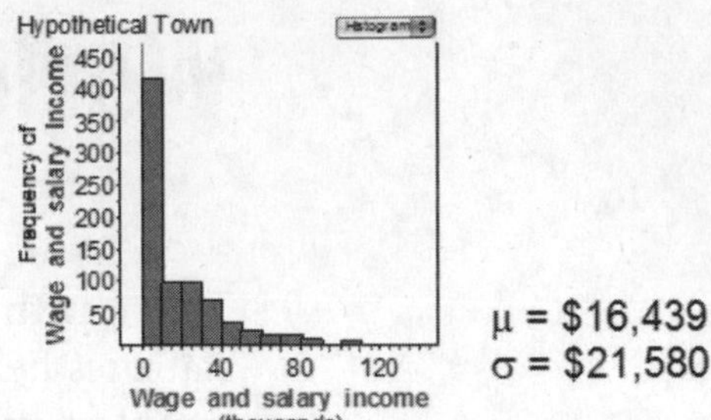

Suppose we did not have this data but needed to *estimate* the mean wage and salary income by taking an SRS of 50 adult residents. In order to arrive at a conclusion based on our *single* SRS of 50 adult residents, it is helpful to know how *our* sample compares to *all* of the possible samples of size 50 from this population. In *theory*, we could calculate the mean for each of these samples; the result would be the ***sampling distribution of sample means of size n = 50***. Like any distribution, this sampling distribution can be described by its center, shape, and spread.

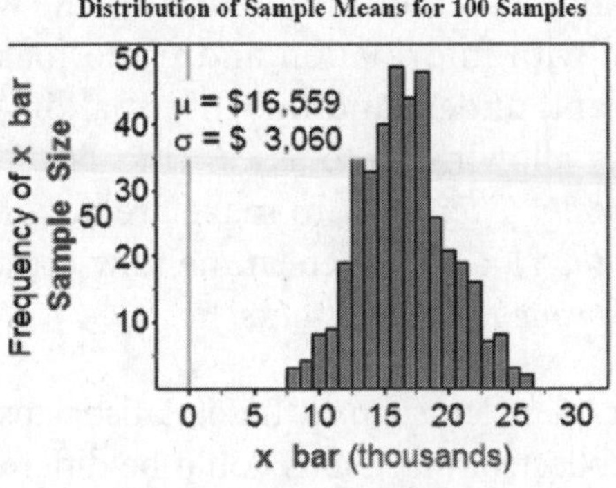

A simulation of 100 random samples of size $n = 50$ was taken from this population, and the mean of each of these samples was calculated. The distribution of 100 sample means of size $n = 50$ is given in the histogram at left. The shape of the distribution is roughly unimodal and symmetric. The mean of this distribution is $16,559 (a good estimate of the true mean), and the standard deviation of this distribution is $3,060 (approximately $\frac{\sigma}{\sqrt{n}}$).

The graphs below show the distributions of sample means for various sample sizes.

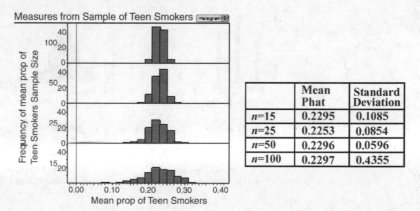

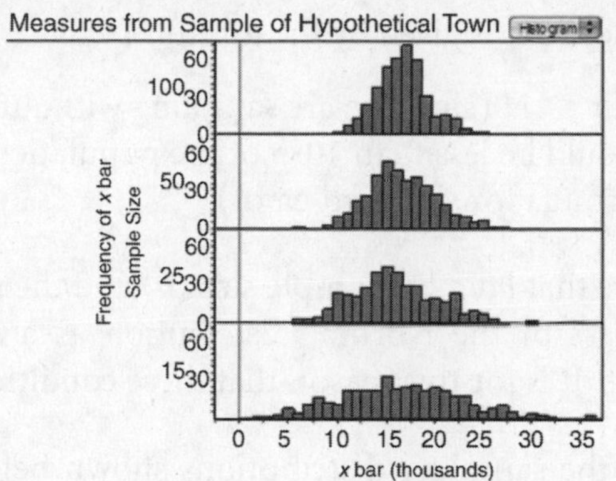

	Mean	Standard Deviation
n=15	16,259	5,632
n=25	16,179	4,382
n=50	16,559	3,060
n=100	16,573	2,175

Suppose our parameter of interest is a population *proportion* (the proportion of teen smokers in a certain town). The graphs below show the distributions of sample proportions for various sample sizes taken from a distribution with population proportion $p = 0.23$.

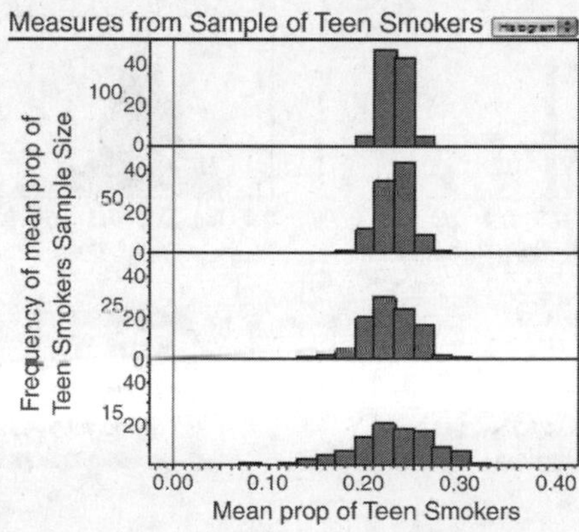

	Mean Phat	Standard Deviation
n=15	0.2295	0.1085
n=25	0.2253	0.0854
n=50	0.2296	0.0596
n=100	0.2297	0.4355

Armed with these ideas about distributions of sample means and sample proportions, we can make decisions regarding a population parameter based on a ***single*** sample of size n. Under certain conditions, the Normal distribution can be used to model the behavior of the sampling distribution, certain formulas can be used, and we can make predictions and discuss the likelihood of outcomes.

Modeling the Distribution of Sample Proportions

The sampling distribution of sample proportions has these characteristics.

- **SHAPE**—The distribution of sample proportions is approximately normally distributed provided that
    - $np \geq 10$ (there are at least 10 successes)

      and
    - $n(1 - p) \geq 10$ (there are at least 10 failures).
- **CENTER**—The mean of the sampling distribution of sample proportions, $\mu_{\hat{p}}$, is centered at the mean of the population, p, regardless of sample size. (We say that $\hat{p}$ is an **unbiased estimator** of p.)

- **SPREAD**—The standard deviation of the sampling distribution of sample proportions is given by the formula $\sigma_{\hat{p}} = \sqrt{\frac{p(1-p)}{n}}$, provided that
  - $10n \leq N$ (since we are sampling without replacement, the sample size should be less than 10% of the population size in order to use this formula for standard error).

Observe that *both* the sample size (n) and the proportion (p) affect the appropriateness of the Normal distribution as a model for the behavior of the samples. It is for this reason that these conditions must be checked!

Notice the sampling distributions shown below. The center of the distribution, *no matter what the sample size*, is the population parameter, p, that is, $\mu_{\hat{p}} = p = 0.23$. But as the sample size increases, the distribution of sample proportions (the sampling distribution) more closely resembles a normal distribution, making the use of Normal calculations safe.

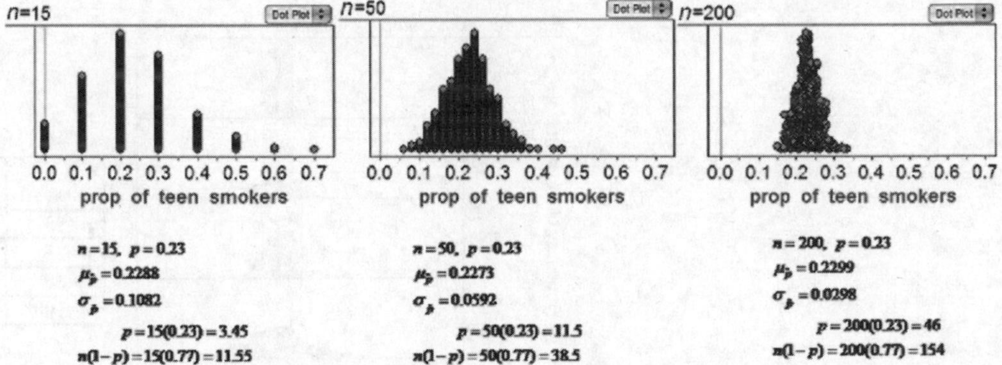

We can also notice that as n increases, the variability of the distribution of $\hat{p}$'s changes—as n increases, the variability decreases. That variability is measured by the standard deviation of the sampling distribution, $\sigma_{\hat{p}}$.

Now look at the conditions. If we choose a sample of size 15, our number of successes, np, will not be large enough to satisfy the condition for using a Normal model, although the number of failures, $n(1 - p)$, *is* large enough. (Again, this shows the importance of checking *all* conditions.)

The Sampling Distribution Model for a Proportion

Provided that the sampled values are independent and the sample size is large enough, the sampling distribution of $\hat{p}$ is modeled by a Normal model with *mean* $\mu_{\hat{p}} = \mu(\hat{p}) = p$, and *standard deviation*

$$\sigma_{\hat{p}} = \text{SD}(\hat{p}) = \sqrt{\frac{p(1-p)}{n}}.$$

Clues for Clarity *Some texts replace the quantity $(1 - p)$ with the letter q.*

Using a Sampling Distribution as a Model for Proportions

Example: Past records show that, on average, 65% of visitors will spend money in the gift shop at a local attraction on any given day. If there are 525 visitors on a given day, what is the probability that at least 70% of these visitors purchase something in the gift shop?

THINK

State what we want to know.

We want to find the probability that in a group of 525 visitors, 70% or more would make a purchase in the gift shop.

SHOW

Check the conditions.

✓ **10% condition: $10n < N$**
Consider the 525 visitors to be a random sample of visitors. It is reasonable to expect the attraction to draw at least 5250 visitors.

✓ **Success/failure condition:**
$\boldsymbol{np \geq 10}$
$np = 525(0.65) = 341.25 > 10$
$\boldsymbol{n(1 - p) \geq 10}$
$n(1 - p) = 525(0.35)$
$= 183.75 > 10$

State the parameters and the sampling distribution model.

The population proportion is $p = 0.65$. The conditions allow us to use a Normal probability model for the sampling distribution of $\hat{p}$. The *mean* of this Normal model is 0.65, and the *standard deviation* is

$$\sigma_{\hat{p}} = \sqrt{\frac{p(1-p)}{n}}$$

$$= \sqrt{\frac{(0.65)(0.35)}{525}} \approx 0.0208.$$

Our model for $\hat{p}$ is $N(0.65, 0.0208)$.

Make a picture.

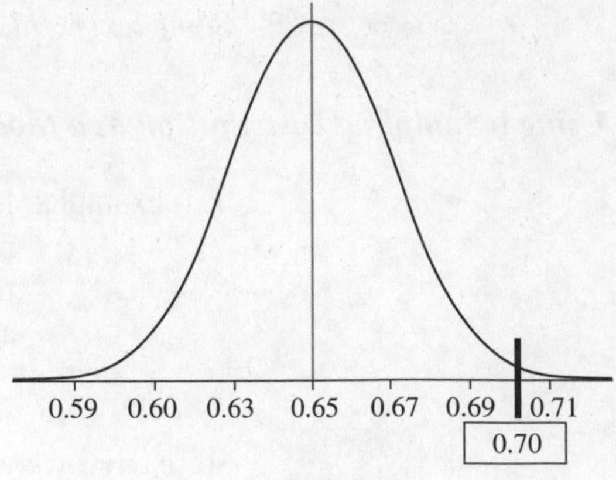

Find the z-score.

$$z = \frac{\hat{p} - p}{\sigma_{\hat{p}}} = \frac{0.70 - 0.65}{0.0208} \approx 2.40$$

Find the resulting probability.

$$P(\hat{p} \geq 0.70) = P(z \geq 2.40) \approx 0.0082$$

Discuss the probability in the context of the question.

There is a probability of only about 0.0082 that for a random sample of 525 visitors, at least 70% of the visitors will buy something in the gift shop.

Modeling the Distribution of Sample Means

For *categorical* variables, we are interested in a *proportion* (p). For *quantitative* variables, a parameter of interest is the average or *mean* (μ). (In our introductory example, we looked at the average income for residents of a certain town.)

The sampling distribution of sample means has these characteristics.

- **SHAPE**—As the sample size increases, the distribution of sample means tends toward an approximately normal distribution (Central Limit Theorem).
- **CENTER**—The mean of the sampling distribution of sample means, $\mu_{\bar{x}}$, is centered at the mean of the population, μ, regardless of sample size. (We say that $\bar{x}$ is an **unbiased estimator** of μ.)
- **SPREAD**—The standard deviation of the sampling distribution of sample means is given by the formula $\sigma_{\bar{x}} = \dfrac{\sigma}{\sqrt{n}}$.

The Central Limit Theorem
(The Fundamental Theorem of Statistics)

As the sample size, n, increases, the mean of n independent values has a sampling distribution that tends toward a Normal model with *mean*, $\mu_{\bar{x}} = \mu(\bar{x}) = \mu$ and *standard deviation*,

$$\sigma_{\bar{x}} = SD(\bar{x}) = \frac{\sigma}{\sqrt{n}}$$

The Central Limit Theorem (CLT) says that **means** of **repeated** samples will tend to follow a Normal model ***if the sample size is "large enough"***; this is true no matter what shape the population distribution has! If the population is Normal, then *any* size sample is "large enough." If the population is *not* Normal, most texts suggest that the sample size be *at least 30* for the CLT to apply.

Clues for Clarity *Avoid confusing the distribution of a sample with the sampling distribution model for sample means. The distribution of* ***a*** *(one) sample will, as* n *increases, look more like the population from which it was taken.*

Using a Sampling Distribution Model for the Mean

Example: Of 500 people attending an international convention, it was determined that the average distance traveled by the conventioneers was 1917 miles with a standard deviation of 2500 miles. What is the probability that a random sample of 40 of the attendees would have traveled an average distance of 900 miles or less to attend this convention?

State what we want to know.

We want to find the probability that in a group of 40 attendees, the *average* distance traveled to the convention was 900 miles or less.

Check the conditions.

✓ **10% random sample condition:** $\mathbf{10n < N}$
We are told 500 people attended the conference and the sample was chosen randomly.
$10(40) = 400 < 500$

✓ **Independence assumption:**
Convention attendees traveled from many different places, so independence is a reasonable assumption in this case.

State the parameters and the sampling distribution model.

The CLT tells us that we can model the sampling distribution of $\bar{x}$ with a Normal model: mean: $\mu_{\bar{x}} = 1917$ and standard deviation:

$$\sigma_{\bar{x}} = \frac{\sigma}{\sqrt{n}} = \frac{2500}{\sqrt{40}} \approx 395.28$$

when the sample size is large enough.

Since $n = 40$, the sample size is large enough.

Make a picture.

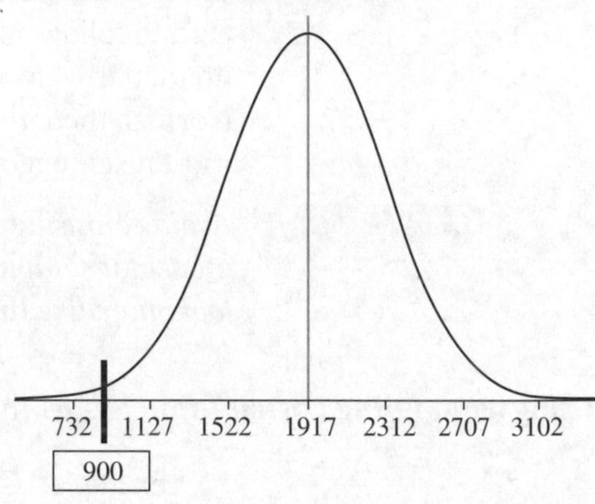

Find the z-score.

$$z = \frac{\bar{x} - \mu}{\sigma_{\bar{x}}} = \frac{900 - 1917}{395.28} \approx -2.57$$

Find the resulting probability.

$P(\bar{x} < 900) = P(z < -2.57) \approx 0.005$

Discuss the probability in the context of the question.

In a sample of size 40, the probability that the average distance traveled was less than 900 miles is only about 0.005.

Standard Error

For both sampling distribution models (proportions and means), we have assumed that we know the population parameters p or μ and σ. In most cases, it is not possible to know these values. Consequently, we must use what we *do* know and *estimate* the standard deviations of the sampling distributions. When this happens, we call the *estimated standard deviation* the **standard error.**

For a *proportion*, the **standard error of $\hat{p}$ is** $SE(\hat{p}) = s_{\hat{p}} = \sqrt{\frac{\hat{p}(1-\hat{p})}{n}}$.

For the *sample mean*, the **standard error of $\bar{x}$ is** $SE(\bar{x}) = s_{\bar{x}} = \frac{s}{\sqrt{n}}$.

We estimate a population parameter, p, by using a sample statistic, $\hat{p}$. For this reason, $\hat{p}$ is called a **point estimate** for p. In general, if the expected value of the estimator equals the corresponding parameter, the statistic is called an **unbiased estimator**. Since $\mu_{\hat{p}} = p$, $\hat{p}$ is an unbiased estimator for p. (Similarly, $\bar{x}$ is a point estimate for μ, and since $\mu_{\bar{x}} = \mu$, $\bar{x}$ is an unbiased estimator for μ.)

We have seen that sample statistics vary. So rather than simply giving a *single* value for our estimate of the population proportion, we use our sample estimate, $\hat{p}$, to build a range of plausible values. To do this, we want to establish an **interval** that we believe (at least with some degree of certainty) contains the true value of our population parameter. This interval forms an interval estimate for the parameter, p, and is called a **confidence interval**. Because of sampling variability, we can never say we are 100% certain; therefore, the confidence level we choose indicates the *degree* of certainty we have that our interval captures the true value of the parameter.

Let's think about how we can accomplish this. We know that under *certain* conditions, the CLT guarantees that the sampling distributions for both sample proportions ($\hat{p}$) and sample means ($\bar{x}$) are ***approximately*** Normal. The good news is that now the Empirical Rule applies. Remember that when we take a sample of size n, it is only one of all the possible samples of that size, and $\hat{p}$ or $\bar{x}$ is only one of all of the possible sample statistics. Consider a 95% confidence level. If we were able to repeatedly take samples of the same size and build ranges of plausible values around our sample statistics, about 95% of all such intervals (*statistic* ± 2 SE) will capture the true parameter, p or μ.

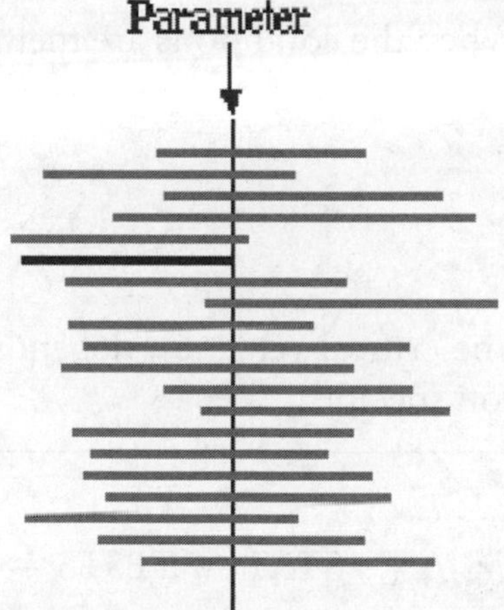

$\frac{19}{20}$ or 95% of the intervals contain the parameter.

5-2 Confidence Intervals for Proportions

Creating and Interpreting a Confidence Interval

What We Can Say

If we choose 95% as our confidence **level**, we build an interval that stretches about 2 SEs from $\hat{p}$ in either direction. Then we can say: *We are 95% confident that the true proportion is between (calculated lower limit) and (calculated upper limit).* This is a correct interpretation of the confidence **interval**.

It is also possible to interpret the confidence **level.** A correct interpretation of the confidence **level** would be: *95% confidence means that, in the long run, 95 out of 100 intervals calculated using the same procedure would (using random samples of the same size from the same population) capture the true population proportion.* Commonly used values for confidence levels are 90%, 95%, and 99%, but other levels may be chosen.

The general form of all confidence intervals is

estimate ± (*Critical Value*) (*Standard Error*).

The desired confidence level determines the **critical value** (the *number* of standard deviations on either side of the estimate). The **critical value (CV)** is denoted by z^*. The most commonly used values are:

Level	CV
90%	1.645
95%	1.960
99%	2.576

One-Proportion *z*-Interval

When the conditions are met, the confidence interval is

$$\hat{p} \pm z^* \times s_{\hat{p}},$$

$$\text{where } s_{\hat{p}} = \sqrt{\frac{\hat{p}(1-\hat{p})}{n}}.$$

The critical value, z^*, depends on the particular confidence level, *C*, that you specify.

TI-83/84 STAT ⇒ TESTS ⇒ 1-PropZInt

TI-*nspire* **Home** ⇒ Calculator ⇒ **Menu** ⇒ Statistics ⇒ Confidence Intervals ⇒ 1-Prop z Interval (**tab** through selections to choose Successes, x:, n:, Clevel:) ⇒ OK (click key or enter)

Clues for Clarity *Know the difference between confidence **interval** and confidence **level** and be sure to give the interpretation requested. It's easy to get **interval** and **level** confused!*

Margin of Error

The distance of the endpoints of the interval from $\hat{p}$ is called the **margin of error (ME)**, in this case $z^* \times s_{\hat{p}}$. The margin of error is tied to the level of confidence. (Surveys in the newspaper or on TV usually report a margin of error based on a 95% confidence level.) The more confident you want to be, the larger the margin of error will be. More confidence implies a wider interval. Since the standard error of $\hat{p}$ is tied to the sample size, as the sample size increases, the value of the standard error decreases and results in a narrower interval.

Assumptions/Conditions for a One-Proportion z-Interval

- **Plausible Independence Condition**—Is it reasonable to assume that the data values are independent of one another?
- **Randomization Condition**—Were proper randomization techniques used to collect the data?
- **10% Condition**—Unless the sample size is less than 10% of the population, the Normal model may not be appropriate.
- **Success/Failure Condition**—We must have at least 10 "successes" ($n\hat{p} \geq 10$) and 10 "failures" ($n(1 - \hat{p}) \geq 10$).

Using a One-Proportion z-Interval

Example: We want to estimate the proportion of Philadelphia families with children enrolled in preschool. In a random sample of 50 Philadelphia families with children of preschool age, 35 had children enrolled in preschool. Find a 95% confidence interval for the current true proportion of Philadelphia families with children enrolled in preschool.

Identify the ***parameter*** **we wish to estimate.** Choose and state a *confidence level.*

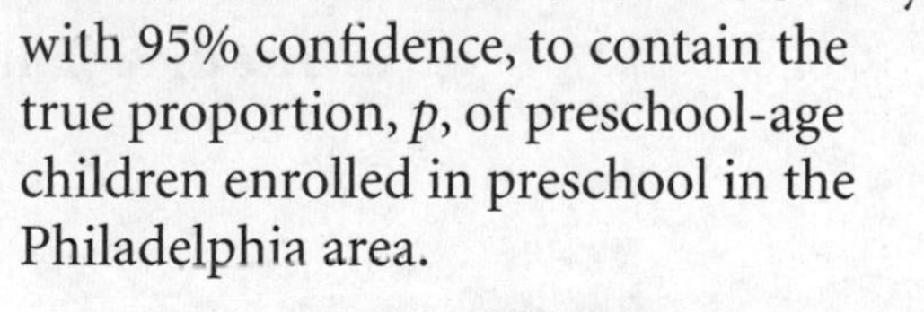

We wish to find an interval that is likely, with 95% confidence, to contain the true proportion, p, of preschool-age children enrolled in preschool in the Philadelphia area.

Check the conditions.

✓ **Plausible independence condition:** It is unlikely these families influenced each other.

✓ **Random condition:** The claim is that the sample was taken randomly.

✓ **10% condition: $10n < N$** The number of preschool-age children in the Philadelphia area is much larger than 500 or 10(50).

✓ **Success/failure condition:**

$\hat{p} = \frac{35}{50} = 0.70$

$n\hat{p} = 50(.70) = 35 > 10$

$n(1 - \hat{p}) = 50(.30) = 15 > 10$

so the sample size is large enough.

State the sampling distribution model for the statistic.

Under these conditions, the sampling distribution of the proportion can be modeled by a Normal model.

Choose your method.

We will find a **one-proportion** ***z*-interval.**

Mechanics

Construct the confidence interval.

$n = 50, \hat{p} = 0.7$

- First, find the **standard error.**

$$SE(\hat{p}) = \sqrt{\frac{\hat{p}(1-\hat{p})}{n}} = \sqrt{\frac{(0.7)(0.3)}{50}} \approx 0.0648$$

- Next, find the **margin of error.**

$$ME = z^* \times SE(\hat{p}) \approx 1.96(0.0648) \approx 0.127$$

Write the confidence interval.

The 95% confidence interval is: 0.7 ± 0.127 or (0.573, 0.827).

Interpretation

We can be 95% confident that between approximately 57.3% and 82.7% of preschool-age children in the Philadelphia area are currently enrolled in preschool.

Clues for Clarity

Things to remember about a parameter:

- *A **parameter** does not vary—there is only ONE true value of a parameter.*
- *You DO NOT KNOW the true value of the **parameter**. If you did, you would not need a confidence interval.*
- *NEVER use $\hat{p}$ when referring to the value of the **parameter**, p.*

Things to remember about interpreting a confidence interval:

- *A confidence interval makes a statement about the true population proportion, and your interpretation of the interval should be about the* ***population*** *proportion.*
- *Keep your* ***interpretation*** *to what you know—do not claim to know too much. A sentence or two should be sufficient.*
- *Sample statistics vary with each sample. Not every interval you compute will capture the true population proportion. Your interpretation of the confidence interval should reflect how confident you are that your interval has managed to capture the true value; your confidence is in the* ***method used*** *to produce the interval.*

5-3 Testing Hypotheses About Proportions

Confidence Intervals and Hypothesis Tests

Confidence intervals, just one form of statistical inference, allow us to use a sample statistic to make a statement about how confident we are that a population parameter lies within certain limits. Another form of statistical inference is a **hypothesis test** or **test of significance.** We use this form of statistical inference when a particular conjecture or claim (hypothesis) has been made about the true value of a population parameter.

Again, we plan to use sample statistics to help us decide whether or not to believe the hypothesis. We want to know if there is enough evidence to support (NOT *prove*) the hypothesis or to reject it. The hard part is that "convincing evidence" is not the same to all people. In the U.S. justice system, the assumption is that a defendant is innocent until proved guilty. Juries declare a person "guilty" or "not guilty"; note that they do not declare a person "innocent." The decision is based on the evidence. A verdict of guilty implies that there was sufficient evidence to convict (reject the claim of innocence), while a verdict of not guilty implies that there was not sufficient evidence to convict. But a not guilty verdict still cannot determine innocence.

The Reasoning of Hypothesis Testing

- **Hypotheses**
  - **The *null* hypothesis:** We start with the particular conjecture or claim that was made about the population parameter of interest. That conjecture gives us a boundary value for the **null hypothesis** denoted by the symbol H_0. The term *null* comes from the idea that there is "no difference" between the hypothesized value and the true population parameter. For proportions we write:

$$H_0: p = p_0 \text{ (hypothesized value)}.$$

Clues for Clarity *The null hypothesis MUST have a sign that includes equality (≤, =, or ≥) and MUST be written using population parameters and NEVER sample statistics. (Think about it—you have no need to hypothesize about the sample statistic; you found it, you KNOW it—end of story!)*

You MUST use standard notation (don't make up your own symbols).

You are advised to write your hypotheses in both symbols and words.

*Your final decision MUST always be stated in terms of rejecting or failing to reject the **null hypothesis**.*

- **The *alternative* hypothesis:** The **alternative hypothesis** is what would be accepted as true if the null hypothesis were to be rejected. It can take one of three different forms and must be specified *before* any sample data are collected. For proportions, a **one-sided** alternative would be either

$$H_a: p < p_0 \textbf{ or } H_a: p > p_0.$$

A **two-sided** alternative would be:

$$H_a: p \neq p_0.$$

The form used will depend on the study being done and should be clear from the context of the problem.

Plan

- Collect data that can be used to calculate a sample statistic. This statistic will be considered an estimate of the population parameter.
- **Decision Rule**: Decide what will be "convincing evidence" to reject the null hypothesis. Remember, samples vary. How likely is it that our sample produced a statistic as extreme as, or more extreme than, the one we observed if the null hypothesis is really true? Should a result as extreme as ours happen only 10% of the time, 5% of the time, or 1% of the time before we decide to reject H_0? We select a **level of significance**, α, that represents our tolerance level for extreme results. Common values of α are 0.10 (10%) *or less*.

Mechanics

- Check the **conditions** for the sampling distribution model.
- Calculate a **test statistic**. A **test statistic** is the *standardized* value of the sample statistic with respect to the hypothesized value. It will tell us how far our sample statistic is from the hypothesized value (in SE units). In general, it has the form

$$\text{Test statistic} = \frac{\text{statistic} - \text{parameter}}{\text{standard deviation of statistic}}$$

For a proportion, the test statistic is given by

$$z = \frac{(\hat{p} - p_0)}{SD(\hat{p})}, \text{ where } SD(\hat{p}) = \sqrt{\frac{p_0(1 - p_0)}{n}}$$

Note: When computing SD for the *test statistic,* we use p_0, because our model is based on the conjecture or claim (null hypothesis). When computing the SE for a *confidence interval,* we use $\hat{p}$ because we do not have a hypothesized parameter.

- Calculate the ***p*-value**. The ***p*-value** is the *probability* that a value at least as extreme as the observed value could occur if, in fact, the hypothesized value were true. Use the Normal table to convert your test statistic to a *p*-value. The smaller the ***p*-value,** the less likely it is that our sample came from a population with the parameter value stated in our null hypothesis. In other words, the smaller the *p*-value, the stronger the evidence is against the null hypothesis.

Conclusion

- Make a decision about whether to *reject* or *fail to reject* the **null hypothesis** based upon the ***p*-value** or the position of the **test statistic**. There are two ways to carry out your decision.
  - **The *p*-value approach: Reject H_0** if the calculated ***p*-value** is *less than* the chosen α-level. We say that the result is **statistically significant.**
  - **The rejection region approach:** The **rejection region (critical region)** depends on whether the test being performed is *one-sided* or *two-sided* and is determined from the H_a and the **level of significance,** α.

    For example, if the **level of significance** is $\alpha = 0.05$ and the test is *two-sided,* then the **critical values** (the values that cut off the rejection region from the rest of the normal curve) will be -1.96 and $+1.96$. This means that if our test statistic is below -1.96 or above $+1.96$, we will decide to **reject H_0.**

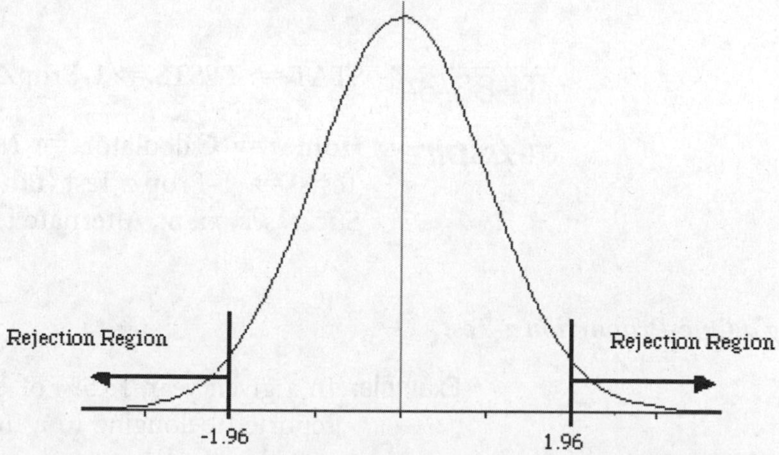

A situation might call for a one-sided test. For a left-tailed test (H_a: $p < p_0$) with $\alpha = 0.05$, the **critical value** is -1.645. This means that if our test statistic is less than -1.645, we will decide to **reject H_0.** Similarly, for a right-tailed test (H_a: $p > p_0$) with $\alpha = 0.05$, the

critical value is 1.645. This means that if our test statistic is greater than 1.645, we will decide to **reject H_0**.

- Write a statement about your decision in the CONTEXT of the situation.

Clues for Clarity *Your statement MUST include*

✓ *Decision (**reject** H_0 in favor of H_a or **fail to reject** H_0)*

✓ *Criteria for decision (p-value compared with α-level or test statistic compared with critical value)*

✓ *Context (use the **words of the problem** to restate your decision)*

One-Proportion z-Test

The conditions for the one-proportion *z*-test are nearly the same as for the one-proportion *z*-interval. We test the hypothesis H_0: $p = p_0$ using the statistic

$$z = \frac{(\hat{p} - p_0)}{SD(\hat{p})},$$

$$\text{where } SD(\hat{p}) = \sqrt{\frac{p_0(1 - p_0)}{n}}.$$

When the conditions are met and the null hypothesis is true, this statistic follows the standard Normal model, so we can use that model to obtain a *p*-value.

- We use p_0 to check the sample size conditions and also in the standard deviation formula since the Normal model is centered at p_0.

TI-83/84 STAT ⇒ TESTS ⇒ 1-PropZTest

TI-*nspire* **Home** ⇒ Calculator ⇒ **Menu** ⇒ Statistics ⇒ Stat Tests ⇒ 1-Prop z Test (**tab** through selections to choose P_0:, Successes, x:, n:, Alternate Hyp:) ⇒ OK (click key or enter)

Using a One-Proportion z-Test

Example: In a given year, 13.5% of employed people in the United States reported belonging to a union. Officials from a large city contacted a random sample of 2000 city workers and 240 claimed union membership. Is there sufficient evidence to conclude that the proportion of workers in this city who are union members is different from the national rate?

THINK

State what we want to know.

We want to know if the proportion of union workers in a particular city is different from the national rate.

Hypotheses

- The **null hypothesis**: NO difference

H_0: $p = 0.135$
H_0: The proportion of union members in this city is equal to the national rate of 0.135.

- The **alternative hypothesis**: There IS a difference.

H_a: $p \neq 0.135$
H_a: The proportion of union members in this city is different from the national rate of 0.135.

Check the conditions.

✓ **Randomization:**
A random sample is stated.

✓ **Population size: 10% condition:**
$10n \leq N$.
20,000 is less than all the city workers if the city is truly large.

✓ **Sample size:**
$np_0 = 2000(0.135) = 270 > 10$
$n(1 - p_0) = 2000(0.865)$
$= 1730 > 10$

Specify the sampling distribution.

Because the conditions are satisfied, it is appropriate to model the sampling distribution of the proportion with $\sim N(p_0, SD(\hat{p}))$.

Tell what test you plan to use.

One-Proportion *z*-test

Mechanics

- Calculate the standard deviation:

$p_0 = 0.135$

$$SD(\hat{p}) = \sqrt{\frac{p_0(1 - p_0)}{n}}$$

$$= \sqrt{\frac{(0.135)(0.865)}{2000}} \approx 0.0076$$

(Notice that this is a standard deviation value and NOT a standard *error* because we are using the parameter, p_0, not the estimated value, $\hat{p}$.)

- Find the **test statistic.**

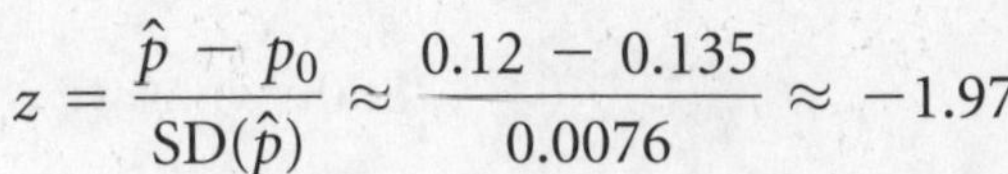

$$z = \frac{\hat{p} - p_0}{SD(\hat{p})} \approx \frac{0.12 - 0.135}{0.0076} \approx -1.97$$

- Make a picture.

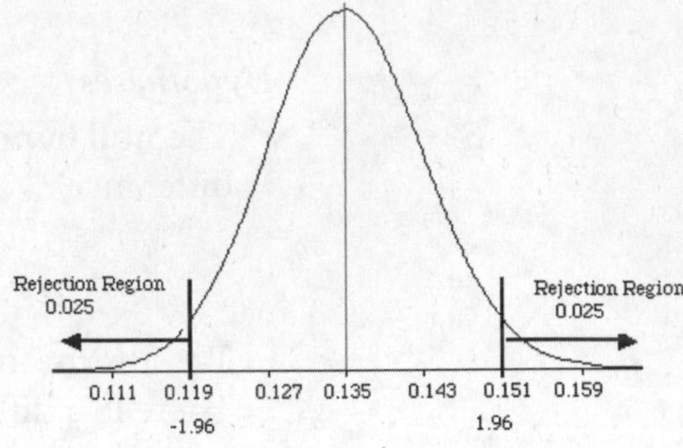

- Calculate the ***p*-value.**

Because we conducted a two-sided test, the p-value $= 2(0.0244)$
$= 0.0488$ (table)

Conclusion

- Link the p-value to a decision about the **null** hypothesis.

The p-value is small enough to reject the null hypothesis in favor of the alternative at the 0.05 level.

- **State a conclusion** in the proper ***context.***

There is sufficient evidence to conclude that, in this city, the proportion of workers who are union members is *different from* the national value.

5-4 More About Tests

Possible Errors When Hypothesis Testing

Because of the variability of sample data, we may draw a wrong conclusion despite having followed correct procedures. Whenever we make decisions based on sample data, there is a risk of error. These errors are of two types, **Type I** and **Type II**. They are not equally serious; the seriousness depends on the situation.

Type I Error

A **Type I Error** is the consequence of rejecting a null hypothesis that is in fact true. The probability of making a **Type I Error** is equal to the value of α, the **level of significance**.

Type II Error

A **Type II Error** is the consequence of failing to reject a null hypothesis that is in fact false. The probability of this type of error is called β. The value of β changes depending on the value of the parameter that is chosen as the alternative.

Note: Knowing how to *calculate* β is NOT a requirement of the AP* curriculum. You ARE expected to understand the difference between α and β and how they affect each other.

Power

The probability that a test will *correctly* reject a null hypothesis that is in fact false is called the **power** of the test.

$$\text{POWER} = 1 - \beta$$

Power is the complement of a **Type II Error**. High power is desired because it indicates the sensitivity of the test to specific values of the alternative hypothesis.

Ways to Reduce Error

- Type I Error (α)—decrease the α-level.
- Type II Error (β)—increase the α-level.
- Type I and Type II Errors—increase the sample size, n.
- Power ($1 - \beta$)—increase the sample size, n, or decrease β, or select a different, more extreme alternative.

The Relationship Between α, β, and Power

	H_0 True	H_0 False
Reject H_0	Type I Error (α)	Power ($1 - \beta$)
Fail to Reject H_0	Correct Decision	Type II Error (β)

Example: The quality-control department of a drug company tests the level of active ingredient of a drug they produce to control blood pressure. They will reject the production lot if there is too much or too little of the active ingredient.

- A **Type I Error** would reject the production lot even though the amount of active ingredient fell within the target range. The company would lose profit.
- A **Type II Error** would accept the production lot when the amount of the active ingredient is really outside of the target range. This would be far worse for the patients—and for the company when it is sued.

5-5 Comparing TWO Proportions

While it is interesting to test a hypothesis about a single proportion, it is more likely that researchers would be interested in a comparison between two proportions. They might compare genders, age groups, treatments, or any other two categories of interest. When comparing proportions of two groups, we usually want to know how those proportions *differ*, so our first step is to find out how these *differences* behave.

The Sampling Distribution for Two Independent Proportions $(\hat{p}_1 - \hat{p}_2)$

The *mean* of the sampling distribution of $\hat{p}_1 - \hat{p}_2$ is $p_1 - p_2$.

The standard deviation of the sampling distribution of $\hat{p}_1 - \hat{p}_2$ is a little trickier. Recall that (the) SQUARE ROOT (operation) IS NOT DISTRIBUTIVE.

$$\sqrt{a^2 + b^2} \neq a + b$$

$$\sqrt{3^2 + 4^2} = \sqrt{9 + 16} = \sqrt{25} = 5$$

$$\sqrt{9 + 16} \neq \sqrt{9} + \sqrt{16} = 3 + 4 = 7$$

The square root of a sum does not equal the sum of the square roots. Standard deviations are square roots of variances. So, we need to **add** the *variances* (the squares of the standard deviations) of the two samples and then take the square root of the sum in order to get the standard deviation of our sampling distribution:

$$SD(X - Y) = \sqrt{Var(X) + Var(Y)}.$$

Just remember, you **CAN add variances**, but you **CANNOT add standard deviations.** So, in our case, for the difference of two proportions:

$$SD(\hat{p}_1 - \hat{p}_2) = \sqrt{\frac{p_1(1 - p_1)}{n_1} + \frac{p_2(1 - p_2)}{n_2}}$$

and

$$SE(\hat{p}_1 - \hat{p}_2) = \sqrt{\frac{\hat{p}_1(1 - \hat{p}_1)}{n_1} + \frac{\hat{p}_2(1 - \hat{p}_2)}{n_2}}.$$

The Sampling Distribution Model for a Difference Between Two Independent Proportions

Provided that the sampled values are independent, the samples are independent, and the sample sizes are large enough, the sampling distribution of $\hat{p}_1 - \hat{p}_2$ is modeled by a Normal model with *mean* $\mu = p_1 - p_2$ and *standard deviation*

$$\sigma(\hat{p}_1 - \hat{p}_2) = SD(\hat{p}_1 - \hat{p}_2) = \sqrt{\frac{p_1(1 - p_1)}{n_1} + \frac{p_2(1 - p_2)}{n_2}}.$$

Assumptions/Conditions for the Difference of Two Proportions

The assumptions/conditions for the difference between two proportions are the same as the assumptions and conditions for one proportion with the exception that each assumption and condition must be checked for EACH data set. As a reminder, those assumptions and conditions are:

- **Plausible Independence Condition**—It is important here to be certain that the two sample groups are independent of one another. If the samples are NOT independent, this procedure is inappropriate.
- **Randomization Condition**—Were proper randomization techniques used to collect the data for each sample?
- **10% Condition**—Unless the size of each sample is less than 10% of its respective population, the Normal model may not be appropriate.
- **Success/Failure Condition**—We must have at least 10 "successes" ($np \geq 10$) and 10 "failures" ($n(1 - p) \geq 10$).

  Note: Some statisticians feel that as long as each of the above computations is at least 5, the success/failure condition has been met. Either 5 or 10 is acceptable for the examination. Just make sure you show which condition you are using and how it applies.

A Two-Proportion z-Interval

If we want to estimate the population difference in proportions based on sample data from two independent populations, we use a confidence interval.

Two-Proportion *z*-Interval

When the conditions are met, we are ready to find the confidence interval for the difference of two proportions, $p_1 - p_2$. The interval is

$$(\hat{p}_1 - \hat{p}_2) \pm z^* \times SE(\hat{p}_1 - \hat{p}_2),$$

$$\text{where } SE(\hat{p}_1 - \hat{p}_2) = \sqrt{\frac{\hat{p}_1(1 - \hat{p}_1)}{n_1} + \frac{\hat{p}_2(1 - \hat{p}_2)}{n_2}}.$$

The critical value z^* depends on the particular confidence level, C, that you specify.

TI-83/84 STAT ⇒ TESTS ⇒ 2-PropZInt

TI-*nspire* **Home** ⇒ Calculator ⇒ **Menu** ⇒ Statistics ⇒ Confidence Intervals ⇒ 2-Prop z Interval (**tab** through selections to choose Successes, x1:, n1:, Successes, x2:, n2:, Clevel:) ⇒ OK (click key or enter)

Example: A recent study of 1000 randomly chosen residents in each of two randomly selected states indicated that the percent of people living in those states who were born in foreign countries was

6.5% for State A and 1.7% for State B. Find a 99% confidence interval for the difference between the proportions of foreign-born residents for these two states.

THINK

Identify the *parameter* we wish to estimate.
Choose and state a confidence level.

We wish to find an interval that we are 99% confident contains the true proportion difference, $p_1 - p_2$, of foreign-born residents in States A and B.

SHOW

Check the conditions.

✓ **Independence:**
Groups from different randomly selected states should be independent of each other.

✓ **Randomization:**
The claim is that each set of sample data was drawn randomly from its respective state.

✓ **Population sizes (10% condition):** $\mathbf{10n_1 \leq N_1}$ **and** $\mathbf{10n_2 \leq N_2}$
It is reasonable to believe that the population of each of these states is greater than 10,000.

✓ **Sample sizes:**

$$n_A\hat{p}_A = 1000(0.065) = 65 > 10$$
$$n_B\hat{p}_B = 1000(0.017) = 17 > 10$$
$$n_A(1 - \hat{p}_A) = 1000(0.935) = 935 > 10$$
$$n_B(1 - \hat{p}_B) = 1000(0.983) = 983 > 10$$

State the sampling distribution model for the statistic.

Under these conditions, the sampling distribution of the difference between the two sample proportions can be modeled by

$$\sim N(p_A - p_B, \mathrm{SE}(\hat{p}_A - \hat{p}_B))$$

Choose your method.

We will find a **two-proportion** ***z*****-interval.**

Mechanics

Construct the confidence interval.

$\hat{p}_A = 0.065 \qquad \hat{p}_B = 0.017$

$\hat{p}_A - \hat{p}_B = 0.065 - 0.017 = 0.048$

$n_A = 1000 \qquad n_B = 1000$

- First find the **standard error.**

$$\text{SE}(\hat{p}_A - \hat{p}_B) = \sqrt{\frac{\hat{p}_A(1-\hat{p}_A)}{n_A} + \frac{\hat{p}_B(1-\hat{p}_B)}{n_B}} \approx \sqrt{\frac{(0.065)(0.935)}{1000} + \frac{(0.017)(0.983)}{1000}} \approx 0.0088$$

- Next find the **margin of error.**

$$\text{ME} = z^* \cdot \text{SE}(\hat{p}_A - \hat{p}_B) \approx 2.576(0.0088) \approx 0.0227$$

- Write the confidence interval.

99% CI: 0.048 ± 0.0227 or $(0.0253, 0.0707)$

Interpretation

We can be 99% confident that the percent difference of foreign-born residents for States A and B is between 2.5% and 7.1%.

A Two-Proportion z-Test

If we want to determine whether there is a significant difference between two population proportions, we take a random sample from each population and conduct a significance test. The procedure for this test is essentially the same as for a one-proportion z-test with one slight difference: Our **null hypothesis** is that there is *no difference* between the two proportions (the *difference is zero*).

$$H_0: p_1 = p_2 \qquad (H_0: p_1 - p_2 = 0)$$

The **alternative hypothesis** is determined by the kind of difference you expect to get in the particular situation ($<$, $\neq$, $>$).

The standard error used in this case is

$$\text{SE}_{\text{pooled}} = \sqrt{\hat{p}_c(1-\hat{p}_c)\left(\frac{1}{n_1} + \frac{1}{n_2}\right)}, \text{ where } \hat{p}_c = \frac{x_1 + x_2}{n_1 + n_2},$$

and $\hat{p}_c$ means the "combined" or "pooled" value of the two proportions. You may wonder why it is okay to combine proportions from two different populations. Remember, the null hypothesis assumes that $p_1 = p_2$ and thus the two populations are identical for the attribute being studied. (For example, the ratio of foreign-born residents is the same in the two states.) Combining the sample data will not distort the proportions.

Two-Proportion z-Test

The conditions for the two-proportion z-test are nearly the same as for the two-proportion interval. The **null hypothesis** is

$$H_0: p_1 = p_2 \text{ or } p_1 - p_2 = 0.$$

The **test statistic** is $z = \dfrac{\hat{p}_1 - \hat{p}_2}{SE_{pooled}}$ using the standard error formula above.

Note: If you have a graphing calculator, it is highly unlikely that you will have to do this calculation by hand. A calculator two-proportion z-test will calculate the z-score automatically and use the correct standard error.

TI-83/84 STAT ⇒ TESTS ⇒ 2-PropZTest

TI-*nspire* **Home** ⇒ Calculator ⇒ **Menu** ⇒ Statistics ⇒ Stat Tests ⇒ 2-Prop z Test (**tab** through selections to choose Successes, x1:, n1:, Successes, x2:, n2:, Alternate Hyp:) ⇒ OK (click key or enter)

Example: A researcher wants to know whether there is a difference in AP* Statistics exam failure rates between rural and suburban students. She randomly selects 107 rural students and 143 suburban students who took the exam. Thirty rural students failed to pass their exam, while 45 suburban students failed to pass. Is there a significant difference in failure rates for these groups?

THINK

State what we want to know. We wish to find out if the failure rates on the AP* Statistics exam for rural and suburban students are significantly different.

Hypotheses

- Null hypothesis: $H_0: p_R = p_S$ or $p_R - p_S = 0$
  There is no difference in failure rates.

- Alternative hypothesis: $H_a: p_R \neq p_S$ or $p_R - p_S \neq 0$
  There is a difference in failure rates.

Check the conditions.

✓ **Independence:**
Rural and suburban student groups are independent.

✓ **Randomization:**
The claim is that the data for each group were drawn randomly.

✓ **Population sizes:**
$10n_1 \leq N_1$ and $10n_2 \leq N_2$
$10n_R \leq N_R$:
$10(107) <$ Rural Exam Takers
$10n_S \leq N_S$:
$10(143) <$ Suburban Exam Takers
It is reasonable to believe that the population of rural exam takers is greater than 1070 and that the population of suburban exam takers is greater than 1430.

✓ **Sample size:**
$30 > 10$
$45 > 10$
$107 - 30 > 10$
$143 - 45 > 10$

State the sampling distribution model for the statistic.

Under these conditions, the sampling distribution of the difference between the two sample proportions can be modeled by

$$\sim N(p_R - p_S, \text{SE}(\hat{p}_R - \hat{p}_S))$$

Choose your method.

We will conduct a **two-proportion *z*-test.**

Mechanics

- Calculate the standard error.

$\hat{p}_R \approx 0.280 \qquad \hat{p}_S \approx 0.315$
$n_R = 107 \qquad n_S = 143$

$$\hat{p}_c = \frac{x_R + x_S}{n_R + n_S}$$
$$= \frac{30 + 45}{107 + 143} = \frac{75}{250} = 0.3$$

$$\text{SE}_{\text{pooled}} = \sqrt{\hat{p}_c(1 - \hat{p}_c)\left(\frac{1}{n_R} + \frac{1}{n_S}\right)}$$

$$\text{SE}_{\text{pooled}} = \sqrt{(0.3)(0.7)\left(\frac{1}{107} + \frac{1}{143}\right)}$$
$$\approx 0.059$$

- Find a *z*-score.

$$z = \frac{\hat{p}_R - \hat{p}_S}{\text{SE}_{\text{pooled}}} = \frac{-0.035}{0.059} \approx -0.59$$

- Make a picture.

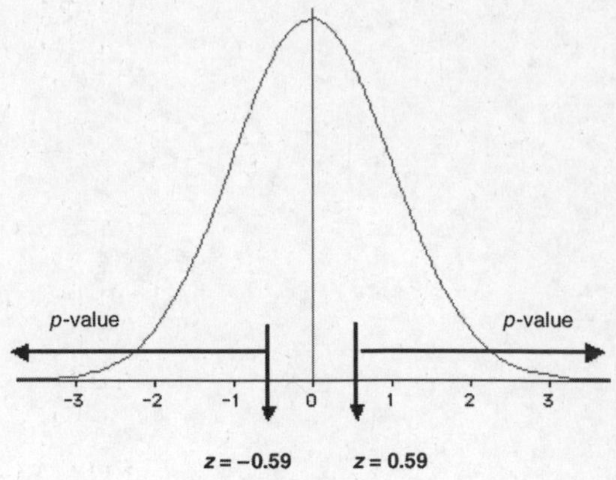

- Find the p-value.

$$p\text{-value} = 2P(|z| \geq 0.59) = 2(0.2776) = 0.5552 \text{ (table)}$$

Conclusion

The p-value (0.5552) is too high to reject H_0. There is insufficient evidence at any reasonable α-level to show a difference between the failure rates of rural and suburban students on the AP* Statistics exam based on this sample.

Review Questions for Topic 5—From the Data at Hand to the World at Large

Multiple Choice

1. In the diagram below, Region II is the rejection region for the null hypothesis. The area of which nonoverlapping region(s) represents the probability of committing a Type II Error?

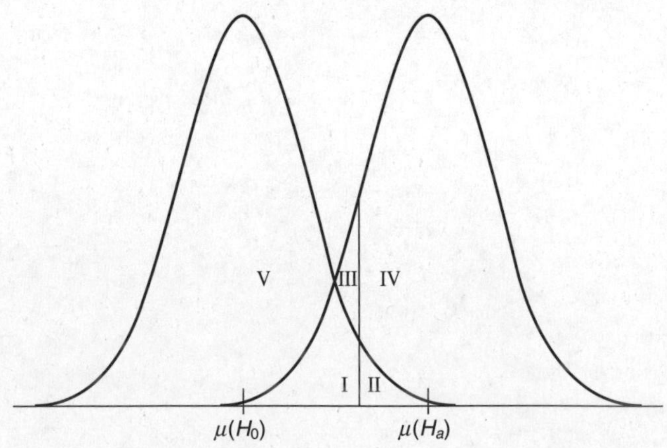

(A) Region I and Region III
(B) Region I and Region V
(C) Region II
(D) Region II and Region IV
(E) None of the above

2. The proportion of orange salamanders along a certain stream is known to be 10%. Use a Normal model to approximate the probability that, for a sample of 100 salamanders along this stream, 20 of them are orange.
(A) 0.0004
(B) 0.1937
(C) 0.3707
(D) 0.6293
(E) 0.9996

3. At a man-made lake in central Pennsylvania, an average of 50 gallons of water flow over the spillway every minute, with a standard deviation of 15 gallons. If the distribution of the number of gallons that flow over the spillway is assumed to be approximately normal, what is the probability that, for any randomly chosen minute, fewer than 20 gallons of water will flow over the spillway?
(A) 0.0228
(B) 0.0456
(C) 0.0968
(D) 0.1936
(E) 0.9772

4. Owners of a chain of ice cream shops recently examined sales figures and noticed that on a randomly selected day, 21 of 103 ice cream customers from their shop located in the eastern part of the state ordered soft-serve ice cream, while 29 of 132 ice cream customers from their shop located in the western part of the state ordered soft-serve ice cream. Construct a 95% confidence interval to find the difference in proportions of customers who favor soft-serve ice cream in the two parts of the state.

(A) $\left(\frac{21}{103} - \frac{29}{132}\right) \pm 1.96\sqrt{\frac{\frac{21}{103}\left(1 - \frac{21}{103}\right)}{103} + \frac{\frac{29}{132}\left(1 - \frac{29}{132}\right)}{132}}$

(B) $\left(\frac{21}{103} - \frac{29}{132}\right) \pm 1.96\sqrt{\frac{\frac{21}{103}\left(1 - \frac{21}{103}\right)}{103} + \frac{\frac{21}{103}\left(1 - \frac{21}{103}\right)}{103}}$

(C) $\left(\frac{21}{103} - \frac{29}{132}\right) \pm 1.96\sqrt{\frac{\frac{29}{132}\left(1 - \frac{29}{132}\right)}{132} + \frac{\frac{29}{132}\left(1 - \frac{29}{132}\right)}{132}}$

(D) $\left(\frac{21}{103} - \frac{29}{132}\right) \pm 1.96\sqrt{\frac{\frac{21}{103}\left(1 - \frac{21}{103}\right)}{103} - \frac{\frac{29}{132}\left(1 - \frac{29}{132}\right)}{132}}$

(E) $\left(\frac{21}{103} - \frac{29}{132}\right) \pm 1.96\sqrt{\frac{50}{235}\left(1 - \frac{50}{235}\right)\left(\frac{1}{103} + \frac{1}{132}\right)}$

5. Use the same information as in the previous problem. Is there a significant difference in the proportions of customers who favor soft-serve ice cream in the eastern and western parts of the state?
   (A) There is a significant difference at the 0.001 level.
   (B) There is a significant difference at the 0.10 level but not at the 0.05 level.
   (C) There is a significant difference at the 0.05 level but not at the 0.01 level.
   (D) There is a significant difference at the 0.01 level but not at the 0.001 level.
   (E) There is no significant difference at the 0.10 level.

6. With an α-level of 5%, what is the power of a test against an alternative for which the probability of a Type II error is 3%?
   (A) 3%
   (B) 5%
   (C) 95%
   (D) 97%
   (E) The power cannot be determined from the information given.

7. A major university expresses 95% confidence that about 90% to 93% of its students find employment in their field within one year of graduation. What is the margin of error implied in this statement?
   (A) 1%
   (B) 1.5%
   (C) 3%
   (D) 5%
   (E) 6%

8. Research indicates that about 30% of all smokers were early smokers, having smoked their first cigarette by age 14. In a random sample of 400 14-year-olds, 140 reported already having smoked their first cigarette. The standard error for a confidence interval for p, the proportion of early smokers, is

   (A) $\sqrt{\frac{(0.30)(0.70)}{140}}$

   (B) $\sqrt{\frac{(0.35)(0.65)}{140}}$

   (C) $\sqrt{\frac{(0.30)(0.70)}{400}}$

(D) 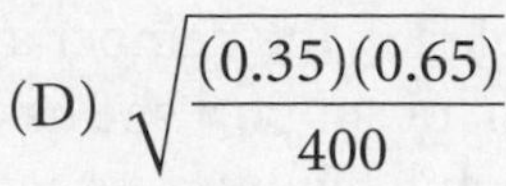 $\sqrt{\dfrac{(0.35)(0.65)}{400}}$

(E) $\dfrac{0.35}{\sqrt{400}}$

9. The histogram at right, with mean of approximately 3.47 and standard deviation of approximately 1.66, represents the distribution of 500 rolls of a fair six-sided die. Samples of size $n = 10$ are taken from this distribution, and the mean for each of those samples is calculated. Which of the following histograms best represents the distribution of sample means of size $n = 10$?

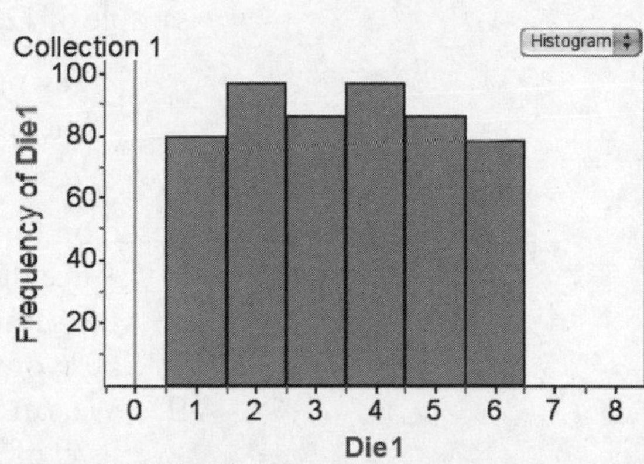

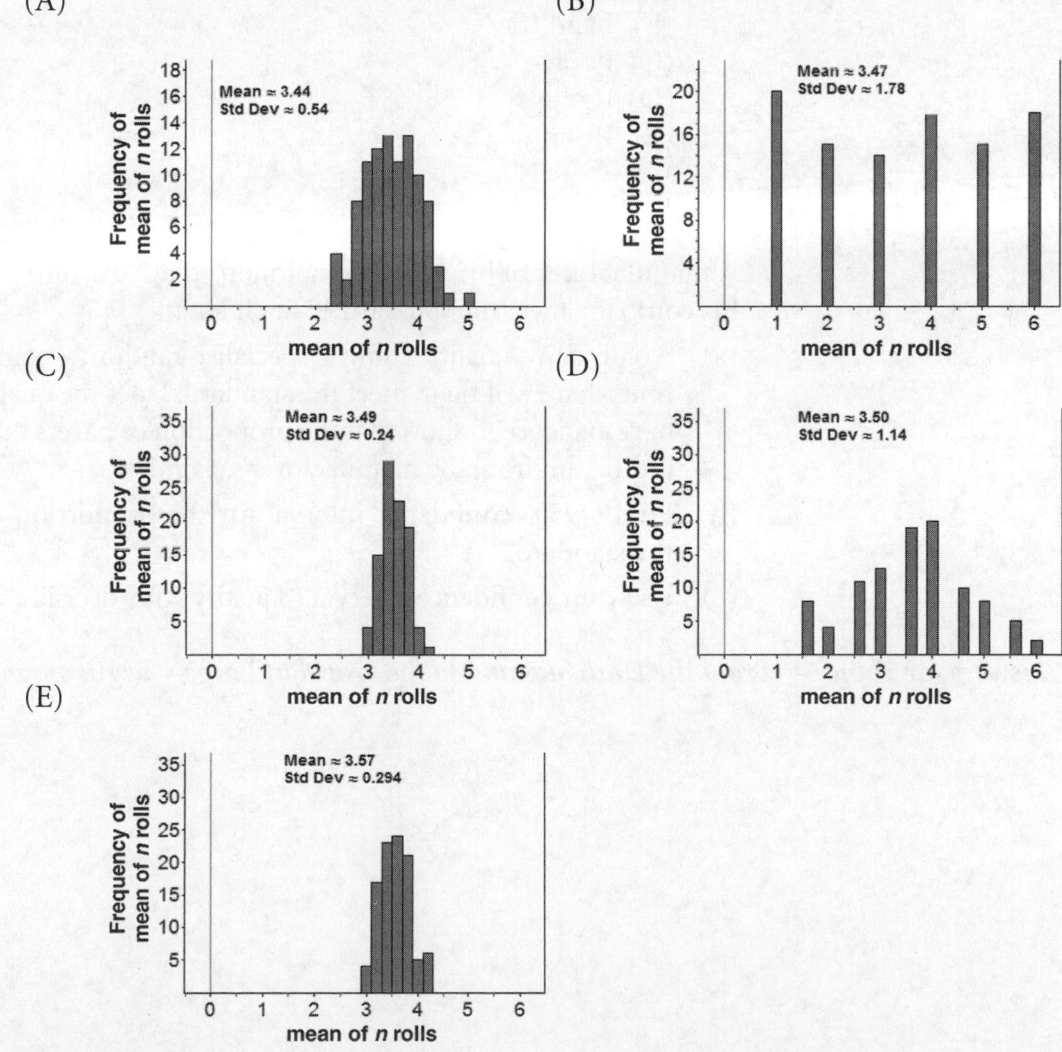

10. In an upcoming mayoral race, the democratic candidate hires a statistician to determine the amount of support she has for the upcoming election. The statistician tests the null hypothesis that the proportion of voters favoring the candidate equals 50% against the alternative hypothesis that the proportion is greater than 50%. The result for a simple random sample of 125 registered voters is displayed in the printout below.

 Test of H_0: $p = 0.5$ *v.* H_A: $p > 0.5$
 Success = for Democratic Candidate
 $n = 125$ $\hat{p} = 0.5623$ $SE = 0.0447$ *p-value* = 0.0818

 Based on this result, which of the following statements is/are valid?

 I. Since the Democratic candidate had well over 50% of the vote in the sample, she can be very confident that she will obtain more than 50% of the vote in the election.
 II. We can find favor for the alternative hypothesis at a significance level of 10% but not at 5%.
 III. The *p*-value of 0.0818 indicates that there is approximately an 8% chance that she will not obtain more than 50% of the vote.

 (A) I and II
 (B) I and III
 (C) I only
 (D) II only
 (E) III only

Free Response

A manufacturer of brick pavers maintains that 80% of the pavers produced by his company meet the standard 15-inch length.

(a) A company quality control specialist randomly samples 51 pavers and finds that 27 of them meet the standard. Does the quality control specialist have evidence to show that the proportion of pavers that meet the standard is different from the manufacturer's claim?
(b) Find a 95% confidence interval for the proportion of pavers that meet the standard.
(c) Use your confidence interval to justify your decision in part (a).

Answers for Topic 5—From the Data at Hand to the World at Large—begin on page 269.

Topic 6

Learning About the World

In the previous section we worked with categorical variables and proportions. We now move to working with quantitative variables. A widely used statistic is the mean. In this section we will look at inference for the mean and the implications of knowing or not knowing the population standard deviation.

6-1 Inferences About Means

When we reviewed the **Central Limit Theorem** (**CLT**), we saw that *means* of *repeated* samples tend to follow a Normal model as long as the population distribution is Normal or the sample size is large enough. To use the *z*-statistic for means, we need to know the population standard deviation, σ. In the real world of data, it is unrealistic to think we will know this. So when we do *not* know σ, is a Normal model still reasonable? If not, what model should we use?

The t-Distributions: A Sampling Distribution for Means

Recall that, according to the CLT, the formula for the standard deviation of the sampling distribution for means is

$$\sigma_{\bar{x}} = \sigma(\bar{x}) = \mathrm{SD}(\bar{x}) = \frac{\sigma}{\sqrt{n}}$$

When we have to estimate σ with s, the standard error of the sampling distribution for means is

$$s_{\bar{x}} = s(\bar{x}) = \mathrm{SE}(\bar{x}) = \frac{s}{\sqrt{n}}$$

Also recall that the smaller the sample, the larger the variation. How can we take into account the larger variation of smaller samples, and what effect does this variation have on the shape of the sampling distribution? The answer comes from an unlikely source, William S. Gosset, the Guinness Brewery quality-control engineer who studied this problem and figured out that the shape of the sampling distribution changed when the standard error, $\frac{s}{\sqrt{n}}$, was used in place of the standard deviation. The new model that he found was not *one* model but a *family* of distributions called the **Student's *t*-distributions**. The shape of the *t*-distributions (unimodal, symmetric, and bell-shaped) is connected to the sample size by a parameter called the **degrees of freedom**. The degrees of freedom (df) determine the particular *t*-distribution. The increased variation due to small sample sizes increases the probability in the tails. We identify the particular *t*-distribution by noting the degrees of freedom with a subscript: t_{df}.

Sampling Distribution for Means

When the conditions are met, the standardized sample mean,

$$t = \frac{\bar{x} - \mu}{\frac{s}{\sqrt{n}}},$$

follows a Student's t-model with $n - 1$ degrees of freedom.

Assumptions/Conditions for Using Student's t-Distributions

To use the Student's t-distributions, these conditions must be satisfied:

- **Randomization condition**—The data come from a random sample or a randomized experiment.
- **Population-size condition (10% condition)**—The sample size is less than 10% of the population.
- **Nearly normal condition**—The data come from a unimodal, symmetric, bell-shaped distribution. This can be verified by constructing a *histogram* or a *normal probability plot of the data.*

<u>*Note:*</u> The t-procedures are said to be **robust**, meaning they work reasonably well with small sample sizes, provided that there are no extreme outliers or skew. As always, before analyzing data, it is important to look at a visual display.

- If the underlying population is approximately normal, the t-statistic is appropriate regardless of sample size, n.
- For $n \geq 40$, the t-statistic is appropriate provided that there are no outliers.
- For $15 \leq n < 40$, the t-statistic is appropriate provided that there are no outliers or strong skew.
- For $n < 15$, the t-statistic is appropriate provided that the distribution of the data is approximately normal.

A One-Sample Confidence Interval for the Mean (σ unknown)

Because we are using s to estimate σ, we use a ***t**-critical value* for confidence intervals and a ***t**-test statistic* for hypothesis tests.

One-Sample *t*-Interval

When the conditions are met, the **confidence interval for the population mean,** μ, is:

$$\bar{x} \pm t^*_{n-1} \times \frac{s}{\sqrt{n}}$$

The **critical value** t^*_{n-1} depends on the particular confidence level, C, that you specify and on the number of **degrees of freedom,** $n - 1$, which we get from the sample size.

TI-83/84 STAT ⇒ TESTS ⇒ TInterval

TI-*nspire* **Home** ⇒ Calculator ⇒ **Menu** ⇒ Statistics ⇒ Confidence Intervals ⇒ t Interval (**tab** through selections for Data Input Method:) ⇒ OK (click key or enter)

Example: Some AP* Statistics students are concerned about safety near an elementary school. Though there is a 15 MPH SCHOOL ZONE sign nearby, most drivers seem to go much faster than that, even when the warning sign flashes. The students randomly selected 20 flashing zone times during the school year, noted the speeds of the cars passing the school during the flashing zone times, and recorded the averages. They found that the overall average speed during the flashing school zone times for the 20 time periods was 24.6 mph with a standard deviation of 7.24 mph. Find a 90% confidence interval for the average speed of all vehicles passing the school during those hours. A histogram of their data follows.

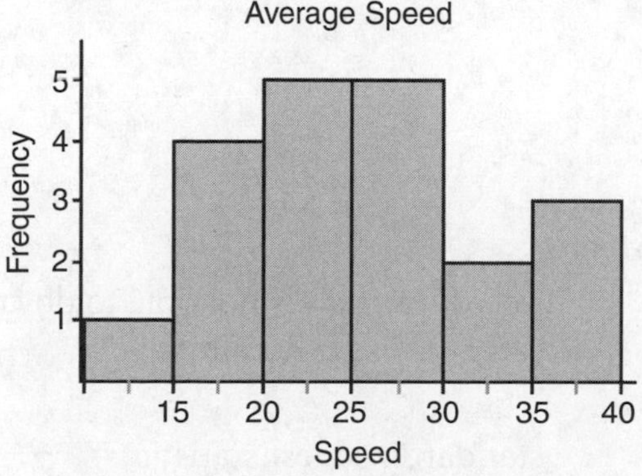

THINK **Identify the parameter being estimated.**

Find a 90% confidence interval for the mean speed, μ, of vehicles that pass the school when the sign is flashing.

Check the conditions.

✓ **Randomization:**
It is a random selection of days from the year.

✓ **Population size: 10n ≤ N**
It is reasonable to assume that at least 200 flashing zone times exist during the school year since the sign flashes both morning and afternoon.

✓ **Sample size:**
$n = 20$, the histogram is roughly symmetric and unimodal (no strong skew or outliers).

Choose your method.

One-sample *t*-interval for the mean

Mechanics
Construct the interval.

$n = 20; \bar{x} = 24.6$ mph; $s = 7.24$ mph

$$\text{SE}(\bar{x}) = \frac{s}{\sqrt{n}} = \frac{7.24}{\sqrt{20}} \approx 1.619$$

The 90% critical value is $t^*_{19} = 1.729$

$$\text{ME} = t^*_{19} \times \text{SE}_{\bar{x}} = 1.729(1.619)$$
$$\approx 2.7993$$

90% CI: $24.6 \pm 2.8 = (21.8, 27.4)$

Interpretation
Explain in context.

We are 90% confident that the true average speed of cars passing the school when the warning sign is flashing is between 21.8 and 27.4 mph.

Hypothesis Test for Means

If σ is known, it is possible to do confidence intervals and hypothesis tests using a *z*-statistic. Recall that

$$\text{standardized test statistic} = \frac{\text{statistic} - \text{parameter}}{\text{standard deviation of statistic}} \text{ or } z = \frac{x - \mu}{\sigma}.$$

However, since it is usually the case that σ is unknown, we will concentrate on those cases for our discussion here. Recall that the format for all hypothesis tests is essentially the same as it was for proportions.

One-Sample *t*-Test for the Mean

When the conditions for using the *t*-model are met, we test the hypothesis H_0: $\mu = \mu_0$ using the statistic

$$t_{n-1} = \frac{\bar{x} - \mu_0}{\frac{s}{\sqrt{n}}}$$

TI-83/84 STAT ⇒ TESTS ⇒ T-Test

TI-*nspire* **Home** ⇒ Calculator ⇒ **Menu** ⇒ Statistics ⇒ Stat Tests ⇒ t Test (**tab** through selections for Data Input Method:) ⇒ OK (click key or enter)

Example: A recent report on the evening news stated that teens watch an average of 13 hours of TV per week. A teacher at Central High School believes that the students in her school actually watch more than 13 hours per week. She randomly selects 25 students from the school and directs them to record their TV-viewing hours for one week. The 25 students reported the following number of hours:

5	5	6	18	23
13	0	18	20	5
23	11	0	25	22
13	24	6	14	20
23	20	11	22	11

Is there enough evidence to support the teacher's claim?

State what we want to know.

Do the students at Central High watch an average of more than 13 hours of TV per week?

Hypotheses

- Null hypothesis

H_0: $\mu = 13$ hours
Students in this teacher's school watch an average of 13 hours of TV per week.

- Alternative hypothesis

H_a: $\mu > 13$ hours
Students in this teacher's school watch an average of more than 13 hours of TV per week.

Make a picture.

Display the data (some choices are histogram, modified boxplot, and normal probability plot).

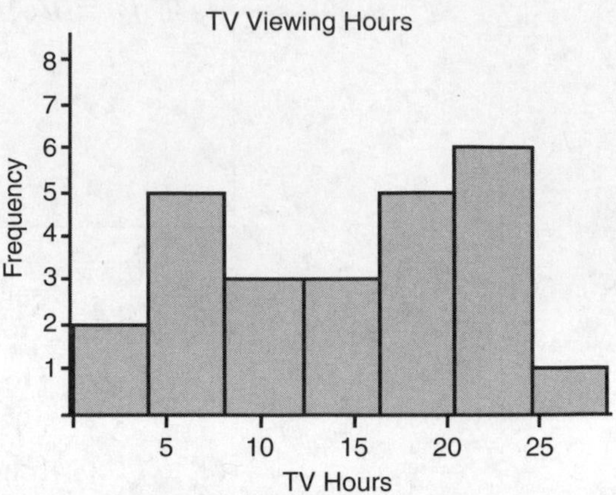

Check conditions.

✓ **Randomization:**
It is stated that the students were selected randomly.

✓ **Population size:**
It is reasonable to think that there are more than 250 students in the school.

✓ **Sample size:**
The histogram shows no outliers or strong skew, so we can use a t-distribution with 24 *df*.

Tell what test you plan to use.

One-sample t-test for the mean

Mechanics

$n = 25; \bar{x} = 14.32; s \approx 7.96$

$$t_{24} = \frac{\bar{x} - \mu_0}{\frac{s}{\sqrt{n}}}$$

$$\approx \frac{14.32 - 13}{\frac{7.96}{\sqrt{25}}}$$

$$= \frac{1.32}{1.592} \approx 0.83$$

p-value $= P(t_{24} > 0.83)$

$= 0.2077$ (calculator)

$0.20 < p\text{-value} < 0.25$ (table)

TELL

Conclusion

With a p-value of 0.2077, our result is not significant at any of the common significance levels. We cannot reject the null hypothesis. There is not enough evidence to conclude that the true mean hours of TV viewing per week for students in this school is greater than 13 hours.

Determining Sample Size

We know that sample size is important in most cases. The Student's t-distributions arose from problems that occurred when small samples displayed different characteristics from larger ones. The question was how to define what was "large enough" for the Normal model to apply. Therefore, it is a good idea to determine a sample size *before* collecting data. The degree of confidence you want to have in your results and the margin of error you are willing to accept will help you to determine the sample size you need.

Once you have decided on your confidence level and acceptable margin of error, you can calculate your sample size from the appropriate formula. For **proportions**, you will need to know a value for $\hat{p}$. Either use an estimated value (p^*) based on past experience or use the conservative value, 0.5, which yields the largest sample size for a given confidence level and margin of error. For **means**, you need to guess a value for s. Without knowing n, you cannot determine the degrees of freedom, so it is not possible to determine a value for t^*. The thing to do is to substitute the value of z^* that corresponds to your confidence level.

Here are two examples, one for proportions and one for means. In the proportions example, we chose to use a 95% confidence level and 4% margin of error with the conservative estimate of $p^* = 0.5$. In the means example, we chose a 90% confidence level and margin of error of 2.

Sample Size for *Proportions*	**Sample Size for *Means***
$\text{ME} = z^* \sqrt{\frac{\hat{p}\hat{q}}{n}}$	$\text{ME} = t^*_{n-1} \frac{s}{\sqrt{n}}$
Let ME = 4%, $\hat{p} = 0.5$, $C = 95\%$	Let ME = 2, $s = 68.2$, $C = 90\%$
$0.04 = 1.96\sqrt{\frac{(0.5)(0.5)}{n}}$	$2 = 1.645\frac{68.2}{\sqrt{n}}$, where $z^* = 1.645$
$0.04\sqrt{n} = 1.96\sqrt{(0.5)(0.5)}$	$2\sqrt{n} = 68.2(1.645)$
$\sqrt{n} = \frac{1.96\sqrt{(0.5)(0.5)}}{0.04} \approx 24.5$	$\sqrt{n} = \frac{(68.2)(1.645)}{2} \approx 56.0945$
$n = (24.5)^2 \approx 600.25$ or 601	$n = (56.0945)^2 \approx 3146.59$ or 3147

Clues for Clarity *You should always round the sample size (n) UP to the nearest integer. Sample size should be a whole number.*

6-2 Inference for Two Independent Samples

Comparing Two Means

As in the case of proportions, the parameter of interest is the difference between two population means, $\mu_1 - \mu_2$. The mechanics are the same.

The Sampling Distribution for Two Independent Means $(\bar{x}_1 - \bar{x}_2)$

- The *mean* of the sampling distribution of $\bar{x}_1 - \bar{x}_2$ is $\mu_1 - \mu_2$.
- The *standard deviation* of the sampling distribution is

$$SD(\bar{x}_1 - \bar{x}_2) = \sqrt{\frac{\sigma_1^2}{n_1} + \frac{\sigma_2^2}{n_2}}.$$

- When we substitute s for σ, which will happen most of the time, then we get the *standard error* of the sampling distribution:

$$SE(\bar{x}_1 - \bar{x}_2) = \sqrt{\frac{s_1^2}{n_1} + \frac{s_2^2}{n_2}}.$$

- The assumptions and conditions for inference for two-sample means are the same as those for one-sample means, but you must check the conditions for *each* independent sample.

A Two-Sample t-Interval for Means (σ unknown)

Two-Sample *t*-Interval for Means (σ unknown)

When the conditions are met, we are ready to find the confidence interval for the difference between means of two independent groups, $\mu_1 - \mu_2$. The interval is

$$(\bar{x}_1 - \bar{x}_2) \pm (t^*_{df} \times SE(\bar{x}_1 - \bar{x}_2)),$$

$$\text{where } SE(\bar{x}_1 - \bar{x}_2) = \sqrt{\frac{s_1^2}{n_1} + \frac{s_2^2}{n_2}}.$$

The critical value t^* depends on the particular confidence level, C, that you specify and on the degrees of freedom; df = at least the smaller of $n_1 - 1$ and $n_2 - 1$ and at most $n_1 + n_2 - 2$.

TI-83/84 STAT ⇒ TESTS ⇒ 2-SampTInt

TI-nspire **Home** ⇒ Calculator ⇒ **Menu** ⇒ Statistics ⇒ Confidence Intervals ⇒ 2-Sample t Interval (**tab** through selections for Data Input Method:) ⇒ OK (click key or enter)

Clues for Clarity *The formula for calculating the actual degrees of freedom is rather complicated, and generally the value is not a whole number (the TI calculators give this number). It is more accurate to use the calculator value to find t^*.*

Example: Manufacturers make claims about their products and usually try to convince you that their product is better than that of a competitor. Most brands of paper towels claim to pick up more liquid than any other brand. How much of a difference, on average, can be expected between Brand A and Brand B? This calls for a confidence interval to find the true difference, $\mu_A - \mu_B$, between the mean number of milliliters of water absorbed by each towel. A random sample of 16 of each type of towel was tested for absorbency. The mean number of mL for Brand A was 15.625 mL with a standard deviation of 3.12 mL, while for Brand B the mean was 14 mL with a standard deviation of 2.53 mL.

THINK

Identify the *parameter* we wish to estimate.
Choose and state a confidence level.

We wish to find a 95% confidence interval that contains the true difference $\mu_A - \mu_B$ between the mean number of milliliters of water absorbed by each towel.

Check the conditions.

✓ **Independence:**
Two different brands should be independent.

✓ **Randomization:**
The towels were selected randomly.

✓ **Population sizes:**
There are more than 160 towels of each brand.

✓ **Sample sizes:**
It is reasonable to assume that the population of both brands of towel have distributions of absorbency that are approximately normal.

Select a model.

We can safely use a Student's t-model with 15 degrees of freedom $(n_1 - 1)$.

Name your method.	**Two-sample *t*-interval for means**

Mechanics

Construct the CI.

$n_A = 16 \quad n_B = 16$

$\bar{x}_A = 15.625 \quad \bar{x}_B = 14$

$s_A = 3.12 \quad s_B = 2.53$

$$\begin{aligned} SE(\bar{x}_A - \bar{x}_B) &= \sqrt{\frac{s_A^2}{n_A} + \frac{s_B^2}{n_B}} \\ &= \sqrt{\frac{(3.12)^2}{16} + \frac{(2.53)^2}{16}} \\ &= \sqrt{\frac{9.7344}{16} + \frac{6.4009}{16}} \\ &\approx \sqrt{1.00846} \\ &\approx 1.004 \end{aligned}$$

$$\begin{aligned} ME&: t_{df}^{*} \cdot SE(\bar{x}_A - \bar{x}_B) \\ &\approx (2.131)(1.004) \\ &\approx 2.14 \end{aligned}$$

State the CI.

$(15.625 - 14) \pm 2.14 = 1.625 \pm 2.14 \approx (-0.515, 3.765)$

TI-83/84 $(-0.4296, 3.6796)$

Remember, the calculator uses the exact degrees of freedom.

Interpretation

We are 95% confident that the mean difference in the true amount of water absorbed by the two brands is between −0.515 mL and 3.765 mL.

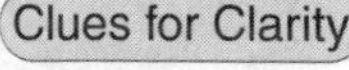

- *When you use the TI calculators, you are asked to choose* Pooled: No Yes. Choose No. *The word* pooled *here does not have the same meaning as it did in two proportions.*
- *Since zero is contained in the interval we calculated, it is possible that, in fact, there is no difference in the amount of water absorbed by the two brands. A two-sided hypothesis test would turn out to be **not significant** for* $\alpha = 0.05$.

A Test for the Difference Between Two Means (σ's unknown)

When we need to conduct a hypothesis test for the difference between the means of two independent groups, the appropriate test is a **two-sample *t*-test for means.**

Two-Sample t-Test for the Difference Between the Means of Two Independent Groups

The conditions for this test are the same as the conditions for the two-sample t-interval. We test the hypothesis H_0: $\mu_1 = \mu_2$ or H_0: $\mu_1 - \mu_2 = 0$. The test statistic is:

$$t_{df} = \frac{(\bar{x}_1 - \bar{x}_2) - (\mu_1 - \mu_2)}{\sqrt{\frac{s_1^2}{n_1} + \frac{s_2^2}{n_2}}}$$

Find the p-value from the t-distribution using the appropriate degrees of freedom.

TI-83/84 **STAT ⇒ TESTS ⇒ 2-SampTTest**

TI-nspire **Home** ⇒ Calculator ⇒ **Menu** ⇒ Statistics ⇒ Stat Tests ⇒ 2-Sample t Test (**tab** through selections for Data Input Method:) ⇒ OK (click key or enter)

Example: It is a common belief that women tend to live longer than men. Random samples from the death records for men and women in Montgomery County were taken, and age at the time of death was recorded. The average age of the 48 males was 68.33 years with a standard deviation of 12.49 years, while the average age of the 40 females was 78.7 years with a standard deviation of 16.43 years. Do women in this county tend to live longer than men? Give appropriate statistical evidence to support your answer.

THINK

State what we want to know.

Is there sufficient evidence to support the claim that women live longer than men?

SHOW

Hypotheses

- Null hypothesis

  H_0: $\mu_M = \mu_F$ or $\mu_M - \mu_F = 0$
  There is no difference in the mean ages at death between men and women in this county.

- Alternative hypothesis

  H_a: $\mu_M < \mu_F$ or $\mu_M - \mu_F < 0$
  The average age at death for men in this county is less than that for women. *(If you choose to put women first and then men, the difference would be in the opposite direction, so the alternative hypothesis would have the opposite sign $>$.)*

Check the conditions.

✓ **Independence:** Males and females are independent groups.

✓ **Randomization:** Records for each group were randomly selected.

✓ **Population size:** Obviously, there are more than 480 and 400 death records.

✓ **Sample size:** Both sample sizes are large enough ($n \geq 40$).

Select a model.

We can safely use a Student's t-model for the difference of means with 39 degrees of freedom ($n_F - 1$) or the calculated *df*.

Name your method.

Two-sample t-test for means

Mechanics

Find the standard error.

$n_M = 48 \qquad n_F = 40$

$\bar{x}_M = 68.33 \qquad \bar{x}_F = 78.7$

$s_M = 12.49 \qquad s_F = 16.43$

$$SE(\bar{x}_M - \bar{x}_F) = \sqrt{\frac{s_M^2}{n_M} + \frac{s_F^2}{n_F}} = \sqrt{\frac{(12.49)^2}{48} + \frac{(16.43)^2}{40}} \approx \sqrt{9.999} \approx 3.162$$

The observed difference is $\bar{x}_M - \bar{x}_F = 68.33 - 78.7 = -10.37$. The difference is *negative* because males are listed first.

Find the test statistic.

$$t = \frac{(\bar{x}_M - \bar{x}_F) - (\mu_M - \mu_F)}{\sqrt{\frac{s_M^2}{n_M} + \frac{s_F^2}{n_F}}}$$

$$t \approx \frac{(-10.37) - 0}{3.162} \approx -3.28$$

Find the p-value.

p-value $= P(t_{71.79} < -3.28) = 0.0008$ (calculator)

Note: Your calculator output is 8.0285E-4.

$0.001 < p\text{-value} < 0.0025$ (table, $df = 30$)

Conclusion

The p-value of 0.0008 means that if there were no difference in the mean ages at time of death, we would have observed such a difference in only 8 samples out of 10,000. We *reject* the null hypothesis at any reasonable level of significance and conclude that women in Montgomery County do tend to live longer than men.

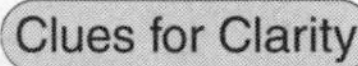

*When you record a p-value, be **certain** that it is a number from 0 to 1. Do NOT carelessly copy the calculator output! In the previous example, you might hastily record the p-value as 8.03. This is **ridiculous**—probabilities cannot exceed 1!*

6-3 A Special Case: Two Samples or One?

Matched Pairs

What should we do when the two samples are *not independent*? What if the data at hand are data for the same people at two different times, such as **before** and **after** going on a diet? It would not make sense to get the average of all the weights *before* the diet and the average of all the weights *after* the diet and do a two-sample t-test for means. Why not? It would violate the condition of independence necessary for a two-sample procedure. We really want to know if the diet was effective based on the amount of change for EACH individual. So we **subtract first** and create a single set of data. Now we use a one-sample procedure.

This method is called **matched pairs**. There are many situations that call for data to be treated in this way, but we must have a good reason for pairing the data. Just because two samples have the same number of data values is NOT a reason for pairing them. It is up to you to recognize when a **matched pairs** procedure is called for. For **matched pairs**, we use the same procedures we used for the **one-sample t-interval** or the **one-sample t-test for the mean**.

Confidence Intervals for Matched Pairs

Example: Over the ten-year period 1990–2000, the unemployment rates for Australia and the United Kingdom were reported as follows:

	1990	1991	1992	1993	1994	1995	1996	1997	1998	1999	2000
Australia	7.3	9.6	10.7	10.9	9.7	8.5	8.6	8.6	8.0	7.2	6.3
UK	6.9	8.8	10.1	10.5	9.7	8.7	8.2	7.0	6.4	6.0	5.5

Find a 90% confidence interval for the mean difference in unemployment rates for Australia and the United Kingdom. The paired differences are (AU − UK) = 0.4, 0.8, 0.6, 0.4, 0, −0.2, 0.4, 1.6, 1.6, 1.2, 0.8.

THINK

State what we want to know.

Find an interval that we are 90% confident will contain μ_d, the true mean difference in unemployment rates for AU and UK.

Check the conditions.

✓ **Independence:**
The data sets for the two countries are paired by year. Thus the data sets are NOT independent. Matched pairs is the method to use.

✓ **Randomization:**
We have no reason to believe that this sequence of years is not representative of the mean of the differences in unemployment rates of these two countries.

✓ **Sample size:**
With $n < 15$, we must check a display for skew and outliers.

Make a picture.

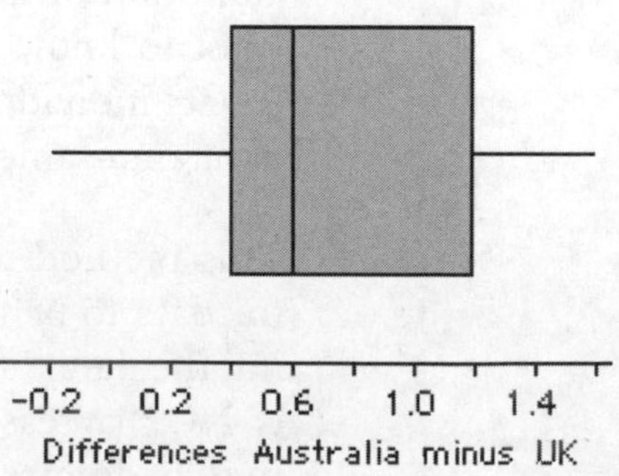

This modified boxplot shows moderate (not strong) skew and no outliers. Use a *t*-model with 10 *df*.

Choose your method.	Find a **paired *t*-interval.**
Mechanics	$n = 11; \bar{x}_d \approx 0.691; s_d \approx 0.589$
Compute the interval.	$\bar{x}_d \pm t^*_{n-1}\left(\frac{s_d}{\sqrt{n}}\right)$ $\approx 0.691 \pm 1.812\left(\frac{0.589}{\sqrt{11}}\right)$ $\approx 0.691 \pm 0.322 = (0.369, 1.013)$

Interpretation

We are 90% confident that the mean difference in the unemployment rates between Australia and the United Kingdom is, on average, between 0.369 and 1.013.

Using a One-Sample t-Test for Matched Pairs

For a test of significance for matched pairs, the null hypothesis is

$$H_0: \mu_d = 0$$

or

H_0: The differences do not differ significantly from zero.

Example: The following chart shows the number of men and women employed in randomly selected professions.

Occupation	Males	Females
Engineers	1902	221
Math/Computer Sci.	1470	633
Natural Scientist	382	200
Health Diagnosing	778	312
Health Assessment	423	629
Teachers, Higher Ed	568	435
Teachers, 7–12	1375	2098
Lawyers & Judges	682	283

Do these data suggest that there is a significant difference in gender in the workplace?

State what we want to know.

We want to measure the mean difference in number of males and number of females in the workplace. The data are reported based on occupation, so we need to keep the data paired and find the differences in each pair.

Those differences are
(Males − Females) = 1681, 837, 182, 466, −206, 133, −723, 399.

SHOW

Hypotheses

- Null hypothesis

H_0: $\mu_d = 0$
The mean gender difference in the workplace is 0.

- Alternative hypothesis

H_a: $\mu_d \neq 0$; d = Males − Females
The mean gender difference in the workplace is not 0.

Check the conditions.

✓ **Independence:**
The data are paired because they count employees in the same occupations.

✓ **Randomization:**
Occupations were randomly selected.

✓ **Population size:**
There are certainly more than 80 occupations.

✓ **Sample size:**
For n = 8, a small sample size, we must check a display for skew and outliers.

Make a picture.

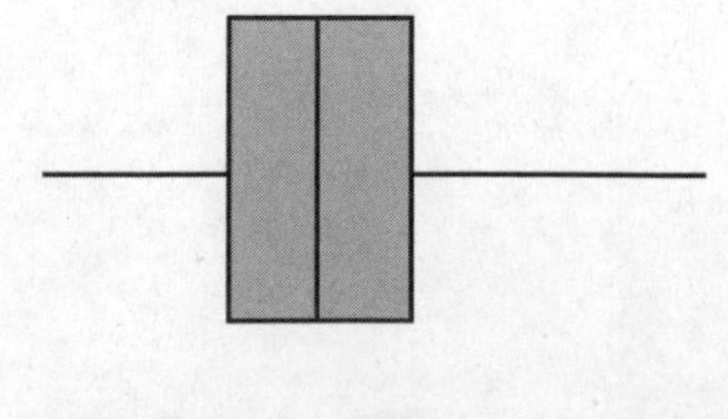

-500 500 1500
Difference Males minus Females

Choose the method.

The modified boxplot shows only slight skew with no outliers, so we use a paired t-test with df = 7.

Mechanics

$n = 8$ pairs $\quad \bar{x}_d \approx 346.125$

$s_d \approx 713.166$

$$s_{\bar{x}_d} \approx \frac{713.166}{\sqrt{8}} \approx 252.1423$$

Find the *t*-statistic.

$$t_{n-1} = \frac{\bar{x}_d - \mu_d}{\frac{s_d}{\sqrt{n}}}$$

$$\approx \frac{346.125 - 0}{252.142} \approx 1.373$$

Find the *p*-value.

p-value $= 0.21$ (calculator)
From the table, a one-sided p-value is $0.1 < p\text{-value} < 0.15$, so the *two*-sided p-value is $0.2 < p\text{-value} < 0.3$.

Interpretation

The p-value is too large at any of the commonly accepted levels to convince us to reject the null hypothesis. There is insufficient evidence to support a difference in gender in the workplace.

Review Questions for Topic 6—Learning About the World

Multiple Choice

1. The bookstore of a large university wants to determine how much money full-time first-year students spend, on average, in the university bookstore. At the end of the school year, a random sample of bookstore bills for 40 first-year students is obtained. A 95% confidence interval for the mean is calculated to be ($450, $1300). Which of the following is a correct interpretation of this interval?
   (A) We can be 95% confident that the average bookstore bill for full-time first-year students in our sample is between $450 and $1300.
   (B) We can be 95% confident that the average bookstore bill for full-time first-year university students is between $450 and $1300.
   (C) We can be 95% confident that the average bookstore bill for full-time first-year students at this university is between $450 and $1300.
   (D) The average bookstore bill for full-time first-year students at this university will be between $450 and $1300 about 95% of the time.
   (E) About 95 out of 100 full-time first-year students at this university will have bookstore bills between $450 and $1300.

2. A survey is to be conducted to determine the proportion of U.S. voters who support additional aid to African nations to fight poverty and HIV/AIDS. Of the proposed sample sizes, which is the smallest that will guarantee a margin of error of no more than 4% for a 90% confidence level?
(A) 225
(B) 325
(C) 425
(D) 525
(E) 625

3. A sample of 45 Turkey De-Lite hot dogs yielded a mean sodium content of 290 mg with a standard deviation of 28 mg. Construct a 98% confidence interval for the average sodium content in Turkey De-Lite hot dogs.
(A) $290 \pm 1.96(4.174)$
(B) $290 \pm 2.02(4.174)$
(C) $290 \pm 2.33(4.174)$
(D) $290 \pm 2.41(4.174)$
(E) $290 \pm 2.69(4.174)$

4. The creators of a discovery-based learning system for statistics claim that students who are taught using their method experience greater success than students taught with a strictly lecture-based method. To test the claim, Professor Myers decided to teach one of his introductory courses using the discovery-based method and the other using a lecture-based course. Eighty introductory statistics students were randomly assigned to one of Professor Myers' two sections. The summary statistics for his end-of-course assessment appear below. At an $\alpha = 0.01$ level, test the claim that students who learn introductory statistics using a discovery-based approach show higher achievement than those taught using a lecture-based approach.

	$\bar{x}$	s	n
Lecture Method	80.6	5.2	40
Discovery-based Method	84.2	3.9	40

(A) Reject H_0, p-value < 0.01
(B) Fail to reject H_0, p-value < 0.01
(C) Reject H_0, p-value > 0.01
(D) Fail to reject H_0, p-value > 0.01
(E) There is not enough information to test the claim.

5. Use the data from question 4 to construct a 95% confidence interval for the mean difference in scores of students taught using a lecture-based method versus a discovery-based method.

(A) $-3.60 \pm 1.99\sqrt{\frac{(5.2)^2}{40} + \frac{(3.9)^2}{40}}$

(B) $-3.60 \pm 1.99\sqrt{\frac{(5.2)^2}{40} - \frac{(3.9)^2}{40}}$

(C) $-3.60 \pm 1.99\left(\frac{5.2}{\sqrt{40}} + \frac{3.9}{\sqrt{40}}\right)$

(D) $-3.60 \pm 1.96\left(\frac{5.2}{\sqrt{40}} - \frac{3.9}{\sqrt{40}}\right)$

(E) $-3.60 \pm 1.96\left(\frac{5.2}{\sqrt{40}} + \frac{3.9}{\sqrt{40}}\right)$

6. Which of the following is an appropriate reason to choose a *t*-distribution as the model for a sampling distribution?
   (A) The sample contains outliers.
   (B) The sample size is less than 30.
   (C) The population standard deviation is not known.
   (D) The numbers of successes and failures are not both at least 10.
   (E) All of the above are appropriate reasons.

7. A random sample of 24 army recruits has a mean height of 68 inches with a standard deviation of 2.5 inches. If a 98% confidence interval is constructed, with all conditions having been met, the margin of error is
   (A) 0.51
   (B) 1.19
   (C) 1.27
   (D) 1.96
   (E) 2.33

8. An analyst is comparing data collected from randomly assigned test subjects who used two different types of hand cream (designated I and II), each for a period of six months. The subjects used one type of cream on one hand and the second on the other and reported a "softness" factor on a scale of 1 to 10 for each hand. What steps should the analyst take to determine which cream is more effective?
   (A) Calculate the mean difference between the right-hand results and the left-hand results, then carry out a one-sample *z*-test.
   (B) Calculate the difference in means between the right-hand results and the left-hand results, then carry out a two-sample *z*-test.
   (C) Calculate the mean difference between the right-hand results and the left-hand results, then carry out a one-sample *t*-test.
   (D) Calculate the difference in means between the right-hand results and the left-hand results, then carry out a two-sample *t*-test.
   (E) Calculate the individual differences between the Type I and Type II results for each subject, then carry out a one-sample *t*-test for the mean difference.

9. A 95% confidence interval for the population mean is (98.52, 101.48). What is the 90% confidence interval constructed from the same data?
   (A) (98.02, 101.98)
   (B) (98.22, 101.78)
   (C) (98.35, 101.65)
   (D) (98.44, 101.55)
   (E) (98.76, 101.23)

10. A random sample of 100 married couples, in which both partners are currently employed, is obtained. State the hypotheses to test whether, on average, men take more sick days than women.
   (A) $H_0 : \mu_w - {}_m = 0;\ H_a : \mu_w - {}_m > 0$
   (B) $H_0 : \mu_w - {}_m = 0;\ H_a : \mu_w - {}_m < 0$
   (C) $H_0 : \mu_w - \mu_m = 0;\ H_a : \mu_w - \mu_m > 0$
   (D) $H_0 : \mu_w - \mu_m = 0;\ H_a : \mu_w - \mu_m < 0$
   (E) $H_0 : \mu_w - \mu_m = 0;\ H_a : \mu_w - \mu_m \neq 0$

Free Response

For a certain year, SAT* Verbal scores for 15 randomly selected high schools in urban and suburban areas in the United States are given below.

Urban	565	550	549	536	535	535	522	516
		504	497	495	489	445	444	435
Suburban	575	563	540	529	528	507	504	498
		482	476	472	463	431	412	375

Is there a statistically significant difference in the average SAT* Verbal scores for these two areas?

Answers for Topic 6—Learning About the World—begin on page 272.

Topic 7

Inference When Variables Are Related

We have already reviewed *inference for proportions* (z-intervals and tests) and *inference for means* (t-intervals and tests). In this part of our review, we look at tests for one and two categorical variables. The data for these tests are usually presented in some form of table divided into categories and *must* be in the form of counts for each category.

7-1 Comparing Counts

The Chi-Square Statistic

There are three inference tests involving *categorical variables* and counts. These tests introduce a new statistic called the **chi-square statistic**, which has the *same form* for all three tests:

$$\chi^2 = \sum_{\textit{all cells}} \frac{(O - E)^2}{E},$$

where O stands for the observed value and E stands for the expected value. In some texts, this statistic is called "chi-squared." Whether the name has a "d" on the end or not, it is the same statistic.

The Chi-Square Distribution

Of course, there is a new statistical distribution to go with this statistic. Like the Student's t-distribution, the χ^2 distribution is really a *family of distributions.* Each individual distribution is specified by its **degrees of freedom.** Unlike the t-distribution, the value of n in this case is *not* the sample size but rather the **number of categories.** The χ^2 distribution is *skewed to the right* and has only positive values. Because there are only positive values, the p-value for the test is computed by calculating the area under the curve *to the right* of the computed χ^2 test statistic.

The Chi-Square Tests

Chi-Square (χ^2) Goodness-of-Fit Test (One Categorical Variable—One Sample)

The goodness-of-fit test is used to determine how well a set of observed values matches a set of expected values. In other words, how well does a sample distribution match the hypothesized population distribution?

The *degrees of freedom* is the number of divisions of the category minus 1 (# cells − 1). The *expected* values are calculated in one of two ways: Either the values for each category are *expected* to all have a uniform distribution, or they are *expected* to follow a distribution specified according to some stated condition.

Assumptions/Conditions for Chi-Square Test for Goodness-of-Fit

- **Counted Data Condition:** Make sure the data are listed in the form of *counts* for each category. Percents or proportions JUST WON'T DO—convert them to counts (rounded to whole numbers) if necessary.
- **Randomization Condition:** The individual cases should be a random sample from the population of interest.
- ***Expected* Cell-Frequency Condition:** There are *at least five* cases in each *expected* cell. Some statisticians use the condition that no more than 20% of expected counts be less than 5 *and NO expected cell count be less than 1.*

A Chi-Square Test for Goodness-of-Fit

When the conditions are met, we test the hypothesis of either a uniform distribution over the categories or some other specified distribution across the categories with the statistic

$$\chi^2_{df} = \sum_{\textit{all cells}} \frac{(O - E)^2}{E}$$

Find the p-value from the χ^2 table or (χ^2 cdf) on your calculator.

For this test, *the null and alternative hypotheses are usually written in words*; however, there are some texts that do use symbols. For example, let k = number of categories of the categorical variable; let p_k = the true proportion for each category, 1 through k. Then the null hypothesis can be written using H_0: $p_1 = \text{prop}_1, p_2 = \text{prop}_2, \ldots, p_k = \text{prop}_k$.

Note that $p_1 + p_2 + p_3 + \cdots + p_k = 1$.

The TI-84 and TI-Nspire both have a goodness-of-fit test on their TESTS menu. You must enter the *observed counts* and the *expected values* into lists, and you will be prompted to enter the *degrees of freedom*. The calculator reports the χ^2 test statistic, the p-value, and the value for each individual component.

The TI-83 calculator does *not* have a goodness-of-fit test on its TESTS menu. The test statistic must be calculated by hand. BUT, you can use the LISTS on your calculator to make the calculation more efficient. There is a chi-square *distribution* on the TI-83 that can be used to obtain the p-value once you have calculated the test statistic.

How to Calculate the χ^2 Test Statistic (using LISTS)

- Enter the *observed* count values into L1.
- Find the *expected values* (based on your null hypothesis) and enter these into L2.
- Let L3 = $(L1 - L2)^2/L2$.
- Sum L3.

TI-83/84 2nd ⇒ STAT ⇒ MATH ⇒ sum(L3)

- This sum is your χ^2 test statistic.

TI-*nspire* **Home** ⇒ Calculator ⇒ **Menu** ⇒ Statistics ⇒ Stat Tests ⇒ χ^2 GOF, (**tab** through selections for Observed List:, Expected List:, Deg of Freedom,df:) ⇒ OK (click key or enter)

Find the *degrees of freedom* (*# cells* − 1). Now you are ready to complete a hypothesis test. Once you have your test statistic, calculate the *p*-value using (χ^2 cdf) on your calculator or look up the critical value with the correct *degrees of freedom* in a table of chi-square values. Then make a decision and draw a conclusion.

Using a Chi-Square Test for Goodness-of-Fit

Example: A Philadelphia newspaper report claims that 24.1% of 18- to 24-year-olds who attend a local college are from Delaware, 15.4% are from New Jersey, 50.7% are from Pennsylvania, and the remaining 9.8% are from other states in the region. Suppose that a random sample (size 150) of 18- to 24-year-olds is taken at the college and the number from each state/region is recorded.

State	Number of Students
Delaware	30
New Jersey	39
Pennsylvania	71
Other	10

Do these data provide evidence at the $\alpha = 0.05$ level that the newspaper report is correct?

THINK

Is the distribution of students at this school consistent with the distribution reported in the claim?

Hypotheses

- Null hypothesis

H_0: The distribution of students is consistent with that given in the report

or

$$H_0: p_D = 24.1\%, \quad p_N = 15.4\%, \quad p_P = 50.7\%, \quad p_O = 9.8\%.$$

- Alternative hypothesis

H_a: The distribution of students is NOT consistent with that given in the report (at least one of the percentages is different)

or

$$H_a: p_D \neq 24.1\%, \text{ or } p_N \neq 15.4\% \text{ or } p_P \neq 50.7\% \text{ or } p_O \neq 9.8\%.$$

Check the conditions.

✓ **Counts:**
The data are counts of students in the given categories.

✓ **Randomization:**
The claim is that the students were selected randomly.

✓ **Expected cell counts (sample size):**
150 times each given percent is: 36.15, 23.1, 76.05, 14.7. So, each cell is greater than 5. The sample size is large enough for this test.

Name the test you will use.

Chi-square goodness-of-fit-test conditions are satisfied, so use a χ^2 distribution with $4 - 1 = 3df$.

Mechanics

- Calculate the test statistic.

$$\chi^2_{df} = \sum_{all\ cells} \frac{(O - E)^2}{E}$$

$$\chi^2_{df=3} = \frac{(30 - 36.15)^2}{36.15} + \frac{(39 - 23.1)^2}{23.1} + \frac{(71 - 76.05)^2}{76.05} + \frac{(10 - 14.7)^2}{14.7}$$

$$\approx 1.05 + 10.94 + 0.34 + 1.50 = 13.83$$

- Calculate the p-value.

The p-value is the area to the right of 13.83 in the χ^2 distribution.
p-value ≈ 0.003 (calculator)
p-value < 0.005 (table)

State your conclusion.

The p-value of 0.003 is much lower than the significance level of 0.05, so we *reject* H_0 that the percentages ("proportions") reported by the newspaper for the states of residency of the students at this college are as stated, and we conclude (in favor of the alternative) that at least one of the percentages is different.

Clues for Clarity

- *If the expected distribution is uniform, the percentages would be* $\frac{100\%}{\text{number of cells}}$. *For example, we expect digits in a random-number table to appear with equal frequencies. The percentage for each digit would be 10%. We would use these percentages to calculate the expected counts.*
- *If you are asked to identify the cell that contributes the most to the* χ^2 *test statistic, just look at the individual components that contribute to your sum. In a computer printout, these components will be listed. (In the example above, New Jersey contributed 10.94 to the* χ^2*-value of 13.83.)*

Chi-Square (χ^2) ***Test for Homogeneity (More than Two Groups—Independent Samples)***

Homogeneity (Equal Proportions) means "the same" or *composed of like parts.* It is used when we have *more than two* groups and we want to know if the category proportions are the same for each group. (Recall that to compare proportions from *two* groups we could use a *two-proportion z-test.*) Because there are more than two groups and there may be several categories, the data usually appear in the form of a two-way table.

The *null hypothesis* is that the distribution of the *counts* is the same (homogeneous) *for each group*. The test statistic compares the observed counts with what the expected counts would be if there were *no differences* between the various groups. The *expected* counts and the *degrees of freedom* are calculated differently than they were in the goodness-of-fit test.

$$\text{Expected cell count} = \frac{(\text{row total})(\text{column total})}{\text{grand total}}$$

$$\text{Degrees of freedom} = (\#\text{ rows } - 1)(\#\text{ columns } - 1) = (r-1)(c-1)$$

The *test for homogeneity* and the *chi-square test of independence* (explained later) can be performed on your calculator. Only the observed values must be entered into a matrix, for example MATRIX [A]. After the test is performed, the expected values will appear in MATRIX [B]. These are the values that must be checked (and shown) to verify sample size conditions.

TI-83/84 STAT ⇒ TESTS ⇒ χ^2 *TEST*

TI-*nspire* **Home** ⇒ Calculator ⇒ **Menu** ⇒ Statistics ⇒ Stat Tests ⇒ χ^2 2-way Test, (**tab** through selections for Observed Matrix:) ⇒ OK (click key or enter)

Assumptions/Conditions for the Chi-Square Test for Homogeneity

- **Counted Data Condition:** The data must be *counts*. A test of homogeneity cannot be done with measurements or proportions.
- **Randomization Condition:** As long as we only intend to compare the data at hand, it is not necessary to check this condition. If we intended to generalize to a larger population, we would need a random sample.
- ***Expected* Cell-Frequency Condition:** The *expected* count in each cell must be at least 5.

Using a Chi-Square Test for Homogeneity

Example: The table below shows the number of Central High School students who passed the AP* Calculus AB exam. Has the distribution of scores changed over the past three years? Give appropriate statistical evidence to support your answer.

Score	Year 1	Year 2	Year 3
5	18	15	11
4	13	12	11
3	12	14	13

Has there been a change in the distribution of passing grades on the AB Calculus exam over these three years?

SHOW

Hypotheses

- Null hypothesis — H_0: The passing scores on the Calculus AB exam have the same distribution (are homogeneous) for these three years.
- Alternative hypothesis — H_a: The passing scores on the Calculus AB exam for these three years do *not* have the same distribution.

Check the conditions.

✓ **Counts:**
The data are counts of the number of students in each category.

✓ **Randomization:**
Not needed here since no generalization is intended.

✓ **Expected cell counts (sample size):**
See the following table, where expected counts are all greater than 5.

	Year 1	Year 2	Year 3	Total
5	18(15.9)	15(15.2)	11(12.9)	44
4	13(13.0)	12(12.4)	11(10.6)	36
3	12(14.1)	14(13.4)	13(11.5)	39
Total	**43**	**41**	**35**	**119**

Name the test.

The sampling distribution of the test statistic is χ^2 with $(3 - 1)(3 - 1) = 4df$. Chi-square test of homogeneity

Mechanics

- Calculate the test statistic.

$$\chi^2_{df=4} = \sum_{all\ cells} \frac{(O - E)^2}{E}$$

$\chi^2 \approx 1.138$ (calculator)

- Determine the p-value.

p-value $= P(\chi^2_{df=4} > 1.138) \approx 0.888$ (calculator)

State your conclusion.

The p-value is very large. There is insufficient evidence to reject the null hypothesis that the passing grades for the AP* Calculus AB exam for the past three years have the same distribution.

Chi-Square χ^2 Test of Independence (Two Categorical Variables—One Sample)

The test called a "Chi-Square χ^2 Test of Independence" is used to determine if, in a *single* population, there is an association between *two* categorical variables. The data are presented in a two-way table called a contingency table. It is called a contingency table because it classifies individuals according to two *categorical* variables so that we can see whether the distribution of counts on one variable is *contingent* on the other.

Clues for Clarity

- *The test for homogeneity compares* ***several*** *populations using the same categories from* ***one variable.***

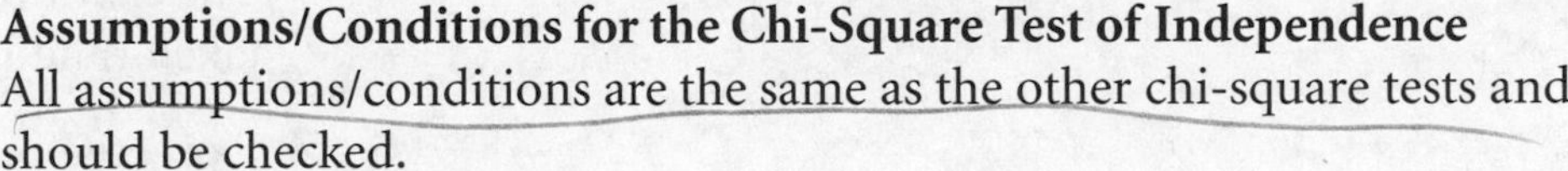

- *The test of independence uses a* ***single*** *population and determines if there is an association between two* ***different categorical variables.***

Assumptions/Conditions for the Chi-Square Test of Independence

All assumptions/conditions are the same as the other chi-square tests and should be checked.

- The data should be **counts.**
- We should have a **random sample** from the population of interest if we are trying to generalize.
- The sample size should be large enough so that the **expected counts** are at least five in each cell.

Note: The procedure and calculations for this test are the same as those for the test of homogeneity; however, the null and alternative hypotheses will be stated differently.

Using a Chi-Square Test of Independence

Example: A survey was taken to determine if there is a relationship between students having computers in their homes and in their school divisions (elementary, middle, secondary). A random sample of size 250 produced the following results:

	Computer in Home	
Division	**Yes**	**No**
Elementary	14	61
Middle	50	25
Secondary	86	14

Is there evidence that school division and having a home computer are independent? Use a 0.05 level of significance.

Are the categorical variables "computer in home" and "school division" *independent*?

Hypotheses

- Null hypothesis — H_0: Computer in home and school division are *independent*.
- Alternative hypothesis — H_a: Computer in home and school division are NOT *independent*.

Check the conditions.

✓ **Counts:**
We have counts of students in two categorical variables.

✓ **Randomization:**
The claim was that the sample was taken randomly.

✓ **Expected cell counts:**
The table below shows all cell counts greater than 5.

	Yes	No	Total
Elementary	14(45)	61(30)	75
Middle	50(45)	25(30)	75
Secondary	86(60)	14(40)	100
Total	150	100	250

Name the test.

The sampling distribution of the test statistic is χ^2 with $(3 - 1)(2 - 1) = 2df$.
Chi-square test of independence

Mechanics

- Calculate the test statistic.

$$\chi^2_{df} = \sum_{all\ cells} \frac{(O - E)^2}{E}$$

$\chi^2_{df=2} \approx 82.94$ (calculator)

- Determine the *p*-value.

$p\text{-value} = P(\chi^2_{df=2} > 82.94) \approx 0$ (calculator)

State your conclusion.

The *p*-value is extremely small (essentially zero), indicating that we have sufficient evidence to *reject* H_0 in favor of H_a.

The two variables "computer in home" and "school division" are NOT *independent.*

Clues for Clarity

Although we rejected the null hypothesis of independence, we cannot interpret our small p-value as proof of causation. A failure of independence does ***not*** *prove a cause-and-effect relationship. There may be lurking variables present.*

7-2 Inference for Regression

In the last two topics, we explored inference for proportions and means. The same principles used for these topics will be applied in our study of Inference for Regression. Just as a sample mean is a random variable with a corresponding sampling distribution (recall that different samples can yield different sample means), so too are the regression slope and intercept. Our inference for regression will focus on the *slope* of the least squares regression equation.

A t-Test for β

When we fit a least squares regression line, $\hat{y} = a + bx$, to a data set of two quantitative variables, we are hoping to predict values of the response variable $(\hat{y})$ for given values of the explanatory variable (x). We know that different samples would produce different estimates for the slope and the intercept of our regression equation. The mean, μ_y, of all the possible responses has a linear relationship (with x) that represents the true regression line where

$$\mu_y = \alpha + \beta x.$$

The parameters α and β are estimated by a and b of the regression equation, this equation having been derived from sample data. The appropriate test is a t-test for slope. Since there are *two* estimates in our equation, the formula for degrees of freedom is $n - 2$.

For the AP* examination, we are interested only in inference for the slope, β, of the regression line.

Hypothesis Test for the Slope of a Least Squares Regression Line

A hypothesis test for the slope of a regression line *generally* tests the null hypothesis, H_0: $\beta = 0$ (x is not a good predictor of y, or there is no linear relationship between x and y), against one of the alternatives, H_a: $\beta(<$ or $\neq$ or $>)0$. (You may wish to take a look at the 2007 Investigative Task - Question 6 for a problem that uses a different set of hypotheses.)

The slope b is an unbiased estimator of the true slope β. It has a sampling distribution with standard deviation σ. The standard deviation of the sampling distribution of the slope is estimated from the data. Because the standard deviation is estimated from the data, it is a standard error, and the distribution is the t-distribution. Sometimes called the "residual standard error" or the "root Mean Square Error," s is an unbiased estimator of σ.

The standard error about the line is

$$s = \sqrt{\frac{1}{n-2}\sum residual^2} = \sqrt{\frac{1}{n-2}\sum (y - \hat{y})^2}.$$

We divide by $n - 2$ since we are estimating *two* parameters, β *and* α (slope and intercept).

> Note: You won't have to calculate SE_b. Usually, it will be provided as part of a computer printout.

Our test statistic, $t_{df=n-2}$, is calculated in the same manner as the test statistic for means and proportions.

$$\text{Standardized test statistic: } \frac{\text{statistic} - \text{parameter}}{\text{standard deviation of statistic}}$$

$$t_{df=n-2} = \frac{\text{observed slope } (b) - \text{expected slope } (\beta_0)}{\text{standard error of } b} = \frac{b - 0}{SE_b}$$

Example of Computer Output for Regression Analysis on Population versus Tons of Garbage

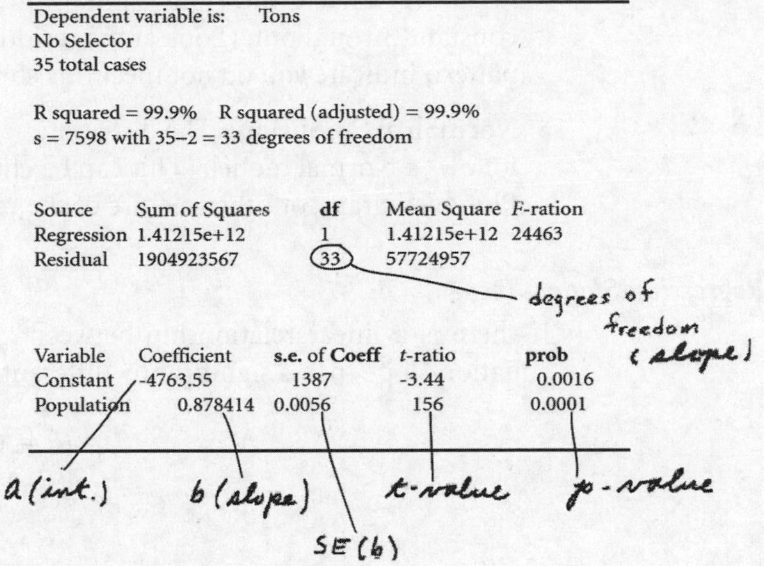

Dependent variable is: Tons
No Selector
35 total cases

R squared = 99.9% R squared (adjusted) = 99.9%
s = 7598 with 35–2 = 33 degrees of freedom

Source	Sum of Squares	df	Mean Square	F-ration
Regression	1.41215e+12	1	1.41215e+12	24463
Residual	1904923567	33	57724957	

Variable	Coefficient	s.e. of Coeff	t-ratio	prob
Constant	-4763.55	1387	-3.44	0.0016
Population	0.878414	0.0056	156	0.0001

From the computer printout:

$$\text{Predicted (Tons)} = -4763.55 + 0.878414\,\text{(Population)}$$

$$t_{df=33} = \frac{0.878414 - 0}{0.0056} \approx 156$$

p-value ≤ 0.0001

There are several measures of variability given in the printout, and it is critical to understand the distinctions between them.

$s =$ 7598 is the standard error **about the line**. It is the standard deviation of the residuals and tells us how close the *sample* data are, on average, to the *model* created from the data.

SE(b) $=$ 0.0056 is the standard error **of the slope**. It tells us how reliably we can estimate the slope (β). In general, standard error is a measure of the variability of a statistic. In *this* case it is an estimate of the standard deviation of a *sampling distribution of sample slopes.*

While s tells us how our sample data vary from our line's predicted values, SE(b) tells us how our regression slope might vary with different samples. We use s in our calculation of SE(b). The variability of our data affects the reliability of our slope.

Assumptions/Conditions for a Linear Regression *t*-Test for Slope

- **Linearity Condition:** The scatterplot must look as if a line will be a good fit. If the shape of the scatter is not linear, then we can try to re-express the data or, if transformations fail, forget about *linear* regression completely.

- **Randomization Condition:** The set of observations (x, y) is a representative sample from the population of interest.
- **Equal-Variance Condition:** The spread around the line is nearly constant throughout. (Look at the residual plot. Outliers or a fan-shaped pattern indicate you do not meet this condition.)
- **Normality Condition:** The distribution of y-values for each x-value follows a Normal model. (This can be checked with a Normal Probability Plot, histogram, or other picture of the residuals.)

Using a Regression Slope t-Test

If there is a linear relationship between x and y, we look for a regression-equation slope that is significantly different from zero. Our hypotheses are

$$H_0: \beta = 0$$
$$H_a: \beta\ (< \text{ or } \neq \text{ or } >) 0.$$

A Linear Regression *t*-Test for Slope

When conditions are met, the standardized estimated regression slope follows a t-distribution with $n - 2$ degrees of freedom, and the t-statistic is

$$t = \frac{b - \beta}{SE_b}, \text{ where } SE_b = \frac{s}{\sqrt{\Sigma(x - \bar{x})^2}}$$

TI-83/84 STAT ⇒ F:LinRegTTest

TI-*nspire* **Home** ⇒ Calculator ⇒ **Menu** ⇒ Statistics ⇒ Stat Tests ⇒ A:Linear Reg t Test, (**tab** through selections for x-List:, Y List:, Save RegEqn to:, Frequency List:, Alternate Hyp:) ⇒ OK (click key or enter)

Example: A researcher from the state department of agriculture wants to know if there is a relationship between the number of farms in operation and the amount of acreage devoted to soybeans. He collects data from a random sample of 21 counties in the state and records the number of farms (Farms) and the amount of acreage devoted to soybean cultivation (Acreage) in each of those counties. The scatterplot is shown in the following figure.

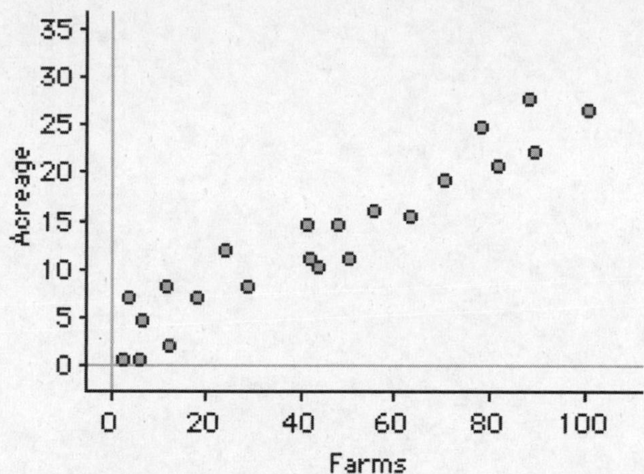

Is there a significant relationship between the amount of acreage devoted to soybean cultivation and the number of farms in this state? Give statistical justification to support your response. (Use $\alpha = 0.01$.)

THINK

Is there a linear relationship between Acreage and Farms in this state?

SHOW

Hypotheses

- Null hypothesis

H_0: $\beta = 0$
There is no linear relationship between Acreage and Farms.

- Alternative hypothesis

H_a: $\beta \neq 0$
There is a linear relationship.

Check the conditions.

✓ **Linearity:**
The scatterplot appears *fairly* linear.

✓ **Randomization:**
State counties were chosen randomly.

✓ **Equal variance:**
The residual plot shows no obvious pattern (the spread is nearly constant with no fan shape).

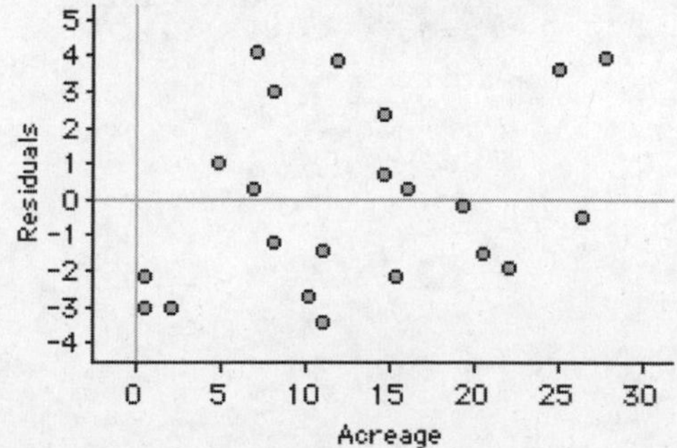

✓ **Normality:**
A normal probability plot of the residuals is fairly linear, indicating that the normality condition is reasonably met.

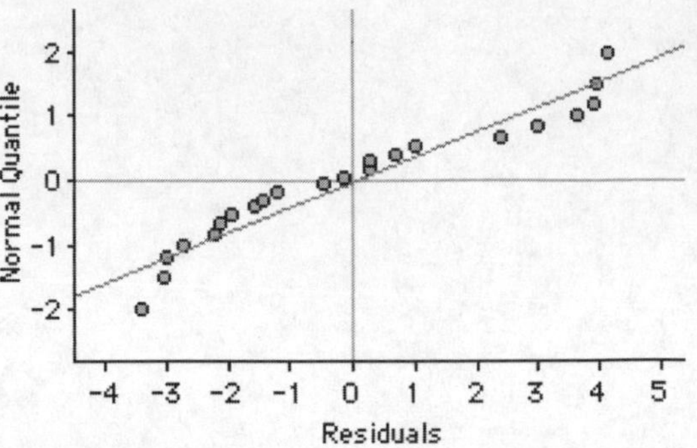

Name the test.

The sampling distribution will be a Student's t-model with $n - 2 = 19$ degrees of freedom.
Use a regression-slope t-test.

Mechanics

- State the regression equation.

The computer output is
Predicted (Acreage) $= -0.64 + 0.292$(Farms)

Predictor	Coef	Stdev	t-ratio	p
Constant	−0.636	1.458	−0.44	0.667
No Farms	0.29184	0.02641	11.05	0.000

$s = 4.120$
R-sq $= 85.9\%$
R-sq(adj) $= 85.2\%$

- Find the p-value.

p-value ≈ 0.000

Conclusion

The p-value of approximately zero means that, at any reasonable α-level, we should *reject* the null hypothesis.

There is strong evidence to conclude that, on average, there is indeed a linear relationship between acreage devoted to soybean cultivation and farms in operation in this state.

Clues for Clarity *Remember that, in general, a relationship does not imply cause and effect. A randomized controlled experiment is necessary to assess cause and effect.*

Building a Confidence Interval for the Slope β

To build a confidence interval for β, the true slope of the least squares regression line, we use the usual format for a confidence interval:

$$\text{statistic} \pm (\text{critical value})(\text{standard deviation of statistic}).$$

Example: Find a 95% confidence interval for β using the information from the previous problem.

Since the necessary assumptions and conditions were already verified in the previous problem, we can proceed with the mechanics of the confidence interval.

$$95\% \text{ CI for } \beta\text{: } b \pm t^*_{n-2}(\text{SE}_b) \approx 0.292 \pm 2.093(0.0264) \approx (0.237, 0.347)$$

Note: The values for b and SE_b were obtained from the computer output. The t^*_{n-2} critical value (2.093) was obtained from the t-distribution with 19 degrees of freedom.

We are 95% confident that the true slope of the regression line for number of farms versus acreage devoted to soybean cultivation is contained in the interval (0.237, 0.347).

Review Questions for Topic 7—Inference When Variables Are Related

Multiple Choice

1. A χ^2 test of independence is appropriate when we want to test the hypothesis that
   (A) two quantitative variables measured on the same subjects are related.
   (B) two categorical variables measured on the same subjects are related.
   (C) a distribution of counts in one categorical variable matches the distribution predicted by a model.
   (D) the distribution of counts for two or more groups on the same categorical variable is the same.
   (E) the means of two distinct populations are statistically significantly different.

2. Below appears a portion of the table showing who survived the sinking of the *Titanic*, based on whether they were crew members or passengers booked in first-, second-, or third-class staterooms.

	Crew	First	Second	Third	Total
Alive	212				710
Dead				528	
Total		325	285		2201

The expected value for the number of first-class passengers who died on the *Titanic* is

(A) 104.8
(B) 162.5
(C) 220.2
(D) 285.5
(E) There is not enough information to determine the expected value.

3. The table shows the number of students absent for the past school year at Bell Baxter High School, broken down by the day of the week. The dean of students would like to know if student absenteeism is related to the day of the week.

Monday	Tuesday	Wednesday	Thursday	Friday
98	84	92	86	76

The *p*-value for this test is

(A) p-value < 0.01
(B) $0.01 < p$-value < 0.05
(C) $0.05 < p$-value < 0.10
(D) $0.10 < p$-value < 0.15
(E) p-value > 0.15

Regression analysis for average SAT Math scores versus per-student spending for 22 school districts in Montgomery County, Pennsylvania, is given in the table below. Use the table to answer questions 4–6.*

```
Dependent variable is     SAT-Math
No Selector
R squared = 21.9%    R squared (adjusted) = 18.0%
s =  27.99 with 22 - 2 = 20 degrees of freedom

Source        Sum of Squares   df    Mean Square   F-ratio
Regression      4401.65         1      4401.65      5.62
Residual       15666.9         20       783.347

Variable       Coefficient    s.e. of Coeff   t-ratio    prob
Constant        446.990       37.66           11.9       ≤ 0.0001
Per Student     7.33145e-3    0.0031          2.37       0.0279
```

4. The Pennsylvania Department of Education is interested in the relationship between per-student spending and average SAT* Math scores. A scatterplot of the data suggests average SAT* Math scores tend to increase as per-student spending in a school district increases. The Department of Education is interested in whether or not this increase is significant. Assuming the conditions for inference are satisfied, the *p*-value for the linear regression *t*-test is approximately

(A) 0.0001
(B) 0.0031
(C) 0.0140

(D) 0.0279
(E) 0.2799

5. Construct a 95% confidence interval for the slope of the regression line in question 4.
(A) $0.00733 \pm 1.96(0.0031)$
(B) $0.00733 \pm 2.086(0.0031)$
(C) $0.00733 \pm 2.086\left(\frac{27.99}{\sqrt{22}}\right)$
(D) $7.33145 \pm 1.96\left(\frac{27.99}{\sqrt{22}}\right)$
(E) $7.33145 \pm 2.086(0.0031)$

6. Which of the following gives the appropriate hypotheses for the test of significance in question 4?
(A) $H_0: b = 0; H_A: b > 0$
(B) $H_0: \mu = 0; H_A: \mu > 0$
(C) $H_0: \alpha = 0; H_A: \alpha > 0$
(D) $H_0: \beta = 0; H_A: \beta > 0$
(E) None of the above.

7. A least squares regression line for y versus x is calculated, and the corresponding residual graph is shown below.

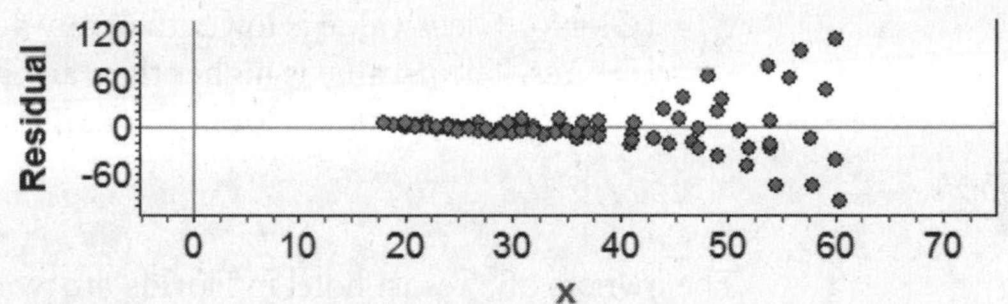

Which of the following is a correct statement?
(A) The model is more accurate for smaller values of x than for larger values.
(B) The condition of constant variance of the residuals is violated.
(C) A linear model is appropriate.
(D) Both A and B are correct.
(E) Both A and C are correct.

Faculty and administrators in a school district were surveyed regarding proposed changes in the school's new health care program. A summary of their responses to the question "Are the proposed changes in the health care program acceptable?" is given in the following table. Use the table to answer questions 8–10.

	Agree	Neutral	Disagree	Total
Faculty	22	15	88	125
Administrators	22	10	1	33
Total	44	25	89	158

8. An appropriate hypothesis test to determine whether there is sufficient statistical evidence to conclude that the faculty and administrators differ in their opinions about the proposed new health care program is a
   (A) two-proportion z-test.
   (B) linear regression t-test.
   (C) χ^2 test of independence.
   (D) χ^2 test of goodness-of-fit.
   (E) χ^2 test of homogeneity (equal proportions).

9. The number of degrees of freedom for the appropriate test of significance in question 8 is
   (A) 2
   (B) 4
   (C) 12
   (D) 147
   (E) not applicable; the appropriate test does not require degrees of freedom.

10. Is there sufficient statistical evidence that the faculty and administrators differ in their opinions about the proposed new health care program?
   (A) No. The same number of faculty and administrators (22) agree that the proposed health care program is acceptable.
   (B) No. The p-value is higher than any acceptable α-level.
   (C) No. The p-value is lower than any acceptable α-level.
   (D) Yes. The p-value is higher than any acceptable α-level.
   (E) Yes. The p-value is lower than any acceptable α-level.

Free Response

The owners of a resort hotel in Florida are wondering whether their customers' preferred method of booking their stays during the peak season has changed significantly for the given time periods. Records for peak season rentals for 1995, 2000, and 2005 appear below.

	1995	**2000**	**2005**
Travel Agent	112	103	57
Book Online	42	77	123
Other	56	30	30

Is there evidence to suggest that customers' booking preferences for these time periods have changed?

Answers for Topic 7—Inference When Variables Are Related—begin on page 275.

Part III

Practice Examinations

The directions shown before each section in Practice Examination 1 are those that you will see on the actual examination. Please refer to these directions for subsequent examinations. For these practice examinations, we have not provided answer sheets, inserts, or the same amount of space below each question that you may see on the actual examination. We encourage you to show your work for each problem so that your teacher and classmates can review your responses and help you correct any weaknesses. Formulas and tables follow, and you may refer to these at any time. For additional formulas and tables, go to the College Board Web site: *http://apcentral.collegeboard.com/apc/members/exam/exam_questions/8357.html.* Click on the most recent exam, and then click on *All Questions* (Formulas start on page 3).

Solutions for each exam, *with explanations*, appear at the end of the book.

Selected Formulas and Tables

$Range = Max - Min$

$IQR = Q3 - Q1$

Outlier Rule-of-Thumb: $y < Q1 - 1.5 \times IQR$ or $y > Q3 + 1.5 \times IQR$

$$\bar{y} = \frac{\sum y}{n}$$

$$s = \sqrt{\frac{\sum(y - \bar{y})^2}{n - 1}}$$

$$z = \frac{y - \mu}{\sigma} \text{ (model based)}$$

$$z = \frac{y - \bar{y}}{s} \text{ (data based)}$$

$$r = \frac{\sum z_x z_y}{n - 1}$$

$$\hat{y} = b_0 + b_1 x \quad \text{where } b_1 = r\frac{s_y}{s_x} \text{ and } b_0 = \bar{y} - b_1\bar{x}$$

$$P(\mathbf{A}) = 1 - P(\mathbf{A}^C)$$

$$P(\mathbf{A} \cup \mathbf{B}) = P(\mathbf{A}) + P(\mathbf{B}) - P(\mathbf{A} \cap \mathbf{B})$$

$$P(\mathbf{A} \cap \mathbf{B}) = P(\mathbf{A}) \times P(\mathbf{B}|\mathbf{A})$$

$$P(\mathbf{B}|\mathbf{A}) = \frac{P(\mathbf{A} \cap \mathbf{B})}{P(\mathbf{A})}$$

If **A** and **B** are independent, $P(\mathbf{B}|\mathbf{A}) = P(\mathbf{B})$

$E(X) = \mu = \sum x \cdot P(x)$ | $Var(X) = \sigma^2 = \sum(x - \mu)^2 P(x)$

$E(X \pm c) = E(X) \pm c$ | $Var(X \pm c) = Var(X)$

$E(aX) = aE(X)$ | $Var(aX) = a^2 Var(X)$

$E(X \pm Y) = E(X) \pm E(Y)$ | $Var(X \pm Y) = Var(X) + Var(Y)$, if X and Y are independent

Geometric: $P(x) = q^{x-1}p$ $\quad \mu = \frac{1}{p}$ $\quad \sigma = \sqrt{\frac{q}{p^2}}$

Binomial: $P(x) = \binom{n}{x} p^x q^{n-x}$ $\quad \mu = np$ $\quad \sigma = \sqrt{npq}$

$\hat{p} = \frac{x}{n}$ $\quad \mu(\hat{p}) = p$ $\quad SD(\hat{p}) = \sqrt{\frac{pq}{n}}$

Sampling distribution of $\bar{y}$:

(CLT) As n grows, the sampling distribution approaches the Normal model with

$$\mu(\bar{y}) = \mu_y \qquad SD(\bar{y}) = \frac{\sigma}{\sqrt{n}}$$

Inference:

Confidence interval for parameter = ***statistic ± critical value × SD(statistic)***

$$\text{Test statistic} = \frac{\textit{Statistic} - \textit{Parameter}}{SD(\textit{statistic})}$$

Parameter	Statistic	*SD*(statistic)	*SE*(statistic)
p	$\hat{p}$	$\sqrt{\frac{pq}{n}}$	$\sqrt{\frac{\hat{p}\hat{q}}{n}}$
$p_1 - p_2$	$\hat{p}_1 - \hat{p}_2$	$\sqrt{\frac{p_1q_1}{n_1} + \frac{p_2q_2}{n_2}}$	$\sqrt{\frac{\hat{p}_1\hat{q}_1}{n_1} + \frac{\hat{p}_2\hat{q}_2}{n_2}}$
μ	$\bar{y}$	$\frac{\sigma}{\sqrt{n}}$	$\frac{s}{\sqrt{n}}$
$\mu_1 - \mu_2$	$\bar{y}_1 - \bar{y}_2$	$\sqrt{\frac{\sigma_1^2}{n_1} + \frac{\sigma_2^2}{n_2}}$	$\sqrt{\frac{s_1^2}{n_1} + \frac{s_2^2}{n_2}}$
μ_d	$\bar{d}$	$\frac{\sigma_d}{\sqrt{n}}$	$\frac{s_d}{\sqrt{n}}$
σ_ε	$s_e = \sqrt{\frac{\Sigma(y - \hat{y})^2}{n - 2}}$		
β_1	b_1		$\frac{s_e}{s_x\sqrt{n - 1}}$
$^*\mu_\nu$	$\hat{y}_\nu$		$\sqrt{SE^2(b_1) \cdot (x_\nu - \bar{x})^2 + \frac{s_e^2}{n}}$
$^*y_\nu$	$\hat{y}_\nu$		$\sqrt{SE^2(b_1) \cdot (x_\nu - \bar{x})^2 + \frac{s_e^2}{n} + s_e^2}$

Pooling: For testing difference between proportions: $\hat{p}_{pooled} = \frac{y_1 + y_2}{n_1 + n_2}$

For testing difference between means: $s_p = \sqrt{\frac{(n_1 - 1)s_1^2 + (n_2 - 1)s_2^2}{n_1 + n_2 - 2}}$

Substitute these pooled estimates in the respective SE formulas for both groups when assumptions and conditions are met.

Chi-square: $\chi^2 = \sum \frac{(obs - exp)^2}{exp}$

Table Z

Areas under the standard normal curve

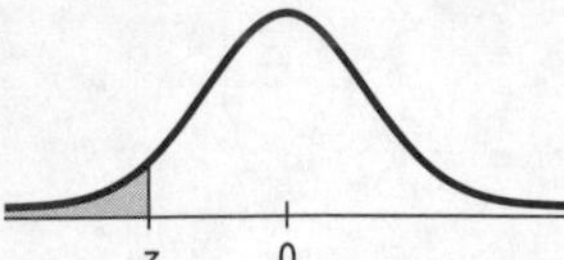

Second decimal place in z										
0.09	*0.08*	*0.07*	*0.06*	*0.05*	*0.04*	*0.03*	*0.02*	*0.01*	*0.00*	*z*
0.0001	0.0001	0.0001	0.0001	0.0001	0.0001	0.0001	0.0001	0.0001	0.0001	*−3.8*
0.0001	0.0001	0.0001	0.0001	0.0001	0.0001	0.0001	0.0001	0.0001	0.0001	*−3.7*
0.0001	0.0001	0.0001	0.0001	0.0001	0.0001	0.0001	0.0001	0.0002	0.0002	*−3.6*
0.0002	0.0002	0.0002	0.0002	0.0002	0.0002	0.0002	0.0002	0.0002	0.0002	*−3.5*
0.0002	0.0003	0.0003	0.0003	0.0003	0.0003	0.0003	0.0003	0.0003	0.0003	*−3.4*
0.0003	0.0004	0.0004	0.0004	0.0004	0.0004	0.0004	0.0005	0.0005	0.0005	*−3.3*
0.0005	0.0005	0.0005	0.0006	0.0006	0.0006	0.0006	0.0006	0.0007	0.0007	*−3.2*
0.0007	0.0007	0.0008	0.0008	0.0008	0.0008	0.0009	0.0009	0.0009	0.0010	*−3.1*
0.0010	0.0010	0.0011	0.0011	0.0011	0.0012	0.0012	0.0013	0.0013	0.0013	*−3.0*
0.0014	0.0014	0.0015	0.0015	0.0016	0.0016	0.0017	0.0018	0.0018	0.0019	*−2.9*
0.0019	0.0020	0.0021	0.0021	0.0022	0.0023	0.0023	0.0024	0.0025	0.0026	*−2.8*
0.0026	0.0027	0.0028	0.0029	0.0030	0.0031	0.0032	0.0033	0.0034	0.0035	*−2.7*
0.0036	0.0037	0.0038	0.0039	0.0040	0.0041	0.0043	0.0044	0.0045	0.0047	*−2.6*
0.0048	0.0049	0.0051	0.0052	0.0054	0.0055	0.0057	0.0059	0.0060	0.0062	*−2.5*
0.0064	0.0066	0.0068	0.0069	0.0071	0.0073	0.0075	0.0078	0.0080	0.0082	*−2.4*
0.0084	0.0087	0.0089	0.0091	0.0094	0.0096	0.0099	0.0102	0.0104	0.0107	*−2.3*
0.0110	0.0113	0.0116	0.0119	0.0122	0.0125	0.0129	0.0132	0.0136	0.0139	*−2.2*
0.0143	0.0146	0.0150	0.0154	0.0158	0.0162	0.0166	0.0170	0.0174	0.0179	*−2.1*
0.0183	0.0188	0.0192	0.0197	0.0202	0.0207	0.0212	0.0217	0.0222	0.0228	*−2.0*
0.0233	0.0239	0.0244	0.0250	0.0256	0.0262	0.0268	0.0274	0.0281	0.0287	*−1.9*
0.0294	0.0301	0.0307	0.0314	0.0322	0.0329	0.0336	0.0344	0.0351	0.0359	*−1.8*
0.0367	0.0375	0.0384	0.0392	0.0401	0.0409	0.0418	0.0427	0.0436	0.0446	*−1.7*
0.0455	0.0465	0.0475	0.0485	0.0495	0.0505	0.0516	0.0526	0.0537	0.0548	*−1.6*
0.0559	0.0571	0.0582	0.0594	0.0606	0.0618	0.0630	0.0643	0.0655	0.0668	*−1.5*
0.0681	0.0694	0.0708	0.0721	0.0735	0.0749	0.0764	0.0778	0.0793	0.0808	*−1.4*
0.0823	0.0838	0.0853	0.0869	0.0885	0.0901	0.0918	0.0934	0.0951	0.0968	*−1.3*
0.0985	0.1003	0.1020	0.1038	0.1056	0.1075	0.1093	0.1112	0.1131	0.1151	*−1.2*
0.1170	0.1190	0.1210	0.1230	0.1251	0.1271	0.1292	0.1314	0.1335	0.1357	*−1.1*
0.1379	0.1401	0.1423	0.1446	0.1469	0.1492	0.1515	0.1539	0.1562	0.1587	*−1.0*
0.1611	0.1635	0.1660	0.1685	0.1711	0.1736	0.1762	0.1788	0.1814	0.1841	*−0.9*
0.1867	0.1894	0.1922	0.1949	0.1977	0.2005	0.2033	0.2061	0.2090	0.2119	*−0.8*
0.2148	0.2177	0.2206	0.2236	0.2266	0.2296	0.2327	0.2358	0.2389	0.2420	*−0.7*
0.2451	0.2483	0.2514	0.2546	0.2578	0.2611	0.2643	0.2676	0.2709	0.2743	*−0.6*
0.2776	0.2810	0.2843	0.2877	0.2912	0.2946	0.2981	0.3015	0.3050	0.3085	*−0.5*
0.3121	0.3156	0.3192	0.3228	0.3264	0.3300	0.3336	0.3372	0.3409	0.3446	*−0.4*
0.3483	0.3520	0.3557	0.3594	0.3632	0.3669	0.3707	0.3745	0.3783	0.3821	*−0.3*
0.3859	0.3897	0.3936	0.3974	0.4013	0.4052	0.4090	0.4129	0.4168	0.4207	*−0.2*
0.4247	0.4286	0.4325	0.4364	0.4404	0.4443	0.4483	0.4522	0.4562	0.4602	*−0.1*
0.4641	0.4681	0.4721	0.4761	0.4801	0.4840	0.4880	0.4920	0.4960	0.5000	*−0.0*

For $z \leq -3.90$, the areas are 0.0000 to four decimal places.

Table Z (cont.)
Areas under the standard normal curve

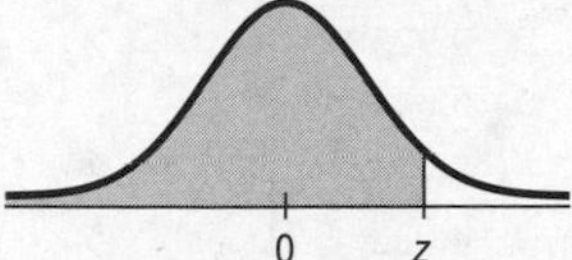

z	0.00	0.01	0.02	0.03	0.04	0.05	0.06	0.07	0.08	0.09
	Second decimal place in z									
0.0	0.5000	0.5040	0.5080	0.5120	0.5160	0.5199	0.5239	0.5279	0.5319	0.5359
0.1	0.5398	0.5438	0.5478	0.5517	0.5557	0.5596	0.5636	0.5675	0.5714	0.5753
0.2	0.5793	0.5832	0.5871	0.5910	0.5948	0.5987	0.6026	0.6064	0.6103	0.6141
0.3	0.6179	0.6217	0.6255	0.6293	0.6331	0.6368	0.6406	0.6443	0.6480	0.6517
0.4	0.6554	0.6591	0.6628	0.6664	0.6700	0.6736	0.6772	0.6808	0.6844	0.6879
0.5	0.6915	0.6950	0.6985	0.7019	0.7054	0.7088	0.7123	0.7157	0.7190	0.7224
0.6	0.7257	0.7291	0.7324	0.7357	0.7389	0.7422	0.7454	0.7486	0.7517	0.7549
0.7	0.7580	0.7611	0.7642	0.7673	0.7704	0.7734	0.7764	0.7794	0.7823	0.7852
0.8	0.7881	0.7910	0.7939	0.7967	0.7995	0.8023	0.8051	0.8078	0.8106	0.8133
0.9	0.8159	0.8186	0.8212	0.8238	0.8264	0.8289	0.8315	0.8340	0.8365	0.8389
1.0	0.8413	0.8438	0.8461	0.8485	0.8508	0.8531	0.8554	0.8577	0.8599	0.8621
1.1	0.8643	0.8665	0.8686	0.8708	0.8729	0.8749	0.8770	0.8790	0.8810	0.8830
1.2	0.8849	0.8869	0.8888	0.8907	0.8925	0.8944	0.8962	0.8980	0.8997	0.9015
1.3	0.9032	0.9049	0.9066	0.9082	0.9099	0.9115	0.9131	0.9147	0.9162	0.9177
1.4	0.9192	0.9207	0.9222	0.9236	0.9251	0.9265	0.9279	0.9292	0.9306	0.9319
1.5	0.9332	0.9345	0.9357	0.9370	0.9382	0.9394	0.9406	0.9418	0.9429	0.9441
1.6	0.9452	0.9463	0.9474	0.9484	0.9495	0.9505	0.9515	0.9525	0.9535	0.9545
1.7	0.9554	0.9564	0.9573	0.9582	0.9591	0.9599	0.9608	0.9616	0.9625	0.9633
1.8	0.9641	0.9649	0.9656	0.9664	0.9671	0.9678	0.9686	0.9693	0.9699	0.9706
1.9	0.9713	0.9719	0.9726	0.9732	0.9738	0.9744	0.9750	0.9756	0.9761	0.9767
2.0	0.9772	0.9778	0.9783	0.9788	0.9793	0.9798	0.9803	0.9808	0.9812	0.9817
2.1	0.9821	0.9826	0.9830	0.9834	0.9838	0.9842	0.9846	0.9850	0.9854	0.9857
2.2	0.9861	0.9864	0.9868	0.9871	0.9875	0.9878	0.9881	0.9884	0.9887	0.9890
2.3	0.9893	0.9896	0.9898	0.9901	0.9904	0.9906	0.9909	0.9911	0.9913	0.9916
2.4	0.9918	0.9920	0.9922	0.9925	0.9927	0.9929	0.9931	0.9932	0.9934	0.9936
2.5	0.9938	0.9940	0.9941	0.9943	0.9945	0.9946	0.9948	0.9949	0.9951	0.9952
2.6	0.9953	0.9955	0.9956	0.9957	0.9959	0.9960	0.9961	0.9962	0.9963	0.9964
2.7	0.9965	0.9966	0.9967	0.9968	0.9969	0.9970	0.9971	0.9972	0.9973	0.9974
2.8	0.9974	0.9975	0.9976	0.9977	0.9977	0.9978	0.9979	0.9979	0.9980	0.9981
2.9	0.9981	0.9982	0.9982	0.9983	0.9984	0.9984	0.9985	0.9985	0.9986	0.9986
3.0	0.9987	0.9987	0.9987	0.9988	0.9988	0.9989	0.9989	0.9989	0.9990	0.9990
3.1	0.9990	0.9991	0.9991	0.9991	0.9992	0.9992	0.9992	0.9992	0.9993	0.9993
3.2	0.9993	0.9993	0.9994	0.9994	0.9994	0.9994	0.9994	0.9995	0.9995	0.9995
3.3	0.9995	0.9995	0.9995	0.9996	0.9996	0.9996	0.9996	0.9996	0.9996	0.9997
3.4	0.9997	0.9997	0.9997	0.9997	0.9997	0.9997	0.9997	0.9997	0.9997	0.9998
3.5	0.9998	0.9998	0.9998	0.9998	0.9998	0.9998	0.9998	0.9998	0.9998	0.9998
3.6	0.9998	0.9998	0.9999	0.9999	0.9999	0.9999	0.9999	0.9999	0.9999	0.9999
3.7	0.9999	0.9999	0.9999	0.9999	0.9999	0.9999	0.9999	0.9999	0.9999	0.9999
3.8	0.9999	0.9999	0.9999	0.9999	0.9999	0.9999	0.9999	0.9999	0.9999	0.9999

For $z \geq 3.90$, the areas are 1.0000 to four decimal places.

Two tail probability		0.20	0.10	0.05	0.02	0.01	
One tail probability		0.10	0.05	0.025	0.01	0.005	
Table T	df						df
Values of t_α	1	3.078	6.314	12.706	31.821	63.657	1
	2	1.886	2.920	4.303	6.965	9.925	2
	3	1.638	2.353	3.182	4.541	5.841	3
	4	1.533	2.132	2.776	3.747	4.604	4
	5	1.476	2.015	2.571	3.365	4.032	5
	6	1.440	1.943	2.447	3.143	3.707	6
	7	1.415	1.895	2.365	2.998	3.499	7
	8	1.397	1.860	2.306	2.896	3.355	8
	9	1.383	1.833	2.262	2.821	3.250	9
	10	1.372	1.812	2.228	2.764	3.169	10
	11	1.363	1.796	2.201	2.718	3.106	11
	12	1.356	1.782	2.179	2.681	3.055	12
	13	1.350	1.771	2.160	2.650	3.012	13
	14	1.345	1.761	2.145	2.624	2.977	14
	15	1.341	1.753	2.131	2.602	2.947	15
	16	1.337	1.746	2.120	2.583	2.921	16
	17	1.333	1.740	2.110	2.567	2.898	17
	18	1.330	1.734	2.101	2.552	2.878	18
	19	1.328	1.729	2.093	2.539	2.861	19
	20	1.325	1.725	2.086	2.528	2.845	20
	21	1.323	1.721	2.080	2.518	2.831	21
	22	1.321	1.717	2.074	2.508	2.819	22
	23	1.319	1.714	2.069	2.500	2.807	23
	24	1.318	1.711	2.064	2.492	2.797	24
	25	1.316	1.708	2.060	2.485	2.787	25
	26	1.315	1.706	2.056	2.479	2.779	26
	27	1.314	1.703	2.052	2.473	2.771	27
	28	1.313	1.701	2.048	2.467	2.763	28
	29	1.311	1.699	2.045	2.462	2.756	29
	30	1.310	1.697	2.042	2.457	2.750	30
	32	1.309	1.694	2.037	2.449	2.738	32
	35	1.306	1.690	2.030	2.438	2.725	35
	40	1.303	1.684	2.021	2.423	2.704	40
	45	1.301	1.679	2.014	2.412	2.690	45
	50	1.299	1.676	2.009	2.403	2.678	50
	60	1.296	1.671	2.000	2.390	2.660	60
	75	1.293	1.665	1.992	2.377	2.643	75
	100	1.290	1.660	1.984	2.364	2.626	100
	120	1.289	1.658	1.980	2.358	2.617	120
	140	1.288	1.656	1.977	2.353	2.611	140
	180	1.286	1.653	1.973	2.347	2.603	180
	250	1.285	1.651	1.969	2.341	2.596	250
	400	1.284	1.649	1.966	2.336	2.588	400
	1000	1.282	1.646	1.962	2.330	2.581	1000
	∞	1.282	1.645	1.960	2.326	2.576	∞
Confidence levels		80%	90%	95%	98%	99%	

$\frac{\alpha}{2}$ $\frac{\alpha}{2}$ $-t_{\alpha/2}$ 0 $t_{\alpha/2}$

Two tails

α 0 t_α

One tail

Table X

Values of χ^2_α

Right tail probability df	0.10	0.05	0.025	0.01	0.005
1	2.706	3.841	5.024	6.635	7.879
2	4.605	5.991	7.378	9.210	10.597
3	6.251	7.815	9.348	11.345	12.838
4	7.779	9.488	11.143	13.277	14.860
5	9.236	11.070	12.833	15.086	16.750
6	10.645	12.592	14.449	16.812	18.548
7	12.017	14.067	16.013	18.475	20.278
8	13.362	15.507	17.535	20.090	21.955
9	14.684	16.919	19.023	21.666	23.589
10	15.987	18.307	20.483	23.209	25.188
11	17.275	19.675	21.920	24.725	26.757
12	18.549	21.026	23.337	26.217	28.300
13	19.812	22.362	24.736	27.688	29.819
14	21.064	23.685	26.119	29.141	31.319
15	22.307	24.996	27.488	30.578	32.801
16	23.542	26.296	28.845	32.000	34.267
17	24.769	27.587	30.191	33.409	35.718
18	25.989	28.869	31.526	34.805	37.156
19	27.204	30.143	32.852	36.191	38.582
20	28.412	31.410	34.170	37.566	39.997
21	29.615	32.671	35.479	38.932	41.401
22	30.813	33.924	36.781	40.290	42.796
23	32.007	35.172	38.076	41.638	44.181
24	33.196	36.415	39.364	42.980	45.559
25	34.382	37.653	40.647	44.314	46.928
26	35.563	38.885	41.923	45.642	48.290
27	36.741	40.113	43.195	46.963	49.645
28	37.916	41.337	44.461	48.278	50.994
29	39.087	42.557	45.722	59.588	52.336
30	40.256	43.773	46.979	50.892	53.672
40	51.805	55.759	59.342	63.691	66.767
50	63.167	67.505	71.420	76.154	79.490
60	74.397	79.082	83.298	88.381	91.955
70	85.527	90.531	95.023	100.424	104.213
80	96.578	101.879	106.628	112.328	116.320
90	107.565	113.145	118.135	124.115	128.296
100	118.499	124.343	129.563	135.811	140.177

AP Statistics Practice Examination 1

Multiple Choice Statistics Section I

Time: 1 hour and 30 minutes
Number of questions: 40
Percent of total grade: 50

Directions: Solve each of the following problems using the available space for scratchwork. Decide which is the best of the choices given and fill in the corresponding oval on the answer sheet. No credit will be given for anything written in the test book. Do not spend too much time on any one problem.

1. A random sample of 25 birthweights (in ounces) is taken, yielding the following summary statistics:

Variable	N	Mean	Median	TrMean	StDev	SE Mean
Birthwt	25	129.40	129.00	128.35	17.41	3.48

Variable	Minimum	Maximum	Q1	Q3
Birthwt	96.00	187.00	119.50	135.50

What can be said about the number of outliers for this data set?

(A) 0
(B) At least 1
(C) No more than 1
(D) At least 2
(E) No more than 2

2. Given two events, A and B, if $P(A) = 0.43$, $P(B) = 0.26$, and $P(A \cup B) = 0.68$, then the two events are
   (A) mutually exclusive but not independent.
   (B) independent but not mutually exclusive.
   (C) mutually exclusive and independent.
   (D) neither mutually exclusive nor independent.
   (E) Not enough information is given to determine whether A and B are mutually exclusive or independent.

3. In a certain county, a newspaper reports that the average family income in the county is $45,000. First-time home buyers believe that the average income is less than reported. Which of the following hypotheses would be appropriate for a significance test?
   (A) H_0: $\mu = 45{,}000$; H_a: $\mu \neq 45{,}000$
   (B) H_0: $\mu = 45{,}000$; H_a: $\mu > 45{,}000$
   (C) H_0: $\mu = 45{,}000$; H_a: $\mu < 45{,}000$
   (D) H_0: $\mu \neq 45{,}000$; H_a: $\mu = 45{,}000$
   (E) H_0: $\mu > 45{,}000$; H_a: $\mu = 45{,}000$

4. Weights for a box of cereal are normally distributed with a mean of 14.10 oz and a standard deviation of 0.04 oz. Which of the following illustrates the probability of selecting a box with at *least* the advertised weight of 14 oz?

(A)

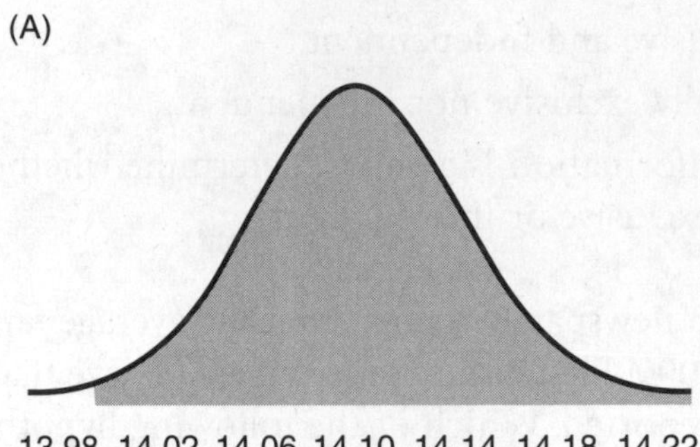

(B)

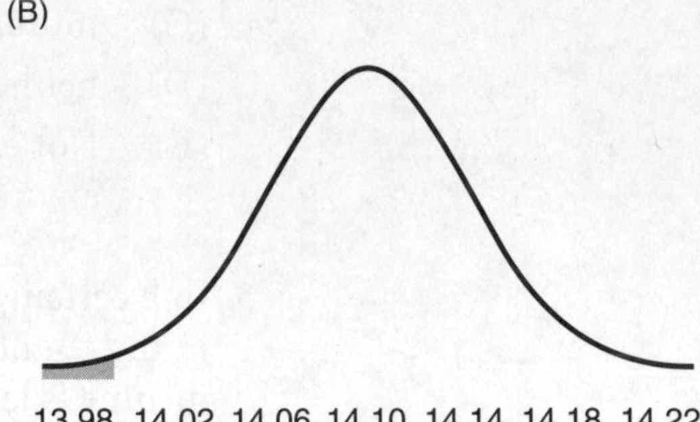

(C)

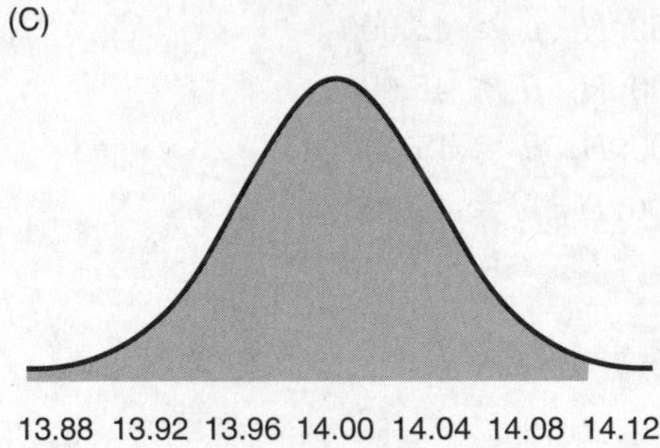

(D)

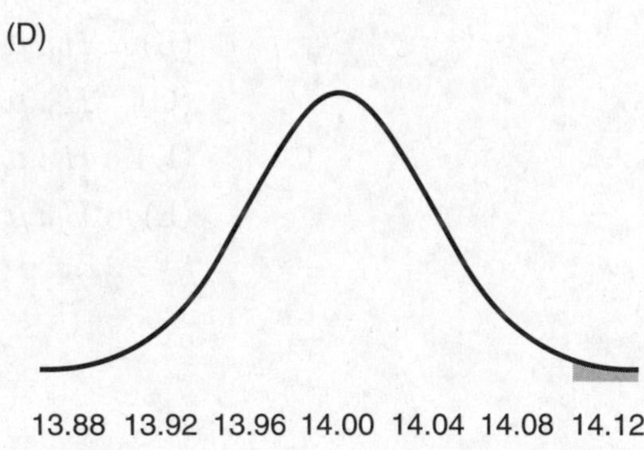

(E)

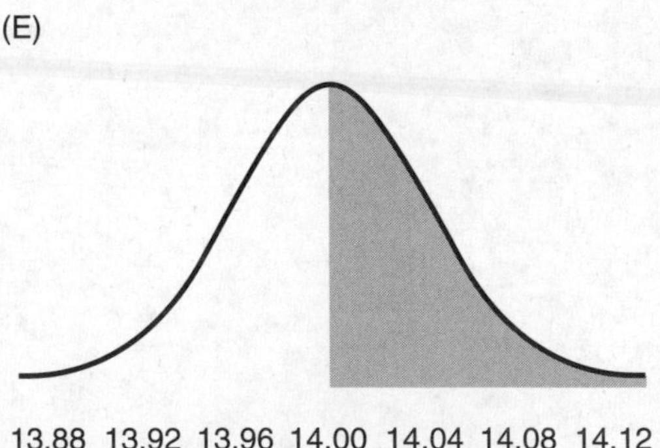

5. The following boxplots summarize two data sets, X and Y. Which of the following MUST be true?

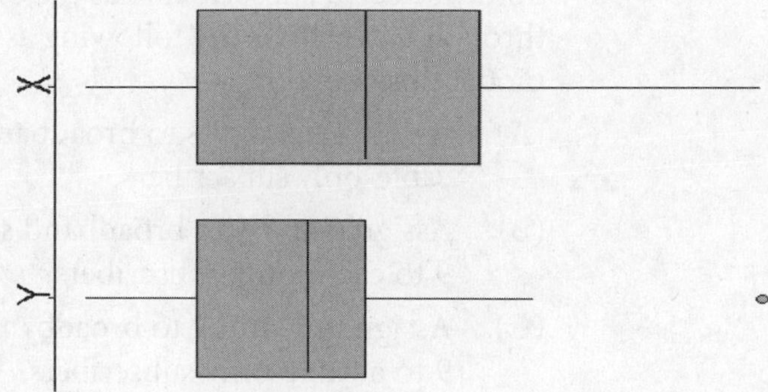

(A) Set X and set Y have the same number of data points.
(B) The box of set X contains more data points than the box of set Y.
(C) The data in set X have a larger range than the data in set Y.
(D) About 50% of the values in set X are greater than about 75% of the values in set Y.
(E) The median of set X is less than the median of set Y.

6. A newlywed couple is trying to choose one of two neighborhood supermarkets for their grocery shopping. They decide to randomly select 20 items, check their prices at each store, and then conduct a test to determine if one store is significantly less expensive than the other. What test should they conduct?

(A) Two-sample z-test
(B) Two-sample t-test
(C) Matched-pairs t-test
(D) χ^2 goodness-of-fit test
(E) Linear regression t-test

7. In a certain community, 20% of cable subscribers also subscribe to the company's broadband service for their Internet connection. You would like to design a simulation to estimate the probability that one of six randomly selected subscribers has the broadband service. Using digits 0 through 9, which of the following assignments would be appropriate to model this situation?

   (A) Assign even digits to broadband subscribers and odd digits to cable-only subscribers.

   (B) Assign 0 and 1 to broadband subscribers and 2, 3, 4, 5, 6, 7, 8, and 9 to cable-only subscribers.

   (C) Assign 0, 1, and 2 to broadband subscribers and 3, 4, 5, 6, 7, 8, and 9 to a cable-only subscribers.

   (D) Assign 1, 2, 3, 4, 5, and 6 to broadband subscribers and 7, 8, 9, and 0 to cable-only subscribers.

   (E) Assign 0, 1, and 2 to broadband subscribers; 3, 4, 5, and 6 to cable-only subscribers; and ignore digits 7, 8, and 9.

8. The number of T-shirts a school store sells monthly has the following probability distribution:

# of T-shirts, *X*	0	1	2	3	4	5	6	7	8	9	10
P(X)	0.02	0.15	0.18	0.21	0.14	0.08	0.08	0.04	0.03	0.02	0.05

   If each T-shirt sells for $10 but costs the store $4 to purchase, what is the expected monthly T-shirt *profit*?

   (A) $ 3.78

   (B) $15.12

   (C) $22.68

   (D) $30.00

   (E) $37.80

9. A population has a distribution that is strongly skewed right. For the sampling distribution of means for samples of size 5, which of the following are true about the shape, center, and spread of the sampling distribution?

	Shape	Mean	Standard Deviation
(A)	Skewed right	Equal to that of the population	Less than that of the population
(B)	Skewed right	Equal to that of the population	Equal to that of the population
(C)	Skewed right	Equal to that of the population	Greater than that of the population
(D)	Approximately normal	Equal to that of the population	Less than that of the population
(E)	Approximately normal	Equal to that of the population	Equal to that of the population

10. A young woman works two jobs and receives tips for both jobs. As a hairdresser, her distribution of weekly tips has mean \$65 and standard deviation \$5.75. As a waitress, her distribution of weekly tips has mean \$154 and standard deviation \$8.02. What are the mean and standard deviation of her combined weekly tips? (Assume independence for the two jobs.)
   (A) mean \$167.16; standard deviation \$9.87
   (B) mean \$167.16; standard deviation \$13.77
   (C) mean \$219.00; standard deviation \$2.27
   (D) mean \$219.00; standard deviation \$9.87
   (E) mean \$219.00; standard deviation \$13.77

11. A cause-and-effect relationship between two variables can best be determined from which of the following?
   (A) A survey conducted using a simple random sample of individuals
   (B) A survey conducted using a stratified random sample of individuals
   (C) An association with a correlation coefficient near 1 or −1
   (D) An observational study where the observational units are chosen randomly
   (E) A controlled experiment where the observational units are assigned randomly

12. Moving times (in minutes) and weights (in pounds) were recorded for a random sample of 20 moving jobs requiring three-man crews, and the results of the regression analysis are shown below.

Predictor	Coef	StDev	T	P
Constant	21.84	25.54	0.86	0.404
Weight	0.036538	0.002977	12.27	0.000

S = 30.32   R − Sq = 89.3%   R − Sq(adj) = 88.7%

Analysis of Variance

Source	DF	SS	MS	F	P
Regression	1	138434	138434	150.60	0.000
Residual Error	18	16546	919		
Total	19	154980			

The equation for the least squares regression line is

(A) $\widehat{\text{Weight}} = 21.84 + 0.037(\text{Time})$.

(B) $\widehat{\text{Time}} = 21.84 + 0.037(\text{Weight})$.

(C) $\widehat{\text{Weight}} = 25.54 + 0.003(\text{Time})$.

(D) $\widehat{\text{Time}} = 25.54 + 0.003(\text{Weight})$.

(E) $\widehat{\text{Time}} = 0.037 + 21.84(\text{Weight})$.

13. Which of the following is not a condition for a geometric setting?

(A) There are only two possible outcomes for each trial.

(B) The probability of success is the same for each trial.

(C) The trials are independent.

(D) There are a fixed number of observations.

(E) The variable of interest is the number of trials required to reach the first success.

14. Two random samples of American adults are taken, and the religious affiliations of the individuals involved are recorded. In the first sample of 200 adults, 66 of the individuals are Christians. In the second sample of 140 adults, 12 of the individuals are Buddhists. Assume the two samples are independent. Which of the following should be used to construct a 95% confidence interval for the difference in proportions for adult Americans who practice the two religions?
 (A) $0.0786 \pm 1.96\sqrt{0.0005}$
 (B) $0.2443 \pm 1.96\sqrt{0.0017}$
 (C) $0.33 \pm 1.96\sqrt{0.0011}$
 (D) The conditions necessary for computing a confidence interval have not been met; therefore, a confidence interval should not be computed.
 (E) Because the sample sizes for the two proportions are not equal, a confidence interval cannot be computed.

15. For a set of values, suppose the mean is 10 and the standard deviation is 2. If each value is multiplied by 9, what will be the mean and standard deviation for this new set of values?
 (A) mean 10; standard deviation 2
 (B) mean 10; standard deviation 18
 (C) mean 90; standard deviation 2
 (D) mean 90; standard deviation 6
 (E) mean 90; standard deviation 18

16. Two measures, x and y, are taken on numerous subjects, and a least squares regression equation is computed.
 The resulting equation is $\hat{y} = 382.1 - 12.25x$. A correct interpretation for the slope and intercept is
 (A) for every increase of 100 units in x, y increases approximately 1225 units; when $x = 0$, y is predicted to be 382.1.
 (B) for every increase of 100 units in x, y decreases approximately 1225 units; when $x = 0$, y is predicted to be 382.1.
 (C) for every increase of 100 units in x, y increases approximately 32,810 units; when $x = 0$, y is predicted to be 12.25.
 (D) for every increase of 100 units in x, y decreases approximately 32,810 units; when $x = 0$, y is predicted to be 12.25.
 (E) for every increase of 100 units in x, y increases approximately 32,810 units; when $x = 0$, y is predicted to be -12.25.

17. High school students on a closed campus recently petitioned their school board to allow students to leave the campus for lunch. In order to support their opinion, the students randomly polled students and teachers with the following question: "Do you think that students should be allowed to leave campus for lunch?" The results are as follows:

	Agree	Disagree	No Opinion	Total
Students	123	37	4	164
Teachers	16	3	3	22
Total	139	40	7	186

Which of the following best describes the responses of students and teachers on the issue?

(A) There is insufficient evidence that students and teachers have different opinions on the issue.
(B) There is evidence that students and teachers have different opinions on the issue at the 0.10 level but not at the 0.05 level.
(C) There is evidence that students and teachers have different opinions on the issue at the 0.05 level but not at the 0.01 level.
(D) There is evidence that students and teachers have different opinions on the issue at the 0.01 level but not at the 0.001 level.
(E) The conditions for conducting an appropriate test of homogeneity between students and teachers on the issue have not been met.

18. A random sample of fireworks shows was selected, and the number of shells used for each show (Shells), along with the length of the show (Length), were recorded. The following output was generated:

Bivariate Fit of Length by Shells

Linear Fit
Length = 20.162164 + 0.0002513 Shells

Summary of Fit

RSquare	0.073444
RSquare Adj	0.021969
Root Mean Square Error	5.116423
Mean of Response	22.85
Observations (or Sum Wgts)	20

What is the correlation between the number of shells and the length of the show?

(A) 0.022
(B) 0.073
(C) 0.148
(D) 0.271
(E) Not enough information is given to determine the correlation.

19. Two friends become roommates. Before deciding whether or not to combine their grocery shopping, they examine a random sample of previous weekly grocery bills for each to determine whether one spends significantly more money on groceries than the other. Assume all conditions for conducting a significance test have been met. The results of the test are:

H_0: Population mean of roommate A *equals that* of roommate B

H_a: Population mean of roommate A is *greater than that* of roommate B

	Roommate A	**Roommate B**
Count:	**10**	**10**
Mean:	**38**	**32**
Std dev:	**8.56**	**8.56**
Std error:	**2.70**	**2.70**

Using **unpooled variances**

Student's *t*:	**1.567**
df:	**18**
p-value:	**0.067**

Based upon the results of the test, which of the following conclusions should the roommates make?

(A) The results show that roommate A spends more than roommate B approximately 6.7% of the time.

(B) The results show that roommate A spends more than roommate B approximately 93.3% of the time.

(C) The results show that roommate A spends more than roommate B at the 0.10 level. If the null hypothesis is true, one could expect to get a test statistic at least as extreme as that observed 6.7% of the time.

(D) The results show that roommate A spends more than roommate B at the 0.10 level. If the null hypothesis is true, one could expect to get a test statistic at least as extreme as that observed 93.3% of the time.

(E) The results do not show that roommate A spends more than roommate B at any of the commonly accepted significance levels.

20. In a game of chance, three fair coins are tossed simultaneously. If all three coins show heads, then the player wins \$15. If all three coins show tails, then the player wins \$10. If it costs \$5 to play the game, what is the player's expected net gain or loss at the end of two games?
(A) The player can expect to gain \$15 after two games.
(B) The player can expect to gain \$1.88 after two games.
(C) The player can expect to gain \$3.75 after two games.
(D) The player can expect to lose \$1.88 after two games.
(E) The player can expect to lose \$3.75 after two games.

21. Senior citizens make up about 12.4% of the American population. If a random sample of 200 Americans is selected, what is the probability that more than 180 of them are *not* senior citizens?
(A) $\binom{200}{180}(0.124)^{180}(0.876)^{20}$
(B) $\binom{200}{180}(0.876)^{180}(0.124)^{20}$
(C) $P\left(z > \dfrac{180 - 175.2}{\dfrac{0.124}{\sqrt{200}}}\right)$
(D) $P\left(z > \dfrac{0.9 - 0.124}{\sqrt{\dfrac{(0.124)(0.876)}{200}}}\right)$
(E) $P\left(z > \dfrac{0.9 - 0.876}{\sqrt{\dfrac{(0.124)(0.876)}{200}}}\right)$

22. An avid tennis fan wishes to determine the average number of points per game in tennis. He takes a random sample of 20 games and finds the mean length to be 5.65 points with a standard deviation of 1.69 points. Which of the following would yield a 95% confidence interval for μ?

(A) $5.65 \pm 1.96\frac{1.69}{\sqrt{20}}$

(B) $5.65 \pm 2.086\frac{1.69}{\sqrt{20}}$

(C) $5.65 \pm 2.093\frac{1.69}{\sqrt{20}}$

(D) $5.65 \pm 2.086\frac{1.69}{\sqrt{19}}$

(E) $5.65 \pm 2.093\frac{1.69}{\sqrt{19}}$

23. In this year's county mathematics competition, a student scored 40; in last year's competition, the student scored 35. The average score this year was 38 with a standard deviation of 2. Last year's average score was 34 with a standard deviation of 1. In which year did the student score better?

(A) The student scored better on this year's exam.

(B) The student scored better on last year's exam.

(C) The student scored equally well on both exams.

(D) Without knowing the number of test items, it is impossible to determine the better score.

(E) Without knowing the number of students taking the exam in the county, it is impossible to determine the better score.

24. There are 39 known moons orbiting the planet Jupiter. The diameter (in kilometers) and distance from Jupiter (in thousands of kilometers) are recorded for the moons discovered prior to May 2002. The conditions for regression analysis were met, and the results follow.

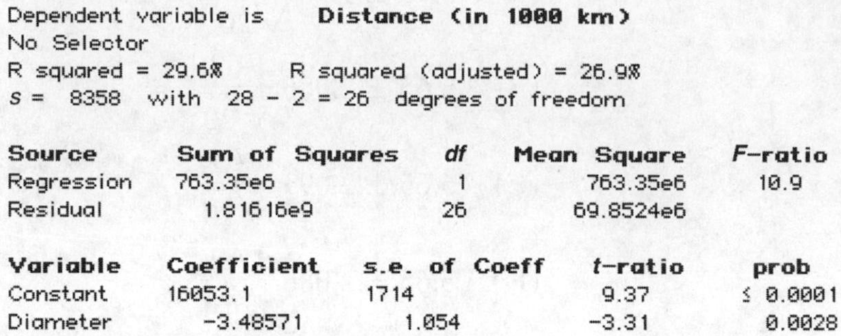

Dependent variable is **Distance (in 1000 km)**
No Selector
R squared = 29.6%   R squared (adjusted) = 26.9%
s = 8358 with 28 − 2 = 26 degrees of freedom

Source	Sum of Squares	df	Mean Square	F-ratio
Regression	763.35e6	1	763.35e6	10.9
Residual	1.81616e9	26	69.8524e6	

Variable	Coefficient	s.e. of Coeff	t-ratio	prob
Constant	16053.1	1714	9.37	≤ 0.0001
Diameter	−3.48571	1.054	−3.31	0.0028

Is there evidence of a relationship between diameter and distance?

(A) There is no evidence of a relationship between diameter and distance at any of the commonly accepted levels.

(B) There is evidence of a relationship between diameter and distance at the 0.10 level but not at the 0.05 level.

(C) There is evidence of a relationship between diameter and distance at the 0.05 level but not at the 0.01 level.

(D) There is evidence of a relationship between diameter and distance at the 0.01 level but not at the 0.001 level.

(E) There is evidence of a relationship between diameter and distance at the 0.001 level.

25. Shown below is a distribution with mean 12.262 and standard deviation 9.610.

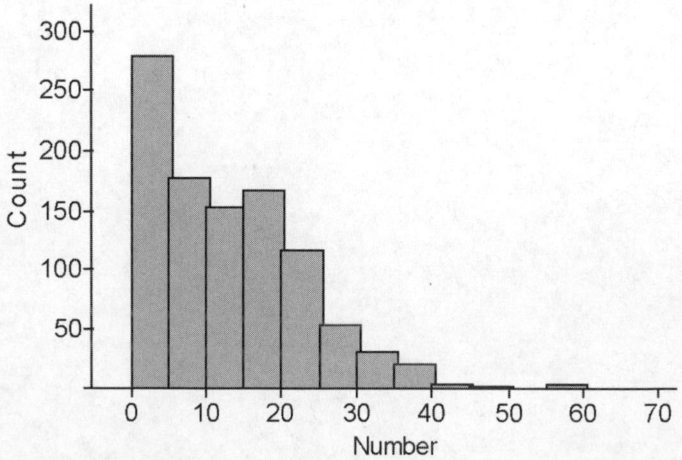

One hundred samples of size 9 are drawn from this population, and the sample means are recorded. Which of the following is most likely to represent this distribution of sample means?

(A)

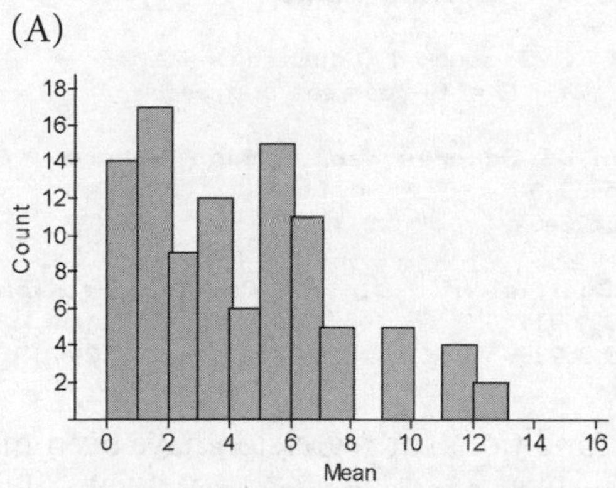

(B)

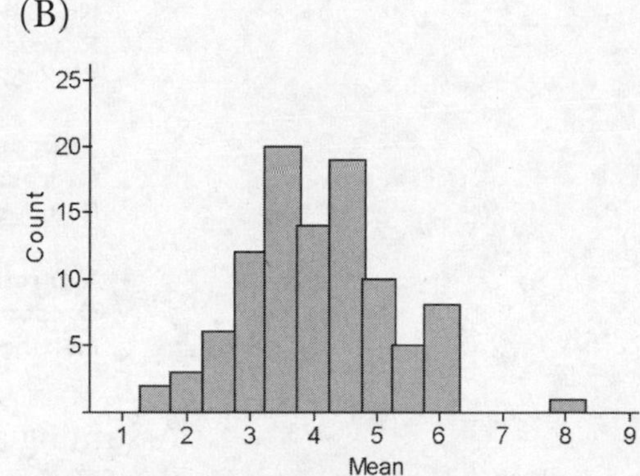

(C)

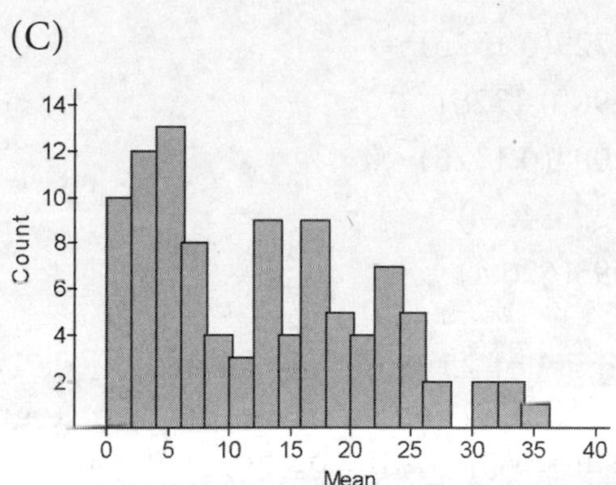

(D)

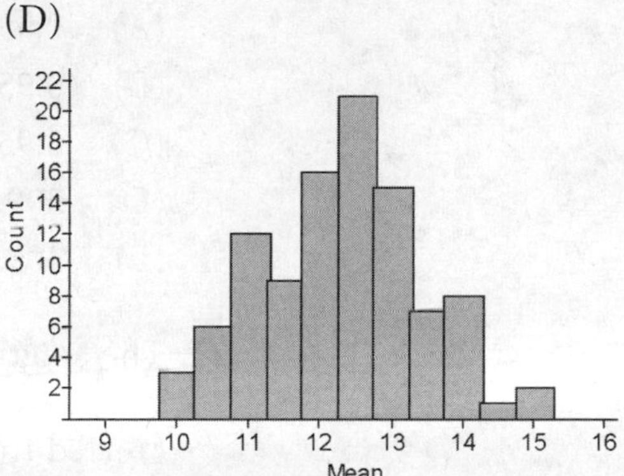

(E)

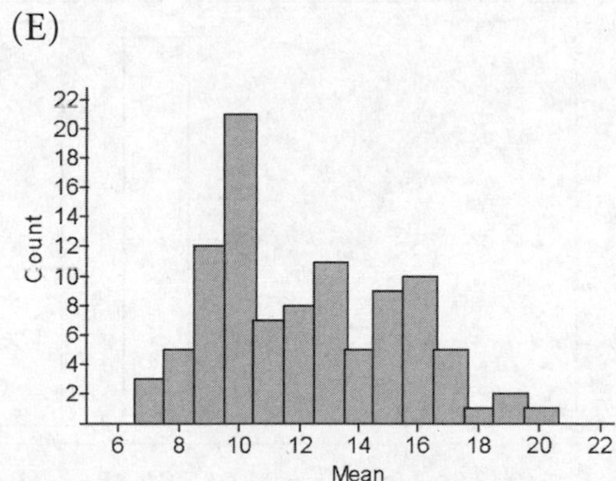

26. Boiling and melting points (in degrees Celsius) are recorded for selected substances, and regression analysis is used to describe the relationship between them. The results of the analysis are shown below:

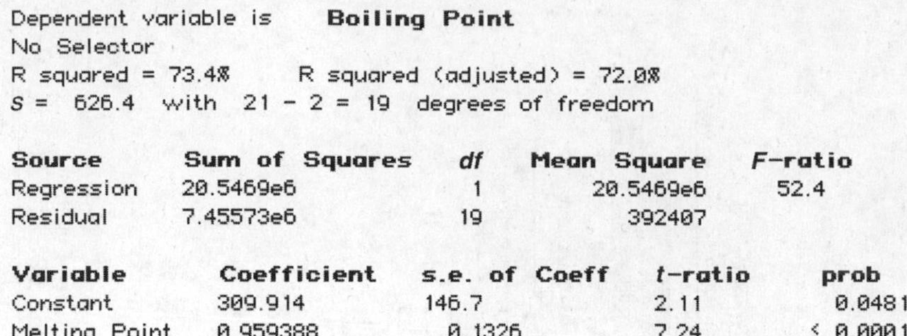

Dependent variable is **Boiling Point**
No Selector
R squared = 73.4% R squared (adjusted) = 72.0%
s = 626.4 with 21 - 2 = 19 degrees of freedom

Source	**Sum of Squares**	*df*	**Mean Square**	*F*-**ratio**
Regression	20.5469e6	1	20.5469e6	52.4
Residual	7.45573e6	19	392407	

Variable	**Coefficient**	**s.e. of Coeff**	*t*-**ratio**	**prob**
Constant	309.914	146.7	2.11	0.0481
Melting Point	0.959388	0.1326	7.24	≤ 0.0001

Assuming all of the conditions for regression have been met, which of the following gives the 95% confidence interval for the slope of the regression line?

(A) $0.959388 \pm 1.729(0.1326)$

(B) $0.959388 \pm 1.96(0.1326)$

(C) $0.959388 \pm 2.093(0.1326)$

(D) $309.914 \pm 1.729(146.7)$

(E) $309.914 \pm 2.093(626.4)$

27. The lengths (in innings) of 25 randomly selected Little League baseball games were recorded, and a *cumulative* frequency histogram was created from the results. What is the best conclusion that can be made from the graph?

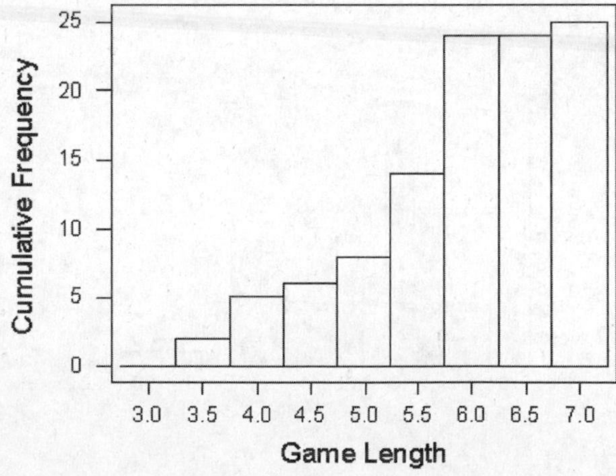

(A) The median game length is 5 innings.

(B) Fourteen games lasted 5.5 innings.

(C) A majority of the games lasted 6 or more innings.

(D) The distribution of game lengths is severely skewed left.

(E) Games lasting more than 6 innings occurred least frequently.

28. For which of the following distributions is the mean greater than the median?

(A)

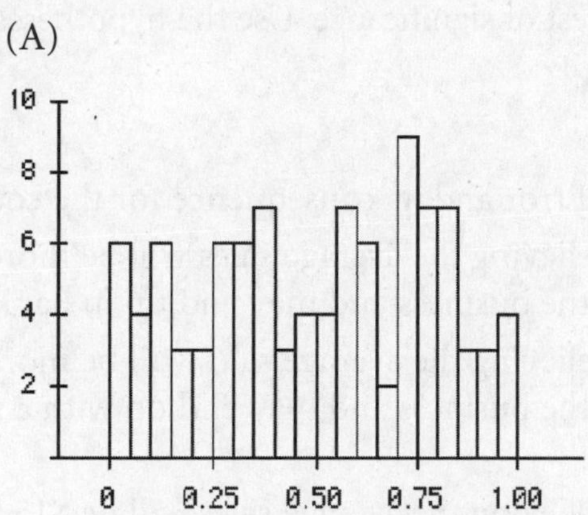

(B)

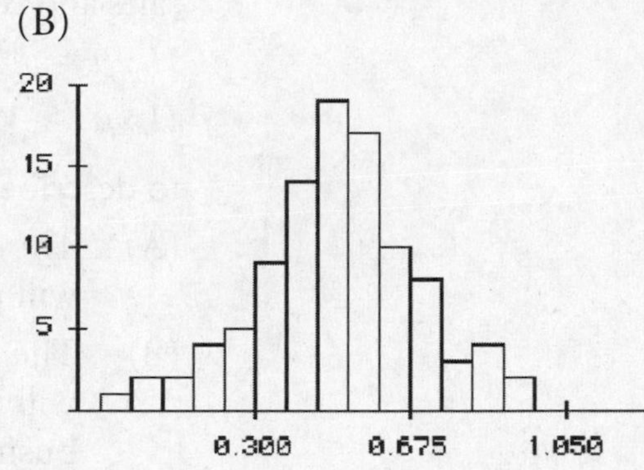

(C)

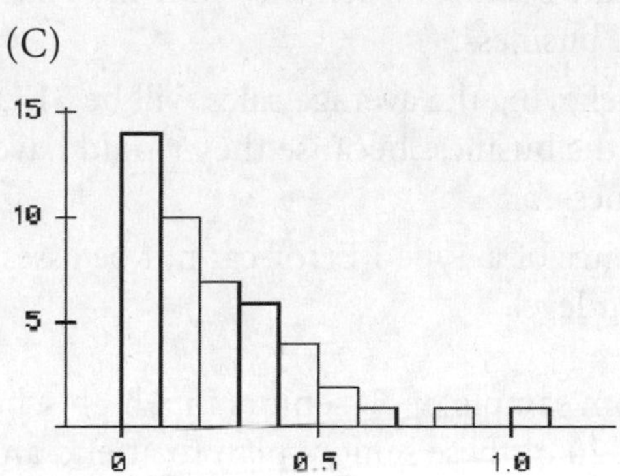

(D)

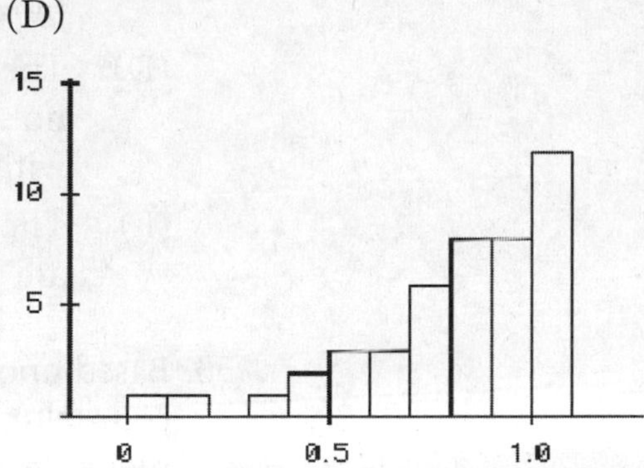

(E)

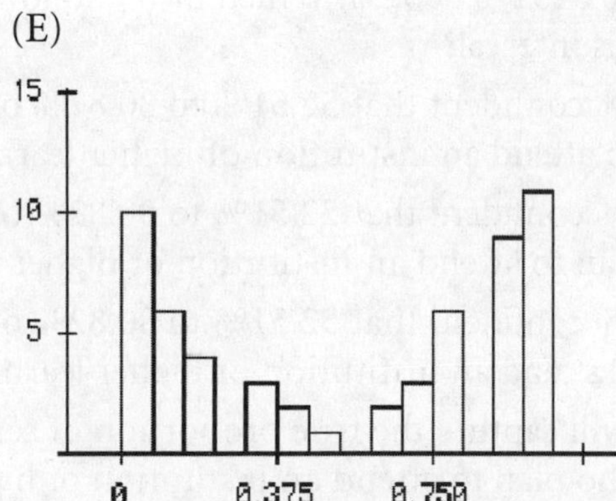

29. A young couple plans to purchase a business. In order to avoid bankruptcy, the couple needs to average more than $15,000 in sales each week. Before signing the deal, they take a random sample (size 30) from previous weeks' sales and conduct a test of significance. Use the hypotheses

H_0: $\mu = 15000$

H_a: $\mu > 15000$

to describe a Type I Error and its consequence for the couple.

(A) The couple, believing the average sales will be more than $15,000, will purchase the business and may end up in bankruptcy.

(B) The couple, believing the average sales will be more than $15,000, will purchase the business and may end up with a successful business.

(C) The couple, believing the average sales will be $15,000 or less, will not purchase the business when they may have succeeded had they purchased the business.

(D) The couple, believing the average sales will be $15,000 or less, will not purchase the business because they would have gone bankrupt with the business.

(E) The consequence of a Type I Error cannot be assessed unless we are given the α level.

30. Based upon a random sample of 30 seniors in a high school, a guidance counselor finds that 20 of these seniors plan to attend an institution of higher learning. A 90% confidence interval constructed from this information yields (0.5251, 0.80823). Which of the following is a correct interpretation for this interval?

(A) We can be 90% confident that 52.51% to 80.82% of our sample seniors plan to attend an institution of higher learning.

(B) We can be 90% confident that 52.51% to 80.82% of seniors at this high school plan to attend an institution of higher learning.

(C) We can be 90% confident that 52.51% to 80.82% of seniors in any school plan to attend an institution of higher learning.

(D) This interval will capture the true proportion of seniors from this high school who plan to attend an institution of higher learning 90% of the time.

(E) This interval will capture the proportion of seniors in our sample who plan to attend an institution of higher learning 90% of the time.

31. As a promotional gimmick, a cereal manufacturer packages boxes of cereal with CD-ROMs of popular games. There are five different games distributed equally among the boxes, but the purchasers do not know which game they are receiving when they purchase the cereal. A child would like to receive one game in particular. What is the probability that the child opens three boxes of cereal before receiving the desired game?

    (A) $\binom{5}{3}(0.2)^3(0.8)^2$

    (B) $\binom{5}{3}(0.2)^2(0.8)^3$

    (C) $\binom{5}{1}(0.6)(0.4)^4$

    (D) $(0.8)^2(0.2)$

    (E) $(0.2)^2(0.8)$

32. A random variable has a standard deviation of 1.3. A new variable is created by transforming the values of the random variable using the following rule: Multiply each value by 2 and then add 5. What is the value of the standard deviation for this transformed variable?

    (A) 1.3
    (B) 2.6
    (C) 6.3
    (D) 7.6
    (E) 8.5

33. Suppose the probability of encountering an American who practices a particular religion is 0.014. What are the mean and standard deviation for the *number* of Americans in a random sample of 500 who practice this religion?

    (A) mean 0.014; standard deviation 0.0006
    (B) mean 0.014; standard deviation 0.0053
    (C) mean 7; standard deviation 0.0006
    (D) mean 7; standard deviation 0.0053
    (E) mean 7; standard deviation 2.627

34. A manufacturer constructs a 95% confidence interval for the average weight of the items he manufactures. His results need to be included in a report to his superiors, and the resulting interval is wider than he would like. In order to decrease the size of the interval the *most*, the manufacturer should take a new sample and
    (A) increase the confidence level and increase the sample size.
    (B) decrease the confidence level and increase the sample size.
    (C) increase the confidence level and decrease the sample size.
    (D) decrease the confidence level and decrease the sample size.
    (E) The manufacturer will not be able to decrease the size of the interval.

35. A least squares regression line was fitted to the weekly cost of groceries in dollars (cost) versus the number of household members (number) for a group of families. The resulting equation is

$$\widehat{\text{cost}} = -33.22 + 44.77\,(\text{number}).$$

A randomly selected family of four spends $135 on groceries in an average week. What is the difference between this family's actual cost and the predicted average family cost?
    (A) −$10.86
    (B) −$0.24
    (C) $0.24
    (D) $10.86
    (E) $145.86

36. A random sample of adults is taken in a rural county. Of the 120 adults sampled, 16 live in poverty. The poverty rate for the entire state is 8.9%. Is there statistical evidence to show that the poverty rate of this county is higher than that of the state?
    (A) Since 13.33% is greater than 8.9%, there is sufficient evidence at the $\alpha = 0.05$ level to show that the poverty rate of the county is higher than that of the state.
    (B) Since 4.40% is less than 8.9%, there is insufficient evidence at the $\alpha = 0.05$ level to show that the poverty rate of the county is higher than that of the state.
    (C) Since 1.706 is less than 8.9, there is insufficient evidence at the $\alpha = 0.05$ level to show that the poverty rate of the county is higher than that of the state.
    (D) Since 1.706 is greater than 1.645, there is sufficient evidence at the $\alpha = 0.05$ level to show that the poverty rate of the county is higher than that of the state.
    (E) Since 0.044 is less than 0.05, there is insufficient evidence at the $\alpha = 0.05$ level to show that the poverty rate of the county is higher than that of the state.

37. Which of the following distributions has a mean of 30 and a standard deviation of 7?

(A)

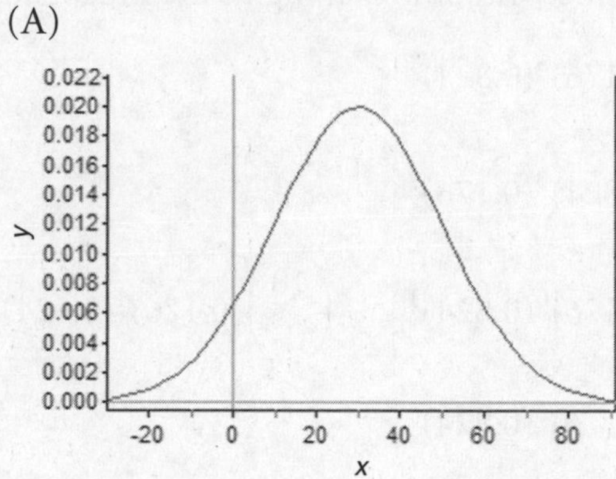

(B)

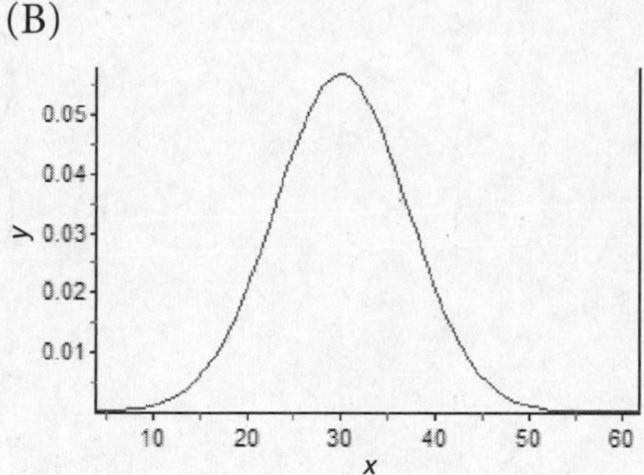

(C)

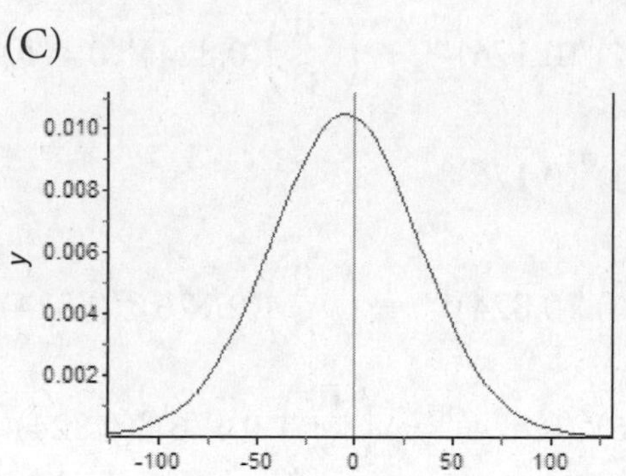

(D)

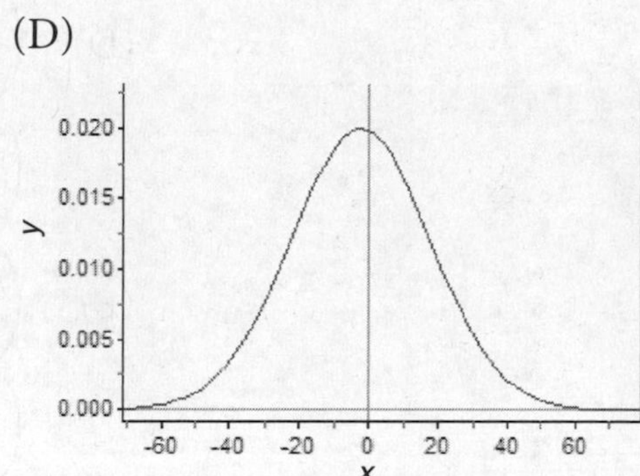

(E)

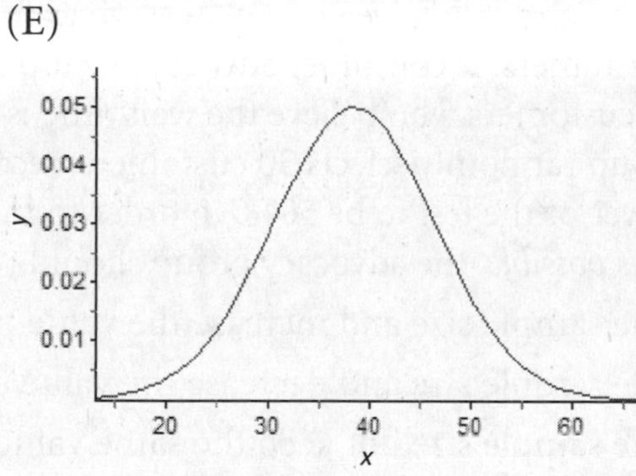

38. Two manufacturers of canned goods add different amounts of water to their canned vegetables. For a 15.25-oz can of vegetables, one manufacturer adds a mean of 4.5 oz with a standard deviation of 0.63 oz. The other manufacturer adds a mean of 5.1 oz with a standard deviation of 0.57 oz. What are the mean and standard deviation for the difference in the amount of water added? (Assume independence for the manufacturers.)

(A) mean 0.6 oz; standard deviation 0.06 oz

(B) mean 0.6 oz; standard deviation 0.85 oz

(C) mean 0.6 oz; standard deviation 0.072 oz

(D) mean 9.6 oz; standard deviation 0.06 oz

(E) mean 9.6 oz; standard deviation 1.20 oz

39. An airline has an on-time probability of 82.4%. What is the probability that, if you travel on this airline, no more than 3 of your next 10 flights will *not* be on time? (Assume that flights are independent.)

(A) $\binom{10}{3}(0.176)^3(0.824)^7$

(B) $\binom{10}{3}(0.824)^3(0.176)^7$

(C) $\binom{10}{0}(0.176)^0(0.824)^{10} + \binom{10}{1}(0.176)^1(0.824)^9 + \binom{10}{2}(0.176)^2(0.824)^8$

(D) $\binom{10}{0}(0.824)^0(0.176)^{10} + \binom{10}{1}(0.824)^1(0.176)^9 + \binom{10}{2}(0.824)^2(0.176)^8$

(E) $\binom{10}{0}(0.176)^0(0.824)^{10} + \binom{10}{1}(0.176)^1(0.824)^9 + \binom{10}{2}(0.176)^2(0.824)^8 + \binom{10}{3}(0.176)^3(0.824)^7$

40. A no-appointment haircutter advertises an average wait time of 15 minutes for customers. A consumer advocacy group has received several complaints from customers who believe the wait time is really 30 minutes. The advocacy group randomly selects 30 customers, records wait times, and calculates the power of the test to be 50%. In order to increase the power of the test *as much as possible,* the advocacy group should

(A) increase the sample size and increase the value of α.
(B) increase the sample size and decrease the value of α.
(C) increase the sample size but keep the same value for α.
(D) decrease the sample size and increase the value of α.
(E) decrease the sample size and decrease the value of α.

STATISTICS
SECTION II

Time: 1 hour and 30 minutes
Number of problems: 6
Percent of total grade: 50

GENERAL INSTRUCTIONS

There are two parts to this section of the examination. Part A consists of five equally weighted problems that represent 75 percent of the total weight of this section. Spend about 65 minutes on this part of the exam. Part B consists of one longer problem that represents 25 percent of the total weight of this section. Spend about 25 minutes on this part of the exam. Since it is not expected that everyone will be able to complete all parts of all problems, you may wish to look over all the problems before you begin to work. The questions are printed in the booklet and on the green insert: It may be easier for you to look over all the problems on the insert. Statistical tables and useful formulas are printed in both the booklet and on the green insert.

- You should write all work for each part of each problem in the space provided for that part in this booklet. Be sure to write clearly and legibly. If you make an error, you may save time by crossing it out rather than trying to erase it. Erased or crossed-out work will not be graded. *No credit will be given for any work shown on the green insert.*
- Show all your work. Indicate clearly the methods you use because you will be graded on the correctness of your methods as well as the accuracy of your final answers. Correct answers without supporting work may not receive credit.

STATISTICS SECTION II Part A

Questions: 1–5
Spend about 65 minutes on this part of the exam.
Percent of Section II grade: 75

Directions: Show all your work. Indicate clearly the methods you use, because you will be graded on the correctness of your methods as well as on the accuracy of your results and explanations.

1. The graph shows the percentage of the population with access to safe drinking water (Water) and the persons per doctor (PPD) for randomly selected regions of the world. Also given is the regression analysis for these variables.

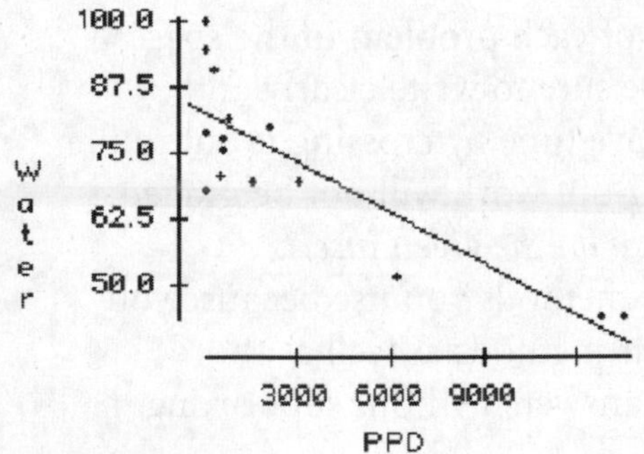

Dependent variable is: **Water**
No Selector
R squared = 70.4% R squared (adjusted) = 68.3%
s = 9.58 with 16 − 2 = 14 degrees of freedom

Source	**Sum of Squares**	**df**	**Mean Square**	**F-ratio**
Regression	3060.62	1	3060.62	33.3
Residual	1284.82	14	91.773	

Variable	**Coefficient**	**s.e. of Coeff**	**t-ratio**	**prob**
Constant	83.4851	2.838	29.4	≤ 0.0001
Doctors	−0.00323837	0.0005608	−5.77	≤ 0.0001

a. What is the equation of the least squares regression line that describes the relationship between the percentage with access to safe drinking water and the persons per doctor? Define any variables used in this equation.

b. Record *and* interpret the value of the correlation coefficient for percentage with access to safe drinking water and persons per doctor.

c. Record *and* interpret the value of the coefficient of determination for percentage with access to safe drinking water and persons per doctor.

2. A random sample of construction workers was taken in a large city. Of the 150 workers sampled, 16 were unemployed.
   a. Construct *and* interpret a 90% confidence interval for the proportion of unemployed construction workers in this city.

   b. At the time this sample was taken, the overall unemployment rate for the city was 6.8%. Based on your confidence interval in part (a), is there evidence at the 0.05 level to show that the unemployment rate for city construction workers is significantly higher than the overall city rate? Explain your reasoning.

3. Wrestling is a somewhat unique sport in that it can be viewed as both an individual and a team sport. The Anytown High School wrestling team consists of five wrestlers, each competing in a different weight class. The point differentials (difference in points between these wrestlers and their opponents) for the first ten meets are recorded for these five wrestlers, and the distributions of their individual results are approximately normal with the following means and standard deviations. (For matches resulting in pins, the point differential was recorded as 15, the same as for a technical fall.)

Weight Class	Mean Point Differential	Standard Deviation
125 lb	7.4	3.2
140 lb	7.9	5.1
152 lb	7.2	4.7
189 lb	8.1	5.3
215 lb	6.4	4.9

   a. What is the probability that the 215-lb wrestler will beat his next opponent by *at least* 14 points?

b. Suppose the team score is calculated directly from the point differentials. What would be the mean score and standard deviation for *this* team?

c. Team scores are *not* calculated directly from the point differentials. If the *real* team score average for last season was 39.5 with a standard deviation of 13.202, do you have any reservations about using this information and part (b) to determine if there is a significant difference in the two scoring methods? Explain.

4. A tennis racquet manufacturer has designed a new racquet. The manufacturer claims the new racquet will allow the user to return more serves than any racquet currently sold. A group of male volunteers who currently play tennis and own their own racquets agree to participate in the study.
   a. Design an experiment that would test the manufacturer's claim.

   b. Suppose the volunteer group had included both men and women. Would you adjust the design of your experiment? If so, provide the new design.

5. A public opinion poll was conducted with 200 randomly selected individuals to determine the level of satisfaction with the president's handling of the economy, foreign affairs, and domestic affairs. The following are the results of the survey.

	Approve	Disapprove	No Opinion
Economy	96	100	4
Foreign Affairs	110	84	6
Domestic Affairs	124	68	8

Is there evidence that the public's opinion on the three issues is the same? Give appropriate statistical evidence to support your answer.

STATISTICS SECTION II Part B

Question: 6
Spend about 25 minutes on this part of the exam.
Percent of Section II grade: 25

Directions: Show all your work. Indicate clearly the methods you use, because you will be graded on the correctness of your methods as well as on the accuracy of your results and explanations.

6. About 48% of U.S. women of all ages engage in walking for physical activity.
   a. Explain *how* you would conduct a simulation using the random-number table displayed in part (b) to estimate the number of walkers from a sample of 10 women.

   b. Perform your simulation 20 times. Start at the leftmost digit in the first row and move across. By marking directly on or above the table, make your procedure clear enough that someone else can follow what you did. Record the number of walkers for each of your trials.

69165	01210	02156	38425	02216	90078	41061	02463	40374	13298	80188	21906
44194	01096	29950	16306	92255	75170	57400	09191	80522	09235	86386	78007
47007	72848	02846	46633	41906	59357	03933	19473	37483	01769	76267	78340
52435	85822	33415	94602	99499	42195	24360	06706	10948	34268	66144	10375
39832	85409	14239	61405	40866	17083	53189	10901	62926	85304	64067	56177
69221	41200	84407	48185	96361	09404	60255	56996	41696	84481	27388	82125
64091	81760	78188	76031	43483	81928	05945	93758	49307	66038	23405	10343
94975	14597	66416	01014	05406	65230	00456	62101	94834	35086	99930	75912

c. From your results, create a frequency table showing the number of women who walk.

d. Another researcher collected 20 random samples of size 10 and recorded the number of women who walk for physical activity.

Number of Walkers	Frequency
1	1
2	2
3	3
4	3
5	2
6	4
7	4
8	1

Create an appropriate graphical display of the researcher's data *and* the data from *your* simulation so that the two data sets can be compared.

e. Write a few sentences comparing the two data sets. Use your display from part (d).

Answers for Examination 1 begin on page 278.

AP Statistics Practice Examination 2

Multiple Choice
Statistics
Section I

Time: 90 minutes

1. For the given scatterplot, what is the correct regression output?

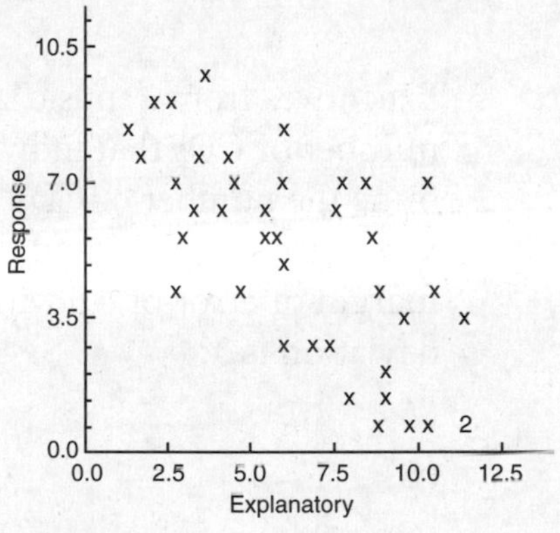

(A)

Predictor	Coef	SE Coef	T	P
Constant	9.1104	0.7745	11.76	0.000
Explanatory	0.6181	0.1085	−5.70	0.000
$S = 2.02551$	R-Sq = 46.1%	R-Sq(adj) = 44.7%		

(B)

Predictor	Coef	SE Coef	T	P
Constant	9.1104	0.7745	11.76	0.000
Explanatory	−0.6181	0.1085	−5.70	0.000
$S = 2.02551$	R-Sq = 67.9%	R-Sq(adj) = 66.3%		

(C)

Predictor	Coef	SE Coef	T	P
Constant	9.1104	0.7745	11.76	0.000
Explanatory	0.6181	0.1085	−5.70	0.000
$S = 2.02551$	R-Sq = 67.9%	R-Sq(adj) = 66.3%		

(D)

Predictor	Coef	SE Coef	T	P
Constant	9.1104	0.7745	11.76	0.000
Explanatory	−0.6181	0.1085	−5.70	0.000
$S = 2.02551$	R-Sq = 46.1%	R-Sq(adj) = 44.7%		

(E)

Predictor	Coef	SE Coef	T	P
Constant	−0.6181	0.7745	11.76	0.000
Explanatory	9.1104	0.1085	−5.70	0.000
$S = 2.02551$	R-Sq = 46.1%	R-Sq(adj) = 44.7%		

2. A magazine claims that 25.1% of all women enjoy gardening. A researcher believes the percentage is higher and performs a test of H_0: $p = 0.251$ versus H_a: $p > 0.251$. A random sample of 100 women yields significant results at the $\alpha = 0.05$ level. Which of the following statements about the confidence interval used to estimate the true population proportion of women who enjoy gardening must be true?
   (A) A 90% confidence interval contains the proportion 0.251.
   (B) A 90% confidence interval does not contain the proportion 0.251, because the value of 0.251 is above the upper limit of the interval.
   (C) A 90% confidence interval does not contain the proportion 0.251, because the value of 0.251 is below the lower limit of the interval.
   (D) A 95% confidence interval does not contain the proportion 0.251, because the value of 0.251 is above the upper limit of the interval.
   (E) A 95% confidence interval does not contain the proportion 0.251, because the value of 0.251 is below the lower limit of the interval.

3. Executives from a music label believe they are losing money from the number of CDs that individuals copy illegally. They would like to determine the number of CDs the average computer owner copies in a month. What size sample would they need to take to estimate this number with a margin of error of 0.5 with 95% confidence, if they assume the standard deviation is 3?
   (A) 10
   (B) 17
   (C) 24
   (D) 98
   (E) 139

4. As part of a statistics project, a student decides to find a 95% confidence interval for the difference in average ages of students and faculty. The student, through diligent research, is able to record the age of all faculty members and all students and then calculates the 95% confidence interval using the t-distribution. Which of the following is a consideration the student failed to take into account?
   (A) The group of teachers and students are not independent. Therefore, the assumptions for using the two-sample t-interval are not valid.
   (B) The ages of teachers and students are not likely to be normally distributed. Therefore, the assumptions for using the two-sample t-interval are not valid.
   (C) The distribution of student ages is likely to have a few large outliers. Therefore, the assumptions for using the two-sample t-interval are not valid.
   (D) In both cases, the student had data for the entire population. Therefore, the actual difference in average ages can be computed, and a confidence interval is not valid.
   (E) Because there are most likely 40 or more students and 40 or more faculty members, there is nothing the student failed to take into account, and the confidence interval is valid.

5. Randomly selected individuals were asked about their physical activity. Of 75 randomly selected men, 30 had walked for exercise in the preceding two weeks. Of 75 randomly selected women, 36 had walked for exercise in the preceding two weeks. Assume independence between the samples. Is there evidence to show a significant difference in the proportion of men and the proportion of women who walk for exercise?
   (A) Because the proportions are different, there is evidence to show a significant difference in the proportions of men and women who walk for exercise.
   (B) With $p = 0.162$, there is insufficient evidence to show a significant difference in the proportions of men and women who walk for exercise.
   (C) With $p = 0.324$, there is insufficient evidence to show a significant difference in the proportions of men and women who walk for exercise.
   (D) With $p = 0.838$, there is insufficient evidence to show a significant difference in the proportions of men and women who walk for exercise.
   (E) The conditions necessary to perform a significance test have not been met; therefore, a conclusion cannot be drawn.

6. Which of the following is a true statement about experimental design?
   (A) Replication is a key component in experimental design. Thus, an experiment needs to be conducted on repeated *samples* before generalizing results.
   (B) Control is a key component in experimental design. Thus, a control group that receives a placebo is a *requirement* for experimentation.
   (C) Randomization is a key component in experimental design. Randomization is used to *reduce* bias.
   (D) Blocking eliminates the effects of *all* lurking variables.
   (E) The placebo effect is a concern for *all* experiments.

7. An experimenter believes that two new exercise programs are more effective than any current exercise routines and wishes to compare the effectiveness of these two new exercise programs on physical fitness. The experimenter is trying to determine whether or not a control group, which follows neither of these new programs but continues with current exercise routines, would be beneficial. Which of the following can be said about the addition of a control group?
   (A) A control group would eliminate the placebo effect.
   (B) A control group would eliminate the need for blinding in the study.
   (C) A control group would allow the experimenter to determine which of the two exercise programs improves physical fitness the most.
   (D) A control group would allow the experimenter to determine if either of the exercise programs is more effective than current programs for physical fitness.
   (E) There would be no added benefit to having a control group.

8. A large fast-food chain is changing vendors for its children's meal toys. The vendor claims that equal quantities of the four types of toys have been manufactured and will be distributed randomly among the restaurants. One restaurant received 89 of one type of toy, 95 of a second type, 106 of a third type, and 110 of the fourth type of toy in a shipment of 400 toys. If we consider this shipment to be a random sample of toys, does this shipment provide sufficient evidence to contradict the vendor's claim?
   (A) Yes, since the store did not receive 100 of each type of toy.
   (B) Yes, since a test of significance yields significant results at the 0.10 but not at the 0.05 level.
   (C) Yes, since a test of significance yields significant results at the 0.05 but not at the 0.01 level.
   (D) Yes, since a test of significance yields significant results at the 0.01 but not at the 0.001 level.
   (E) No, since a test of significance yielded results that were not significant at even the 0.10 level.

9. Concert attendance for a stadium is normally distributed with a standard deviation of 7641. If a concert with 41,293 people in attendance is in the top 2% of all concert attendance records, what is the mean concert attendance?
   (A) 25,601
   (B) 27,917
   (C) 54,670
   (D) 56,986
   (E) 77,163

10. A congressman mails a questionnaire to his constituents asking if the United States should use military force to overthrow violent dictators in controversial areas of the world. Of the 500 people who respond, 35% believe the United States should use military force in this situation. On a talk show, the politician claims that only 35% of his constituents (with a 4% margin of error) believe in using military force. Which assumption for constructing a confidence interval is violated?
    (A) The population is ten times as large as the sample.
    (B) The data constitute a simple random sample from the population of interest.
    (C) The count of successes, $n\hat{p}$, is 10 or more.
    (D) The count of failures, $n(1 - \hat{p})$, is 10 or more.
    (E) There are no violations for constructing a confidence interval.

11. Owners of a day-care chain wish to determine the proportion of families in need of day care for the town of Bockville. Bockville is estimated to have 1000 families. The owners of the day-care chain randomly sample 50 families and find that 60% of them have a need for day-care services. Which of the following is a condition necessary for constructing a confidence interval for a **proportion** that has *not* been met?
    (A) The data constitute a representative random sample from the population of interest.
    (B) The sample size is less than 10% of the population size.
    (C) The counts of those who need day care and those who don't need day care are 10 or more.
    (D) The distribution of sample values is approximately normally distributed.
    (E) All conditions necessary for constructing a confidence interval for the proportion seem to be met.

12. Which of the following sample designs does *not* contain a source of bias?
    (A) A politician would like to know how her constituents feel about a particular issue. As a result, her office mails questionnaires about the issue to a random sample of adults in her political district.
    (B) A company uses the telephone directory to randomly select adults for a telephone survey to gauge their feelings toward items manufactured by the company.
    (C) An interviewer selects a random sample of individuals to question about a particular issue. Since some of the individuals are not informed about the issue, the interviewer gives background and his personal view on the issue before recording their responses.
    (D) A news show asks viewers to call a toll-free number to express their opinions about a recent high-publicity trial.
    (E) One thousand numbered tickets are sold as a fund-raiser. Five numbers are chosen randomly, and the individuals with the winning ticket numbers each win $10.

13. The cause of death and the age of the deceased are recorded for 454 patients from a hospital.

	15–24	25–34	35–44	45–54	55–64	Total
Accident	14	12	15	12	7	60
Homicide	5	4	3	0	0	12
Heart disease	1	3	14	34	63	115
HIV	0	3	6	4	0	13
Cancer	2	4	17	47	89	159
Other	3	7	16	26	43	95
Total	25	33	71	123	202	454

Use these values to estimate the probability that a person at this hospital died as a result of an accident if it is known the person was between the ages of 45 and 54.
    (A) 0.0264
    (B) 0.0976
    (C) 0.1322
    (D) 0.2000
    (E) 0.4878

14. Two different Internet sites claim to offer the Web's lowest hotel rates for major U.S. cities. To test the claim, a consumer group randomly selects 50 hotels and checks the rate charged for these hotels on both sites. To determine if there is a significant difference in rates between these two sites, which significance test is appropriate?
    (A) Two-sample z-test
    (B) Two-sample t-test
    (C) Matched-pairs test
    (D) χ^2 test of independence
    (E) Linear regression t-test

15. Which of the following does *not* represent a probability density function?
    (A) $f(x) = 1$ for $0 \le x \le 1$
    (B) $f(x) = \frac{1}{3}x$ for $0 \le x \le \sqrt{6}$
    (C) $f(x) = \frac{1}{4}x + \frac{1}{4}$ for $0 \le x \le 2$
    (D) $f(x) = \begin{cases} 0.2, & 0 \le x \le 3 \\ 0.4, & 3 < x \le 4 \\ 0, & \text{elsewhere} \end{cases}$
    (E) $f(x) = \begin{cases} 0.1, & 0 \le x \le 8 \\ 0.2, & 8 < x \le 10 \\ 0, & \text{elsewhere} \end{cases}$

16. The following dotplots show the mean temperature (in degrees Fahrenheit) for a sample of cities in North America. Both January and July temperatures are shown. What is one statement that can be made with certainty from an analysis of the dotplots?

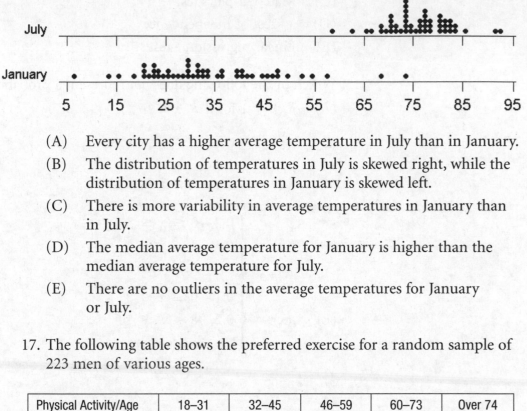

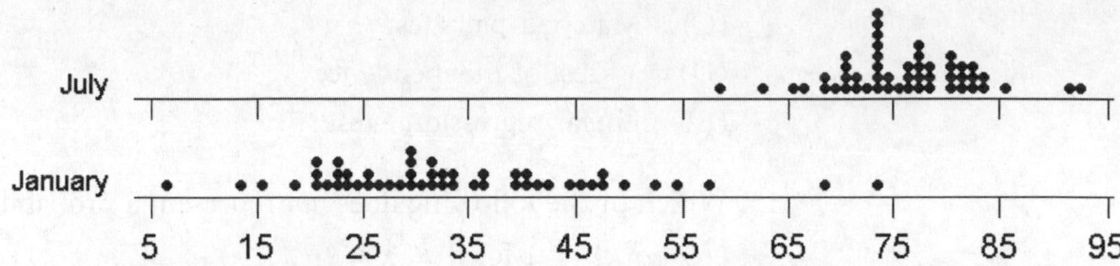

(A) Every city has a higher average temperature in July than in January.

(B) The distribution of temperatures in July is skewed right, while the distribution of temperatures in January is skewed left.

(C) There is more variability in average temperatures in January than in July.

(D) The median average temperature for January is higher than the median average temperature for July.

(E) There are no outliers in the average temperatures for January or July.

17. The following table shows the preferred exercise for a random sample of 223 men of various ages.

Physical Activity/Age	18–31	32–45	46–59	60–73	Over 74
Jogging	23	14	9	1	0
Cycling	19	19	14	11	8
Swimming	10	8	5	3	1
Weight Lifting	34	21	12	6	5

If the type of exercise is independent of age, how many men over the age of 74 would we expect to prefer cycling?

(A) 3

(B) 4

(C) 8

(D) 11

(E) 14

18. A drug company wishes to test a new drug. A researcher assembles a group of volunteers and randomly assigns them to one of two groups—one to take the drug and one to take a placebo. In addition, the company wants the experiment to be double-blind. What is the meaning of double-blind in this situation?
    (A) The volunteers in both groups are blindfolded when they take the drug or placebo.
    (B) The volunteers in both groups do not know whether they are taking the drug or the placebo.
    (C) Neither the volunteers nor the drug company executives know which volunteers are taking the drug and which are taking the placebo.
    (D) Neither the volunteers nor the evaluator know which volunteers are taking the drug and which are taking the placebo.
    (E) As long as the subjects are randomly assigned to the two groups, there is no need to make the experiment double-blind.

19. A baseball recruiter visits a high school where a player has a batting average of 0.450. (This means that he gets a hit in 45% of his at-bats.) What is the probability that the recruiter won't see the player get a hit until his third at-bat?
    (A) $(0.450)^2(0.550)$
    (B) $(0.550)^2(0.450)$
    (C) $\binom{3}{1}(0.450)(0.550)^2$
    (D) $\binom{3}{1}(0.550)(0.450)^2$
    (E) $\binom{3}{2}(0.450)(0.550)^2$

20. The following graph shows the vitamin A content (in IUs, International Units) for 23 types of fruit.

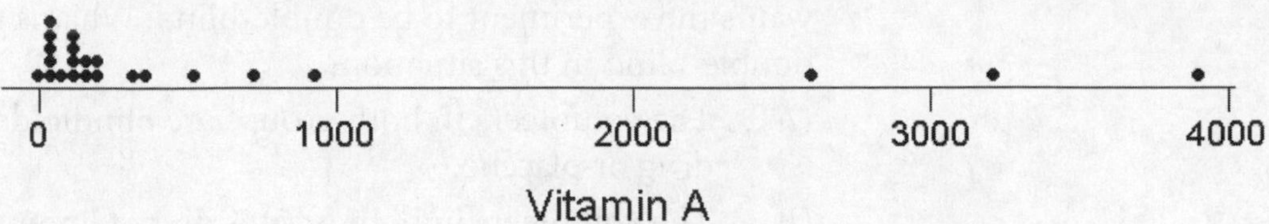

Which of the following is the best measure to describe the center of this distribution?

(A) Mean

(B) Median

(C) Standard deviation

(D) Interquartile range

(E) Range

21. Pearson High School students have cumulative grade point averages as shown in the table.

Class \ GPA	≥ 4.0	3.0–4.0	2.0–3.0	1.0–2.0	< 1.0	Total
Sophomores	43	121	114	22	10	310
Juniors	26	102	84	16	5	233
Seniors	15	87	100	10	7	219
Total	84	310	298	48	22	762

Which of the following statements is *not* true?

(A) About 39% of sophomores have *at least* a 3.0 GPA.

(B) Sophomores represent 39% of GPAs from 3.0 to 4.0.

(C) Seniors represent about 29% of the reported GPAs at Pearson High School.

(D) Only about 3% of seniors have GPAs *less than* 1.0.

(E) About 11% of the reported GPAs are juniors with GPAs from 2.0 to 3.0.

22. The coefficient of determination between two variables is computed to be 81%. Which of the following statements *must* be true?
    (A) Large values of the explanatory variable correspond with large values of the response variable.
    (B) Large values of the explanatory variable correspond with small values of the response variable.
    (C) A cause-and-effect relationship exists between the explanatory and response variables.
    (D) There is a strong, positive, linear relationship between the explanatory and response variables.
    (E) Approximately 81% of the variability in the response variable is explained by linear regression on the explanatory variable.

23. The carbohydrate content (in grams) for serving sizes of select dairy (D), fruit (F), meat (M), and vegetable (V) items is recorded, yielding the following graphical information.

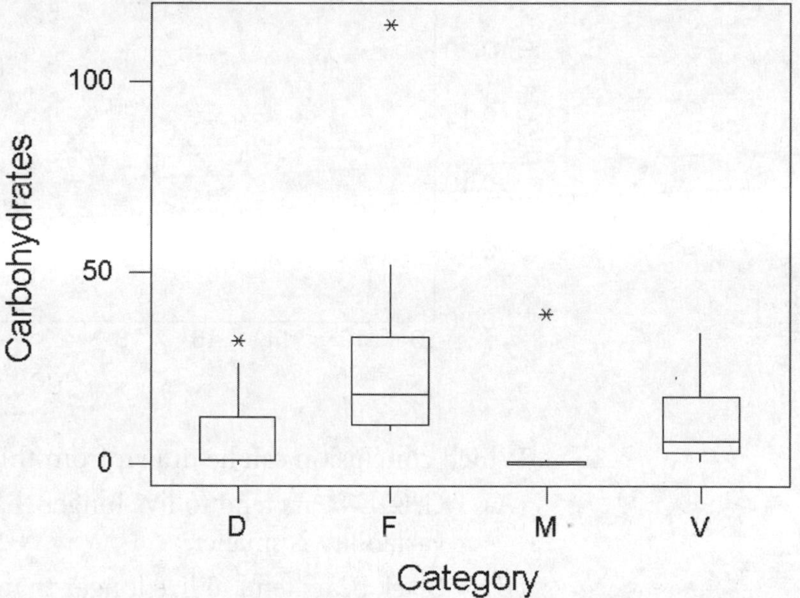

Which of the four food categories would have the smallest value for *all* measures of spread?
    (A) Dairy
    (B) Fruit
    (C) Meats
    (D) Vegetables
    (E) Meats with the outlier removed

24. The correlation between the depth (in feet) and length (in feet) for a sample of caves is found to be −0.346. If the measurement of depth is converted to meters, what will be the resulting correlation? (1 ft = 0.3048 m)
 (A) −0.627
 (B) −0.346
 (C) −0.105
 (D) 0.105
 (E) 0.346

25. Data are collected from zoos for the age at death (in years) for black bears and grizzly bears. The graphs below model the data collected from these zoos.

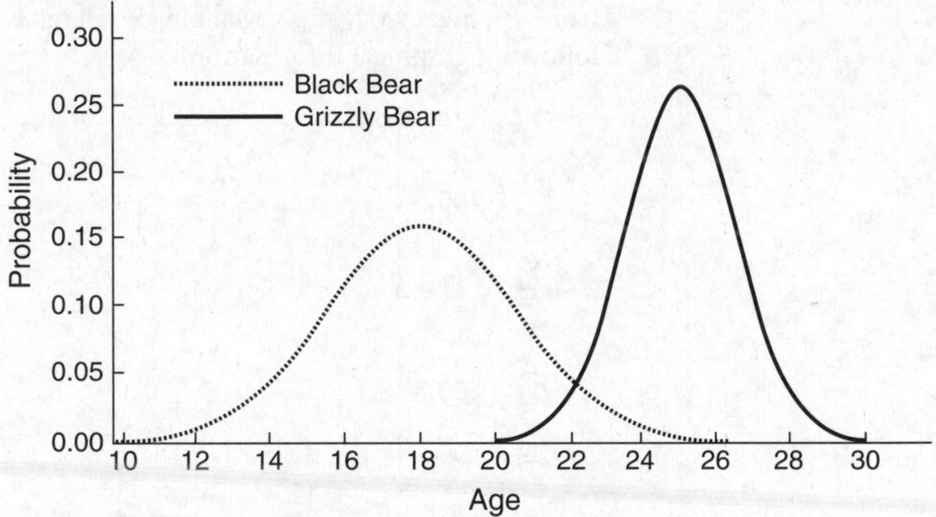

Which conclusion can be drawn from this graph?
 (A) Grizzly bears tend to live longer than black bears, but their variability is smaller.
 (B) Black bears tend to live longer than grizzly bears, but their variability is smaller.
 (C) Grizzly bears tend to live longer than black bears, and their variability is larger.
 (D) Black bears tend to live longer than grizzly bears, and their variability is larger.
 (E) Grizzly bears tend to live longer than black bears, and the two variabilities are approximately equal.

26. In a very large school district, the food services administrator wishes to determine the proportion of students who will buy a school lunch to within ± 0.03. Using the most conservative estimate for p, how many students should this administrator survey to have 90% confidence?
    (A) 164
    (B) 271
    (C) 457
    (D) 752
    (E) 1844

27. If two events, A and B, are mutually exclusive, then the probability that both A and B occur simultaneously is
    (A) 0.
    (B) 1.
    (C) $P(A) + P(B)$.
    (D) $P(A) + P(B) - P(A \cap B)$.
    (E) $P(A)\,P(B)$.

28. Which of the following is *not* a characteristic for t-distributions?
    (A) The t-distributions are mound-shaped.
    (B) The t-distributions are centered at 0.
    (C) The t-distributions have more area in the tails than a normal distribution.
    (D) The t-distributions use s as an estimate of σ.
    (E) As the number of degrees of freedom decreases, the t-distribution approaches the normal distribution.

29. Which of the following is a valid discrete probability distribution?

(A)

x	−10	−9	−8	−7	−6	−5	−4	−3	−2	−1
$P(x)$	0.1	0.1	0.1	0.1	0.1	0.1	0.1	0.1	0.1	0.1

(B)

x	−2	1	2	4
$P(x)$	0.2	0.6	0.2	0.1

(C)

x	1	2	3
$P(x)$	0.3	0.2	0.1

(D)

x	1	2	3	4
$P(x)$	0.1	0.2	0.3	−0.1

(E)

x	−2	−1	1	2
$P(x)$	−0.3	−0.2	0.2	0.3

30. For a given school year, a reporter has been told that the average teacher's salary was \$59,500 with a standard deviation of \$17,200. The reporter also knows that teachers will be receiving raises of 3.25% for the next school year. What would the reporter write for the new average teacher's salary and standard deviation?
    (A) mean \$1934; standard deviation \$559
    (B) mean \$59,500; standard deviation \$17,200
    (C) mean \$59,500; standard deviation \$17,759
    (D) mean \$61,434; standard deviation \$17,200
    (E) mean \$61,434; standard deviation \$17,759

31. The average life expectancy for a male in eastern Africa is 45 years. Ten years ago, a major health organization opened a health clinic in a large village located in eastern Africa. The organizers believe the life expectancy for this village has increased as a result of the health care. What are the appropriate hypotheses for a significance test?
    (A) H_0: $\mu = 45$; H_a: $\mu \neq 45$
    (B) H_0: $\mu = 45$; H_a: $\mu > 45$
    (C) H_0: $\mu = 45$; H_a: $\mu < 45$
    (D) H_0: $\mu \neq 45$; H_a: $\mu = 45$
    (E) H_0: $\mu > 45$; H_a: $\mu = 45$

32. Since many individuals walk around their homes in their socks, a manufacturer has created a material for socks that is believed to be more resistant to wear than cotton. The manufacturer wishes to test this belief over a period of a month. Given a group of volunteers, which of the following designs will *best* test this new material's resistance to wear?
    (A) Have the volunteers wear the socks made from the new material for a month, and check the wear on the socks at the end of the month.
    (B) Allow half of the volunteers to wear cotton socks, while the other half wear socks made of the new material. Compare the wear on the socks at the end of the month.
    (C) Randomly assign half of the volunteers to wear cotton socks, while the other half wear socks made of the new material. Compare the wear on the socks at the end of the month.
    (D) Randomly assign half of the volunteers to wear cotton socks, while the other half wear socks made of the new material. At the end of two weeks, the volunteers should change sock types. Compare the wear on the socks at the end of the month.
    (E) For each volunteer, randomly choose which foot wears a cotton sock, while the other foot wears a sock made of the new material. Compare the wear on the socks at the end of the month.

33. Given the information below, which of the statements is true?

X	2	4	6	8	10
$P(X)$	0.3	0.2	0	0.4	0.1

(A) The expected value of the random variable is 6.
(B) The expected value of the random variable is 0.
(C) The variance of the random variable is 1.
(D) The expected value of the random variable is 11.6.
(E) The variance of the random variable is 8.64.

34. Residual plots and their corresponding linear regression equations are shown for a set of data. Using the equation with the best fit, find the predicted value of y when $x = 7$.

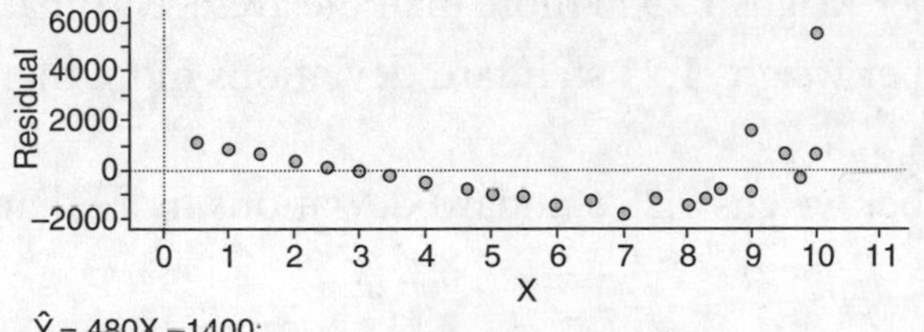

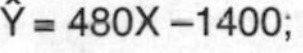

$\hat{Y} = 480X - 1400;$

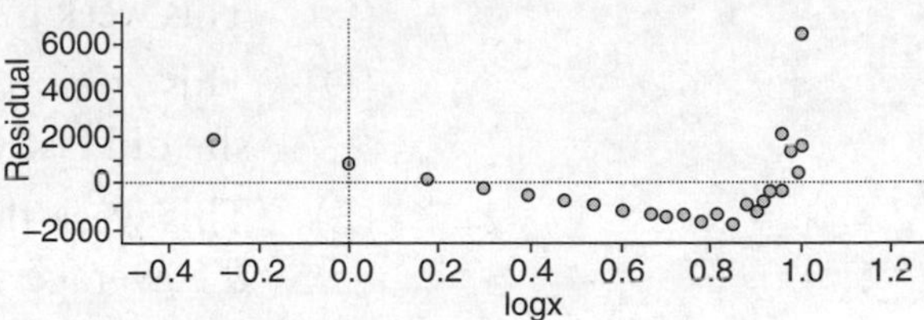

$\hat{Y} = 3310\log x - 850;$

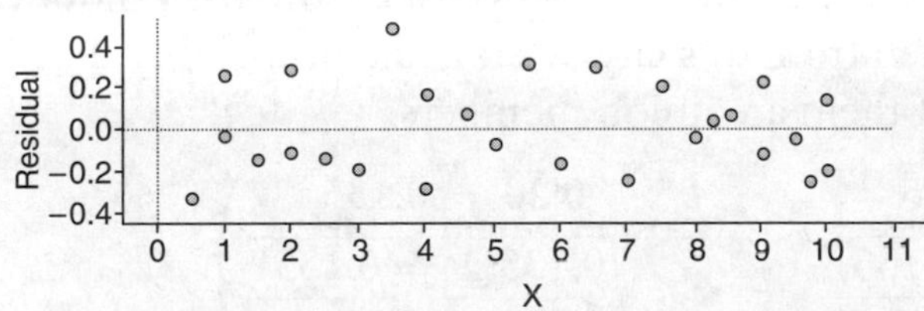

$\log\hat{y} = 0.387X - 0.051;$

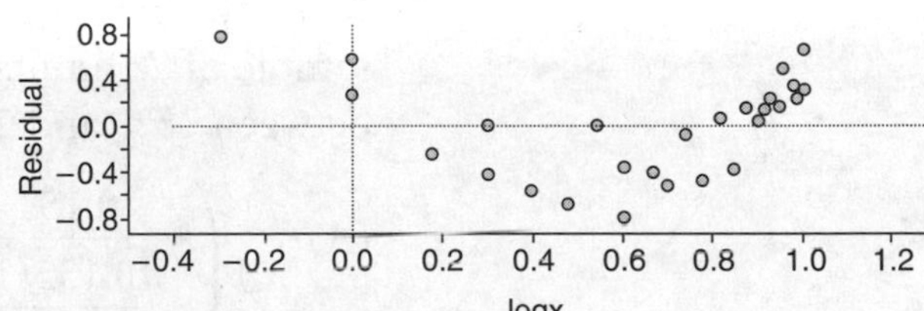

$\log\hat{y} = 3.27\log x + 0.011;$

(A) 454.988
(B) 594.936
(C) 1947.275
(D) 1960.000
(E) Not enough information is given to determine the predicted value for y.

35. A university is proposing a new procedure for professors to gain tenure. To gauge sentiment about the proposal, the university intends to randomly sample five professors, five assistant professors, five associate professors, five adjunct professors, and five visiting professors. This is an example of what type of sampling design?
   (A) Simple random sample
   (B) Stratified random sample
   (C) Systematic random sample
   (D) Cluster sample
   (E) Convenience sample

36. The weights of women are approximately normally distributed. This week, the *z*-score of weight for a member of a weight-watching group is 1.25. Which of the following is a correct interpretation of this *z*-score?
   (A) This week the member weighs 1.25 lb more than last week.
   (B) This week the member weighs 1.25 lb less than last week.
   (C) This week the member weighs 1.25 lb more than the average woman.
   (D) This week the member weighs 1.25 standard deviations more than she did last week.
   (E) This week the member weighs 1.25 standard deviations more than the average woman.

37. In a city, 13.5% of the labor force are members of a union. If a random sample of 75 adults is taken from this city, what is the probability that between 15% and 20% of them are union members?

   (A) $$P\left(\frac{0.15 - 0.135}{\sqrt{\frac{0.135(1 - 0.135)}{75}}} < z < \frac{0.20 - 0.135}{\sqrt{\frac{0.135(1 - 0.135)}{75}}}\right)$$

   (B) $$P\left(\frac{0.15 - 0.135}{\sqrt{\frac{0.15(1 - 0.15)}{75}}} < z < \frac{0.20 - 0.135}{\sqrt{\frac{0.15(1 - 0.15)}{75}}}\right)$$

   (C) $$P\left(\frac{0.15 - 0.135}{\sqrt{\frac{0.15(1 - 0.15)}{75}}} < z < \frac{0.20 - 0.135}{\sqrt{\frac{0.2(1 - 0.2)}{75}}}\right)$$

   (D) $$P\left(\frac{0.15 - 0.135}{\sqrt{\frac{0.2(1 - 0.2)}{75}}} < z < \frac{0.20 - 0.135}{\sqrt{\frac{0.2(1 - 0.2)}{75}}}\right)$$

   (E) $$P\left(\frac{0.135 - 0.15}{\sqrt{\frac{0.15(1 - 0.15)}{75}}} < z < \frac{0.135 - 0.2}{\sqrt{\frac{0.2(1 - 0.2)}{75}}}\right)$$

38. Having read about the positive effects of gingko biloba on memory, some precocious statistics students decide to conduct their own experiment to test the herb's effects. Close to 50 of their classmates, all in good health and representing a variety of ethnic groups, volunteer to take part in the experiment, and the students randomly assign half of the volunteers to take gingko. The other half take a placebo. The students perform a memory test on the volunteers at the beginning of the experiment and a second test eight weeks later. After analyzing their results, they find no memory improvement in the gingko group versus the placebo group. Assuming the students followed all aspects of good experimental design, which of the following can be concluded?

    (A) Gingko biloba does not improve memory, and no one should take it to improve memory.

    (B) Gingko biloba does not improve memory in healthy individuals and should only be taken by individuals exhibiting signs of dementia.

    (C) Gingko biloba does not improve memory in healthy teenagers and should only be taken by adults.

    (D) Gingko biloba does not improve memory in healthy teenagers and should only be taken by adults in poor health.

    (E) Gingko biloba does not improve memory in healthy teenagers, and further studies should be conducted to determine its effectiveness in other groups.

39. For the given boxplot, which are the correct summary statistics?

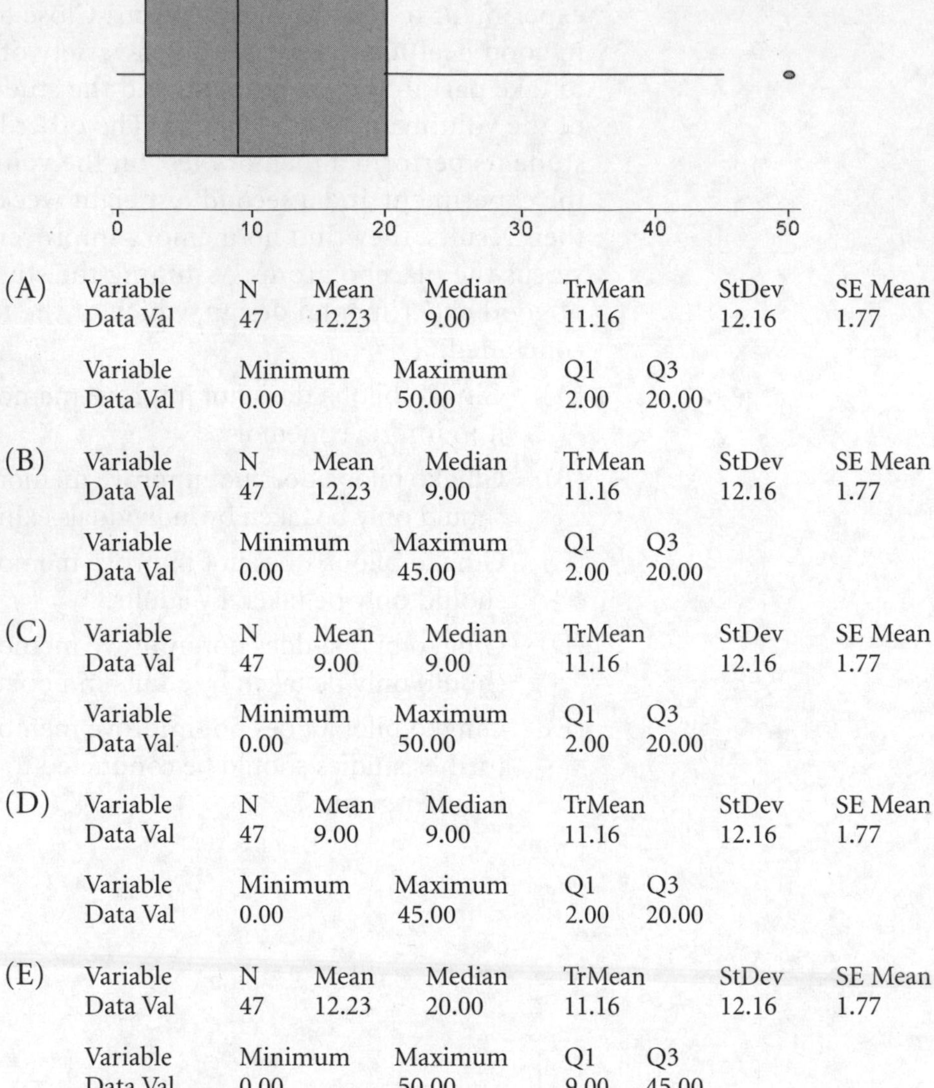

(A)

Variable	N	Mean	Median	TrMean	StDev	SE Mean
Data Val	47	12.23	9.00	11.16	12.16	1.77

Variable	Minimum	Maximum	Q1	Q3
Data Val	0.00	50.00	2.00	20.00

(B)

Variable	N	Mean	Median	TrMean	StDev	SE Mean
Data Val	47	12.23	9.00	11.16	12.16	1.77

Variable	Minimum	Maximum	Q1	Q3
Data Val	0.00	45.00	2.00	20.00

(C)

Variable	N	Mean	Median	TrMean	StDev	SE Mean
Data Val	47	9.00	9.00	11.16	12.16	1.77

Variable	Minimum	Maximum	Q1	Q3
Data Val	0.00	50.00	2.00	20.00

(D)

Variable	N	Mean	Median	TrMean	StDev	SE Mean
Data Val	47	9.00	9.00	11.16	12.16	1.77

Variable	Minimum	Maximum	Q1	Q3
Data Val	0.00	45.00	2.00	20.00

(E)

Variable	N	Mean	Median	TrMean	StDev	SE Mean
Data Val	47	12.23	20.00	11.16	12.16	1.77

Variable	Minimum	Maximum	Q1	Q3
Data Val	0.00	50.00	9.00	45.00

40. Data have been collected, and a statistician conducts a test of significance using the data. The statistician is considering the effects associated with Type I and Type II errors under these circumstances. Which of the following is true?

I. Reducing the probability of a Type I error increases power.
II. Reducing power increases the probability of a Type II error.
III. Reducing the probability of a Type I error increases the probability of a Type II error.

(A) I only
(B) II only
(C) III only
(D) I and II only
(E) II and III only

SECTION II: FREE RESPONSE
Part A

90 minutes
Suggested time: 65 minutes

1. A shipment of computer chips consists of 10,000 units. The manufacturer claims that the probability of selecting a defective unit is 0.003.
   a. How many defective units should the receiver of the shipment expect?

   b. What is the probability that the receiver of the shipment will get more defective units than expected?

   c. What is the probability that fewer than 18 units will be defective in this shipment?

2. A manufacturer has created a pole from a new material and believes that pole-vaulters can improve the heights of their vaults by using this new type of pole.
   a. In order to test this hypothesis, the manufacturer visits Kennett High School. He selects a student who is new to vaulting. He records a sample of 25 vaults where the student uses a pole made from the customary material. Then he records a sample of 25 vaults where the student uses a pole constructed from the new material. He analyzes the data and finds a significant improvement in heights with the new pole. Comment on the design of this experiment.

b. Could you improve upon the design of the experiment in part (a)? If you answer yes, describe *your* design.

c. As pole-vaulters improve their performances, longer poles become a necessity. Describe an experiment to test the new material that takes different pole lengths into account.

3. Suppose that the weights of a name-brand cereal vary normally with mean $\mu = 11.13$ oz and standard deviation $\sigma = 0.08$ oz. The advertised weight is 11 oz. For the equivalent generic brand with an advertised weight of 11 oz, the weights vary normally with mean $\mu = 11.15$ oz and standard deviation $\sigma = 0.16$ oz.

   a. For each of the brands, find the probability that the weight of a box of cereal will be less than the advertised weight.

   b. For each of the brands, find the probability that the average weight for a purchase of four boxes of cereal will exceed 11.25 oz.

   c. If you believe strongly in getting what you pay for, that is, you want to make sure you get at least the weight advertised on the box, which brand of cereal are you more likely to buy and why?

   d. If you wanted to get the most for your money, that is, you would like to get much more than the advertised weight, which brand of cereal are you more likely to buy and why?

4. Based on results from a random sample of 35 individuals, a company advertises that individuals who use its diet supplement lose an average of 4.6 lb with a standard deviation of 1.2 lb during the first week of dieting.

   a. A graph of the data reveals no strong skew or outliers. Does this provide evidence of a significant weight loss?

   b. The advertisement fails to mention that these results were part of a double-blind experiment to compare the supplement with a placebo. In the control group, the weight loss was 3.7 lb with a standard deviation of 2.3 lb in the first week of dieting. The control group consisted of a random sample of 32 individuals. A graph of the data for the control group reveals no strong skew or outliers. Is there evidence to show that the group taking the diet supplement lost more weight than the control group in the first week?

5. In eastern Pennsylvania, the peak migration for red-shouldered hawks is October 15–31. During 2001 and 2002, the owner of a mountaintop home recorded the number of these hawks that migrated past her home each day during the peak migration season. The following summary statistics resulted:

Variable	Year	N	Mean	Median	TrMean	StDev
Red Shoulder	2001	16	6.81	4.50	6.00	7.62
	2002	16	8.25	4.50	5.93	12.53

Variable	Year	SE Mean	Minimum	Maximum	Q1	Q3
Red Shoulder	2001	1.90	0.00	25.00	1.00	11.75
	2002	3.13	0.00	49.00	0.50	10.00

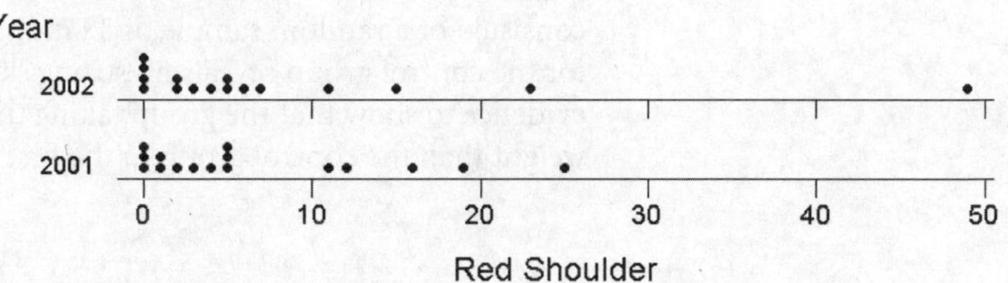

a. It appears that 49 is an outlier for 2002. Describe a procedure you would use to determine if this value is an outlier, and justify your answer based on that procedure.

b. Compare the migration of red-shouldered hawks in 2001 and 2002.

Part B

Suggested time: 25 minutes

6. A hiker records distances (in miles) and times (in hours) for a random sample of 25 of her hikes, resulting in the following information.

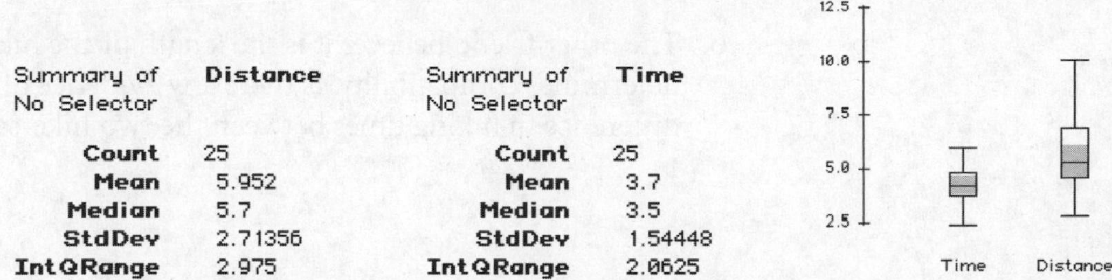

Summary of	**Distance**
No Selector	
Count	25
Mean	5.952
Median	5.7
StdDev	2.71356
IntQRange	2.975

Summary of	**Time**
No Selector	
Count	25
Mean	3.7
Median	3.5
StdDev	1.54448
IntQRange	2.0625

Dependent variable is: **Time**
No Selector
R squared = 77.3% R squared (adjusted) = 76.3%
s = 0.7515 with 25 - 2 = 23 degrees of freedom

Source	**Sum of Squares**	**df**	**Mean Square**	**F-ratio**
Regression	44.2594	1	44.2594	78.4
Residual	12.9906	23	0.564807	

Variable	**Coefficient**	**s.e. of Coeff**	**t-ratio**	**prob**
Constant	0.721346	0.3685	1.96	0.0625
Distance	0.500446	0.05653	8.85	≤ 0.0001

A friend also records distances (in miles) and times (in hours) for a random sample of 20 of his hikes, resulting in the following information.

Summary of	**Distance2**
No Selector	
Count	20
Mean	7.585
Median	7.65
StdDev	2.4577
IntQRange	3.7

Summary of	**Time2**
No Selector	
Count	20
Mean	4.5875
Median	4.5
StdDev	1.2677
IntQRange	1.375

12.5
10.0
7.5
5.0
2.5
Time2
Distance2

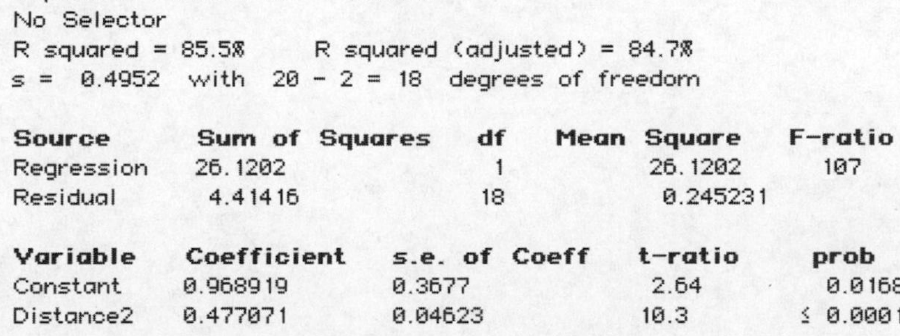

Dependent variable is: **Time2**
No Selector
R squared = 85.5% R squared (adjusted) = 84.7%
s = 0.4952 with 20 - 2 = 18 degrees of freedom

Source	**Sum of Squares**	**df**	**Mean Square**	**F-ratio**
Regression	26.1202	1	26.1202	107
Residual	4.41416	18	0.245231	

Variable	**Coefficient**	**s.e. of Coeff**	**t-ratio**	**prob**
Constant	0.968919	0.3677	2.64	0.0168
Distance2	0.477071	0.04623	10.3	≤ 0.0001

These friends are trying to determine whether or not they would be well suited to hike together.

a. One of the friends believes that hiking distances are important to determining compatibility. Is there any evidence of a significant difference in hiking distances between the two hikers?

b. The other friend believes it is the length of the hike in time that best determines compatibility. Is there any evidence of a significant difference in hiking times between the two hikers?

c. Should the two friends hike together? Use your results from parts (a) and (b) to support your answer.

d. Rather than look at the choice of hikes, which would be reflected in the distances and times of the hikes reported, a mutual friend suggests that the two should instead look at their hiking rate. This friend conjectures that hikers with rates of speed within 0.1 mph of one another make compatible hikers. Record the speed at which these friends hike. Would your answer to part (c) change if their mutual friend is correct in his conjecture?

Answers for Examination 2 begin on page 286.

AP Statistics Practice Examination 3

Multiple Choice Statistics Section I

Time: 90 minutes

1. According to the U.S. Bureau of the Census, the distribution of ages for senior citizens is as follows:

Age	65–74	75–84	85–94	95 and over
Percentage	58.0	32.2	9.0	0.8

Of a random sample of 626 senior residents from a large community, 300 are ages 65–74, 232 are ages 75–84, 92 are ages 85–94, and 2 are over 95. Is there evidence to show that the distribution of residents in the community is different from the distribution of senior citizens in the nation?

(A) There is evidence of a significant difference in distributions at the 0.10 level but not at the 0.05 level.

(B) There is evidence of a significant difference in distributions at the 0.05 level but not at the 0.01 level.

(C) There is evidence of a significant difference in distributions at the 0.01 level but not at the 0.001 level.

(D) There is evidence of a significant difference in distributions at the 0.001 level.

(E) There is insufficient evidence of a significant difference in distributions at any of the commonly accepted levels.

2. A high school administrator wishes to compare state assessment results of male and female students.

   Which graphical display *wouldn't* you recommend to him?

   (A) Comparative dotplots
   (B) Back-to-back stemplot
   (C) Scatterplot
   (D) Parallel boxplots
   (E) Histograms drawn side by side with the same scale

3. In a small town of 500, the last census reported the average family income as $34,000. Before the next census, the town wants to determine whether its average income has significantly increased. To accomplish this, a town administrator could

   (A) randomly sample 70 families, compute the average income, and perform a one-sample z-test.
   (B) randomly sample 50 families, compute the average income, and perform a one-sample t-test with 50 degrees of freedom.
   (C) randomly sample 50 families, compute the average income, and perform a one-sample t-test with 500 degrees of freedom.
   (D) randomly sample 30 families, compute the average income, and perform a one-sample t-test with 29 degrees of freedom.
   (E) randomly sample 30 families, compute the average income, and perform a one-sample t-test with 499 degrees of freedom.

4. Two random variables, X and Y, are independent. X has expected value 2.5 and standard deviation 0.3, while Y has expected value 4.7 and standard deviation 0.4. Which of the following is true?

   (A) The mean of $X + Y$ is 6.2.
   (B) The standard deviation of $X + Y$ is 0.7.
   (C) The variance of $X + Y$ is 0.7.
   (D) The mean of $X + Y$ is 11.75.
   (E) The standard deviation of $X + Y$ is 0.5.

5. Which of the following is true?

   (A) The value of a random variable must always be positive.
   (B) The expected value of a random variable must always be positive.
   (C) The variance of a random variable must always be positive.
   (D) The expected value of a random variable must be nonzero.
   (E) The variance of a random variable must be nonnegative (0 or positive).

6. In 2000, women comprised 15.1% of the Army's active duty troops. In a random sample of 100 recent graduates who enlisted in the Army, 20 were women. Construct a 95% confidence interval for the proportion of women who currently enlist in the Army, and determine whether or not this proportion is significantly different from the proportion in 2000 at the $\alpha = 0.05$ level.

(A) $0.151 \pm 1.96\sqrt{\frac{(0.151)(0.849)}{100}}$;

since 0.151 is contained in the 95% confidence interval, there is insufficient evidence to show that this proportion is significantly different than in 2000.

(B) $0.20 \pm 1.645\sqrt{\frac{(0.20)(0.80)}{100}}$;

since 0.151 is contained in the 95% confidence interval, there is insufficient evidence to show that this proportion is significantly different than in 2000.

(C) $0.20 \pm 1.645\sqrt{\frac{(0.20)(0.80)}{100}}$;

since 0.151 is contained in the 95% confidence interval, there is sufficient evidence to show that this proportion is significantly different than in 2000.

(D) $0.20 \pm 1.96\sqrt{\frac{(0.20)(0.80)}{100}}$;

since 0.151 is contained in the 95% confidence interval, there is insufficient evidence to show that this proportion is significantly different than in 2000.

(E) $0.20 \pm 1.96\sqrt{\frac{(0.20)(0.80)}{100}}$;

since 0.151 is contained in the 95% confidence interval, there is sufficient evidence to show that this proportion is significantly different than in 2000.

7. Home pregnancy test kits have grown in popularity. Research shows that only 30% of those using a particular kit are actually pregnant. When a pregnant woman uses this kit, it correctly indicates pregnancy 96% of the time. A woman who is not pregnant gets a correct indication 90% of the time. What is the probability that a woman is pregnant given that this test gives a positive result?
   (A) About 96%
   (B) About 86%
   (C) About 80%
   (D) About 36%
   (E) About 21%

8. Which of the following statements is true for the construction of a bar graph?
   (A) The scale of the horizontal axis should be the frequency.
   (B) There can be no gaps between bars.
   (C) Bar graphs are used to depict categorical data.
   (D) Mention of the shape, center, and spread should be made when describing bar graphs.
   (E) The width of the bars should differ according to the frequency of the class.

9. The histograms below represent average weekly job income for students in two high school classes.

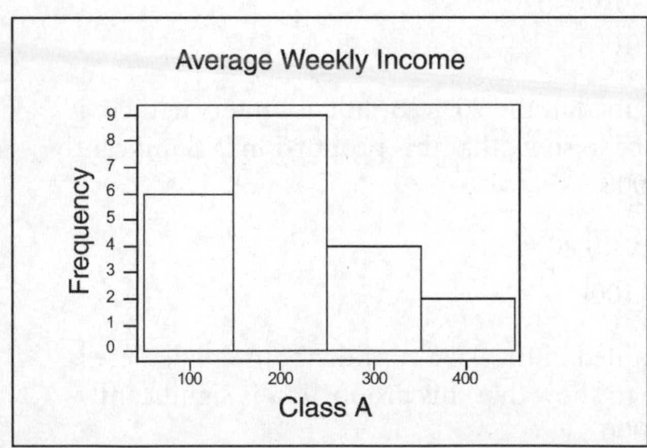

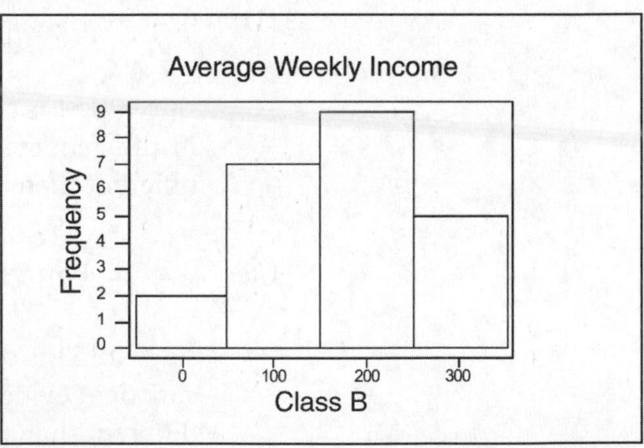

What conclusion is reasonable based on the displays? *Note:* Both classes have medians in the $200 range.
   (A) The mean weekly income for class A is higher than for class B.
   (B) The mean weekly income for class B is higher than for class A.
   (C) More students in class B earn wages in excess of $250 than in class A.
   (D) More students in class B have higher paying jobs than in class A.
   (E) All students in both classes have paying jobs.

10. Two friends, Tom and Janice, have cars in desperate need of repair. On any given day, the probability that Tom's car will break down is 0.5, the probability that Janice's car will break down is 0.5, and the probability that both of their cars will break down is 0.3. What is the probability that Tom or Janice's car will break down?
    (A) 1.3
    (B) 1.0
    (C) 0.7
    (D) 0.4
    (E) 0.2

11. In a state where young adults can obtain learner's permits for driving 6 months before their 16th birthdays, a random sample of young adults applying for their permits is taken, and their ages in years are recorded. The cumulative proportions are plotted against age, resulting in the following graph.

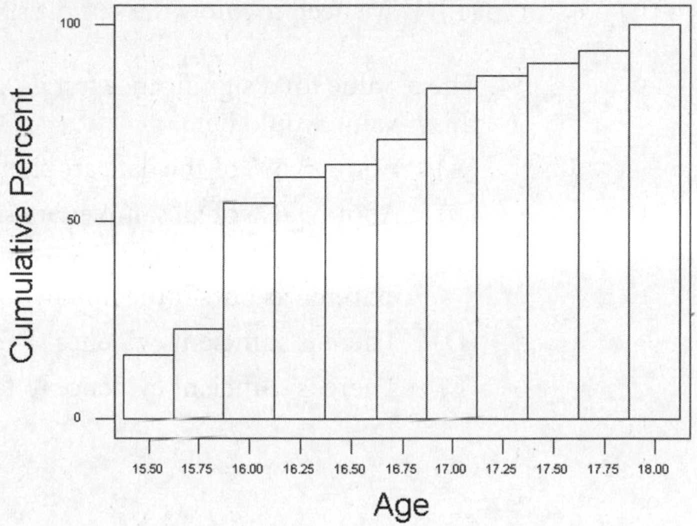

The median and interquartile range for this group of individuals are
    (A) 16 and 1 year.
    (B) 16 and 1.5 years.
    (C) 16.75 and 1 year.
    (D) 16.75 and 1.5 years.
    (E) 50 and 50 years.

12. A local senior center would like to estimate the average life expectancy for men in the local community accurate to within 0.5 year. Assuming a standard deviation of 10 years and a confidence level of 90%, how many local male death records would need to be sampled?
    (A) 33
    (B) 658
    (C) 1083
    (D) 1536
    (E) 108,241

13. In general, how does quadrupling the sample size affect the width of a confidence interval?
    (A) The width of the interval becomes four times as large.
    (B) The width of the interval becomes two times as large.
    (C) The width of the interval becomes half as large.
    (D) The width of the interval becomes one-quarter as large.
    (E) We need to know the sample size to be able to determine the effect.

14. The *p*-value for a significance test is 0.0358. A correct interpretation of this *p*-value would be:
    (A) About 3.6% of the data are significant.
    (B) About 3.6% of all samples are significant.
    (C) About 3.6% of all samples would produce a test statistic at least as extreme as ours if the null hypothesis is true.
    (D) There is sufficient evidence to reject the null hypothesis.
    (E) There is sufficient evidence to fail to reject the null hypothesis.

15. In order to ease parking problems in a community containing a university, university officials propose purchasing one acre of community parkland that is adjacent to the university to build a parking garage. The officials believe community members will overwhelmingly support this proposal, and they would like to conduct a survey of 100 community members to confirm their belief. Which of the following will produce a simple random sample?
   (A) Recording the opinion of the first 100 people who call the university regarding this issue
   (B) Randomly selecting 100 people from the local phone directory
   (C) Surveying every third person who walks past the administrative offices until 100 people have responded
   (D) Using the latest census data from the community, numbering the residents, and using a random-number table to choose 100 people
   (E) Using the latest census data from the community and randomly choosing 25 residents ages 18–25, 25 residents ages 26–39, 25 residents ages 40–64, and 25 residents ages 65 and over

16. Summary statistics are calculated for a data set that includes an outlier. If the outlier is removed, which summary statistic would be least affected?
   (A) Mean
   (B) Median
   (C) Range
   (D) Standard deviation
   (E) Variance

17. Recently, news channels in Montana and California randomly polled adults in their states about their belief that air quality was negatively affecting their health. The results showed that 5% of the adults in Montana believed that air quality was a serious problem, while in California the results showed that 43% believed the issue was serious. The reporter concluded that 24% of all adults from these two states believe there is a problem with air quality. Which of the following statements best describes the problem with this reporter's conclusion?
   (A) We do not know if a simple random sample was conducted in Montana and California.
   (B) The reporter should have stated that 48% of all adults believe there is a problem with air quality.
   (C) The size of the population in Montana differs from that in California.
   (D) The reporter should have included a statement about the margin of error with the result.
   (E) There is no problem with the reporter's conclusion.

18. Order the correlation coefficients from least to greatest for the given scatterplots.

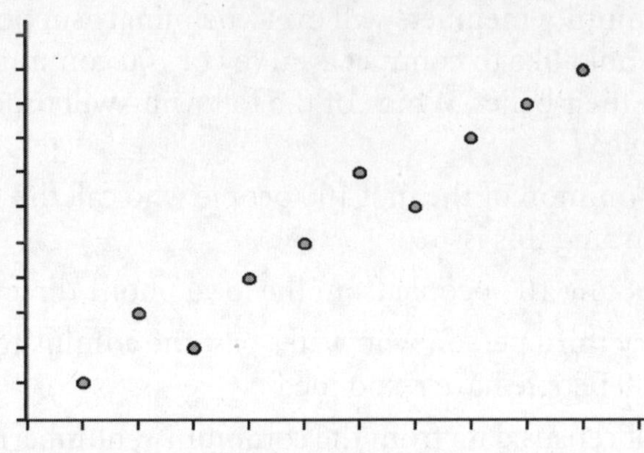

Plot 1 with correlation r_1

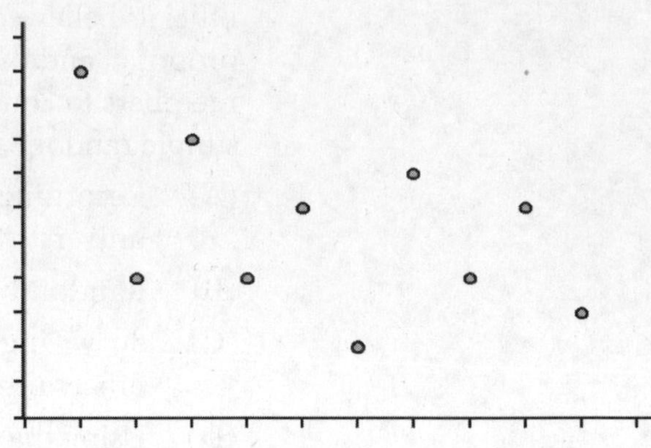

Plot 2 with correlation r_2

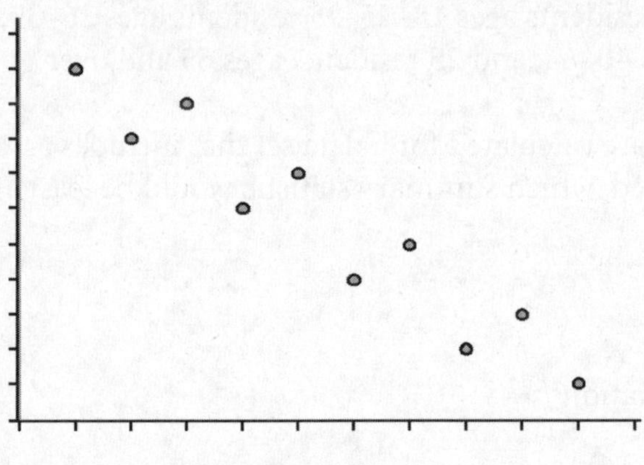

Plot 3 with correlation r_3

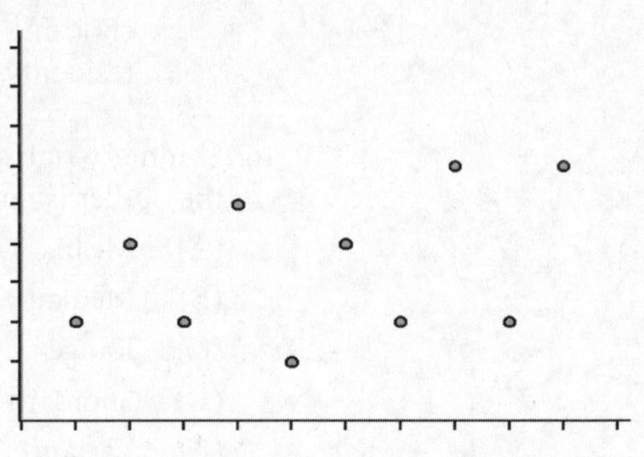

Plot 4 with correlation r_4

(A) $r_4 < r_3 < r_2 < r_1$
(B) $r_4 < r_2 < r_3 < r_1$
(C) $r_3 < r_2 < r_4 < r_1$
(D) $r_2 < r_3 < r_4 < r_1$
(E) $r_1 < r_2 < r_3 < r_4$

19. Which boxplot matches the given frequency histogram?

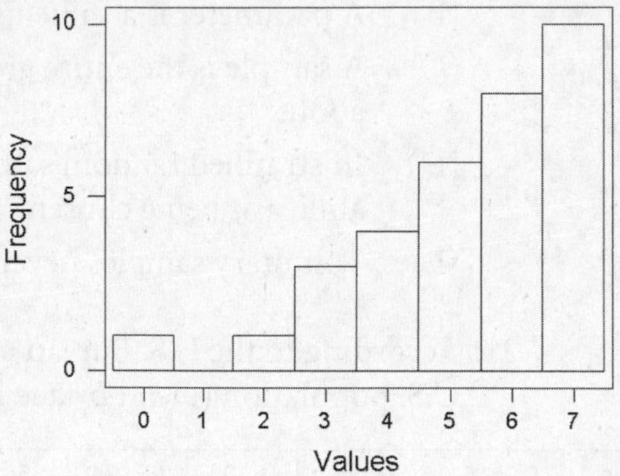

(A)

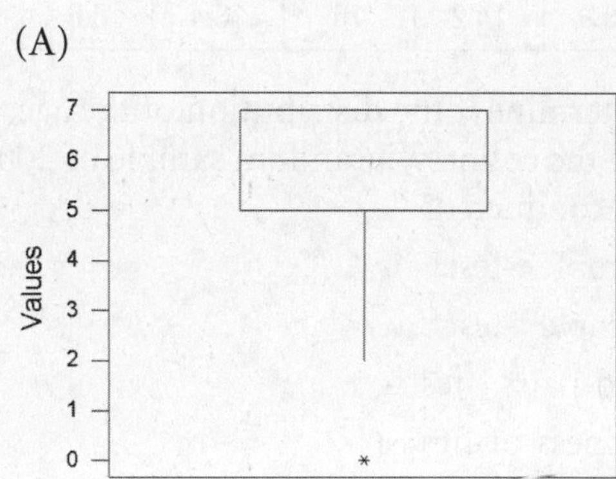

(B)

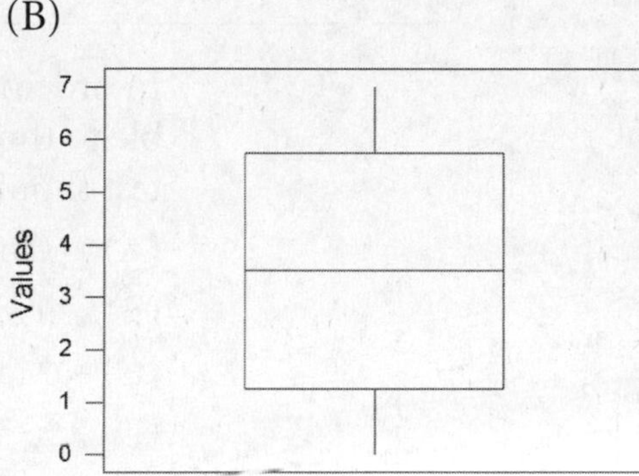

(C)

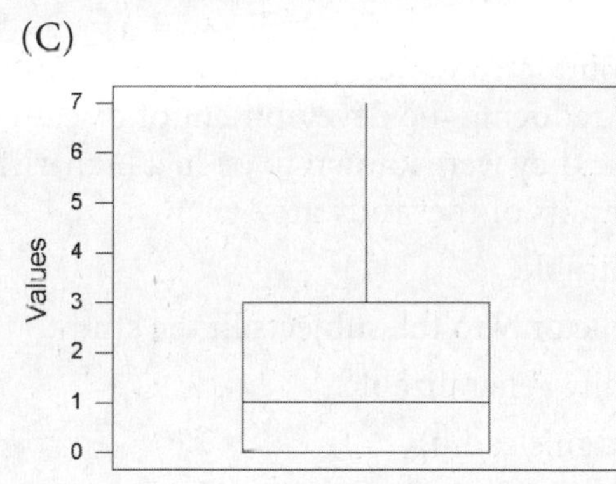

(D)

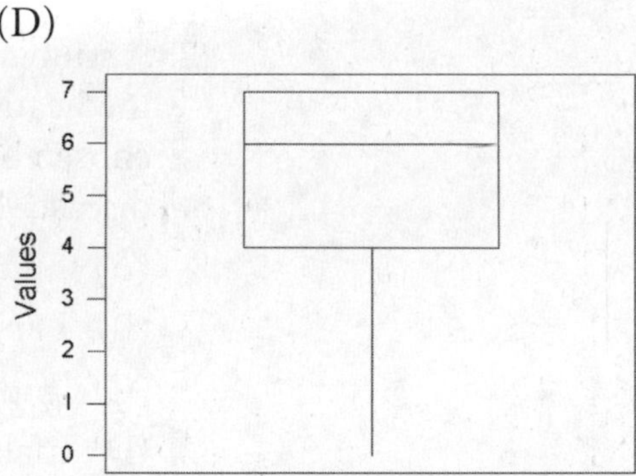

(E)

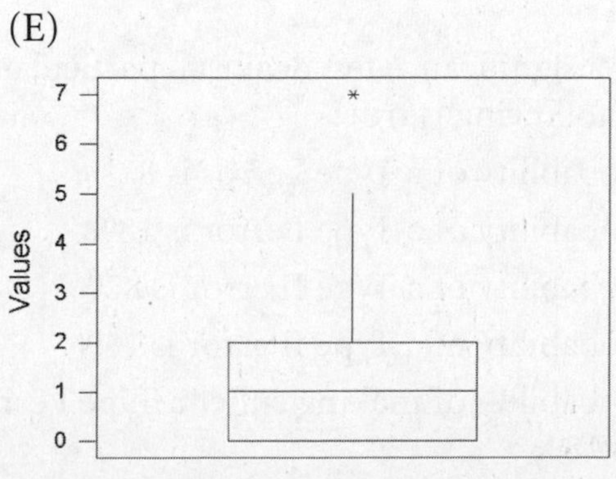

20. Which of the following statements is true?
   (A) A census is an experiment that involves the entire population.
   (B) A parameter is a value used to describe a sample.
   (C) A sample is the entire group of individuals we want information about.
   (D) In stratified random sampling, every individual has the same probability of being chosen.
   (E) Voluntary samples never introduce bias.

21. According to the U.S. Bureau of the Census, in 2000 the breakdown of the U.S. population (in %) by age is as follows.

Age	< 5	5–14	15–24	25–34	35–44	45–54	55–64	65–74	75–84	> 85
Percent	6.8	14.6	13.9	14.2	16	13.4	8.6	6.5	4.4	1.5

In order to determine if the distribution of the ages in a city are comparable to those of the country, a random sample of 200 ages are found. What test should be conducted?
   (A) One-sample *t*-test
   (B) Two-sample *t*-test
   (C) Matched-pairs *t*-test
   (D) χ^2 goodness-of-fit test
   (E) Inference for regression *t*-test

22. A study was conducted to determine the benefit of an over-the-counter medication in reducing the development of disease. Subjects selected were chosen because they were known to be in a high-risk group for the disease. The results of the study are
   (A) not replicable.
   (B) applicable only to the subjects in the study.
   (C) not readily generalizable.
   (D) false and misleading.
   (E) valid for all takers of this over-the-counter medication.

23. The power of a significance test against a particular alternative is 82%. Which of the following is true?
   (A) The probability of a Type I error is 82%.
   (B) The probability of a Type I error is 18%.
   (C) The probability of a Type II error is 82%.
   (D) The probability of a Type II error is 18%.
   (E) The probability of making either a Type I error or a Type II error is 18%.

24. A t-distribution with 30 degrees of freedom is an appropriate statistical model when
    (A) constructing a confidence interval based on a random sample of size 29.
    (B) constructing a confidence interval based on two independent random samples of sizes 13 and 17.
    (C) using a t-statistic based on a random sample of size 30.
    (D) using a t-statistic based on a random sample of size 31.
    (E) we do not know μ, σ, or the sample size.

25. A random sample of 32 games is chosen for a professional basketball team, team A, and their results are recorded. The team averaged 88 points per game with a standard deviation of 8. The same is done for a second team, team B, with this team averaging 90 points per game with a standard deviation of 6. A 95% confidence interval is constructed for the difference in points scored per game between the two teams. What do the results of the confidence interval show?
    (A) We can be 95% confident that, on average, team A scores between 1.54 and 5.54 more points per game than team B.
    (B) We can be 95% confident that, on average, team A scores between 1.54 and 5.54 fewer points per game than team B.
    (C) We can be 95% confident that, on average, team A scores between 1.54 points fewer than and 5.54 points more than team B.
    (D) We can be 95% confident that, on average, team A scores between 5.54 points fewer than and 1.54 points more than team B.
    (E) The conditions necessary to find a 95% confidence interval have not been met.

26. What is the probability that on five rolls of a fair die you will roll three or more 1s?
    (A) 99.7%
    (B) 96.5%
    (C) 40.2%
    (D) 3.5%
    (E) 0.3%

27. A class of statistics students scored the following grades on a 10-point quiz: 5, 2, 4, 6, 7, 9, 8, 10, 10, 6, 7, 7, 10, 4, 2. Their teacher, who sets a passing grade at 70%, looks at the distribution and sees that it is
    (A) skewed right with about 50% of the class passing.
    (B) skewed left with about 50% of the class passing.
    (C) skewed right with about 50% of the class failing.
    (D) nearly symmetric with one outlier.
    (E) nearly symmetric with no outliers.

28. A 95% confidence interval for the proportion of female athletes in college programs is constructed based on sample data from 30 randomly selected coeducational colleges. If the confidence interval is (0.38, 0.52), we can say
    (A) 95% of the time, colleges have between 38% and 52% female athletes.
    (B) 95% of colleges have an average of 45% female athletes.
    (C) 95% of the time, the true proportion of female college athletes is somewhere between 38% and 52%.
    (D) we are 95% confident that all colleges have between 38% and 52% female athletes.
    (E) we are 95% confident that the proportion of female athletes in college programs is between 38% and 52%.

29. Given the tree diagram shown, what is the probability that event B will happen given that event A has already occurred?

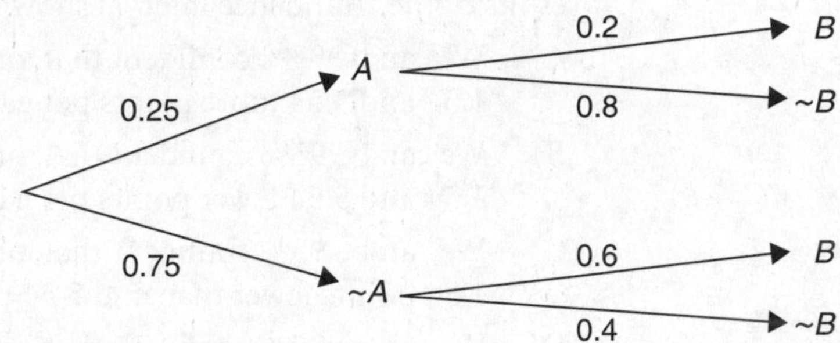

    (A) 10%
    (B) 20%
    (C) 45%
    (D) 50%
    (E) 75%

30. Patients afflicted with a debilitating disease took part in a study to measure the effectiveness of a new drug in controlling the progress of the disease. The patients were divided into two groups: an experimental group who received the drug and a control group who received a placebo. The results of the experimental group were so positive that the study was stopped early. This was most likely because
    (A) the researchers stopped getting useful information.
    (B) the researchers realized that their subjects were poorly chosen.
    (C) the researchers felt that it was too expensive to continue the study.
    (D) the researchers felt it was unethical to use only patients who had the disease in the study.
    (E) the researchers felt it was unethical to withhold an effective treatment from the placebo group.

31. Statistics students decided to analyze the relationship between hours spent studying per night and average grades on tests. Their data display is shown below.

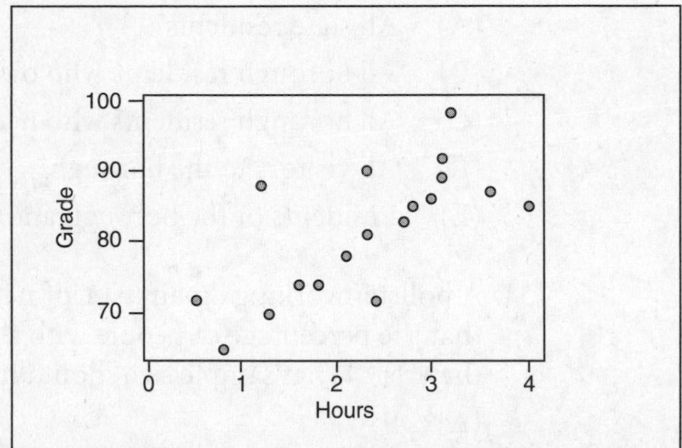

The correlation coefficient for the least squares regression line is most nearly

(A) 0.95
(B) 0.70
(C) −0.55
(D) −0.30
(E) 0.10

32. The weekly beef consumption for a random sample of 15 adults is 1.25 lb with a standard deviation of 0.39 lb. A modified boxplot of the data reveals a slight skew with no outliers. Find a 98% confidence interval for the average weekly beef consumption of adults.

(A) $0.39 \pm 2.326\frac{1.25}{\sqrt{15}}$

(B) $0.39 \pm 2.624\frac{1.25}{\sqrt{15}}$

(C) $1.25 \pm 2.326\frac{0.39}{\sqrt{15}}$

(D) $1.25 \pm 2.602\frac{0.39}{\sqrt{15}}$

(E) $1.25 \pm 2.624\frac{0.39}{\sqrt{15}}$

33. The president of a borough council is trying to determine whether or not there is a need to build a parking garage rather than a parking lot on borough property. The president conducts a survey of borough residents to assess their parking needs. What is the population of interest?
    (A) All state residents
    (B) All borough residents who own cars
    (C) All borough residents who need additional parking
    (D) All visitors to the borough
    (E) Residents of the borough and nearby communities

34. A pollster working on an issue of national importance wants to be sure that the percentage of people with a certain opinion differs by no more than 3%. What sample size should he use for the poll?
    (A) 9
    (B) 17
    (C) 278
    (D) 556
    (E) There is not enough information to determine sample size.

35. A study randomly assigned patients to treatment groups to determine the effect of taking aspirin in preventing the development of colon polyps. One group took an aspirin daily, and the other group took a placebo. Neither the patients nor the doctors knew who was getting which pill. This study is best described as a
    (A) block design with random assignment.
    (B) double-blind comparative experiment.
    (C) blinded block design observational study.
    (D) blind experiment with random assignment.
    (E) randomly assigned observational study.

36. There are 100 students enrolled in various AP* courses at Addison High School. There are 31 students enrolled in AP* Statistics, 52 students enrolled in AP* English, and 15 students enrolled in AP* French. Ten students study both AP* Statistics and AP* English, 5 students study both AP* Statistics and AP* French, 8 students study both AP* English and AP* French, and 3 students study all three AP* subjects. What is the probability that a student takes an AP* course other than these three?
    (A) 9%
    (B) 12%
    (C) 22%
    (D) 78%
    (E) 93%

37. Two professors, A and B, got into an argument about who grades tougher. Professor A insisted that his grades were lower than those for Professor B. In order to test this theory, each professor took a random sample of 25 student grades and conducted a test of significance. The graphical displays showed that each grade distribution was approximately normal. The results are recorded below.

H_o: Population mean of **Professor A** equals that of **Professor B**
H_a: Population mean of **Professor A** is less than that of **Professor B**

	Professor A	**Professor B**
Count:	25	25
Mean:	79	82
Std dev:	6	4
Std error:	1.2	0.8

Using unpooled variances

Student's t:	−2.08
DF:	41.8144
P-values:	0.022

Which of the following conclusions is/are supported by the results of the significance test?

I. At the $\alpha = 0.05$ level, we have evidence to show that every student in Professor A's class scored lower than every student in Professor B's class.

II. If there were no difference in grades between the two professors, then we could get results as extreme as those from the samples approximately 2.2% of the time.

III. The test results are not valid, since the conditions necessary to perform the test were not met.

(A) I only
(B) II only
(C) III only
(D) I and II
(E) II and III

38. An athlete has recorded his heart rate (in beats per minute) during training for several years. He wishes to determine his average training heart rate. In order to do so, he randomly selects heart rates from 15 days and calculates a 95% confidence interval from the data. If the rates are 111, 116, 118, 119, 127, 129, 132, 132, 134, 135, 138, 141, 146, 152, and 182, what is the 95% confidence interval for his average heart rate during training?

(A) $134 \pm 1.645\dfrac{17.431}{\sqrt{15}}$

(B) $134 \pm 1.761\dfrac{17.431}{\sqrt{15}}$

(C) $134 \pm 1.960\dfrac{17.431}{\sqrt{15}}$

(D) $134 \pm 2.145\dfrac{17.431}{\sqrt{15}}$

(E) The conditions for finding a 95% confidence interval have not been met.

39. Regression analysis is performed on two variables, *X* and *Y*. A residual plot is graphed, and summary statistics are found for the residuals.

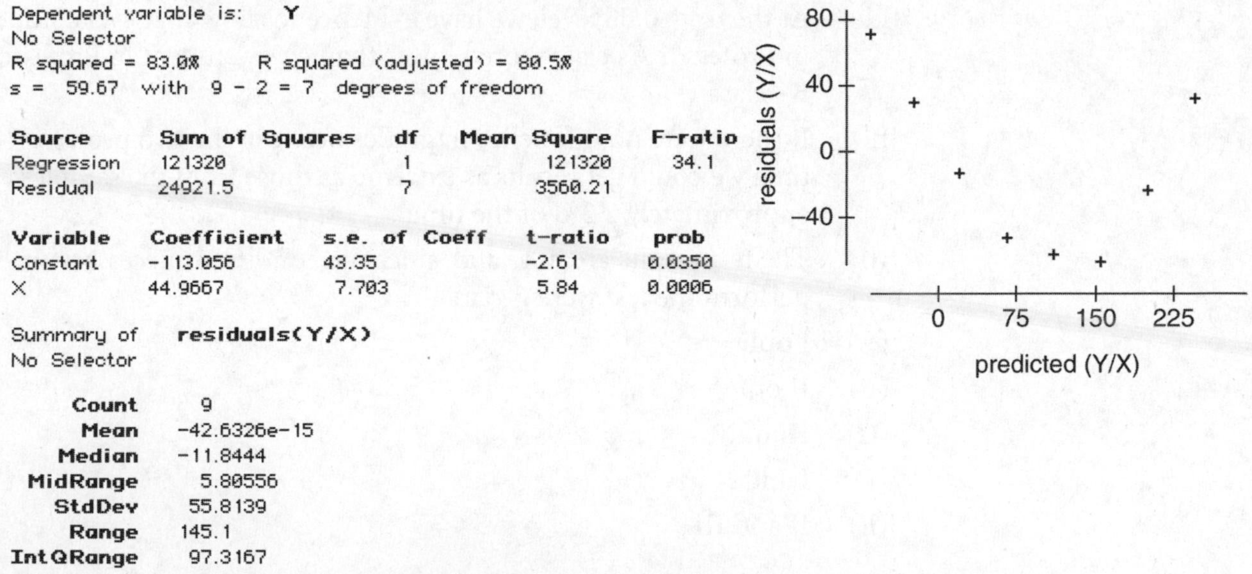

Dependent variable is: **Y**
No Selector
R squared = 83.0% R squared (adjusted) = 80.5%
s = 59.67 with 9 - 2 = 7 degrees of freedom

Source	Sum of Squares	df	Mean Square	F-ratio
Regression	121320	1	121320	34.1
Residual	24921.5	7	3560.21	

Variable	Coefficient	s.e. of Coeff	t-ratio	prob
Constant	-113.056	43.35	-2.61	0.0350
X	44.9667	7.703	5.84	0.0006

Summary of **residuals(Y/X)**
No Selector

Count	9
Mean	-42.6326e-15
Median	-11.8444
MidRange	5.80556
StdDev	55.8139
Range	145.1
IntQRange	97.3167

What tells you there is a better fit for the data?

(A) The mean residual value is 0.

(B) A significant relationship does not exist for *X* and *Y*.

(C) There is a low correlation between *X* and *Y*.

(D) There is a pattern in the residual plot.

(E) The linear regression model for *X* and *Y* is appropriate; a better fit does not exist.

40. The following information resulted from regression analysis for the percentage of white children under the age of 18 versus the percentage of black children under the age of 18 who live in poverty in several large cities.

```
Dependent variable is:     Black
No Selector
R squared = 79.5%      R squared (adjusted) = 77.8%
s =  1.072  with  14 - 2 = 12  degrees of freedom

Source        Sum of Squares    df    Mean Square    F-ratio
Regression    53.5882            1      53.5882       46.6
Residual      13.7889           12       1.14907

Variable    Coefficient    s.e. of Coeff    t-ratio    prob
Constant    30.4954        1.942            15.7       ≤ 0.0001
White       0.911941       0.1335           6.83       ≤ 0.0001
```

If the data were reevaluated using the percentage of white children as the dependent variable, the correlation coefficient would be which of the following?

(A) 0.778

(B) 0.795

(C) 0.882

(D) 0.892

(E) Not enough information is given to calculate the correlation coefficient.

SECTION II: FREE RESPONSE
Part A

90 minutes
Suggested time: 65 minutes

1. A high school administrator wants to determine whether positive reinforcement improves student performance. A group of students is randomly selected from the high school population. Their last year's records are examined for their GPAs. Beginning the first day of the school year and continuing through the first semester, the selected students receive a reward (free movie tickets) whenever they pass a major test. At the end of the first semester, their GPAs for the semester are calculated and compared with the last year's GPAs.
   a. Comment on this design.

   b. Suggest an improved design.

2. A baseball player's overall batting average is 0.320. His average with runners on base decreases to 0.275. Assuming that there is a 40% chance of a runner on base whenever the player comes up to bat, what is his batting average without runners on base?

3. If the probability that the Germantown Academy Patriots football team will lose any game next year is 0.125 and each game is independent, determine:

   a. the probability that the team's first loss will be in the seventh game.

b. the probability that the team will have exactly one loss in the first five games.

c. the expected number of games it will take to get the first loss.

4. A company rates customer satisfaction on a scale from 1 to 10, with 10 indicating the highest level of satisfaction. The company randomly selects 20 first-time customers and asks them to rate their satisfaction. The following year, after the company has made some changes in its customer service policy, a second group of 20 first-time customers is surveyed.

Before Changes	After Changes
4	7
7	3
6	7
8	6
4	5
2	5
9	8
9	9
4	10
5	7
7	7
3	5
8	9
4	7
6	6
8	9
9	10
1	7
6	9
8	8

From the point of view of the Customer Service Department Supervisor, report on the success or failure of the company's policy changes. Provide statistical evidence.

5. Male and female life expectancies (in years) are given for 15 regions of the world.

Male: 51.1, 76.0, 65.2, 63.8, 70.3, 61.3, 64.5, 65.8, 64.1, 74.9, 76.3, 76.9, 67.0, 74.2, 77.5

Female: 53.2, 83.0, 72.2, 71.5, 74.6, 62.4, 69.5, 70.3, 73.9, 81.5, 82.3, 82.7, 72.2, 79.9, 84.1

a. Create a back-to-back stemplot to compare male and female life expectancies.

b. Create parallel boxplots to compare male and female life expectancies.

c. Based on an examination of your graphical displays, write a few sentences comparing the life expectancies of men and women.

d. Give one advantage to using the back-to-back stemplot over the parallel boxplot.

e. Give one advantage to using the parallel boxplot over the back-to-back stemplot.

Part B

Suggested time: 25 minutes

6. A random sample of car owners are polled to determine how many days before (or after) their car inspection is due they wait until they get the car inspected. We let 0 represent getting their car inspected *on* the due date, and *n* represents getting their car inspected *n* days *before* the due date (3 = inspected 3 days before the due date). Summary statistics for the days are listed.

Variable	N	Mean	Median	TrMean	StDev	SE Mean
Days	20	13.65	3.00	11.28	22.09	4.94

Variable	Minimum	Maximum	Q1	Q3
Days	−5.00	75.00	1.00	18.75

a. The summary statistics show a minimum value of −5. Could this occur, or do you believe there was an error in data reporting? Explain your answer.

b. An inspection station owner believes that the average person waits until less than a week (7 days) before inspection is due to have his car inspected. What procedure would you choose to test his theory and why? (Do *not* actually test the theory.)

c. Do the data satisfy the conditions necessary to test the theory? Explain your answer.

d. The inspection station owner collects his own data on how long people wait. He randomly chooses 40 customers and records the days. The summary statistics for his data are shown below.

Variable	N	Mean	Median	TrMean	StDev	SE Mean
Station	40	12.85	7.00	11.86	13.28	2.10

Variable	Minimum	Maximum	Q1	Q3
Station	–5.00	48.00	3.00	22.00

Find a 95% confidence interval for the average number of days before inspection until people have their cars inspected.

e. The inspection station owner does not understand confidence intervals and again claims the average time is less than 7 days. State the hypotheses you would use to conduct a test of significance, but, without conducting the test, explain to the station owner the conclusions of the test and how you can be certain of these conclusions.

Answers for Examination 3 begin on Page 294.

AP Statistics Practice Examination 4

Multiple Choice
Statistics
Section I

Time: 90 minutes

1. Which of the following statements is (are) correct?

   I. Correlation makes no distinction between explanatory and response variables.
   II. The sign of r reflects the strength of the association.
   III. r measures the strength of a *linear* relationship only.

   (A) I only
   (B) II only
   (C) III only
   (D) I and II
   (E) I and III

2. In a random sample of 500 women, 120 are college graduates. With what confidence can we assert that between 22% and 26% of women are college graduates?

   (A) 2%
   (B) 4%
   (C) 14.75%
   (D) 24%
   (E) 70.49%

3. The median of a distribution is 150, and the interquartile range is 50. Identify the statement(s) that *must* be true.

   I. 50% of the data are between 125 and 175.
   II. 50% of the data are less than or equal to 150.
   III. 75% of the data are greater than 125.

   (A) I only
   (B) II only
   (C) I and II only
   (D) II and III only
   (E) I, II, and III

4. Twenty-five men were polled, and their annual incomes were recorded. The cumulative frequency histogram below shows the results.

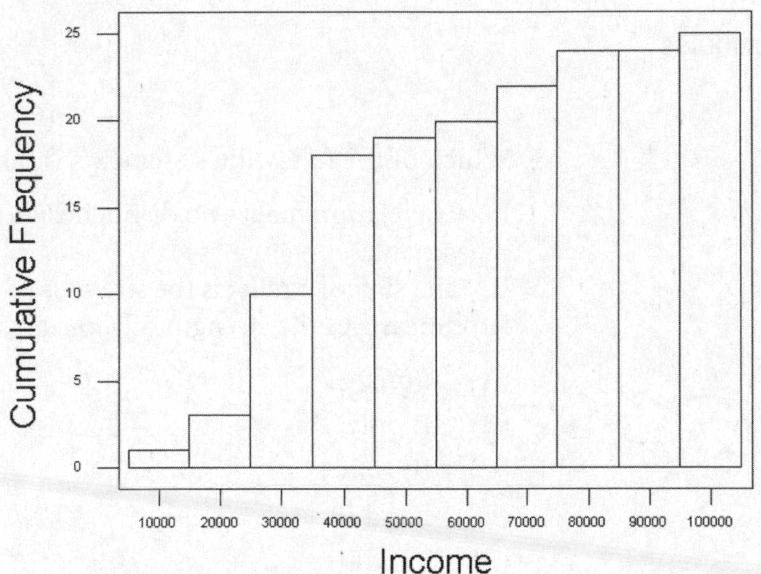

   Which of the following statements can be made upon examination of the histogram?

   (A) The same number of men had incomes between \$75,000 and \$85,000 as between \$85,000 and \$95,000.
   (B) The median income was \$55,000.
   (C) The mean income was less than the median income.
   (D) The modal income was between \$35,000 and \$45,000.
   (E) No men had incomes between \$75,000 and \$85,000.

5. Only 6 out of every 100 people have blood type O^+. What is the probability that in a random sample of individuals, the first person with type O^+ blood will be the eighth person tested?
   (A) $C(8, 8)(0.06)^8(0.94)^0$
   (B) $C(8, 1)(0.06)^1(0.94)^7$
   (C) $C(1, 8)(0.06)^1(0.94)^7$
   (D) $(0.06)^1(0.94)^7$
   (E) $(0.06)^7(0.94)^1$

6. Mr. DeVeaux teaches two sections of AP* Physics. He has 38 seniors in one section and 24 juniors in the other section. The overall mean for both sections on the midterm exam was 87. If the junior section had a mean of 92, what was the approximate mean for the senior section on the midterm exam?
   (A) 82.6
   (B) 83.8
   (C) 89.5
   (D) 87.0
   (E) 90.4

7. Which of the following is/are acceptable ways to express your decision at the end of a hypothesis test?

   I. Fail to reject H_0; accept H_a
   II. Accept H_0; reject H_a
   III. Reject H_0; accept H_a

   (A) I only
   (B) II only
   (C) III only
   (D) All are acceptable.
   (E) None are acceptable.

8. The following table gives the percentage of nursing home residents by age.

Age	under 65	65–74	75–84	85 and older
Percentage	9.8	12	31.8	46.5

In a random sample of 150 families with a relative in a nursing home, the following was the distribution of the relatives' ages: 10 under 65, 20 ages 65–74, 52 ages 75–84, and 68 ages 85 and older. If a goodness-of-fit test were performed, what would be the value of the χ^2 statistic?

(A) 0.541
(B) 0.707
(C) 2.156
(D) 2.810
(E) 28.110

9. If $P(A) = 0.7$, $P(not\ B) = 0.4$, and $P(A \text{ and } B) = 0.5$, find $P(A \text{ or } B)$.

(A) 1.3
(B) 0.6
(C) 0.8
(D) 0.1
(E) 1.1

10. If you wanted to find the average GPA for seniors at your school who have been accepted into college, what would be the most appropriate technique to use to gather the data?

(A) Census
(B) Simple random sample
(C) Stratified random sample
(D) Systematic random sample
(E) Controlled experiment

11. Given that a population has a standard deviation of 0, which of the following statements *must* be true?

    I. The standard deviation of a sample drawn from the population is also 0.
    II. The sample mean of a sample drawn from the population is also 0.
    III. The sample mean and median are equal for a sample drawn from the population.

    (A) I only
    (B) III only
    (C) I and II only
    (D) I and III only
    (E) I, II, and III

12. A meteorologist wants to simulate 20 days of weather in a region where the probability of precipitation during the season being simulated is 40%. She uses a random-number table as shown.

    23091 05892 21007 43902 62973 29940 69630 91312

    If *R* represents a rainy day and *N* represents a day without rain, which of the following could be the meteorologist's simulation result?

    (A) *NRNRR* *RNRNR* *NRNNR* *NRRNN* 10 of the 20 days will be rainy.
    (B) *RRRNN* *RRNRR* *NNRNR* *NNRRR* 12 of the 20 days will be rainy.
    (C) *RRRNR* *RNNNR* *RRRRN* *NRNRR* 13 of the 20 days will be rainy.
    (D) *RRRNR* *RNNNR* *RRRRN* *RRNRR* 14 of the 20 days will be rainy.
    (E) There is an insufficient number of random digits to conduct this simulation.

13. The American judicial system is based on the assumption that a person is innocent until proved guilty. A defendant is accused of a crime. What is the consequence of a Type II error?

    (A) The jury finds the defendant innocent; he is innocent.
    (B) The jury finds the defendant innocent; he is guilty.
    (C) The jury finds the defendant guilty; he is innocent.
    (D) The jury finds the defendant guilty; he is guilty.
    (E) The jury declares a mistrial because an error has been made.

14. A random sample of 27 individuals is selected, and the age and income of each individual is recorded. Regression analysis is performed, with the following results.

```
Dependent variable is:     Income
No Selector
R squared = 2.0%        R squared (adjusted) = -1.9%
s =  2.734e4  with  27 - 2 = 25  degrees of freedom
```

Source	Sum of Squares	df	Mean Square	F-ratio
Regression	3.90728e8	1	3.90728e8	0.523
Residual	1.86828e10	25	7.4731e8	

Variable	Coefficient	s.e. of Coeff	t-ratio	prob
Constant	27300.4	1.576e4	1.73	0.0956
Age	244.203	337.7	0.723	0.4763

Is there a significant relationship between age and income?

(A) A significant relationship exists between age and income at the $\alpha = 0.10$ level but not at the $\alpha = 0.05$ level.

(B) A significant relationship exists between age and income at the $\alpha = 0.05$ level but not at the $\alpha = 0.01$ level.

(C) A significant relationship exists between age and income at the $\alpha = 0.01$ level but not at the $\alpha = 0.001$ level.

(D) A significant relationship exists between age and income at the $\alpha = 0.001$ level.

(E) A significant relationship between age and income does not exist at any of the commonly accepted levels.

15. Suppose that 25% of horses live over 23.4 years, while 85% live less than 25.2 years. Assuming the ages of horses are normally distributed, what are the mean and standard deviation for the life expectancy of horses?

(A) mean 20.14; standard deviation 4.86

(B) mean 22.690; standard deviation 1.052

(C) mean 22.690; standard deviation 4.97

(D) mean 24.110; standard deviation 1.052

(E) Not enough information is given to find the mean and standard deviation.

16. Statistics show that 7.3% of workers between the ages of 16 and 24 earn the minimum wage or less. What is the probability that if three young adults between the ages of 16 and 24 are polled, two or more will earn the minimum wage or less?

(A) 0.0004

(B) 0.0148

(C) 0.0152

(D) 0.0627

(E) 0.0677

17. To work in the word-processing department at Dewey, Cheatem, and Howe, a large center-city law firm, you must be able to type at least 80 words per minute. The director of the human resources department is revising the job description for word processors. She believes that it is possible to adjust the typing speed upward and still have a sufficient number of qualified candidates. She takes a random sample of 15 employees from the word-processing department and gives them a typing test. The mean typing speed is 93 words per minute with a standard deviation of 7 words per minute. Assume that typing speeds follow an approximately normal distribution. A 98% confidence interval for the mean number of words typed by word processors at this law firm is (88.26, 97.74). What is the t^* critical value used to compute this interval?
    (A) 2.131
    (B) 2.145
    (C) 2.249
    (D) 2.264
    (E) 2.624

18. Two random samples from two independent populations are taken with the following results.

Sample 1	Sample 2
$n = 30$	$n = 40$
$\bar{x} = 26$	$\bar{x} = 31$
$s = 3.2$	$s = 3.8$

    The standard error of the sampling distribution of the differences of the means is
    (A) 0.594
    (B) 0.838
    (C) 4.968
    (D) 7.000
    (E) 24.646

19. Of the registered voters in a community, 58% are female. A local politician running for office has the support of 48% of the registered women and 53% of the registered men. What percentage of the vote can the politician expect to get?
    (A) 49.8%
    (B) 50.1%
    (C) 50.5%
    (D) 58.58%
    (E) Not enough information is given to determine the percentage of support for the politician.

20. The percentages of children living below poverty levels for white and Asian children in the United States from 1987 to 2000 are given in the back-to-back stemplot.

White		Asian
	10	
	11	8
9	12	
5	13	
8 5	14	4
9 3 1	15	
9 8 3 2 1	16	4
8 4	17	5 6
	18	0 2 3
	19	5 5 8
	20	3
	21	
	22	
	23	5
	24	1

11 | 8 = 11.8%

Which of the following is a statement that can be made from an examination of the back-to-back stemplot?

(A) For every year from 1987 to 2000, the percentage of white children living in poverty is lower than the percentage of Asian children.

(B) If the outliers are removed from the distribution of Asian poverty-level percentages, the range for the distribution of white children will be larger than that for Asian children.

(C) The mean poverty-level percentage for both white and Asian children is less than the respective median value.

(D) The poverty-level percentages for both white and Asian children have increased over time.

(E) There is more variability in the poverty-level percentages for Asian children than for white children.

21. Which of the statements listed below is/are correct?

I. The slope of a regression line can be calculated from the formula $b = \dfrac{r \cdot s_y}{s_x}$.

II. Residual = actual value − fitted value

III. Causation is demonstrated by the correlation coefficient.

(A) I only

(B) II only

(C) III only

(D) I and II only

(E) II and III only

22. A set of numbers contains five values. The largest value is 500, and the range is 100. Which of the following statements is *not* true?
    (A) The largest possible value for the mean is 480.
    (B) The smallest possible value for the mean is 420.
    (C) The largest possible value for the median is 500.
    (D) The smallest possible value for the median is 400.
    (E) The smallest possible value for the standard deviation is 0.

23. Which of the following could represent the sampling distribution of sample proportions if $p = 0.40$ and $n = 16$?

(A)

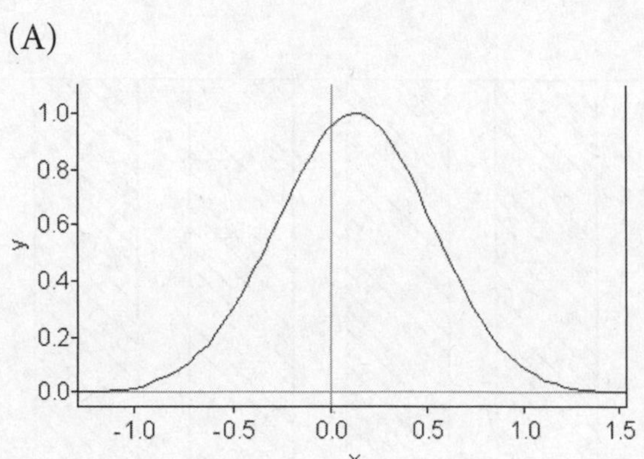

(B)

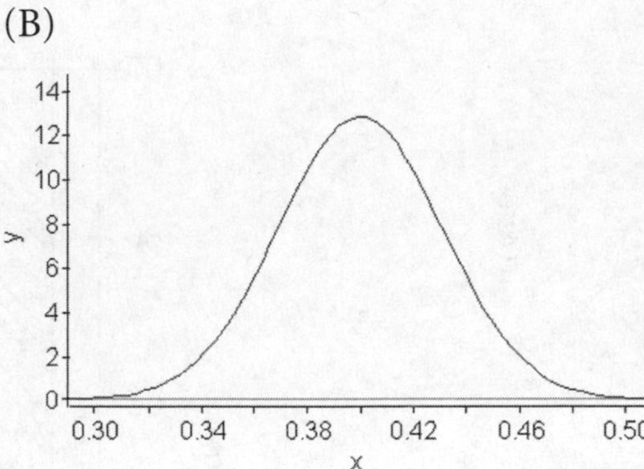

(C)

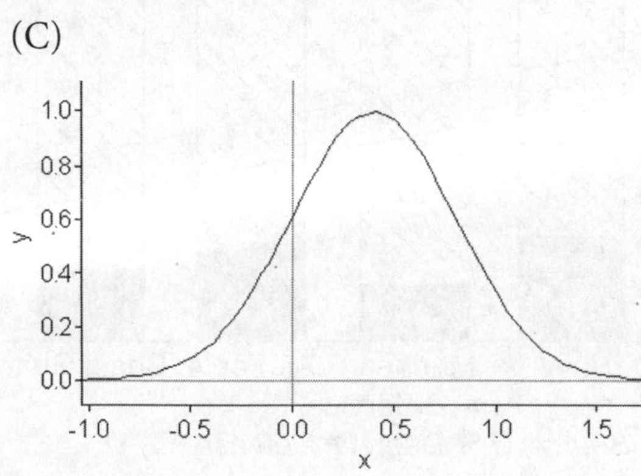

(D)

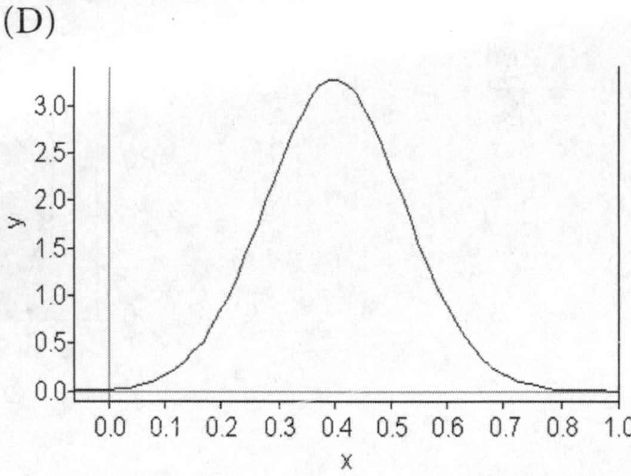

24. A population is normally distributed with mean 42.3 and standard deviation 2.8. The variance for the sampling distribution of sample means for samples of size 10 is
    - (A) 0.028
    - (B) 0.280
    - (C) 0.784
    - (D) 0.885
    - (E) 2.479

25. The breakdown of percentages of men and women in the various branches of the armed services is given in the following segmented bar graph.

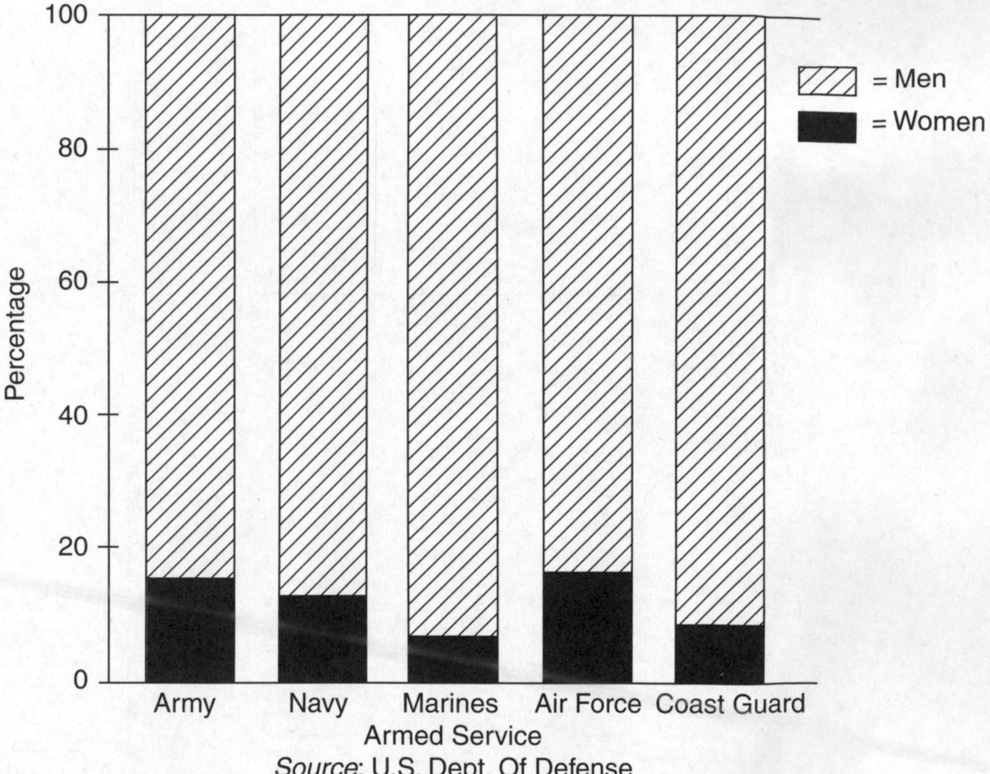

Which of the following can be stated from an observation of the chart?
- (A) The number of women in the Marines is less than the number of women in any other armed service.
- (B) The number of men in the Air Force is less than the number of men in any other armed service.
- (C) The percentage of women in the Marines is less than the percentage of women in any other armed service.
- (D) The proportion of men in each of the services is the same.
- (E) The percentage of women in the armed services is changing over time.

26. If $P(B) = 0.4$ and $P(A \cap B) = 0.21$, then find $P(A)$ if A and B are independent.
    (A) 0.084
    (B) 0.475
    (C) 0.525
    (D) 0.600
    (E) Not possible

27. For Hospital A, the average waiting time (time between walking in the door and seeing a doctor) in the emergency room is 135 minutes with a standard deviation of 45 minutes. For Hospital B, the average waiting time in the emergency room is 90 minutes with a standard deviation of 22.5 minutes. In which hospital are you more likely to wait less than 45 minutes? Assume the distributions of waiting times are normally distributed.
    (A) Hospital B, because the average wait-time is only 90 minutes, rather than 135 minutes in Hospital A.
    (B) Hospital A, because with twice the standard deviation of Hospital B, it has twice the spread.
    (C) Neither, because for both hospitals, the probability of waiting less than 45 minutes is 2.275%.
    (D) Neither, because for both hospitals, the probability of waiting less than 45 minutes is 97.725%.
    (E) It is impossible for any patient to wait less than 45 minutes in either hospital unless the patient is in critical condition.

28. Suppose the adult unemployment rate of a city is 4.8%. If you had taken a survey of 100 adults and constructed a 95% confidence interval for the proportion of unemployed adults, which of the following would have been true?
    (A) The interval would have contained 4.8%.
    (B) The center of the interval would have been 4.8%.
    (C) You would have had a 95% probability that the interval contained 4.8%.
    (D) Increasing the sample size would have ensured capturing 4.8%.
    (E) Approximately 95% of similarly constructed intervals would have captured 4.8%.

29. A recent news program reported that the presidential approval rate was 51% with a margin of error of ±4%.

What is meant by ±4%?

(A) 4% of the respondents were undecided.

(B) The proportion of Americans who approve of the president is between 49% and 53%.

(C) The president's approval rating from those sampled was between 47% and 55%.

(D) The proportion of Americans who approve of the president is between 47% and 55%.

(E) Unless the true proportion of Americans who approve of the president is between 47% and 55%, it is unlikely we could have obtained these sample results.

30. An aspirin maker claims that 4 out of 5 doctors recommend its product. A consumer advocacy group believes the proportion is lower. To test the claim, a random sample of 50 doctors is selected, and 35 recommend this manufacturer's product. An appropriate test outcome is

(A) $z = -1.768$ and $p = 0.039$

(B) $z = -1.768$ and $p = 0.077$

(C) $z = -1.768$ and $p = 0.961$

(D) $t = -1.768$ and $p = 0.042$

(E) $t = -1.758$ and $p = 0.083$

31. Ruth plans to sell the jewelry she makes at an outdoor craft festival this coming Saturday. Based on her experience from past years, she can expect to make a profit of $400 if it is a sunny day, $275 if the weather is overcast, and $100 if it is raining. The weather forecaster (based on historical records) has estimated the chance of a sunny day for the day of the craft festival to be 0.65, the chance of an overcast day to be 0.15, and the chance of a rainy day to be 0.20. What is Ruth's expected profit from the sale of her jewelry?

(A) $400.00

(B) $321.25

(C) $275.00

(D) $258.33

(E) $100.00

38. A χ^2-distribution with 14 degrees of freedom is a correct model for
    (A) a comparison of the production percentage distribution of 7 car model colors with the statistically determined national preferences for those colors.
    (B) testing the question of whether 14 genetic traits are equally distributed in a population.
    (C) testing whether choice of color is independent of age among 3 age groups and 5 color choices.
    (D) testing whether the choice to smoke cigarettes or not to smoke cigarettes is independent of ethnicity among 7 different ethnic groups.
    (E) a comparison of the equality of proportions of 8 sports activities for 3 high school grade levels.

39. Starting time for hourly wage employees at a large manufacturing plant is 7 A.M. If an employee clocks in before 7:15 A.M., he is not marked as being late for work and his pay is not reduced. A random sample of 15 daily time sheets from the past two years showed that the average number of employees who arrived at work between 7 A.M. and 7:15 A.M. each day was 23 with a standard deviation of 6. Assume that the assumptions for inference have been met. Construct a 90% confidence interval for the mean number of employees who arrive at work during this time frame each day.
    (A) 23 ± 2.728
    (B) 23 ± 3.315
    (C) 23 ± 2.630
    (D) 23 ± 3.301
    (E) 23 ± 2.894

40. For the given probability distribution, find the standard deviation of X.

X	1	3	5	7	9
$P(x)$	0.13	0.17	0.25	0.24	0.21

    (A) 0.050
    (B) 2.621
    (C) 3.162
    (D) 5.460
    (E) 6.868

SECTION II: FREE RESPONSE
Part A

90 minutes
Suggested time: 65 minutes

1. The following table shows the number of hours spent studying for final examinations by a randomly selected group of seniors and freshmen.

Seniors	6	5	5	4	5	7	8	3	4	15
Freshmen	5	12	13	7	4	8	10	4	11	12

   a. Construct an appropriate graphical display to compare the study times for the two classes.

   b. Write a few sentences comparing the study times for the two classes.

2. The owner of a synthetic motor oil company claims that his oil maintains viscosity and protects engines up to ten times as long as petroleum motor oil in gas-powered vehicles.
   a. Describe an experimental design that would test the effectiveness of the synthetic motor oil, using viscosity as a measure of effectiveness.

   b. Describe any possible confounding variables.

   c. Viscosity is measured numerically in units called centipoise (cP). Explain what hypothesis test you would use to test whether there is a difference in average viscosity between the synthetic motor oil and the petroleum motor oil. List both your null and alternative hypotheses.

3. A triathlon is a sports competition with three distinct components. Some triathlons consist of a 2.4-mile swim, followed by a 112-mile bike ride, and end with a 26.2-mile run. The mean times (in minutes) and standard deviations for these portions of the race are recorded below.

Component	Mean	Standard Deviation
Swim	75.465	12.378
Bike	403.506	45.023
Run	287.497	49.894

a. In a recent event, the fastest swimming time recorded was 49 minutes. If the swimming times are normally distributed, what is the probability that a randomly chosen triathlete will record a time of 49 minutes or less?

b. At the same event, the slowest time for the bike portion of the race was 8 hours and 43 minutes. If the bike times are normally distributed, what is the probability that a randomly chosen triathlete will record a time of 8 hours and 43 minutes or more?

c. What is the probability that the average run time for four randomly selected triathletes will be 5 hours or less?

d. The winning time for a recent triathlon was 8 hours and 46 minutes. If we assume the times for the three legs of the race are independent, what is the probability that a person will finish the triathlon in 8 hours and 46 minutes or less?

4. A random sample of U.S. doctors was asked the question, "In general, should a surgeon diagnosed with dementia be allowed to perform surgery?" Of the 921 sampled, 83 indicated "Yes, with close supervision"; 838 indicated "No, not under any circumstance."
   a. Use this information to construct and interpret a 98% confidence interval for the number of doctors who think that a surgeon diagnosed with dementia should be allowed to perform surgery with close supervision.

   b. The same question was asked of a random sample of nurses. Of the 768 sampled, 23 indicated that the surgeons should be allowed to perform surgery with close supervision. Is there significant evidence to suggest that the proportion of nurses who feel that surgeons diagnosed with dementia should be allowed to perform surgery under close supervision is less than the proportion of doctors? Give statistical evidence to support your decision.

5. A manufacturer of potato chips produces large bags of chips. The production weight is approximately normally distributed with a mean of 14.8 oz and a standard deviation of 1.2 oz.
   a. What is the probability of obtaining a bag of this company's chips that weighs less than 14 oz?

b. Round the value you obtained in part (a) to the nearest hundredth. Explain how you would conduct a simulation using the random-number table displayed below to estimate the number of bags of chips you would have to buy before obtaining one that weighs less than 14 oz. Perform your simulation seven times. Start at the leftmost digit in the first row and move across. By marking directly on or above the table, make your procedure clear enough that someone can follow what you did. Record the number of bags of chips for each of your trials.

9 2 1 9 5 6 6 8 0 3 3 1 8 2 5 6 4 6 5 1 0 5 8 2 0 9 3 9

2 3 9 8 9 2 4 8 8 7 9 3 3 2 0 3 6 2 5 0 9 4 4 3 1 1 7 6

8 4 1 6 1 4 0 3 9 7 0 1 9 8 3 7 6 7 9 3 2 6 8 3 2 8 2 3

c. Based on your results in part (b), what is the expected number of bags of potato chips you will have to buy before finding one that weighs less than 14 oz?

Part B

Suggested time: 25 minutes

6. A store that sells cellular telephones opened for business twelve years ago. Total sales of cellular telephones for each year of business are given.

Year	1	2	3	4	5	6	7	8	9	10	11	12
Units Sold	375	566	671	1106	1311	1283	2136	2967	4094	4572	5157	6621

a. Record and interpret the slope of the least squares regression line that describes the relationship between the number of cellular telephones sold and the business year.

b. Record and interpret the value of the correlation coefficient for the year of business and the number of cell phones sold.

c. Use this model to predict the number of cell phones the store will sell in the next business year.

d. Describe any shortcomings you see in this model.

e. Find a better model for predicting the number of units sold for a given business year. Justify your choice, and use three decimal places for your slope and intercept coefficients.

f. Use your model from part (e) to predict the number of cell phones the store will sell in the next business year.

Answers for Examination 4 begin on page 304.

Solutions

Answers to Review Questions for Topic 1

<u>*Multiple Choice*</u>

1. D

   An outlier is any value outside the range of
   Q1 − 1.5 (IQR), Q3 + 1.5 (IQR)
   315 − 1.5 (460), 775 + 1.5 (460)

2. D

   Since the outlier boundaries are −375 and 1465 (from the previous question), the maximum is clearly an outlier. The minimum is not an outlier. It cannot be known how many more outliers may exist without access to the original data set.

3. A

   Rel. Freq. (SA) $= \dfrac{7}{34}$, and Rel. Freq. (SD + D) $= \dfrac{2 + 7}{34} = \dfrac{9}{34}$. The difference is $\dfrac{2}{34} \approx 0.059$.

4. D

   Since there are a total of 50 values, half the values (25/50 or 50%) are less than 110.

5. B

   The five-number summary defines a boxplot. The minimum is the first ordered piece of data, approximately 450. 25% of the data falls below the first quartile (about 560), 50% below the median (slightly more than 600), and 75% below the third quartile (about 660). The maximum is the last data point in an ordered set of data, approximately 775. Remember that an ogive is a *cumulative* relative frequency graph.

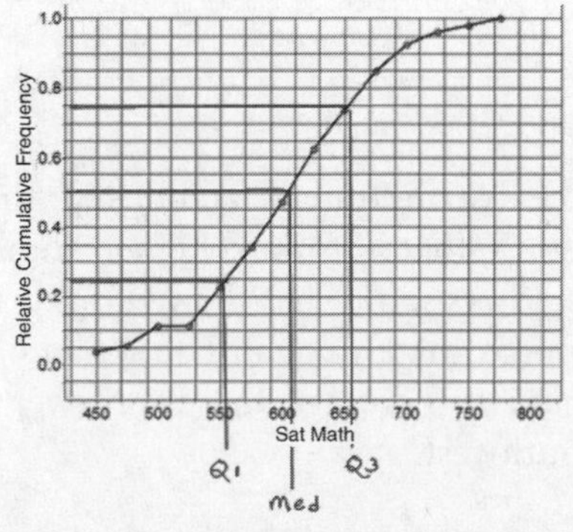

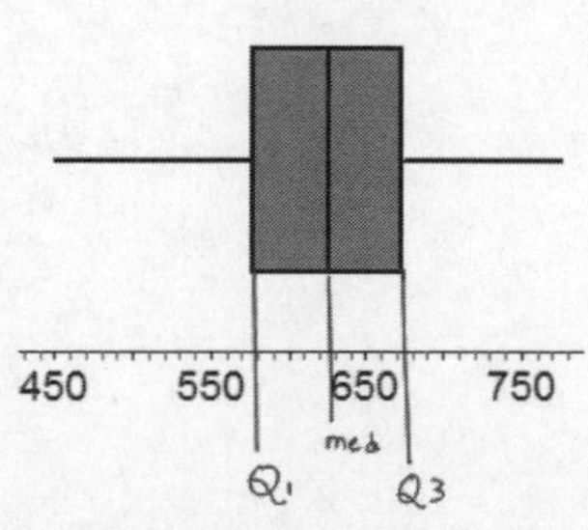

6. B

The Empirical Rule says that approximately 68% of the data will lie *within* one standard deviation of the mean. Since 20–25 is one standard deviation to the *left* of the mean, then approximately 34% of the data will lie between these values.

7. B

$Z = \frac{x - \mu}{\sigma} = \frac{45 - 50}{8}$. All other choices are correct. Note that in choice D, the presence of $\geq$ does not affect the area under the normal curve.

8. D

Using the calculator, *normalcdf* $(-2.31, 1.8) = 0.9536$. Using the table, $P(z < 1.8) - P(z < -2.31) = 0.9641 - 0.0104 = 0.9537$. Both answers round to 0.954. Remember that the probability that $z =$ any *particular* number is zero, i.e., $P(z = -2.31) = 0$. Thus, $P(z \geq -2.31) = P(z > -2.31)$.

9. C

The median and IQR are *resistant* measures. They are not affected by outliers. In a skewed distribution, the mean would be pulled in the direction of the tail.

10. E

Because this is a graph of categorical (not quantitative) data, shape cannot be described. Another person graphing the same data could choose to put the categories in alphabetical order. The "shape" of their graph would be different.

Free Response

(a)

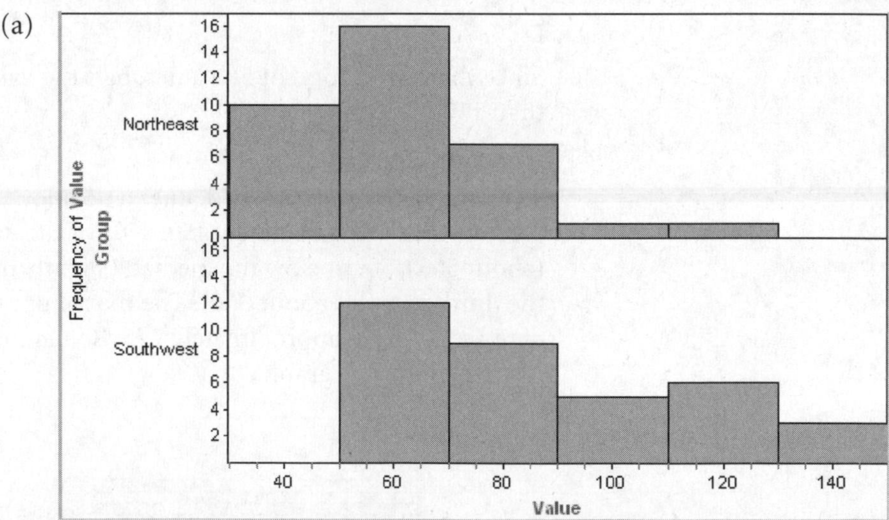

(b) The distribution of fatalities for the northeast region is skewed to the right—that is, toward higher numbers. The distribution for the southwest region is somewhat skewed right. The ranges for the two distributions are approximately equal. The center of the northeast distribution is lower—that is, on average, there are fewer fatalities in the northeast than in the southwest.

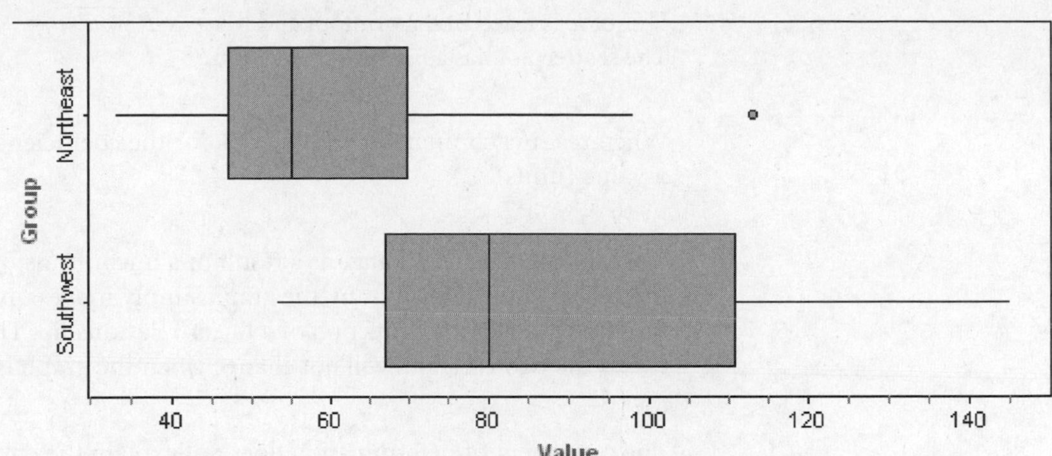

(d) It is more apparent in the boxplot that there is a high outlier in the number of fatalities in the northeast, while there are no outlying values in the southwest. While the histograms showed similar ranges, the boxplots clearly indicate that the IQR for the southwest is far greater than the IQR for the northeast—that is, there is more variability in the middle 50% of fatalities for the southwest. The median of the number of fatalities for the southwest region is higher than 75% of the fatality numbers for the northeast region, a characteristic that was not readily apparent in the histograms.

Answers to Review Questions for Topic 2

Multiple Choice

1. D

   The scatterplot shows a curvilinear pattern that appears to follow a quadratic model.

2. B

   Finding a high correlation between two variables does *not* indicate a causal relationship between the variables.

3. A

   $\hat{y} = a + bx$ or $\hat{y} = b_0 + b_1x$

   $b = b_1 = r\frac{s_y}{s_x} = 0.887\left(\frac{102.43}{22.64}\right) \approx 4.01$

   $a = b_0 = \bar{y} - b\bar{x} = 401.15 - 4.01(156.85) \approx -228.30$

4. B

   The exponential form is $y = ab^x$. When you do a linear regression using $(x, \log y)$

   $$\log \hat{y} = b_0 + b_1x \Rightarrow \hat{y} = 10^{b_0+b_1x} = 10^{b_0}(10^{b_1})^x$$

   where $10^{b_0} = a$ and $10^{b_1} = b$.

5. B

R Square is listed in the printout and $|r| = \sqrt{RSquare} = \sqrt{0.885671399} \approx 0.94$. The scatterplot has a *negative* correlation.

6. C

When reading computer printout, look for the coefficients of the intercept and x-value (units).

7. E

Correlation does not change as a result of a linear transformation. If all costs increase by the same amount, the graph simply moves up. Correlation measures the strength and direction of a linear relationship. The relationship between the two variables will not change when the graph is repositioned.

8. C

The coefficient of determination does not explain the data (the data are what they are). It explains how much of the variability in our y-variable can be attributed to its linear relationship with our x-variable.

9. A

Residuals = Observed − Predicted. Since the residual is negative, the predicted value must be greater than the observed value. If you were tempted to choose (C), remember that a predicted value, if calculated correctly, cannot be wrong. Saying that the predicted value cannot be *wrong* does not mean that the predicted value will *match* an observed value.

10. B

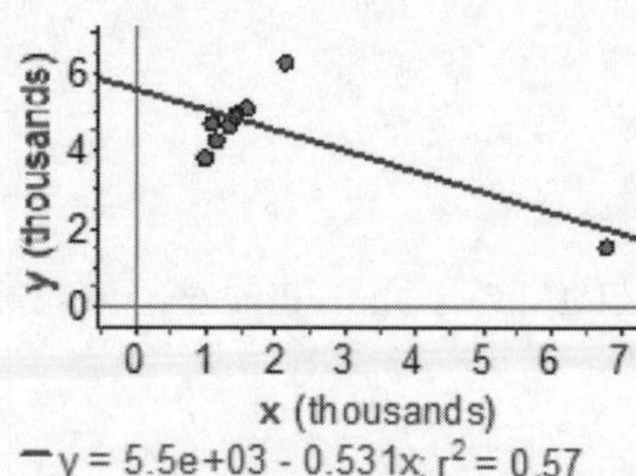

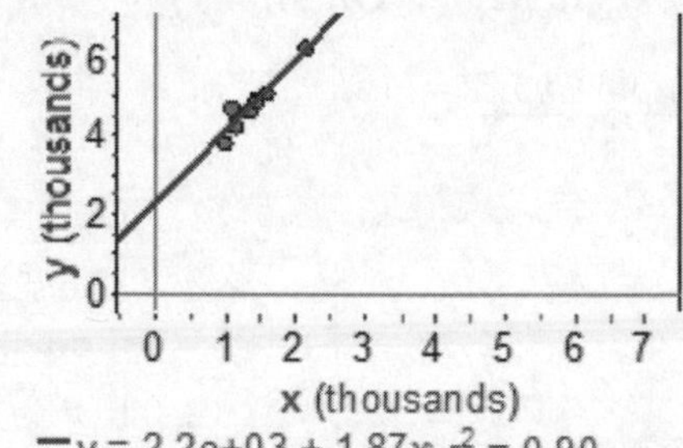

Free Response

(a)

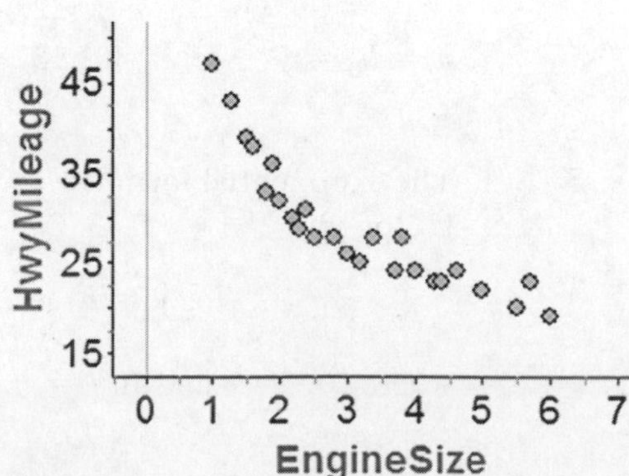

(b) $\hat{y} = 42.875 - 4.389x$, where $\hat{y}$ = predicted Hwy Mileage and x = Engine Size; $r^2 \approx 0.793$

(c) The data follow a curved pattern, so a linear model is not appropriate; furthermore, the residual plot shows a distinct pattern.

(d) $\log \hat{y} = 1.660 - 0.466 \log x$; $r^2 \approx 0.952$

Plotting (x, $\log y$) did not straighten the data enough to use a linear model. In addition, the residual plot showed a curved pattern. Plotting ($\log x$, $\log y$) made the data straighter and produced a residual plot with no discernible pattern. The r^2 value for the power model ($\log x$, $\log y$) was higher than for the exponential model (x, $\log y$).

$$\widehat{\log(\text{Hwy Mileage})} = 1.660 - 0.466 \log(8.0)$$
$$\log(\text{Hwy Mileage}) \approx 1.2392$$
$$\text{Hwy Mileage} = 10^{1.2392}$$
$$\text{Hwy Mileage} \approx 17.3 \text{ mpg}$$

We should be cautious when we extrapolate (predict outside the range of our data values) for engine size. We should not use our model, despite its strength, to predict so far outside the range of our data set. Indeed, 8.0 would be an outlier for engine size.

(e) $$\text{Residual} = \text{Actual Value} - \text{Predicted Value} \approx 32 - 33.1 \approx 1.1$$

The residual for a 2.0 liter engine is approximately 1.1 mpg.

Answers to Review Questions for Topic 3

Multiple Choice

1. E

   Because there was a treatment imposed within randomized groups, this is a randomized comparative experiment. It is best conducted as double-blind, where neither the women nor the evaluators know which individuals are taking aspirin and which are getting a placebo.

2. C

   Because the suspected variability is associated with age, the study should be blocked on that variable.

3. C

   Because no treatment was imposed, this is an observational study.

4. C

   The question asked links two ideas: the use of nuclear weapons *and* their morality. Respondents may reply yes *or* no because of one or the other of these ideas. The question is worded in such a way that it may influence the response.

5. B

Because this year's students comprise a sample of the whole population, their mean performance is a statistic. The parameter in this context would be the performance of all students in the history of the course.

6. C

We are testing to see whether handedness (explanatory variable) affects ability to memorize facts (response variable).

7. D

Since 93% of the population is right-handed, 7% is left-handed; therefore, 7 out of 100 numbers must represent left-handed teens. Since all numbers selected from the table must have the same number of digits, the easiest scheme is to use 00–06 to represent the left-handed teens. A repeat of 07–99 indicates another right-hander to be counted, so repeats of these numbers must be allowed. (For example, if 23 came up twice, it would *not* represent the same *teen* but rather another right-handed teen.) We are looking for the *first* occurrence of a number from 00–06 indicating the first left-handed teen.

8. D

Although the researchers' conclusion indicates that the average number of words memorized by left-handed teens is greater than that of right-handed teens, this result would only be considered statistically significant if the observed difference was unlikely to have occurred simply as a result of chance variation.

9. A

A sampling frame is a list of all individuals in the population of interest from which the sample is drawn. Our population of interest is college graduates ages 25 to 30 who used online social networks while in college. Registered voters in this age group may or may not fit this profile.

10. B

Randomization is a form of control that helps to distribute chance variation (possibly due to unanticipated variables not controlled for in the experiment) among all groups. If we start with treatment groups that are as similar as possible, any differences observed after treatment may be attributed to the treatment alone.

Free Response

1. There are many possible schemes for using the table to simulate the positions of the parties, but because we are only interested in the first position, perhaps the simplest is

   Let 1 = Innovators (*I*), 2 = Old-timers (*O*), 3 = Preservationists (*P*), and discard all other digits.

   One trial consists of finding the party that appears first.

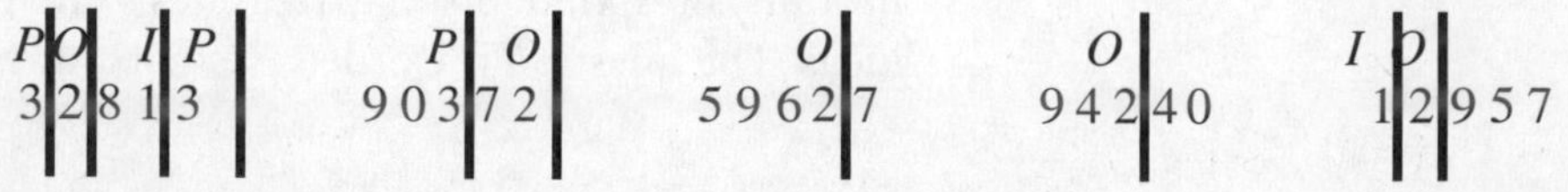

P *O* | *I* *P* | *P* *O* | *O* | *O* | *I* *O*

3 2 | 8 1 3 | 9 0 3 | 7 2 | 5 9 6 2 | 7 9 4 2 | 4 0 1 | 2 | 9 5 7

Since the Innovators appear first in 2 out of the 10 trials, the party may have some evidence to suggest that the process has been unfair. They might also point out that in this simulation, each of the three parties was selected first at least twice. More trials should be conducted, but on the basis of our limited evidence, it is likely that the Innovators would have appeared first on at least one of the ballots in the last 10 years.

2. The researchers did not take into account variations in foot dryness over time (due to seasonal variation, subjects' physical changes, etc.). A better design is a matched-pairs design in which each subject uses the new formula on one foot and the current product on the other. Randomization is accomplished by assigning the formulas to the feet. One way to achieve this random assignment is to toss a coin. Heads indicates that the subject applies the new formula to the left foot and the current product to the right. Tails indicates the opposite application. At the end of the 6-month trial, we will compare the difference in foot dryness between new formula and current product. The experiment should remain double-blind.

Answers to Review Questions for Topic 4

Multiple Choice

1. C

We wish to know the probability that the request came from a school (S) given that it came through e-mail (E). There are 164 e-mails, 2 of which came from schools, or $\frac{2}{164}$. Alternatively, by formula,

$$P(S|E) = \frac{P(S \cap E)}{P(E)} = \frac{\frac{2}{2731}}{\frac{164}{2731}} = \frac{2}{164} = \frac{1}{82}.$$

2. B

Since there are 200 athletes, we take 35% of 200 to find that 70 athletes play no contact sports.

A Venn diagram for this situation is

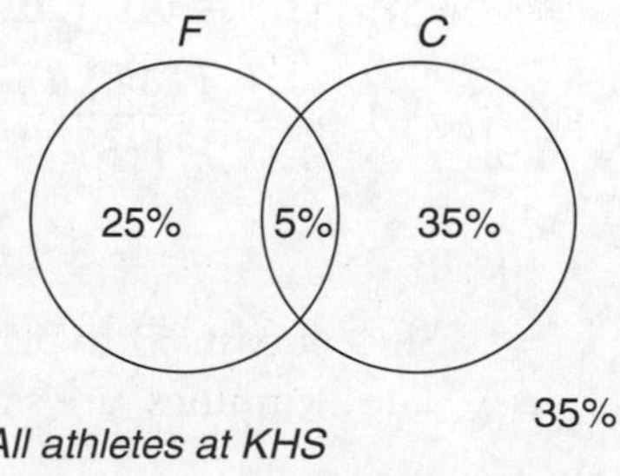

3. A

The error rate is 0.02. This is a geometric probability setting or "wait-time" problem, where we consider a "success" to be finding an error. So $p = 0.02$ and

$q = 0.98$. We want 234 "failures" prior to our first success, or $(0.98)^{234}(0.02)^1 = 0.00017 \approx 0.0002$ or 0.02%.

4. E

The theoretical probability of rolling a particular number on one roll of a die is $\frac{1}{6}$, so the probability of rolling either a 2 or a 6 is $\frac{1}{6} + \frac{1}{6}$ or $\frac{1}{3}$. This theoretical probability is the long-run average. The Law of Large Numbers says that as we increase our number of trials, the empirical probability will approach the theoretical probability.

5. D

We assume that the company's sites act as independent producers. Thus, we can add not only the means but also the *variances*. Thus, for a pair of shoes we create a new random variable whose mean is $\mu_1 + \mu_2 = 0.002 + 0.005 = 0.007$ and whose variance is $\sigma_1^2 + \sigma_2^2 = (0.15)^2 + (0.18)^2 = 0.0225 + 0.0324 = 0.0549$. The *standard deviation* for the new random variable is $\sqrt{0.0549} \approx 0.2343$.

6. A

This is a geometric distribution since we are waiting for the first success (finding a person with the given genetic trait). The formula for the mean or expected value of a geometric distribution is $\mu_x = E(x) = \frac{1}{p} = \frac{1}{.27} \approx 3.7$, so we would need to observe about 4 people, on average, to find one with the given genetic trait.

7. D

This is a binomial distribution with $n = 15$ and $p = 0.18$.

$$P(X \geq 3) = 1 - P(X \leq 2) = 1 - \left[\binom{15}{0}0.82^{15} + \binom{15}{1}(0.18)(0.82)^{14} + \binom{15}{2}(0.18)^2(0.82)^{13}\right]$$

8. C

The new mean is $\mu_{new} = a\mu_x + b = 1.5(42) + 7 = 70$ and the new standard deviation is $\sigma_{new} = \sqrt{b^2\sigma^2} = \sqrt{(1.5)^2(9)} = 4.5$.

9. C

$$P(A \cup B) = P(A) + P(B) - P(A \cap B)$$

$$0.55 = 0.3 + 0.4 - P(A \cap B)$$

$$P(A \cap B) = 0.3 + 0.4 - 0.55 = 0.15$$

$$P(A|B) = \frac{P(A \cap B)}{P(B)} = \frac{0.15}{0.4} = 0.375$$

10. B

Since it costs \$1 to play the game, you must subtract this \$1 from any payout. The "winnings" are shown with their associated probabilities:

X	−\$.50	−\$1.00	\$3.00
P(x)	1/6	4/6	1/6

$$E(X) = \sum x \cdot P(x) = -.50\left(\frac{1}{6}\right) - 1\left(\frac{4}{6}\right) + 3\left(\frac{1}{6}\right) = -.25$$

Free Response

A tree diagram helps us to see the possibilities.

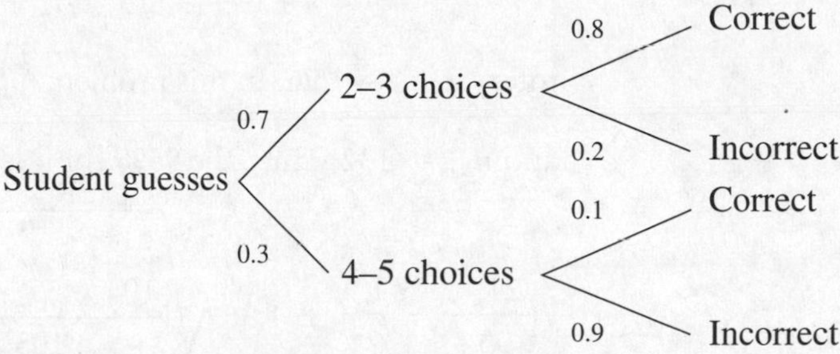

$$\begin{aligned} P(\text{correct guess}) &= P(\text{2–3 choices} \cap \text{correct}) \\ &\quad + P(\text{4–5 choices} \cap \text{correct}) \\ &= (0.7)(0.8) + (0.3)(0.1) = 0.56 + 0.03 = 0.59 \end{aligned}$$

Therefore, the probability that this student will answer correctly by guessing is 59%.

Answers to Review Questions for Topic 5

Multiple Choice

1. A

   A Type II Error occurs when we fail to reject the null hypothesis when the null hypothesis is false. The rejection region for the null hypothesis is represented by the area of Region II. The nonrejection regions are represented by Regions I and V. Since we know that the null hypothesis is false (implying that the alternative is true), the regions representing the probability of a Type II error are the rejection regions under the alternative curve, I and III.

2. A

   It is appropriate to use the Normal model for the sampling distribution for $\hat{p} = 0.2$ since n is large, it is reasonable to assume that the population of salamanders in the stream is greater than 10 times the sample size, and

   $np \geq 10$ and $n(1 - p) \geq 10$
   $100(0.1) \geq 10$ and $100(1 - 0.1) \geq 10$

$$P(p \geq 0.2) = P\left(z \geq \frac{\hat{p} - p}{\sqrt{\frac{p(1-p)}{n}}} = \frac{0.2 - 0.1}{\sqrt{\frac{0.1(1-0.1)}{100}}} \approx 3.33\right)$$
$$\approx 1 - 0.9996 = 0.0004$$

3. A

$$P(x < 20) = P\left(z < \frac{20 - 50}{15}\right) = P(z < -2) \approx 0.0228$$

4. A

The formula for a two-proportion z-interval is

$(\hat{p}_1 - \hat{p}_2) \pm z^* \sqrt{\frac{\hat{p}_1(1 - \hat{p}_1)}{n_1} + \frac{\hat{p}_2(1 - \hat{p}_2)}{n_2}}$. For a 95% confidence interval, $z^* = 1.96$. In this problem, $\hat{p}_E = \frac{21}{103}$, $\hat{p}_W = \frac{29}{132}$, $n_E = 103$, and $n_W = 132$. Thus, the 95% confidence interval is

$$\left(\frac{21}{103} - \frac{29}{132}\right) \pm 1.96 \sqrt{\frac{\frac{21}{103}\left(1 - \frac{21}{103}\right)}{103} + \frac{\frac{29}{132}\left(1 - \frac{29}{132}\right)}{132}}.$$

5. E

Groups from two state regions should be independent of each other, and the claim is that the sample data were randomly selected from each respective part of the state. It is reasonable to believe that the population of each part of the state is greater than 1030 and 1320, respectively. Also,

$103(0.2039) = 21 > 10$, $103(0.7961) = 82 > 10$, and
$132(0.2197) = 29 > 10$, and $132(0.7803) = 103 > 10$.

$$\hat{p}_{\text{Combined}} = \frac{21 + 29}{103 + 132} = \frac{50}{235} \approx 0.2128$$

Our hypotheses are H_0: $p_W = p_E$ and H_a: $p_W \neq p_E$.

$$p = 2P\left(|z| > \frac{0.2039 - 0.7961}{\sqrt{\frac{0.2128(1 - 0.2128)}{235}}}\right) \approx 0.7688$$

Therefore, there is no significant difference in the proportions at the 0.10 level.

6. D

The power of a test is $1 - \beta$, where β is the probability of a Type II error ($100\% - 3\% = 97\%$).

7. B

The endpoints of the confidence interval are 0.90 and 0.93. A confidence interval for a proportion is $\hat{p} \pm ME$; thus, $\hat{p}$ is the center of the interval (0.915), and the margin of error is half of the interval's length (0.015).

8. D

The standard error of the estimate is $\sqrt{\frac{\hat{p}(1 - \hat{p})}{n}}$, where $\hat{p} = 0.35$ and $n = 400$. (Remember that we use $\hat{p}$ for a *confidence interval*, but we use

p, the hypothesized boundary value, when calculating the standard error for a *test statistic.*)

9. A

   The mean of the sampling distribution of sample means will be approximately the same as the mean of the population distribution. The standard deviation of the sampling distribution for samples of size $n = 10$ is calculated by $s = \frac{\sigma}{\sqrt{n}} = \frac{1.66}{\sqrt{10}} \approx 0.54$.

10. D

    $0.05 < 0.0818 < 0.10$

    Just because $\hat{p} > 0.50$, we cannot say that the candidate can be VERY confident. A 95% confidence interval for these results is $\hat{p} \pm z^{*} SE = 0.5623 \pm 1.96(0.0447) \approx 0.5623 \pm 0.0876$ or $(0.4747, 0.6499)$. The candidate can be 95% confident that she will receive between 47% and 65% of the vote, approximately; the left endpoint falls *below* 50%. A p-value of 0.0818 tells us that if the null hypothesis ($p = 0.5$) is true, 8% of *all possible* sample proportions from samples of the same size as ours ($n = 125$) would be *equal to or more extreme* than our result of 0.5623.

Free Response

(a) We want to know if the proportion of pavers that meet the 15-inch standard length is 80%.

Assumptions/Conditions for the One-Proportion z-Test

We are told that the sample of pavers is a random sample, and it is reasonable to believe that more than 510 pavers are manufactured.

$np_0 = 51(0.80) = 40.8 > 10$ and $n(1 - p_0) = 51(0.20) = 10.2 > 10$

Because the conditions are satisfied, it is appropriate to model the sampling distribution of the proportion with $N(p_0, \text{SD}(\hat{p}))$.

Hypotheses

$$H_0: p = 0.80$$

The proportion of manufactured pavers that meet the standard is 0.80.

$$H_a: p \neq 0.80$$

The proportion of manufactured pavers that meet the standard isn't 0.80.

Mechanics for the One-Proportion z-Test

$$p_0 = 0.80, \text{SD}(\hat{p}) = \sqrt{\frac{p_0(1 - p_0)}{n}} = \sqrt{\frac{(0.80)(0.20)}{51}} \approx 0.0560$$

$$z = \frac{\hat{p} - p_0}{\text{SD}(\hat{p})} \approx \frac{0.5294 - 0.80}{0.0560}$$

$$\approx -4.8321 \text{ and the } p\text{-value is approximately } 0.$$

Conclusion

The p-value (essentially 0) is small enough to reject the null hypothesis in favor of the alternative at the 0.05 level. There is sufficient evidence to conclude that the proportion of manufactured pavers that meet the standard is different from 80%.

(b) We wish to find an interval that is likely, with 95% confidence, to contain the true proportion, p, of manufactured pavers that meet the standard.

Conditions for the One-Proportion z-Interval

From part (a), we know we have a random sample and a sufficiently large population for our sample. However, our success/failure conditions must be checked. The number of successes in our sample is 27, and the number of failures is $51 - 27 = 24$. Both are greater than 10.

Because the conditions are satisfied, we can safely construct our confidence interval.

Mechanics for the One-Proportion z-Interval

$$n = 51, \hat{p} = 0.5294, \text{SE}(\hat{p}) = \sqrt{\frac{\hat{p}(1 - \hat{p})}{n}}$$

$$\approx \sqrt{\frac{(0.5294)(0.4706)}{51}} \approx 0.0699$$

$$\text{ME} = z^* \times \text{SE}(\hat{p}) \approx 1.96(0.0699) \approx 0.137$$

So, the 95% confidence interval is 0.5294 ± 0.137 or (0.3924, 0.6664).

Interpretation

We can be 95% confident that between 39.24% and 66.64% of manufactured pavers meet the standard 15-inch length.

(c) Our decision in part (a) was to reject the null hypothesis that 80% of the pavers meet the standard length of 15 inches in favor of the alternative that the percentage differs from 80%. Since our confidence interval (0.3924, 0.6664) does not contain 0.80, this indicates that 80% is not a plausible value for the true proportion of pavers that meet the standard length. Thus, we confirm our decision to reject the null hypothesis.

Answers to Review Questions for Topic 6

Multiple Choice

1. C

A confidence interval estimates a range of plausible values for a *parameter* based on a point estimate from a sample. Choice B is incorrect because the interpretation in context must refer to the population of interest, first-year students at *this* university. Choice A is incorrect because we can be 100% sure about our *sample* mean since we *have* all the data for our sample. Choice D is incorrect because there is no *probability* associated with a population parameter; it is what it is—the uncertainty lies in our methods for estimating it. Choice E is incorrect because a confidence interval allows us to make inferences about a population but not about individuals.

2. C

To guarantee a margin of error no greater than 4% with 90% confidence, the sample size must be at least 424.

$$\text{ME} = z^* \sqrt{\frac{p(1-p)}{n}} \leq 0.04$$

$$= 1.645\sqrt{\frac{0.5(1-0.5)}{n}} \leq 0.04$$

$$= \sqrt{\frac{0.25}{n}} \leq 0.0243$$

$$= \frac{0.25}{n} \leq 0.00059$$

$$= \frac{0.25}{0.00059} \leq n$$

$$= 423.7 \leq n$$

3. D

$$t^*_{df=44} = 2.41$$

$$= 290 \pm 2.41\left(\frac{28}{\sqrt{45}}\right)$$

$$= 290 \pm 2.41(4.174)$$

4. A

$$t_{df=72.3} = \frac{(80.6 - 84.2) - 0}{\sqrt{\frac{5.2^2}{40} + \frac{3.9^2}{40}}} \approx -3.5028$$

p-value $\approx 0.0004 < \alpha = 0.01$

5. A

$$(\bar{x}_L - \bar{x}_D) \pm t^*_{df=72.3}\sqrt{\frac{s_L^2}{n_L} + \frac{s_D^2}{n_D}}$$

$$= (80.6 - 84.2) \pm 1.99\sqrt{\frac{(5.2)^2}{40} + \frac{(3.9)^2}{40}}$$

$$= -3.60 \pm 1.99\sqrt{\frac{(5.2)^2}{40} + \frac{(3.9)^2}{40}}$$

6. C

The t-distribution is used when the population standard deviation is unknown. The standard deviation of the sample is used to estimate the standard deviation of the population.

7. C

The margin of error for a one-sample t-interval is

$$t^*\left(\frac{s}{\sqrt{n}}\right) = 2.49\left(\frac{2.5}{\sqrt{24}}\right) \approx 1.27.$$

8. E

Because each subject received both treatments, the two sets of data are not independent and a matched-pairs one-sample t-test is the appropriate analysis. In order to determine which cream is *better*, the difference must be ordered by TYPE OF CREAM, *not* by hand. (Remember, this was a randomized experiment. In this matched-pairs, the randomization is the hand.) The analysis is based on an experiment for which the population standard deviation is unknown; thus, a z-test is not appropriate in any case.

9. E

Using the same data, a smaller confidence level results in a narrower confidence interval. This means that the *left* endpoint of the 90% confidence interval must be greater than the left endpoint of the 95% interval, and the *right* endpoint of the 90% interval must be less than the right endpoint of the 95% confidence interval. Only E meets both of these criteria. (NOTE: No real computation is necessary!)

10. B

We must test for the mean difference in sick days between men and women. In our sample, the men and women are married, and thus, the males and females are not independent of one another. For example, if the husband gets the flu, he is likely to pass it on to the wife; this would result in both using sick days. While the problem setting asks us to test whether, on average, men take more sick days than women, our alternative hypothesis is stated in the reverse ($w < m$ or $w - m < 0$).

Free Response

Assumptions/Conditions for Two-Sample t-Test for Means

Independent groups assumption: No reason to believe that the SAT* Verbal scores for schools in the two areas are related.

Randomization condition: Both samples were randomly selected.

Nearly normal condition: Boxplots of the two sets of SAT* Verbal scores appear fairly symmetric with no outliers; the linear nature of the Normal Quantile plots confirms that the distributions are approximately normally distributed.

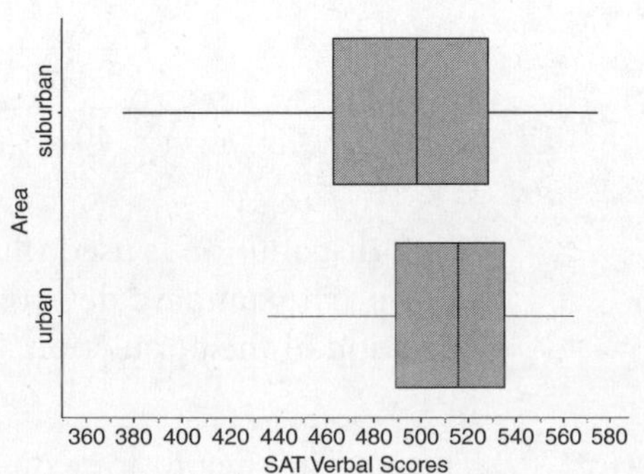

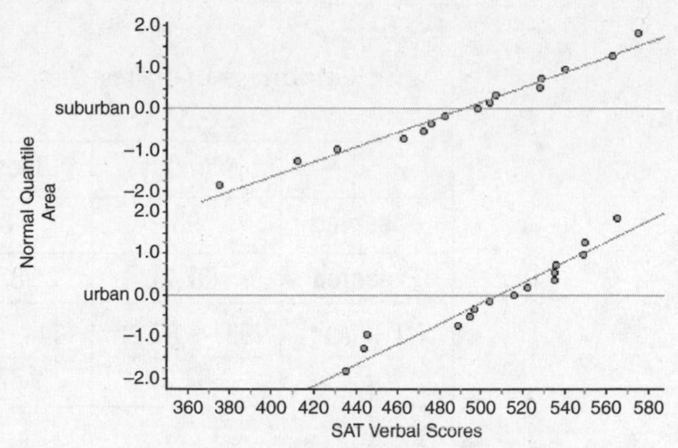

Since the conditions are reasonable, a two-sample t-test is appropriate.

Hypotheses:

H_0: $\mu_U = \mu_S$ or The mean SAT* Verbal scores for the two areas are the same.

H_a: $\mu_U \neq \mu_S$ or The mean SAT* Verbal scores for the two areas are different.

Mechanics:

$n_U = 15 \quad n_S = 15$

$\bar{x}_U \approx 507.8 \quad \bar{x}_S \approx 490.3$

$s_U \approx 40.76 \quad s_S \approx 55.21$

$$t_{df=25.8} \approx \frac{(507.8 - 490.3) - 0}{\sqrt{\frac{(40.76)^2}{15} + \frac{(55.21)^2}{15}}} \approx 0.99$$

p-value ≈ 0.33

Conclusion:

At any reasonable α-level with such a high p-value (0.33), we fail to reject the null hypothesis. There is insufficient evidence to show a statistically significant difference in the average SAT* Verbal scores for urban and suburban areas.

Answers to Review Questions for Topic 7

Multiple Choice

1. B

   χ^2 tests are for categorical data. A χ^2 test of independence examines the distribution of counts for one group of individuals classified according to two categorical variables.

2. C

   $$\text{Expected Value} = \frac{(\text{row total})(\text{column total})}{\text{table total}}$$

   $$\text{Expected Value (First-Class and Dead)} = \frac{(2201 - 710)(325)}{2201} \approx 220.2$$

3. E

χ^2 Goodness-of-fit test

	Monday	Tuesday	Wednesday	Thursday	Friday
Observed	98	84	92	86	76
Expected	(87.2)	(87.2)	(87.2)	(87.2)	(87.2)
$\frac{(O - E)^2}{E}$	$\frac{(98 - 87.2)^2}{87.2}$	$\frac{(84 - 87.2)^2}{87.2}$	$\frac{(92 - 87.2)^2}{87.2}$	$\frac{(86 - 87.2)^2}{87.2}$	$\frac{(76 - 87.2)^2}{87.2}$

$$\chi^2_{df=4} = \sum_{all} \frac{(\text{observed} - \text{expected})^2}{\text{expected}} \approx 3.17$$

p-value ≈ 0.529

4. C

The computer output gives the p-value for a *two*-tailed test as 0.0279. Since we are doing a *one*-tailed test, we need to divide this value in half.

5. B

95% confidence interval for slope:

$b \pm t^*_{df=n-2}\,\mathrm{SE}_{(b)}$

$0.00733 \pm 2.086(0.0031)$

```
Dependent variable is     SAT-Math
No Selector
R squared = 21.9%    R squared (adjusted) = 18.0%
s = 27.99 with 22 - 2 = 20 degrees of freedom

Source        Sum of Squares    df    Mean Square    F-ratio
Regression       4401.65         1      4401.65        5.62
Residual        15666.9         (20)     783.347

Variable      Coefficient      s.e. of Coeff    t-ratio     prob
Constant       446.990          37.66            11.9       ≤ 0.0001
Per Student   (7.33145e-3)     (0.0031)          2.37        0.0279

                  slope          SE(slope)     df(slope)
```

6. D

Hypotheses are always stated in terms of the parameter of interest. The parameter of interest is the population slope β (*not* the statistic b).

7. D

The fan-shaped pattern in the residual plot indicates that as the value of x increases, the model is less accurate in predicting the corresponding y-value, so choice A is correct. The residuals are close to the line $y = 0$ for small values of x, but the residuals are larger as x increases, so choice B is also correct.

Either a curved pattern or unequal variance in the residuals suggests that a nonlinear model may fit the data better than a linear model. In this case we see unequal variance (a fan-shaped pattern), so C is incorrect.

8. E

The appropriate test is a χ^2 test of homogeneity (equal proportions). The data are given as counts, and there are two separate groups (faculty and administrators) with the same variable (response to the question asked) measured on each group. Although the surveyed individuals may not constitute random samples, this is not a problem because we are not trying to generalize to a larger group.

9. A

For a χ^2 test of homogeneity (equal proportions), the degrees of freedom are $(rows - 1)(columns - 1) = (1)(2) = 2$. (Be careful not to include the totals when you count the number of rows and columns.)

10. E

The p-value is approximately 0, lower than any acceptable α-level, so there is ample evidence that at least one of the proportions, and therefore one response group, is significantly different. (It is not enough for table values to be different; they must be *significantly* different. You MUST perform a statistical test.)

Free Response

Hypotheses:

H_0: The booking methods used by customers of this hotel in 1995, 2000, and 2005 have the same distribution (are homogeneous).

H_a: The booking methods used by customers of this hotel in 1995, 2000, and 2005 do not have the same distribution.

Assumptions/Conditions for χ^2 Test of Homogeneity

Counted data condition: I have counts of the number of customers in categories.

Randomization condition: I don't want to draw inferences to other hotels, so there is no need to check for a random sample.

Expected cell-frequency condition: The expected values (shown in the table in parentheses) are all at least 5.

	1995	2000	2005
Travel Agent	112 (90.7)	103 (90.7)	57 (90.7)
Book Online	42 (80.7)	77 (80.7)	123 (80.7)
Other	56 (38.7)	30 (38.7)	30 (38.7)

Since the assumptions and conditions are reasonable, we will proceed with a χ^2 test of homogeneity. (We choose a test of homogeneity because there are three separate samples—one for each year.)

Mechanics:

$$\chi^2_{df=4} = \sum_{all} \frac{(\text{observed} - \text{expected})^2}{\text{expected}}$$

$\chi^2_{df=4} \approx 71.7711$

p-value ≈ 0

Conclusion:

Since the p-value is essentially zero, I reject the null hypothesis at any reasonable α-level and conclude that the booking methods chosen by customers of this hotel have changed over the years examined.

ANSWERS TO PRACTICE EXAMINATION 1

Section I: Multiple Choice

1. B

   IQR = Q3 − Q1. Using the 1.5 IQR Rule:

   Q1 − 1.5 IQR = 119.5 − 1.5(16) = 95.5, which is less than the minimum value *and* Q3 + 1.5 IQR = 135.5 + 1.5(16) = 159.5, which is less than the maximum value. Therefore, there is at least one outlier, the maximum value.

2. D

   $P(A) + P(B) = 0.69$; $P(A \cup B) = 0.68$; $0.69 \neq 0.68$ and thus the two events are not mutually exclusive.

   $P(A \cup B) = P(A) + P(B) - P(A \cap B) = 0.69 - P(A \cap B) = 0.68$; therefore, $P(A \cap B) = 0.01$.

   The two events are not independent. If they were, then either $P(B \mid A) = P(B)$ *or* $P(A)P(B) = P(A \cap B)$ would have to be true. But,

   $$P(B \mid A) = \frac{P(A \cap B)}{(A)} = \frac{0.01}{0.43} = 0.023 \text{ which} \neq P(B), 0.26. \text{ And}$$

   $P(A)P(B) \neq P(A \cap B)$ since $0.11118 \neq 0.01$.

3. C

   The current belief is that the average family income is $45,000. Thus the null hypothesis should set μ equal to 45,000. The first-time home buyers are trying to show that the average family income is less than $45,000; therefore, the alternative hypothesis should set μ less than 45,000.

4. A

   With a mean of 14.1 and a standard deviation of 0.04, the curve should have a peak at 14.1, and the change in curvature should occur 0.04 unit on either side of 14.1. *At least 14 oz* means 14 oz or more. Therefore, the shading should be to the right of 14.

5. D

   The upper quartile of set Y is equivalent to the median of set X. Therefore, approximately 50% of the data values in set X are greater than approximately 75% of the data values in set Y.

6. C

   The data are blocked by grocery item; therefore, the matched-pairs design is appropriate for this test.

7. B

Since 20% of the subscribers also subscribe to broadband, 20%, or two of the ten digits, should represent broadband subscribers.

8. C

The profit for each shirt is $10 − $4 = $6. The expected number of shirts sold can be calculated as follows:

$0(0.02) + 1(0.15) + 2(0.18) + 3(0.21) + 4(0.14) + 5(0.08)$

$+ 6(0.08) + 7(0.04) + 8(0.03) + 9(0.02) + 10(0.05) = 3.78.$

Therefore, the expected profit is (3.78)($6) = $22.68.

9. A

For small sample sizes, the shape of the distribution will mimic that of the population. The mean of the sampling distribution will equal that of the population, and the standard deviation of the sampling distribution will equal that of the population divided by the square root of 5 in this case.

10. D

For independent variables,

$\mu_{A+B} = \mu_A + \mu_B = 65 + 154 = 219$ and

$\sigma_{A+B} = \sqrt{\sigma_A^2 + \sigma_B^2} = \sqrt{5.75^2 + 8.02^2} \approx 9.87.$

11. E

Cause-and-effect relationships can only be determined by a controlled randomized experiment.

12. B

All least squares regression lines are in the form $\hat{y} = a + bx$, where a is the constant (constant coefficient = 21.84) and b is the coefficient of the explanatory variable (weight coefficient = 0.037).

13. D

There are a fixed number of observations in a binomial setting, not a geometric setting.

14. B

The formula for the construction of the confidence interval is

$$(\hat{p}_1 - \hat{p}_2) \pm z^* \sqrt{\frac{\hat{p}_1(1 - \hat{p}_1)}{n_1} + \frac{\hat{p}_2(1 - \hat{p}_2)}{n_2}},$$

where $\hat{p}_1 = \frac{66}{200}$, $\hat{p}_2 = \frac{12}{140}$, $n_1 = 200$, $n_2 = 140$, and $z^* = 1.96$.

15. E

If each of the values is multiplied by 9, then the mean and standard deviation will also be multiplied by 9.

16. B

For the given equation, the intercept is 382.1, and the slope is −12.25. The intercept yields the predicted value for the dependent variable when the independent variable assumes a value of 0. Since the slope is negative, the slope will give the decrease in value of the dependent variable for every unit increase in the independent variable.

17. E

The appropriate significance test would be a chi-square test of independence; however, the conditions have not been met. Two of the six expected counts are 4.731 and 0.828; this violates the condition that no more than 20% of the expected counts can be less than 5. Additionally, all expected counts should be greater than 1.

18. D

Since the slope coefficient is positive, the correlation coefficient will be positive. The correlation coefficient, r, is the square root of R-squared.

19. C

A p-value is the probability of obtaining results like those from your sample (or more extreme) if the null hypothesis is true. Thus, if the two roommates spend equal amounts on groceries, you could get results like those sampled (or more extreme) 6.7% of the time. Since $p = 0.067 < 0.10$, the results are significant at the 0.10 level.

20. E

$$\$10\left(\frac{1}{8}\right) + \$5\left(\frac{1}{8}\right) - \$5\left(\frac{3}{4}\right) = -\$1.875 \approx -\$1.88 \text{ for one game.}$$

Therefore, the player can expect to lose $(2)(1.875) = \$3.75$ for two games.

21. E

$$z = \left(\frac{\hat{p} - p}{\sqrt{\frac{p(1-p)}{n}}}\right) = \left(\frac{0.9 - 0.876}{\sqrt{\frac{(0.876)(0.124)}{200}}}\right)$$

and we wish to find the probability that more than 180 of the 200 individuals are *not* senior citizens. Since 12.4% are senior citizens, 87.6% are not.

22. C

A t-interval with 19 degrees of freedom should be constructed with the given information, and substitutions should be made into this formula:

$$\bar{x} \pm t^*_{19}\frac{s}{\sqrt{n}} = 5.65 \pm 2.093\frac{1.69}{\sqrt{20}}.$$

23. C

Standardized value for this year's test: $\dfrac{40 - 38}{2} = 1$

Standardized value for last year's test: $\dfrac{35 - 34}{1} = 1$

Therefore, in both years, the student scored 1 standard deviation higher than the mean. Thus, the student scored equally well in both years.

24. D

Since $p = 0.0028 > 0.001$ but $p = 0.0028 < 0.01$, there is evidence of a relationship between distance and diameter at the 0.01 level.

25. E

The mean of the distribution of sample means should have a mean of approximately 12.262 and a standard deviation of approximately $9.610/\sqrt{9}$ or 3.1. It is important to check the scale on each axis and not just look at the shape of the distribution.

26. C

The slope of the least squares regression line is 0.959388. With 19 degrees of freedom and 95% confidence, the critical value is 2.093. The standard error of the slope coefficient, as can be seen in the computer output, is 0.1326.

27. E

Remember, this is a *cumulative* frequency histogram. Only one game is added to the histogram in the last two classes (6.5 and 7).

28. C

In a distribution skewed to the right, the mean is greater than the median. Recall that the mean follows the tail of a skewed distribution.

29. A

A Type I error is the error of rejecting the null hypothesis when the null hypothesis is true. In this case, it means the couple rejects the belief that profits are $15,000 or less, believing the average profits are more than $15,000. Since the average profits really are $15,000 or less, the couple will go bankrupt.

30. B

A confidence interval yields an interval of values that one can be reasonably confident will capture the true parameter of interest. In this case, the parameter of interest is the proportion of seniors *at this school* who will attend an institution of higher learning (eliminate answer choice C). We already know the proportion from our sample (eliminate A and E). The true proportion is a fixed value and will either be captured by the interval or not (eliminate D and E).

31. D

This is a geometric setting with $p = 0.2$ and $x = 3$. There are two failures (0.8^2) before the first success (0.2).

32. B

If each value of the distribution is multiplied by 2, then the standard deviation will also be multiplied by 2. Addition of 5 to each of the values only shifts the distribution and does not change the spread of the distribution.

33. E

This is a binomial setting with $p = 0.014$ and $n = 500$. Therefore, the mean is $(500)(0.014) = 7$, and the standard deviation is $\sqrt{(500)(0.014)(1 - 0.014)} \approx 2.627$.

34. B

Increasing the sample size will decrease the width of a confidence interval. Additionally, decreasing the confidence level will decrease the width of a confidence interval. Therefore, the combination that will most decrease the width of the interval would be a combination of increasing the sample size and decreasing the confidence level.

35. A

Predicted grocery cost $= -33.22 + 44.77(4) = \$145.86$

Actual grocery cost $= \$135$

Residual $=$ actual $-$ fitted $= 135 - 145.86 = -10.86$

36. D

Performing a *one-proportion z-test* with H_0: $p = 0.089$ and H_a: $p > 0.089$, $z = 1.706$, and $p = 0.0440$. The critical region boundary for the 0.05 level is $z = 1.645$. Therefore, since $1.706 > 1.645$, or since $.0440 < 0.5$ ($p < \alpha$), there is evidence that the county's poverty rate is higher than that of the state.

37. B

The peak of the curve is at approximately 30, and the change in curvature occurs at 25 and 35, 5 units (or 1 standard deviation) on either side of the mean. Additionally, from the Empirical Rule we know that 99.7% of the values should fall within 3 standard deviations of the mean.

38. B

For independent variables, $\mu_{A-B} = \mu_A - \mu_B = 5.1 - 4.5 = 0.6$ and $\sigma_{A-B} = \sqrt{\sigma_A^2 + \sigma_B^2} = \sqrt{0.57^2 + 0.63^2} \approx 0.85$.

39. E

No more than 3 means 3 or fewer. This is a binomial setting with $p = 0.176$ and $n = 10$.

40. A

Increasing the sample size improves power, and increasing the value of α also improves power. Therefore, overall, power can best be improved by increasing both the sample size and the α value.

Section II: Free Response

1. a. $\hat{y} = 83.4851 - 0.0032x$, where y = percentage of the population with access to safe drinking water and x = the number of persons per doctor in these regions.

   b. $r = -0.839$

   There is a fairly strong, negative, linear relationship between the percentage of the population with access to safe drinking water and the number of persons per doctor in these regions.

   c. The coefficient of determination is $R^2 = 70.4\%$. We can say that 70.4% of the variability in the percentage of the population with access to safe water is accounted for by its linear relationship with the number of persons per doctor in these regions.

2. a. *Conditions for the one-proportion z-interval:*

   (1) **Randomization:** We are told that results are from a random sample of construction workers.

   (2) **Population size:** $10n < N$

   It is reasonable to assume there are more than $(10)(150) = 1500$ construction workers in the city.

(3) **Sample size:** $np \geq 10$ and $n(1 - p) \geq 10$

$$np = (150)\left(\frac{16}{150}\right) = 16 > 10 \text{ and}$$

$$n(1 - p) = (150)\left(\frac{134}{150}\right) = 134 > 10$$

Mechanics:

The construction of a 90% confidence interval for a proportion makes use of the formula

$$\hat{p} \pm z^* \sqrt{\frac{\hat{p}(1 - \hat{p})}{n}}.$$

For this problem, the confidence interval is constructed as

$$\frac{16}{150} \pm 1.645\sqrt{\frac{\left(\frac{16}{150}\right)\left(1 - \frac{16}{150}\right)}{150}} \approx 0.1067 \pm 0.0415.$$

95% CI for p: (0.0652, 0.1482).

Interpretation:

We can be 90% confident that between 6.52% and 14.82% of the construction workers in this city are unemployed.

b. A 90% confidence interval can be used to test the two-sided hypothesis H_a: $p \neq 0.068$ at the $\alpha = 0.10$ level. The 90% confidence interval can also be used to test the one-sided hypothesis H_a: $p > 0.068$ at the $\alpha = 0.05$ level. Since the value $p = 0.068$ is contained in the 90% CI, there is insufficient statistical evidence to show that the unemployment rate for city construction workers is significantly higher than the overall city rate.

3. a. $P(x > 14) = P\left(z > \frac{14 - 6.4}{4.9}\right) = P(z > 1.55) \approx 0.06$

There is a 6% chance that the 215-lb wrestler will beat his next opponent by at least 14 points.

b. Team mean = Sum of means of team members = 7.4 + 7.9 + 7.2 + 8.1 + 6.4 = 37 points

Team standard deviation = $\sqrt{\text{Sum of variances of team members}}$

$\sqrt{3.2^2 + 5.1^2 + 4.7^2 + 5.3^2 + 4.9^2} \approx 10.509$ points

c. The team mean calculated in part (b) was based on the first ten meets. This is not a random sample of the season. A team may have improved over the course of the season, and its first ten meets would not be representative of the season as a whole. We would need to take a *random sample* to calculate the team mean.

4. a. The best design is matched-pairs. Randomly choose whether each volunteer should start with his/her own racquet or the new racquet. Serve balls to the volunteers, recording how many balls are returned. Then, have the volunteers

switch racquet types. Serve balls again, and again record how many balls are returned.

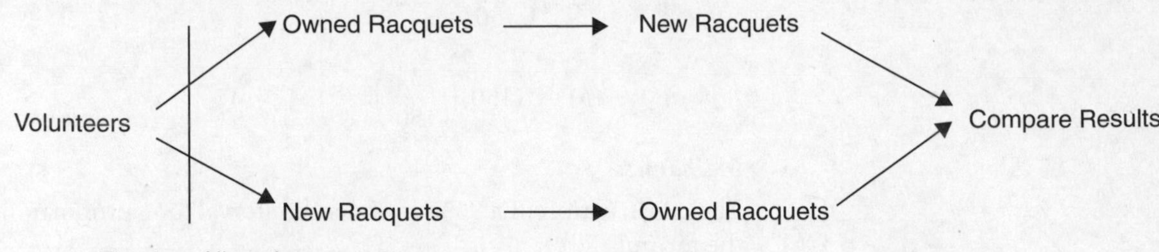

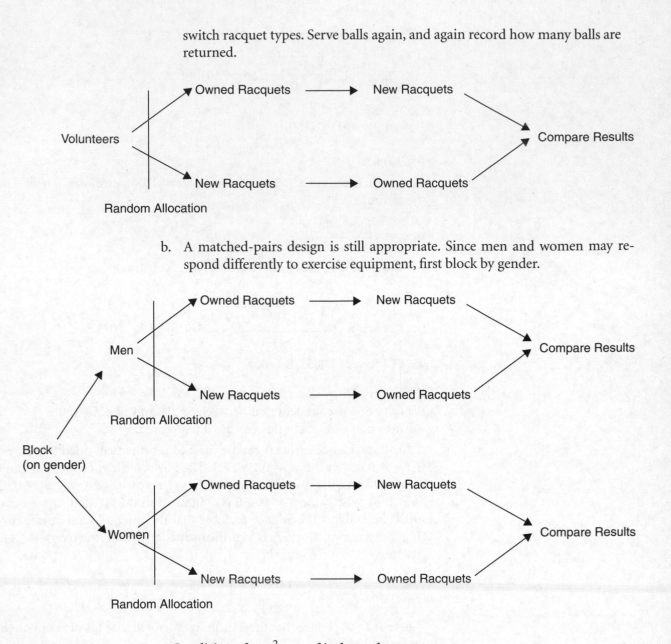

b. A matched-pairs design is still appropriate. Since men and women may respond differently to exercise equipment, first block by gender.

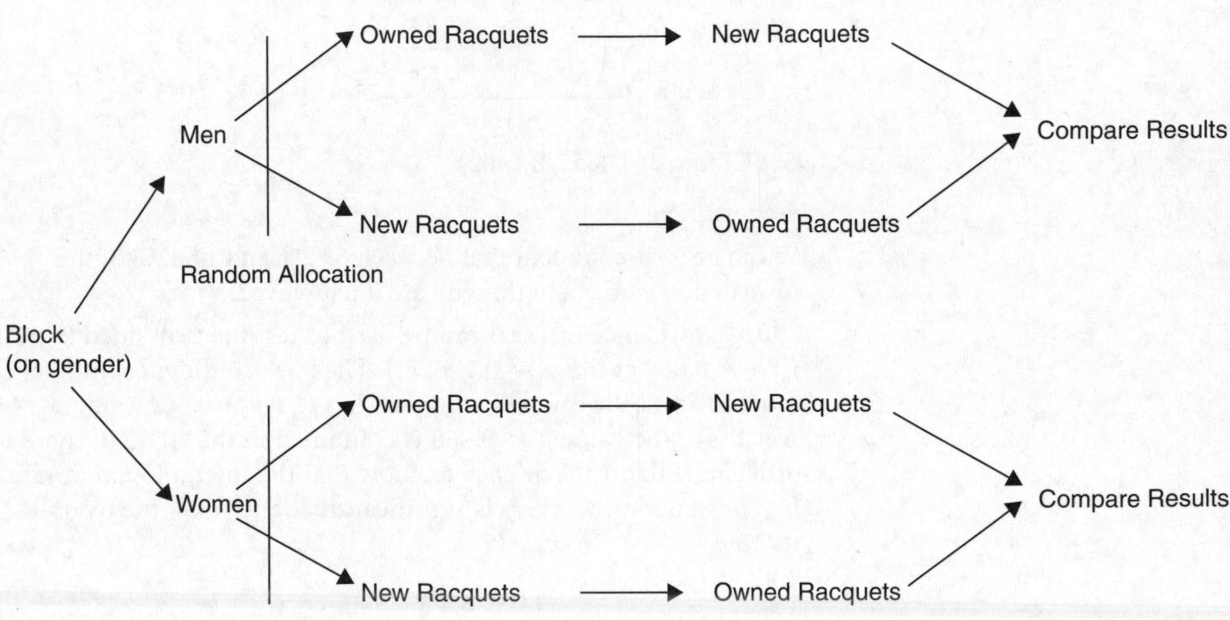

5. *Conditions for χ^2 test of independence:*

(1) **Randomization:** We are told our data are counts from a simple random sample of 600 individuals.

(2) **Sample size:** *Expected* cell counts ≥5. (table)

	Approve	Disapprove	No Opinion
Economy	96 (*110*)	100 (*84*)	4 (*6*)
Foreign Affairs	110 (*110*)	84 (*84*)	6 (*6*)
Domestic Affairs	124 (*110*)	68 (*84*)	8 (*6*)

Hypotheses:

H_0: The public's opinion on the three issues is the same.

H_a: The public's opinion on the three issues is not the same.

Mechanics:

$$\chi^2 = \sum\left(\frac{(Observed - Expected)^2}{Expected}\right) = \chi^2 \text{ test of homogeneity}$$

$$\begin{bmatrix} \frac{(96-110)^2}{110} + \frac{(100-84)^2}{84} + \frac{(4-6)^2}{6} + \\ \frac{(110-110)^2}{110} + \frac{(84-84)^2}{84} + \frac{(6-6)^2}{6} + \\ \frac{(124-110)^2}{110} + \frac{(68-84)^2}{84} + \frac{(8-6)^2}{6} \end{bmatrix} \approx \begin{bmatrix} 1.782 & + & 3.048 & + & .667 & + \\ 0 & + & 0 & + & 0 & + \\ 1.782 & + & 3.048 & + & .667 & \end{bmatrix}$$

≈ 10.994 and $p \approx 0.027$
with 4 degrees of freedom

Conclusion:

Since $p = 0.027 < 0.05$, our results are significant at the 0.05 level. Reject the null hypothesis in favor of the alternative hypothesis. We have evidence that the public's opinion on the three issues is not the same.

6. a. Assign the numbers 00–47 to represent women who walk (W). The numbers 48–99 will represent women who do not walk (N). Start in the upper-left-hand corner of the table, examine every two digits, and record the category of the two-digit number. Move across the table until ten distinct two-digit numbers are examined and record your results. Ignore repeats. This constitutes one trial. Repeat many times and obtain an average.

   b.

Trial 1: 6 walkers — Trial 2: 7 walkers — Trial 3: 7 walkers
N W N W W W W N N W
69|16|5 0|12|10| 02|15|6 3|84|25 | 02|21|6 9|00|78| 41|06|1 0|24|63 | 40|37|4 1|32|98| 80|18|8 2|19|06

Trial 4: 6 walkers — Trial 5: 3 walkers — Trial 6: 4 walkers
44|49|4 0|10|96| 29|95|0 1|63|06 | 92|25|5 7|51|70| 57|40|0 0|91|91 | 80|52|2 0|92|35| 86|38|6 7|80|07

Trial 7: 5 walkers — Trial 8: 3 walkers — Trial 9: 5 walkers
47|00|7 7|28|48| 02|84|6 4|66|33 | 41|90|6 5|93|57| 03|93|3 1|94|73 | 37|48|3 0|17|69| 76|26|7 7|83|40

Trial 10: 6 walkers — Trial 11: 5 walkers — Trial 12: 5 walkers
52|43|5 8|58|22| 33|41|5 9|46|02 | 99|49|9 4|21|95| 24|36|0 0|67|06 | 10|94|8 3|42|68| 66|14|4 1|03|75

Trial 13: 7 walkers — Trial 14: 4 walkers — Trial 15: 2 walkers
39|83|2 8|54|09| 14|23|9 6|14|05 | 40|86|6 1|70|83| 53|18|9 1|09|01 | 62|92|6 8|53|04| 64|06|7 5|61|77

Trial 16: 5 walkers — Trial 17: 4 walkers — Trial 18: 6 walkers
69|22|1 4|12|00| 84|40|7 4|81|85 | 96|36|1 0|94|04| 60|25|5 5|69|96 | 41|69|6 8|44|81| 27|38|8 8|21|25

Trial 19: 5 walkers — Trial 20: 6 walkers
64|09|1 8|17|60| 78|18|8 7|60|31 | 43|48|3 8|19|28| 05|94|5 9|37|58 | 49307 66038 23405 10343

c.

Number of Walkers	Frequency
1	0
2	1
3	2
4	3
5	6
6	5
7	3
8	0

d. Your Results

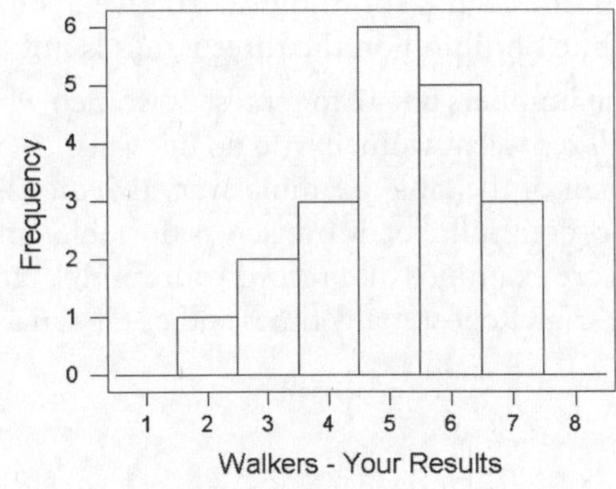

Researcher's Results

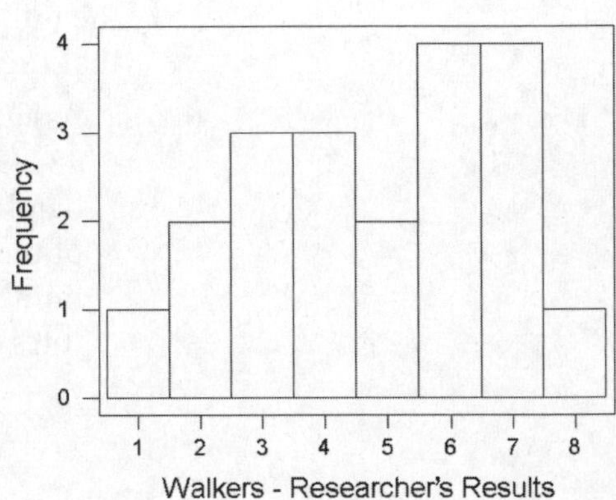

e. Both distributions are somewhat skewed left. The distribution of the simulation results is unimodal, with a high peak at the value of 5. Both distributions have a median value of 5. The spread from the simulation is less than that from the researcher. The range of values from the simulation is 5, while the range from the researcher's results is 7.

<u>*Note:*</u> Other comparative displays like parallel boxplots and comparative dotplots would be acceptable solutions to part (d); however, a scatterplot is NOT appropriate for these data sets since the data involve only one variable.

ANSWERS TO PRACTICE EXAMINATION 2

Section I: Multiple Choice

1. D

The intercept is positive and approximately 9. The slope is negative, and the correlation coefficient is moderate, not strong.

2. C

The given hypotheses were for a one-sided test. A one-sided hypothesis test with a significance level of 0.05 would correspond to a 90% confidence interval.

Significant results would mean the sample results were significantly higher than the hypothesized value of 0.251. Therefore, 0.251 would fall below the lower limit of the interval.

3. E

$\text{ME} = \frac{z^* \sigma}{\sqrt{n}}$. Solving for n yields $n = \left(\frac{z^* \sigma}{\text{ME}}\right)^2$.

$$0.5 = \frac{(1.96)(3)}{\sqrt{n}} \Rightarrow n = \left(\frac{(1.96)(3)}{0.5}\right)^2 \approx 138.2976$$

or 139 computer owners

4. D

The purpose behind finding a confidence interval is to use a statistic to estimate a value for a parameter. If one is able to find the parameter, then there is no need to construct a confidence interval.

5. C

Performing a two-proportion z-test with H_0: $p_M = p_F$ and H_a: $p_M \neq p_F$ yields a p-value of 0.324, insignificant results at any of the commonly accepted levels.

6. C

Control, randomization, and replication are the key principles of experimental design. Randomization is used to reduce bias in results. Replication refers to the need to have an adequate sample size when conducting an experiment as well as the ability of another researcher to repeat your results. The placebo effect only affects humans. A placebo is not always necessary. You may be comparing two treatments. It is impossible to *eliminate all* lurking variables. (These words, "eliminate" and "all," should generally be avoided when describing experimental design.)

7. D

A control group in this situation would add a baseline for comparison.

8. E

A χ^2 goodness-of-fit test should be performed. The conditions for conducting the test are met if we consider this shipment to be a random sample. Expected cell counts are each 100. The test statistic would be

$$\chi^2 = \frac{(89 - 100)^2}{100} + \frac{(95 - 100)^2}{100} + \frac{(106 - 100)^2}{100} + \frac{(110 - 100)^2}{100}$$

$= 2.82$. With three degrees of freedom, the p-value is 0.4202. Thus, the result is not significant at any of the commonly accepted significance levels.

9. A

The top 2% constitute the 98th percentile. The standard normal value for the 98th percentile is $z = 2.0537$. Using the formula for z-scores, the following equation can be set up:

$$2.0537 = \frac{41{,}293 - \mu}{7641}.$$

Solving for μ results in average concert attendance of 25,601.

10. B

These data are from a voluntary response sample, which is generally biased, and do not form a simple random sample of constituents.

11. E

Necessary conditions for a one-proportion z-interval are answer choices A, B, and C. All of these conditions are met.

A: We are told that the families were randomly chosen;

B: $50(10) = 500 < 1000$;

C: $50(0.60) = 30 > 10$ and $50(1 - 0.60) = 20 > 10$.

Answer choice D is *not* a necessary condition for proportions.

12. E

This is an example of a simple random sample. Each individual has the same probability of having his/her number selected, and every sample of size 5 has an equal probability of being selected.

13. B

We are told that the person was between the ages of 45 and 54. Of the 123 people in that category, 12 died as result of accidents. So, the probability is $12/123 \approx 0.0976$.

14. C

The data are paired by hotel. Since the rates are checked for the same hotels, we do not have two independent samples. Thus, a matched-pairs test is appropriate.

15. E

For a continuous probability density function, probability is associated with area. The sum of the areas exceeds 1. The area under the curve from $x = 0$ to $x = 8$ is $(0.1)(8) = 0.8$. The area under the curve from $x = 8$ to $x = 10$ is $(0.2)(2) = 0.4$. The sum of the two areas is $1.2 > 1$.

16. C

The range of average temperatures for July is 34.4 degrees, while the range of average temperatures for January is 66.2 degrees.

17. B

$$\frac{\text{(row total)(column total)}}{\text{table total}} = \frac{(71)(14)}{223} \approx 4.4574 \approx 4$$

18. D

This is the classic definition of double-blind. Neither the subjects nor the experimenters know who is in which group.

19. B

This is a geometric setting where $p = 0.450$ and $x = 3$. There are two failures ($q = 0.550$) before a success ($p = 0.450$).

20. B

The mean is not resistant to outliers; therefore, the mean will be affected by the outlying fruit with high IU content. On the other hand, the median is resistant to outliers and is therefore the better choice for a measure of center. The standard deviation, IQR, and range are measures of spread, not center.

21. A

$121/310 \approx 39\%$ is the proportion of sophomores who have a 3.0 to 4.0 GPA. The statement uses at least 3.0, and we must therefore count all who are 3.0 or more. This includes the cell counts 121 and 43 for a total of 164.

22. E

By definition, the coefficient of determination gives the percentage of the variability in the response variable explained by regression on the explanatory variable. Since we are only given a value for r^2, we cannot determine if the relationship between variables is positive or negative.

23. E

Once we remove the outlier for meat, it has the smallest range, IQR, and standard deviation.

24. B

Changing units will not affect the value of the correlation coefficient.

25. A

The distribution for grizzly bears is located to the right of that for black bears; therefore, grizzly bears tend to live longer. The distribution for grizzly bears is taller and thinner than that for black bears; therefore, there is less variability in the data for grizzly bears than black bears.

26. D

$$\text{ME} = z^* \sqrt{\frac{p(1-p)}{n}} = \frac{z^* \sqrt{p(1-p)}}{\sqrt{n}} \Rightarrow \sqrt{n} = \frac{z^* \sqrt{p(1-p)}}{\text{ME}}$$

$$n = \left(\frac{z^* \sqrt{p(1-p)}}{\text{ME}}\right)^2 = \left(\frac{1.645\sqrt{0.5(1-0.5)}}{0.03}\right)^2 \approx 751.674 \approx 752$$

27. A

By definition, two events are mutually exclusive if they cannot happen on the same outcome; therefore, the probability that both occur simultaneously is 0.

28. E

As the number of degrees of freedom *increases*, the t-distribution approaches the normal distribution.

29. A

All probabilities have values between 0 and 1, inclusive. The sum of the probabilities is 1.

30. E

Both the mean and the standard deviation will increase by 3.25%.

31. B

We wish to see if the average life expectancy in this village is more than 45 years of age.

32. E

A matched-pairs design will yield the best results for this experiment. Both socks will be exposed to the same usage and should give the most accurate results. Answer choice C was a completely randomized design. It is possible that one group would be much more active than the other, skewing the results. For answer choice D, it is possible that the two-week periods involved different activities, which could skew the results.

33. E

$$E(X) = 2(0.3) + 4(0.2) + 6(0) + 8(0.4) + 10(0.1)$$
$$= 0.6 + 0.8 + 0 + 3.2 + 1.0$$
$$= 5.6$$
$$\text{Var}(X) = E(X - \mu)^2 P(x)$$
$$= (2 - 5.6)^2(0.3) + (4 - 5.6)^2(0.2)$$
$$+ (6 - 5.6)^2(0) + (8 - 5.6)^2(0.4) + (10 - 5.6)^2(0.1)$$
$$\approx 3.888 + 0.512 + 0 + 2.304 + 1.936$$
$$\approx 8.64$$

34. A

The residual with the least pattern was created with x and $\log y$ as the variables; therefore, the best fit is the equation $\log \hat{y} = 0.378x - 0.051$.
When $x = 7$, $\log \hat{y} = 0.387(7) - 0.051 \approx 2.658$.

$$\hat{y} \approx 10^{2.658} \approx 454.988$$

35. B

The professors are stratified according to their status because professors of different status may have different feelings about tenure.

36. E

A z-score gives the number of standard deviations that a value falls below the mean for a negative score and above the mean for a positive score.

37. A

For the sampling distribution of sample proportions,
$\mu_{\hat{p}} = p$ and $\sigma_{\hat{p}} = \sqrt{\dfrac{p(1-p)}{n}}$. For this problem, $p = 0.135$ and $n = 75$. Standardize the endpoint values by subtracting this mean and dividing by this standard deviation.

38. E

The results can only be generalized for the population of individuals from which the sample was taken. In this case, that population is healthy teenagers.

39. A

This distribution is skewed right, so the mean will be larger than the median. The minimum is 0, and the maximum is 50. The lower quartile is between 0 and 5, and the upper quartile is 20. The median is between 5 and 10, closer to 10.

40. E

As the probability of a Type I error increases, power increases. As power increases, the probability of a Type II error decreases. Therefore, reducing power increases the probability of a Type II error, and reducing the probability of a Type I error increases the probability of a Type II error.

Section II: Free Response

1. a. This is a binomial model. The items are either defective or not defective. Since n is large (10,000), the conditions for a normal approximation to the binomial are met:

$np = 10{,}000(0.003) = 30 \geq 10$ and

$n(1 - p) = 10{,}000(0.997) = 9970 \geq 10.$

The expected number of defective units in this shipment is given by

$\mu = np = 10{,}000(0.003) = 30$ units.

b. Since the expected number of units is the mean of the distribution, there is a 50% probability that there will be more than 30 defective units in the shipment. (*A simple sketch of the normal curve with the mean of 30 shown and the area to the right shaded would be sufficient to support your answer.*) By formula,

$$P(X > 30) = P\left(z > \frac{x - \mu}{\sqrt{np(1 - p)}}\right)$$

$$= P\left(z > \frac{30 - 30}{\sqrt{10{,}000(0.003)(0.997)}}\right) = P(z > 0) = 0.5.$$

If a binomial approach is used, there is a 45.2% probability that there will be more than 30 defective units in the shipment.

$P(x > 30) = 1 - P(x \leq 30)$

On the TI-83/84, the command would be

$1 - binomcdf(10{,}000, 0.003, 30) \approx 0.452.$

c. $P(x < 18) = P\left(z < \dfrac{18 - 30}{\sqrt{10{,}000(0.003)(0.997)}}\right)$

$\approx P(z < -2.19) \approx 0.0143$ (by table) or 0.0141 by calculator. There is a 1.4% chance that fewer than 18 units in this shipment of 10,000 will be defective. If a binomial approach is used, there is a 0.7% probability that fewer than 18 units in the shipment will be defective. On the TI-83/84, the command would be $binomcdf(10{,}000, 0.003, 17) \approx 0.007.$

2. a. This experiment lacks randomization. There will most likely be a confounding variable of the learning curve of the vaulter. Since the student is only beginning to learn how to vault, his first vaults will most likely be for much lower heights than his later vaults. Therefore, the manufacturer cannot truly attribute the increased height to the pole. It may instead be due to experience.

b. To improve upon the design, for the 50 vaults, the student uses a random method to choose the type of pole to use. In this manner, randomization is introduced into the experiment, and the experience factor is most likely removed.

c. We should use a block design, with the blocks defined by pole length. Within each group of vaulter(s), the vaulter should use a random method to choose which type of pole to use for each vault. Heights should be recorded, and after the vaults are completed, the results between the new type of pole and the old should be compared.

3. a. Name brand: $P(x < 11) = P\left(z < \dfrac{11 - 11.13}{0.08}\right) \approx 0.052$

Generic brand: $P(x < 11) = P\left(z < \dfrac{11 - 11.15}{0.16}\right) \approx 0.174$

b. Name brand:

$$P(\bar{x} > 11.25) = P\left(z > \frac{11.25 - 11.13}{\frac{0.08}{\sqrt{4}}}\right) \approx 0.001$$

Generic brand:

$$P(\bar{x} > 11.25) = P\left(z > \frac{11.25 - 11.15}{\frac{0.16}{\sqrt{4}}}\right) \approx 0.106$$

c. Purchasing the name-brand cereal produces the highest probability of receiving at least 11 oz, as demonstrated in part (a), where there is a higher probability of purchasing less than 11 oz with the generic brand.

d. As demonstrated in part (b), if you are hoping to receive higher weights, the higher probability of this event is associated with purchasing the generic brand.

4. a. *Conditions for the one-sample t-test:*

(1) **Randomization:** We are told that the individuals constitute a random sample.

(2) **Sample size:** Either $n \geq 40$ or the data set should be normally distributed. With no strong skew or outliers, the sample size of 35 is sufficiently large to proceed with the t-procedure.

Hypotheses:

H_0: $\mu = 0$ The average weight loss is zero.

H_a: $\mu > 0$ The average weight loss is greater than zero.

Mechanics:

$$t = \frac{4.6 - 0}{\frac{1.2}{\sqrt{35}}} \approx 22.678 \text{ with 34 degrees of freedom, } p \approx 0$$

Conclusion:

At the $\alpha = 0.05$ level, since $p \approx 0 < 0.05$ our results are significant. Therefore, we reject the null hypothesis in favor of the alternative. We have evidence to show that the average weight loss is significant.

b. *Conditions for the two-sample t-test:*

(1) **Randomization:** We are told that both samples are random. It is reasonable to believe that they are independent as well.

(2) **Sample size:** Either $n_1 \geq 40$ and $n_2 \geq 40$ or both sets of data should be normally distributed. Given that both distributions exhibit no strong skew or outliers, with samples of sizes 35 and 32, the sample sizes are sufficiently large to proceed with the t-procedure.

Hypotheses:

H_0: $\mu_D = \mu_C$ The average weight loss of the diet group is the same as that of the control group.

H_a: $\mu_D > \mu_C$ The average weight loss of the diet group is larger than that of the control group.

Mechanics:

$$t = \frac{4.6 - 3.7}{\sqrt{\frac{1.2^2}{35} + \frac{2.3^2}{32}}} \approx 1.981 \text{ with } 45.766 \text{ degrees of freedom}$$

$p \approx 0.027$

Conclusion:

At the $\alpha = 0.05$ level, since $p = 0.027 < 0.05$, our results are significant. Therefore, we reject the null hypothesis in favor of the alternative. We have evidence to show that those taking the diet supplement lose, on average, significantly more weight in the first week.

5. a. Outliers on the high end are those values that lie more than 1.5 IQRs above Q3. IQR $= 10 - 0.5 = 9.5$

   Q3 + 1.5 IQR $= 10 + (1.5)(9.5) = 24.25$. The maximum value is 49, which is greater than 24.25. Therefore, 49 is an outlier on the high end.

   b. The distributions for the migration of red-shouldered hawks for both 2001 and 2002 are skewed right. Both distributions have the same median value of 4.5; however, the distribution for 2002 has a larger mean (not unexpected since the mean is affected by the high end outlier). The outlier also causes 2002 to have a larger range; however, the IQR for 2001 is larger.

6. a. *Conditions for the two-sample t-test:*

   (1) **Randomization:** We are told that both hikers recorded results from a random sample of hikes. It is reasonable to believe the samples are independent. Since the hikers have not hiked together, their results should be independent.

   (2) **Sample size:** Either $n_1 \geq 40$ and $n_2 \geq 40$ or both sets of data should be normally distributed. The graphs show that both distributions of hiking distances are approximately normal.

Hypotheses:

H_0: $\mu_1 = \mu_2$ The average distances hiked by the two hikers are the same.

H_a: $\mu_1 \neq \mu_2$ The average distances hiked by the two hikers are different.

Mechanics:

$$t = \frac{\bar{x}_1 - \bar{x}_2}{\sqrt{\frac{s_1^2}{n_1} + \frac{s_2^2}{n_2}}}$$

$$= \frac{5.952 - 7.585}{\sqrt{\frac{2.71356^2}{25} + \frac{2.4577^2}{20}}} \approx -2.114 \text{ and } p = 0.0404$$

Conclusion:

Since $p = 0.0404 < 0.05$, our results are significant. Reject the null hypothesis in favor of the alternative. We have evidence to show a difference in average distances hiked by the two hikers.

b. *Conditions for the two-sample t-test:*

(1) **Randomization:** We are told that both hikers recorded results from a random sample of hikes. It is reasonable to assume the samples are independent. Since the hikers have not hiked together, their results should be independent.

(2) **Sample size:** Either $n_1 \geq 40$ and $n_2 \geq 40$ or both sets of data should be normally distributed. The graphs show that both distributions of hiking times are approximately normal.

Hypotheses:

H_0: $\mu_1 = \mu_2$ The average times hiked by the two hikers are the same.

H_a: $\mu_1 \neq \mu_2$ The average times hiked by the two hikers are different.

Mechanics:

$$t = \frac{\bar{x}_1 - \bar{x}_2}{\sqrt{\frac{s_1^2}{n_1} + \frac{s_2^2}{n_2}}} = \frac{3.7 - 4.5875}{\sqrt{\frac{1.5448^2}{25} + \frac{1.2677^2}{20}}} \approx -2.117 \text{ and}$$

$p = 0.0401$

Conclusion:

Since $p = 0.0401 < 0.05$, our results are significant. Reject the null hypothesis in favor of the alternative. We have evidence to show a difference in average times hiked by the two hikers.

c. Given the results in parts (a) and (b), the friends probably should not hike together. They go for hikes that differ significantly in average distance and time.

d. Hiker 1 tends to hike at approximately 0.500 mph, and hiker 2 tends to hike at approximately 0.477 mph. These two speeds differ by 0.023 mph. Thus, according to this mutual friend, these two hikers would be well suited to hike together.

ANSWERS TO PRACTICE EXAMINATION 3

Section I: Multiple Choice

1. D

This is a χ^2 goodness-of-fit test. The null hypothesis is that the distribution of seniors in the community fits the distribution of senior citizens in the United States. The alternative hypothesis is that the distribution of seniors in the community does not fit. The expected counts are as follows.

Age	65–74	75–84	85–94	95 and over
Percentage	363.08	201.57	56.34	5.008

$$\chi^2 = \frac{(300 - 363.08)^2}{363.08} + \frac{(232 - 201.57)^2}{201.57} + \frac{(92 - 56.34)^2}{56.34} + \frac{(2 - 5.008)^2}{5.008} \approx 39.930$$

With 3 degrees of freedom, the resulting p-value is $1.1026 \times 10^{-8} \approx 0 < 0.001$. Therefore, the results are statistically significant at the 0.001 level.

2. C

   A scatterplot is an appropriate graphical display to compare two quantitative variables. For this problem, there is one quantitative variable split into two categories.

3. D

   The population size is 500, so a sample size of either 50 or 30 is appropriate. We are not given σ, so a t-test is appropriate. $df = n - 1$, where n = sample size. If $n = 30$, $df = 29$.

4. E

   The mean of $X + Y = E(X + Y) = E(X) + E(Y) = 2.5 + 4.7 = 7.2$. Because the random variables are independent, we can add the *variances*, but *not* the standard deviations, so
   $\text{Var}(X) = (0.3)^2$, $\text{Var}(Y) = (0.4)^2$, and
   $\text{Var}(X + Y) = 0.09 + 0.16 = 0.25$.
   The standard deviation is $\sqrt{0.25} = 0.5$.

5. E

   Random variables may take on any values; for example, a loss of \$2 at the racetrack may be represented by the random variable value (-2). Expected value to a player at a casino is negative (otherwise the "house" would be losing money). Since the variance is computed by the formula $\text{Var}(X) = E(X - \mu)^2P(x)$, the value will be positive or zero (nonnegative). The variance is zero if the difference between the random variable and the mean is zero.

6. D

   The formula for the construction of the confidence interval is

   $$\hat{p} \pm z^*\sqrt{\frac{\hat{p}(1 - \hat{p})}{n}}, \text{ where } \hat{p} = \frac{20}{100}, z^* = 1.96, \text{ and } n = 100.$$

   If the hypothesized value for the proportion is contained in the 95% confidence interval, the results of the hypothesis test will not be significant. Since 0.151 is contained in the 95% confidence interval, (0.1216, 0.2784), we will not be able to show a significant difference between our sample proportion and the 2000 proportion of women in the Army.

7. C

Make a tree diagram to show the probabilities as stated in the problem.

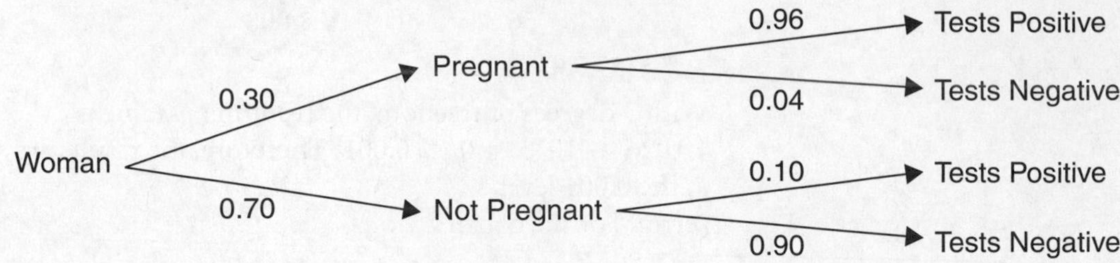

We want to find

$$P(\text{pregnant} \mid \text{tests positive}) = \frac{P(\text{pregnant} \cap \text{tests positive})}{P(\text{tests positive})}$$

$$= \frac{(0.3)(0.96)}{(0.3)(0.96) + (0.7)(0.1)} \approx 0.8045.$$

8. C

Bar graphs are a graphical display for categorical values. Because the variable is categorical, there is no scale for the horizontal axis, and there is a gap between bars. Additionally, it doesn't make sense to assign numerical summaries to categorical data.

9. A

Although the histograms show opposite skew directions, you must be careful to read the labels on any graph. It is clear that some students in class B earn very little or no money and that none of them earns more than \$350. In class A, everyone has a job and earns at least \$50 with some earning in the \$350–\$450 range. While the centers for both distributions lie in the same modal class, these extreme values will pull their means in opposite directions (toward their respective tails). Thus, the mean for class A is higher than for class B.

10. C

The probability that Tom's car will break down is 0.5: $P(T) = 0.5$. The probability that Janice's car will break down is 0.5: $P(J) = 0.5$. The probability that both of their cars will break down is 0.3: $P(T \cap J) = 0.3$. We wish to find the probability that Tom or Janice's car will break down.

$$P(T \cup J) = P(T) + P(J) - P(T \cap J) = 0.5 + 0.5 - 0.3 = 0.7$$

11. A

The median is the value at the 50th percentile, which is 16 years of age for this problem. The interquartile range is found by taking the 75th percentile–25th percentile, in this case, $17 - 16 = 1$. Notice that the median and Q1 are the same in this problem.

12. C

$$n = \left(\frac{z^*\sigma}{\text{ME}}\right)^2 = \left(\frac{1.645 \cdot 10}{0.5}\right)^2$$
$$= 1082.41 \approx 1083$$

Thus, 1083 death records should be examined.

13. C

The width of a confidence interval is determined by doubling the margin of error. For the construction of a confidence interval for means, the margin of error is $t^*\frac{s}{\sqrt{n}}$. If the sample size is quadrupled, the new margin of error becomes

$$t^*\frac{s}{\sqrt{4n}} = t^*\frac{s}{2\sqrt{n}} = \frac{1}{2}t^*\frac{s}{\sqrt{n}}.$$

Therefore, if the margin of error is halved, so too is the width of the confidence interval.

14. C

A p-value outside of the context of a problem setting tells us only the probability that a test statistic at least as extreme as ours occurs when the null hypothesis is true. We cannot reject the null hypothesis without an alpha level or problem setting that suggests an appropriate level.

15. D

A simple random sample is one in which each individual has the same probability of being chosen, and each sample of size 100 has the same probability of being chosen. Only answer choice D satisfies both conditions.

16. B

The mean, range, standard deviation, and variance are not resistant to outliers. The median and interquartile range are resistant to outliers.

17. C

The population of California is much larger than that of Montana. Therefore, 43% of California's residents constitute many more individuals than 43% of Montana's residents. As a result, weighting must be considered to state an overall percentage, and the percentages cannot be added.

18. C

Plot 3 has a strong negative correlation; plot 2 has a moderate negative correlation; plot 4 has a weak positive correlation; and plot 1 has a strong positive correlation.

19. D

From the display, it is evident that 0 is the minimum value and 7 is the maximum value. There are 33 data values, so the median is in the 17th position. The median is 6. The lower quartile is between the 8th and 9th positions and has a value of 4. The upper quartile is 7. Thus, the IQR is $7 - 4 = 3$. Using the 1.5 IQR rule, 1.5 IQR $= 4.5$.

$$Q1 - 1.5\,\text{IQR} = 4 - 4.5 = -0.5$$

Therefore, there are no outliers on the low end.

20. D

A census is not an experiment. A parameter is a value used to describe a population. A population is the entire group of individuals we want information about, and voluntary response samples are generally biased.

21. D

We are trying to determine if the age breakdown in the city fits the distribution of ages in the country.

22. C

Only patients in a high-risk group were part of the study. The results are not readily generalizable to all people who may take this over-the-counter medication.

23. D

Power $= 1 - \beta$, where $\beta =$ the probability of a Type II error.

$82\% = 1 - \beta$, so $\beta = 18\%$.

24. D

The degrees of freedom in a one-sample situation are $df = n - 1$.

25. D

The formula for the confidence interval is

$$(\overline{x}_B - \overline{x}_A) \pm t^* \sqrt{\frac{s_B^2}{n_B} + \frac{s_A^2}{n_A}} = (90 - 88) \pm t^* \sqrt{\frac{6^2}{32} + \frac{8^2}{32}}.$$

Using technology will yield a t^*-value with 57.493 degrees of freedom. When using the t-tables, the more conservative value of 30 degrees of freedom should be used. ($32 - 1 = 31$ *df*, but 31 does not appear on the table.) The resulting interval is $(-1.54, 5.54)$. Thus, the mean for team A is between 5.54 points less than and 1.54 points more than the mean for team B.

26. D

We want to find the probability of rolling three *or* four *or* five 1s. Use the binomial probability formula

$$C(n, r)p^r(1 - p)^{n-r}$$
$$= C(5,3)\left(\frac{1}{6}\right)^3\left(\frac{5}{6}\right)^2 + C(5,4)\left(\frac{1}{6}\right)^4\left(\frac{5}{6}\right)^1 + C(5,5)\left(\frac{1}{6}\right)^5\left(\frac{5}{6}\right)^0$$
$$\approx 0.03215 + 0.00321 + 0.00012 \approx 0.0354.$$

Alternatively, you may use the TI-83/84 command

$binomcdf\left(5, \frac{1}{6}, 2\right) \approx .9645$, which finds the probability of rolling zero, one, or two 1s and subtract from 1.

27. B

The five-number summary is 2, 4, 7, 9, 10. The boxplot of the data is

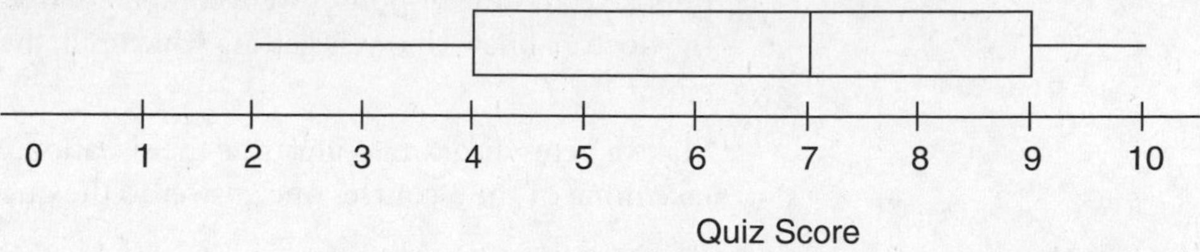

28. E

A confidence interval may or may not contain the true proportion. 95% of intervals constructed with sample data like ours will contain the true proportion. A confidence interval gives a range of plausible values for the population proportion but does not tell us anything about a particular college.

29. B

There is nothing tricky here. Just follow the part of the tree that shows event *A*, then follow to *B*. When event *A* occurs, event *B* will occur 0.2 or 20% of the time. You will get the same result by using

$$P(B \mid A) = \frac{P(B \cap A)}{P(A)} = \frac{(0.25)(0.2)}{(0.25)} = 0.2,$$

but with unnecessary effort.

30. E

Studies that involve human subjects are especially sensitive to ethical issues. In this case, the drug being studied should be available to all involved in the study since the study concerned the effectiveness and the results were very positive.

31. B

The data show a positive, moderately strong linear association.

32. E

We are finding a 98% confidence interval for a mean given a sample of size 15. A *t*-interval with 14 degrees of freedom would be appropriate.

$$\bar{x} \pm t^*_{df}\frac{s}{\sqrt{n}} = 1.25 \pm 2.62\frac{0.39}{\sqrt{15}}$$

33. B

Since the president is interested only in assessing the parking needs of borough residents, the population of interest is borough residents who own cars.

34. E

In order to find a sample size, we could use the conservative value of 0.5 for *p*, but we are still missing the confidence level. Without a confidence level, we cannot find a value for z^*. To find a sample size given the margin of error in a problem dealing with proportions:

$$\text{ME} = z^*\sqrt{\frac{p(1-p)}{n}} = \frac{z^*\sqrt{p(1-p)}}{\sqrt{n}} \Rightarrow$$

$$\sqrt{n} = \frac{z^*\sqrt{p(1-p)}}{\text{ME}} \Rightarrow n = \left(\frac{z^*\sqrt{p(1-p)}}{\text{ME}}\right)^2.$$

35. B

This was a comparative experiment because a treatment (aspirin/placebo) was imposed, and the responses were compared. Because neither the patients nor the doctors knew who was getting which pill, the experiment was double-blind.

36. C

Make a Venn diagram to illustrate the situation. Since 22 of 100 AP* students take none of the 3 courses, the answer to the question asked is 22%.

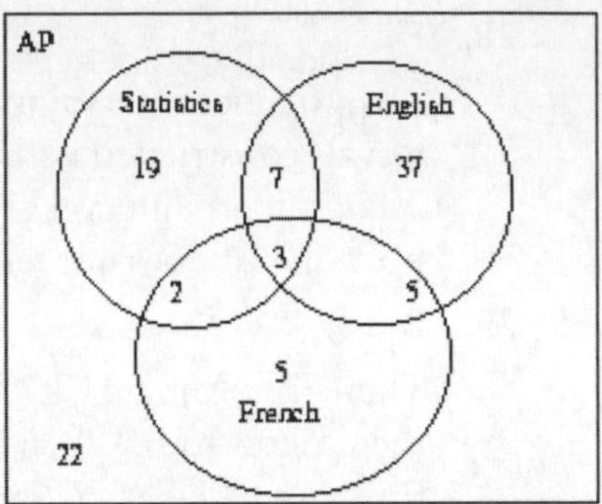

37. B

Only statement II is correct. The two-sample t-test only allows us to make conclusions about the average student grade for each professor, not individual students. Additionally, we were told that we have random samples of grades for each professor, and the distribution of grades is approximately normal for each as well. It is reasonable to conclude that the grades of the two professors are independent. The correct interpretation of a p-value says that if the null hypothesis is true (there is no difference in grades between the two professors), then we can expect to get results as extreme as those from our sample 2.2% of the time (p-value $= 0.022$).

38. E

A modified boxplot reveals an outlier; therefore, the conditions necessary to find a 95% confidence interval for a mean with a sample of size 15 are not met.

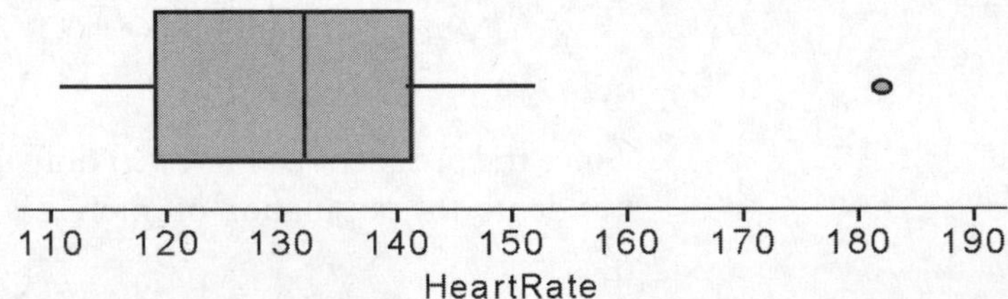

39. D

The mean residual value for *all* regression analyses is 0. With a p-value of 0.0006, there is a significant relationship between X and Y, and the correlation is a high 0.911. A pattern in the residual plot, however, indicates that an even better fit exists.

40. D

Reversing the dependent and independent variables does not change the correlation. Since $R^2 = 0.795$ and the slope is positive,

$r = \sqrt{0.795} \approx 0.892.$

Section II: Free Response

1. a. This design is part observational study and part experiment. There are many possible confounding and lurking variables. Confounding variables may include that students not receiving the rewards may work harder as a form of protest; movie tickets may be a social stressor for those without dates and may actually not be a reward at all if someone does not like movies; courses taken in two different years may have differing degrees of difficulty and result in different GPAs. Lurking variables include the intrinsic motivation of students who simply enjoy getting good grades as well as other rewards that may be provided by the classroom teacher as the normal course of action in the class.

   b. Randomly allocate the students to two groups: one to receive the reward and the other not. Allow students in the reward group to choose from a wide selection of rewards. At the end of the first semester, compare the mean GPAs from both groups. Because the students were randomly assigned to the groups, we expect the groups to have similar GPA distributions. This design is now a true comparative experiment; it does not rely on last year's GPAs and the design will remove most of the confounding variables.

2. A tree diagram illustrates the possibilities. B represents a runner on base. H represents the batter getting a hit.

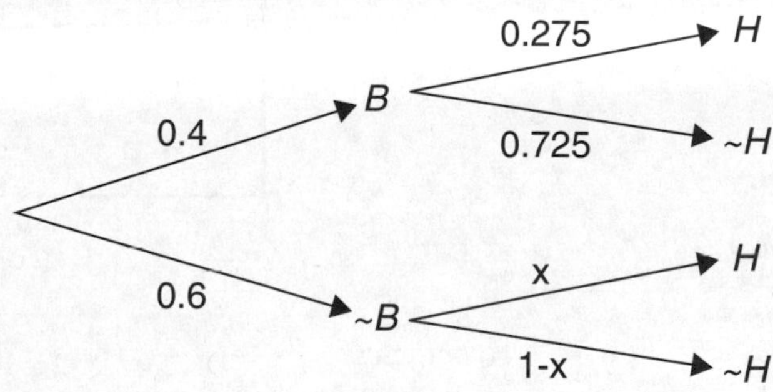

$P(H) = P(B \cap H) + P(\sim B \cap H)$

$0.320 = (0.4)(0.275) + (0.6)(x)$

$0.320 = 0.110 + (0.6)(x)$

$0.210 = 0.6x$

$0.350 = x$

Thus, the player has a 0.350 batting average when there are no runners on base.

3. a. This is a geometric setting with $p = 0.125$ and $k = 7$. Therefore, the probability that the team will not lose until their seventh game is

   $(1 - 0.125)^6(0.125) \approx 0.056.$

b. This is a binomial setting with $n = 5, p = 0.125$, and $k = 1$. Therefore, the probability that GA will lose one game in five is

$$\binom{5}{1}(1 - 0.125)^4(0.125) \approx 0.366.$$

c. This is a geometric setting. The mean for a geometric setting is $\frac{1}{p}$.

Therefore, in the long run, GA can expect to play $\frac{1}{p} = \frac{1}{0.125} = 8$ games until their first loss; that is, they will lose the 8th game.

4. *Conditions for the two-sample t-test:*

(1) **Randomization:** We are told that both samples are random. It is reasonable to believe the second group is independent of the first.

(2) **Sample size:** Either $n_1 \geq 40$ and $n_2 \geq 40$ or both sets of data should be normally distributed. Both data sets show mild skew (parallel boxplots), but the test is robust for $n > 15$ for mild skew. There are no outliers. The population of customers is certainly more than 200 per year.

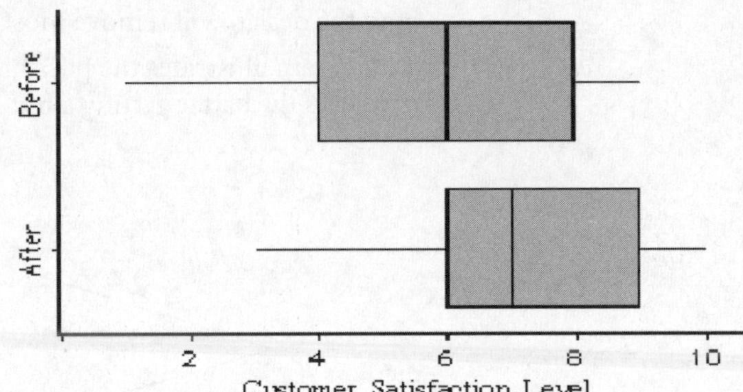

Hypotheses:

H_0: $\mu_A = \mu_B$ There is no difference in the average satisfaction rate before and after policy changes.

H_a: $\mu_A > \mu_B$ The average satisfaction rate increased after the policy changes.

Mechanics:

$$t = \frac{5.9 - 7.2}{\sqrt{\frac{2.426^2}{20} + \frac{1.852^2}{20}}} \approx -1.905 \text{ with 35.537 degrees of freedom,}$$

$p \approx 0.0325$ (calculator results)

(Using the table, $df = 19$ and $0.025 < p < 0.05$.)

Conclusion:

Supervisor: There is evidence to suggest that the policy changes the company has made have resulted in increased customer satisfaction. (Our level of significance is 5% and our p-value of 0.0325 is less than 0.05.)

5. a. Truncate the life expectancies to the nearest integer. (Rounding would be appropriate.)

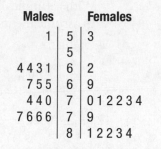

Males		Females
1	5	3
	5	
4 4 3 1	6	2
7 5 5	6	9
4 4 0	7	0 1 2 2 3 4
7 6 6 6	7	9
	8	1 2 2 3 4

b.

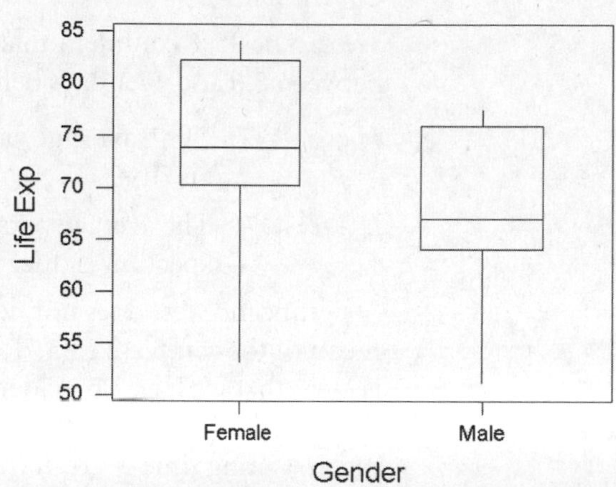

c. Both distributions are skewed left. Women tend to live longer than men; the median age for women is 73.9 years, while for men it is only 67 years. The interquartile ranges of the genders are almost equivalent; women have a slightly larger range in life expectancies than men.

d. The back-to-back stemplot maintains the individual life expectancies. Individual values are lost in the boxplot.

e. The parallel boxplots show the five-number summary; with a stemplot, summary statistics would need to be calculated.

6. a. A value of −5 could occur if a person waits until 5 days *after* his inspection is due to have his car inspected.

b. A one-sample t-test would be appropriate in this situation. You would want to compare the average wait-time with the hypothesized value of 7 days.

c. The conditions to test a one-sample t-test would not be met. Although the car owners were randomly polled and it is a certainty that there are more than 200 car owners, for a sample of size 20, we need to be cautious and check for skew or outliers. There is at least one outlier on the high end for this data set.

$Q3 + 1.5\ IQR = 18.75 + 1.5(17.75) = 45.375$

The maximum of 75 is larger than this value.
Therefore, it is not safe to use a t-procedure.

d. *Conditions for the one-sample t-interval:*

(1) **Randomization:** We are told that the station owner randomly chooses 40 customers.

(2) **Sample size:** Either $n \geq 40$ or the data should be normally distributed. With a sample of size 40, the t-procedure is safe to use. It is reasonable to assume the inspection station owner inspects more than 400 cars.

Mechanics:

$\bar{x} \pm t^*_{39}\frac{s}{\sqrt{n}}$, where $\bar{x} = 12.85$, $s = 13.28$, and $n = 40$

$12.85 \pm 2.0227\frac{13.28}{\sqrt{40}}$

(8.6028, 17.097) using the TI-83/84

Conclusion:

We can be 95% confident that the average person has his/her car inspected between 8.6 and 17.1 days before the inspection is due.

e. H_0: $\mu = 7$ The average person waits until 7 days before inspection is due.

H_a: $\mu < 7$ The average person waits until fewer than 7 days before inspection is due.

A significance test does not need to be conducted in this case because the mean of the sample, 12.85, does not support the alternative hypothesis. It is clear that we have no evidence to support a mean waiting time of less than 7 days. (The only alternative that might be investigated is that the mean waiting time is greater than 7 days.)

ANSWERS TO PRACTICE EXAMINATION 4

Section I: Multiple Choice

1. E

The sign of r indicates the *direction* of the association, not the *strength*.

2. E

For this problem, the margin of error is 0.02, and the sample proportion is 0.24. Thus, the following equation can be used to solve for z^*:

$$0.02 = z^*\sqrt{\frac{(0.24)(1 - 0.24)}{500}},$$

and $z^* = 1.047$. To find the level of confidence, we find

$P(-1.047 < z < 1.047) \approx 0.7049$.

3. B

The IQR tells us the distance between Q1 and Q3. It does not tell us how that distance is distributed about the median.

4. D

There were eight men with incomes between \$35,000 and \$45,000, higher than any other income interval. Remember that this is a *cumulative frequency* histogram.

5. D

We are looking for the geometric probability of a first success on a particular trial where $p = 0.06$ and $q = 0.94$. The formula is $P(X = x) = q^{1-x}p$ or $P(X = 8) = (0.94)^7(0.06)$. Picture a tree diagram where you make eight selections of individuals with the first seven being "failures" with probability 0.94 (having a blood type other that O^+) and the last being a "success" with probability 0.06.

6. B

$$\bar{x}_{\text{juniors}} = \frac{\sum x_{\text{juniors}}}{n_{\text{juniors}}};\ 92 = \frac{\sum x_{\text{juniors}}}{24};\ \sum x_{\text{juniors}} = 2208$$

$$\bar{x}_{total} = \frac{\sum x_{\text{total}}}{n_{\text{total}}};\ 87 = \frac{\sum x_{\text{total}}}{62};\ \sum x_{\text{total}} = 5394$$

$$\sum x_{\text{seniors}} = \sum x_{\text{total}} - \sum x_{\text{juniors}} = 5394 - 2208 = 3186$$

$$\bar{x}_{\text{seniors}} = \frac{\sum x_{\text{seniors}}}{n_{\text{seniors}}};\ \bar{x}_{\text{seniors}} = \frac{3186}{38}$$

$$\approx 83.8$$

7. C

Your decision must always be stated in terms of *rejecting* or *failing to reject* the null hypothesis. If you *reject* the null hypothesis, you are in favor of (accepting) the alternative hypothesis. If you *fail to reject* the null hypothesis, you do NOT accept the alternative hypothesis. (Remember, this statement is part of a fuller statement that includes your reason and the context of the problem.)

8. C

First, the expected counts should be computed.

Age	under 65	65–74	75–84	85 and older
Percentage	14.7	18	47.7	69.75

$$\chi^2 = \sum \frac{(Obs - Exp)^2}{Exp}$$

$$= \frac{(10 - 14.7)^2}{14.7} + \frac{(20 - 18)^2}{18}$$

$$+ \frac{(52 - 47.7)^2}{47.7} + \frac{(68 - 69.75)^2}{69.75} \approx 2.156$$

9. C

$P(B) = 1 - P(not\ B) = 1 - 0.4 = 0.6;$

$P(A \text{ or } B) = P(A) + P(B) - P(A \text{ and } B)$

$= 0.7 + 0.6 - 0.5 = 0.8.$

10. A

Since it is possible in a relatively easy manner to find the GPA for *every* senior who has been accepted to college, a census is the most appropriate technique.

11. D

If the population has a standard deviation of 0, then all values in the population are identical. These values may or may not be 0. Since all of the values are identical, if a sample is drawn from the population, the sample will consist of identical values. Therefore, the standard deviation of the sample is 0, and the mean and median are equal for the sample.

12. C

Answer choice C assigns 0–3 to represent rain (R) and 4–9 to represent no rain (N). If you use a two-digit representation, 00–39 would be rain (R) and 40–99 would be no rain (N). Answer choice B incorrectly assigns both 00 and 40 for rain. Answer choice A uses evens and odds; this would simulate 50%. Answer choice D uses 0–4 to represent rain; this would simulate 50%. Answer choice E incorrectly assumes you must use three digits to simulate percentages so that 100% can be represented.

13. B

A Type II Error is committed when we fail to reject the null hypothesis when the alternative hypothesis is true.

14. E

The null hypothesis would be that there is no relationship between age and income. The alternative hypothesis would be that there is a relationship between age and income. The p-value for the slope can be found in the last row of output corresponding with the explanatory variable age.

Variable	Coefficient	s.e. of Coeff	t-ratio	prob
Constant	27300.4	1.576e4	1.73	0.0956
Age	244.203	337.7	0.723	0.4763

With a p-value of 0.4763, we do not have sufficient evidence at any of the commonly accepted levels to show a relationship between age and income.

15. A

If 25% of horses live over 23.4 years, then 75% of horses live under 23.4 years. From the standard normal table, the z-score associated with 0.75 is 0.67. The z-score associated with 85% living less than 25.2 years is 1.04. Using the formula for standardized scores,

$$0.67 = \frac{23.4 - \mu}{\sigma} \text{ and } 1.04 = \frac{25.2 - \mu}{\sigma}.$$

Solving algebraically gives $\mu = 20.14$ and $\sigma = 4.86$.

16. C

This is a binomial setting with $n = 3$ and $p = 0.073$. We are asked to find the probability that $x = 2$ or $x = 3$.

$$P(x \geq 2) = \binom{3}{2}(0.073)^2(0.927) + \binom{3}{3}(0.073)^3 \approx 0.0152$$

17. E

Looking at a table of the *t*-distribution with 14 degrees of freedom and an upper tail probability of 0.01 yields a t^* critical value of 2.624.

18. B

$$\sigma_{\bar{x}_1 - \bar{x}_2} = \sqrt{\frac{s_1^2}{n_1} + \frac{s_2^2}{n_2}} = \sqrt{\frac{3.2^2}{30} + \frac{3.8^2}{40}} \approx 0.838$$

19. B

The politician can expect 48% of the female vote, and females comprise 58% of the population of interest. Therefore, the politician can expect $(0.58)(0.48) = 27.84\%$ of the vote from registered women. Of the 42% of males, the politician can expect votes from 53% of them. Therefore, the politician can expect $(0.42)(0.53) = 22.26\%$ of the vote from registered men. Overall, the politician expects $27.84\% + 22.26\% = 50.1\%$ of the vote.

20. E

The five-number summary for the percentage of white children living in poverty is: 12.9, 14.8, 16, 16.8, 17.8. The five-number summary for the percentage of Asian children living in poverty is: 11.8, 17.5, 18.25, 19.8, 24.1.

Answer choices A and D can be eliminated since the back-to-back stemplot tells us nothing about any individual year. There are three outliers for the distribution of Asian percentages: 11.8, 23.5, and 24.1. Even with their removal, the range of Asian percentages would be larger than that for white children. Finally, the distribution of white percentages is skewed left, resulting in a mean smaller than the median, but the distribution of Asian percentages shows no clear skew. In fact, the average percentage of Asian children living in poverty is 18.49%. The spread (or variability) of Asian percentages is larger for both the range and the interquartile range.

21. D

Causation *cannot* be demonstrated by the correlation coefficient. Only a randomized, controlled experiment can demonstrate causation.

22. E

With a range of 100, it is not possible for all five values to be identical. In order to have a standard deviation of 0, the values would need to be identical.

23. D

The sampling distribution of sample proportions for $p = 0.40$ and $n = 16$ would be centered at

$\mu_{\hat{p}} = p = 0.4$

with a standard deviation of

$$\sigma_{\hat{p}} = \sqrt{\frac{p(1-p)}{n}} = \sqrt{\frac{(0.4)(0.6)}{16}} \approx 0.122.$$

24. C

The standard deviation of the sampling distribution is $\sigma / \sqrt{n}$. Therefore, the variance, which is the square of the standard deviation, is

$$\frac{\sigma^2}{n} = \frac{(2.8)^2}{10} = 0.784.$$

25. C

The segmented bar graphs represent the percentages in the armed services by gender, not counts. Therefore, we can only compare the percentage of men and women in the various services.

26. C

If A and B are independent, then $P(A \cap B) = P(A) \cdot P(B)$. Thus,

$$0.21 = (0.4)P(A) \text{ and } P(A) = \frac{0.21}{0.4} = 0.525.$$

27. C

In each case, a wait-time of 45 minutes is 2 standard deviations below the mean. For a normal distribution, the probability that a value will fall more than 2 standard deviations below the mean is 2.275%.

$P(z < -2) = 0.0228$ using the table, and on the TI-83/84:

normalcdf$(-1E99, 2, 0, 1) = 0.02275$.

28. E

We cannot state with certainty that our confidence interval will capture the population proportion. The interpretation of the 95% confidence level tells us that in the long run, 95% of similarly constructed intervals will capture the true population proportion.

29. E

The sample result will be contained in the confidence interval, more specifically in the middle. The margin of error provides us with information about confidence in finding a population value. We cannot state with certainty that the population proportion will be contained in the confidence interval. The approval rating of the president is likely to be between 47% and 55%.

30. A

We are testing a null hypothesis of $p = 0.8$ versus an alternative hypothesis of $p < 0.8$. We are performing a one-proportion z-test. The test statistic is

$$z = \frac{0.7 - 0.8}{\sqrt{\frac{0.8(1 - 0.8)}{50}}} \approx -1.768.$$

The p-value is $P(z < -1.768) \approx 0.039$.

31. B

Let $X =$ the amount of profit Ruth makes.

X	\$400	\$275	\$100
P(x)	0.65	0.15	0.20

$E(x) = \mu_x = \$400(0.65) + \$275(0.15) + \$100(0.20) = \$321.25$

32. C

This is a binomial setting with $n = 8$ and $p = (1 - 0.45) = 0.55$. Therefore, the mean is $np = (8)(0.55) = 4.4$ and the standard deviation is $\sqrt{np(1 - p)} = \sqrt{(8)(0.55)(0.45)} \approx 1.41$.

33. C

If $\log \hat{y} = 0.214 - 1.28(2)$, then $\hat{y} = 10^{0.124 - 1.28(2)} \approx 0.0045$.

34. E

We are not told that we have two independent simple random samples. This is one of the necessary conditions for finding a confidence interval for a difference in proportions.

35. C

The residuals show a curved pattern, so the linear model is not a good model for the data. The sum of the residuals is zero. The sum of the squares helps to build the standard deviation and is not zero unless all of the residuals are zero.

36. E

Undercoverage, because not everyone shops at a mall; *nonresponse*, because only people with a strong opinion may be willing to answer; *response bias*, because the different appearances of the two boys may influence the type of response each boy receives.

37. E

Of the listed statistics, only the median is resistant to outliers.

38. E

All of these are appropriately modeled with a χ^2 distribution.

Answer choices A and B are goodness-of-fit tests with $(7 - 1) = 6$ and $(14 - 1) = 13$ degrees of freedom, respectively.

Answer choices C and D are tests of independence. Choice E is a test of homogeneity. These three choices use a two-way table. For a two-way table, $df = (\text{rows} - 1)(\text{columns} - 1)$.

So, $df_C = (5 - 1)(3 - 1) = 8$; $df_D = (7 - 1)(2 - 1) = 6$;
$df_E = (8 - 1)(3 - 1) = 14$.

39. A

$$90\%\ \text{CI: } \bar{x} \pm t^*_{14}\frac{s}{\sqrt{n}} = 23 \pm 1.761\left(\frac{6}{\sqrt{15}}\right) \approx 23 \pm 2.728$$

40. B

Calculate the standard deviation by first finding the expected value and the variance.

$$E(X) = \mu_X = 1(0.13) + 3(0.17) + 5(0.25) + 7(0.24) + 9(0.21) \approx 5.460$$
$$\text{Var}(X) = \sum(x - \mu_X)^2 P(x)$$
$$= (1 - 5.460)^2(0.13) + \cdots + (9 - 5.460)^2(0.21) \approx 6.868$$
$$\text{SD}(X) = \sqrt{\text{Var}(X)} \approx \sqrt{6.868} \approx 2.621$$

Section II: Free Response

1. a. Parallel boxplots are shown.
(Other acceptable displays for comparing two sets of quantitative data are back-to-back stemplots and histograms or dotplots that use the same scales.)

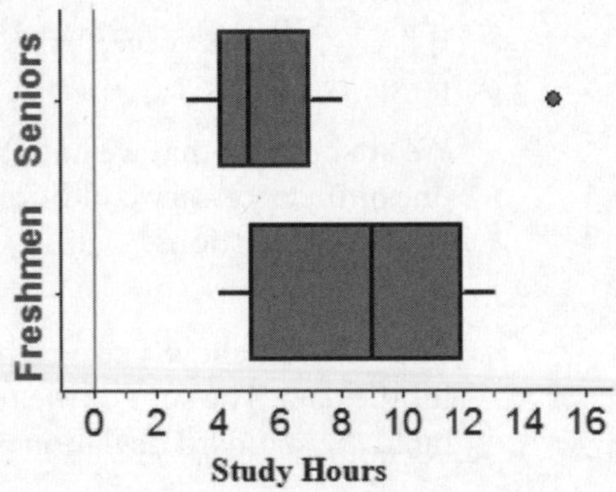

b. The boxplots reveal that freshmen tended to spend **more time** studying for their final exams; their median of about 9 hours is higher than the seniors' median of about 5 hours, and approximately 75% of the freshmen study 5 or more hours compared to only 50% of the seniors. Although the range for seniors (about 12 hours) is larger than the freshmen's range (9 hours), the IQR for the seniors is much **smaller** than the freshmen's IQR. The distribution of freshmen study hours is approximately symmetric, while the seniors' distribution is skewed to the right because of the high outlier.

Note: It is **not** sufficient to just give the values for center and shape for each distribution. You **must** *compare* them by using words such as *smaller, more,* etc. Also, in a description of the shape of a boxplot, it is **never** appropriate to say that it is approximately normal or bell-shaped. This cannot be determined from a boxplot.

2. a. For a given group of cars, randomly choose whether a car should start with synthetic motor oil or petroleum motor oil. Run the cars for three months, and at the next oil change, compare viscosities of the two oil types.

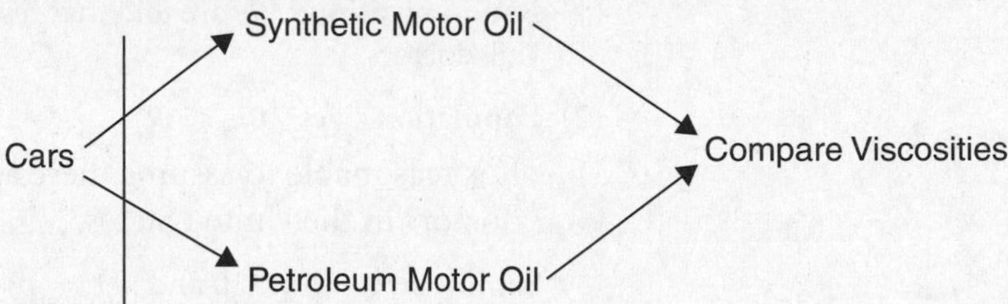

b. There are numerous factors that may affect the breakdown of the oil. Possible confounding variables may include the make of the car, the size of the car's engine, or the age of the car.

c. Since the design shown in part (a) is a completely randomized design, a two-sample *t*-test is appropriate (provided that the conditions are met), where the average viscosity between the synthetic oil and the petroleum oil is compared. The hypotheses are:

H_0: $\mu_S = \mu_P$ There is no difference in average viscosity between the synthetic and petroleum oils.

H_a: $\mu_S \neq \mu_P$ There is a difference in average viscosity between the synthetic and petroleum oils.

3. a. $P(x \leq 49) = P\left(z \leq \frac{49 - 75.465}{12.378}\right) \approx 0.016$

b. 8 hours and 43 minutes is equivalent to 523 minutes.

$$P(x \geq 523) = P\left(z \geq \frac{523 - 403.506}{45.023}\right) \approx 0.0040$$

c. 5 hours is equivalent to 300 minutes.

$$P(\bar{x} \leq 300) = P\left(z \leq \frac{300 - 287.497}{\frac{49.894}{\sqrt{4}}}\right) \approx 0.6919$$

d. 8 hours and 46 minutes is equivalent to 526 minutes.

$$\mu_{S+B+R} = \mu_S + \mu_B + \mu_R$$
$$= 75.465 + 403.506 + 287.497 = 766.468$$

$$\sigma_{S+B+R} = \sqrt{\sigma_S^2 + \sigma_B^2 + \sigma_R^2}$$
$$= \sqrt{12.378^2 + 45.023^2 + 49.894^2} \approx 68.3352$$

$$P(Sum \leq 526) = P\left(z \leq \frac{526 - 766.468}{68.3352}\right) \approx 0.0002$$

4. a. Use a one-proportion z-interval. $\hat{p} = \frac{83}{921}$, $n = 921$

Assumptions/conditions for the one-proportion z-interval:

(1) **Randomization:** We are told that results are from a random sample of U.S. doctors.

(2) **Population size:** $10n < N$

It is reasonable to assume there are more than $(10)(921) = 9210$ doctors in the United States.

(3) **Sample size:** $np \geq 10$ and $n(1 - p) \geq 10$

$\frac{83}{921}(921) > 10$ and $\frac{838}{921}(921) > 10$

Mechanics:

The construction of a 98% confidence interval for a proportion makes use of the formula

$$\hat{p} \pm z^* \sqrt{\frac{\hat{p}(1 - \hat{p})}{n}}.$$

For this problem, the confidence interval is constructed as

$$\frac{83}{921} \pm 2.33\sqrt{\frac{\left(\frac{83}{921}\right)\left(1 - \frac{83}{921}\right)}{921}} \approx 0.0901 \pm 0.0219.$$

98% CI for p: (0.0682, 0.1120)

Conclusion:

We can be 98% confident that the true proportion of doctors who feel that a surgeon diagnosed with dementia should be allowed to perform surgery with close supervision is contained in the interval (0.0682, 0.1120).

b. Use a two-proportion z-test.

$$\hat{p}_D = \frac{83}{921}, n = 921, \quad \hat{p}_N = \frac{23}{768}, \quad \hat{p}_{pooled} = \frac{83 + 23}{921 + 768} = \frac{106}{1689}$$

Assumptions/conditions for the two-proportion z-test:

(1) **Randomization:** We are told that results are from a random sample of doctors and nurses. Additionally, it is reasonable to believe the samples are independent.

(2) **Population size:** $10n < N$

It is reasonable to assume that there are more than 9210 doctors and 7680 nurses in the United States.

(3) **Sample size:** $n\hat{p}_D \geq 10$ and $n(1 - \hat{p}_D) \geq 10$ and

$n\hat{p}_N \geq 10$ and $n(1 - \hat{p}_N) \geq 10$

$\frac{83}{921}(921) > 10$ and $\frac{838}{921}(921) > 10$ and

$\frac{23}{768}(768) > 10$ and $\frac{745}{768}(768) > 10$

Hypotheses:

H_0: $p_N = p_D$ *or* $p_N - p_D = 0$ — The proportion of nurses who feel that surgeons diagnosed with dementia should be allowed to perform surgery under close supervision equals the proportion of doctors.

H_a: $p_N < p_D$ *or* $p_N - p_D < 0$ — The proportion of nurses who feel that surgeons diagnosed with dementia should be allowed to perform surgery under close supervision is less than the proportion of doctors.

Mechanics:

$$z = \frac{\left(\frac{23}{768} - \frac{83}{921}\right) - 0}{\sqrt{\frac{\left(\frac{106}{1689}\right)\left(\frac{1583}{1689}\right)}{768} + \frac{\left(\frac{106}{1689}\right)\left(\frac{1583}{1689}\right)}{921}}}$$

$$\approx \frac{-0.06017}{0.01185} \approx 5.08 \text{ and the } p\text{-value} \approx 0.$$

Conclusion:

Because the p-value ≈ 0, we reject the null hypothesis at any reasonable α-level. There is significant evidence that the proportion of nurses who think that surgeons with dementia should be allowed to perform surgery with supervision is less than the proportion of doctors who feel that way.

5. a. $P(x < 14) = P\left(z < \dfrac{14 - 14.8}{1.2}\right) \approx P(z < -0.67) \approx 0.25$

b. Let success = bag of chips that weighs less than 14 oz with $p = 0.25$. Let 00 − 24 = success and 25 − 99 = failure.

2 3 6 2

9 2 | 1 9 | 5 6 | 6 8 | 0 3 | 3 1 | 8 2 | 5 6 | 4 6 | 5 1 | 0 5 | 8 2 | 0 9 | 3 9 |

2 7 5

2 3 | 9 8 | 9 2 | 4 8 | 8 7 | 9 3 | 3 2 | 0 3 | 6 2 | 5 0 | 9 4 | 4 3 | 1 1 | 7 6 |

8 4 1 6 1 4 0 3 9 7 0 1 9 8 3 7 6 7 9 3 2 6 8 3 2 8 2 3

c. $E(X) = \mu_x = \dfrac{2 + 3 + 6 + 2 + 2 + 7 + 5}{7} \approx 3.9$. On average you would need to purchase about four bags of potato chips before finding one that weighs less than 14 oz.

6. a. The regression equation is $\hat{y} = -1021 + 553x$, where x = year of business and y = units sold. The slope is approximately 553; for each additional year of business the number of cell phones sold increases by about 553.

b. $r \approx 0.958$. There is a strong, positive linear relationship between the year of business and the number of cell phones sold.

c. Predicted Units Sold $= -1021 + 553(13) = 6168$. In the thirteenth year of business, the store can expect to sell approximately 6168 cell phones.

d. There is a curved pattern in the scatterplot in addition to a distinct pattern in the residual plot.

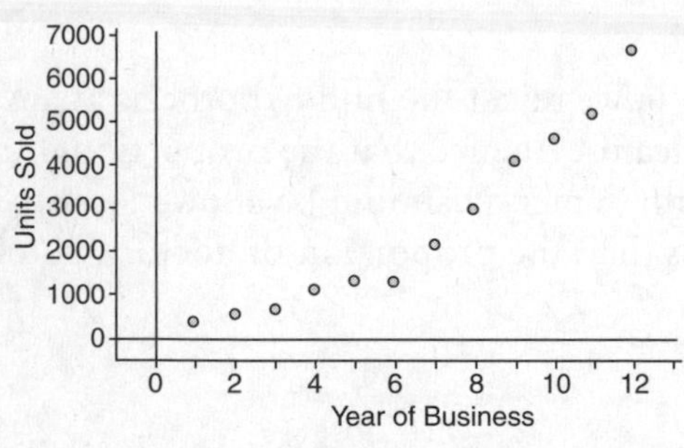

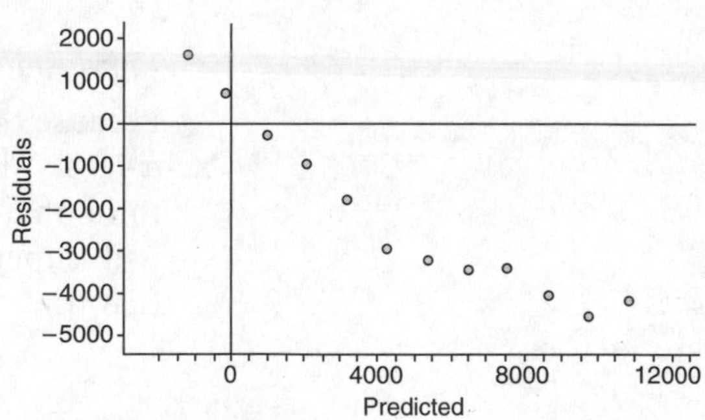

e. There are several possible transformations you could use. An exponential transformation makes the scatterplot more linear and reduces (though does not eliminate) the pattern in the residual plot. It also improves the coefficient of determination (r^2).

log(Units) = 2.518 + 0.113 (Year); $r^2 \approx 0.982$

f. log(Units) = 2.518 + 0.113 (13) = 3.987

$10^{3.987} \approx 9705$ Units Sold